CW01662550

# Praise for *Photography and Phi*

"This is a very valuable collection that gathers together a set of articles and issues that should be of general interest to philosophers of art."

*Notre Dame Philosophical Reviews*

"Will enlighten the student and refresh the informed. Contributes greatly to the literature and will occupy a favorite spot on the book shelves."

*Metapsychology*

"Any adequate aesthetic theory must accommodate facts about the production, interpretation, and evaluation of photographic images. Scott Walden's valuable collection should help bring the realities and significance of photography into the philosophical mainstream; it provides rich and well-informed reflections upon epistemological, ontological, and evaluative aspects of photographic process and product."

Robert Kraut, Ohio State University

"This is a first-rate collection of essays in the philosophy of photography by the leading figures in the analytic literature. Remarkably, it is also the first such collection to appear in English, running from the classic essays by Walton and Scruton right through to current work by leading exponents such as Lopes, Maynard, and Currie. Covering a range of questions foundational to the epistemology, ontology, ethics, and aesthetics of photography, it is probably the most wide-ranging single book available on the philosophy of photography to date. As such it is a real achievement, sure to foster debate."

Diarmuid Costello, University of Warwick

**New Directions in Aesthetics**

Series editors: Dominic McIver Lopes, University of British Columbia, and Berys Gaut, University of St Andrews

Blackwell's New Directions in Aesthetics series highlights ambitious single- and multiple-author books that confront the most intriguing and pressing problems in aesthetics and the philosophy of art today. Each book is written in a way that advances understanding of the subject at hand and is accessible to upper-undergraduate and graduate students.

1. *Interpretation and Construction: Art, Speech, and the Law* by Robert Stecker
2. *Art as Performance* by David Davies
3. *The Performance of Reading: An Essay in the Philosophy of Literature* by Peter Kivy
4. *The Art of Theater* by James R. Hamilton
5. *Cultural Appropriation and the Arts* by James O. Young
6. *Photography and Philosophy: Essays on the Pencil of Nature* ed. Scott Walden
7. *Art and Ethical Criticism* ed. Garry L. Hagberg
8. *Mirrors to One Another: Emotion and Value in Jane Austen and David Hume* by Eva Dadlez
9. *Comic Relief: A Comprehensive Philosophy of Humor* by John Morreall
10. *The Art of Videogames* by Grant Tavinor

# Photography and Philosophy

## Essays on the Pencil of Nature

Edited by Scott Walden

WILEY-BLACKWELL

A John Wiley & Sons, Inc., Publication

This paperback edition first published [2010]
© [2010] Blackwell Publishing Ltd.

Edition history: Blackwell Publishing Ltd (hardback, 2008)

Blackwell Publishing was acquired by John Wiley & Sons in February 2007. Blackwell's publishing program has been merged with Wiley's global Scientific, Technical, and Medical business to form Wiley-Blackwell.

*Registered Office*
John Wiley & Sons Ltd, The Atrium, Southern Gate, Chichester, West Sussex, PO19 8SQ, United Kingdom

*Editorial Offices*
350 Main Street, Malden, MA 02148-5020, USA
9600 Garsington Road, Oxford, OX4 2DQ, UK
The Atrium, Southern Gate, Chichester, West Sussex, PO19 8SQ, UK

For details of our global editorial offices, for customer services, and for information about how to apply for permission to reuse the copyright material in this book please see our website at www.wiley.com/wiley-blackwell.

The right of Scott Walden to be identified as the author of the editorial material in this work has been asserted in accordance with the UK Copyright, Designs and Patents Act 1988.

All rights reserved. No part of this publication may be reproduced, stored in a retrieval system, or transmitted, in any form or by any means, electronic, mechanical, photocopying, recording or otherwise, except as permitted by the UK Copyright, Designs and Patents Act 1988, without the prior permission of the publisher.

Wiley also publishes its books in a variety of electronic formats. Some content that appears in print may not be available in electronic books.

Designations used by companies to distinguish their products are often claimed as trademarks. All brand names and product names used in this book are trade names, service marks, trademarks or registered trademarks of their respective owners. The publisher is not associated with any product or vendor mentioned in this book. This publication is designed to provide accurate and authoritative information in regard to the subject matter covered. It is sold on the understanding that the publisher is not engaged in rendering professional services. If professional advice or other expert assistance is required, the services of a competent professional should be sought.

*Library of Congress Cataloging-in-Publication Data*
Photography and philosophy : essays on the pencil of nature / edited by Scott Walden.
p. cm. — (New directions in aesthetics)
Includes bibliographical references and index.
ISBN 978-1-4051-3924-3 (hardcover : alk. paper) – ISBN 978-1-4443-3508-8 (pbk : alk. paper) 1. Photography—Philosophy. 2. Photography, Artistic—Philosophy. I. Walden, Scott, 1961–
TR183.P483 2007
770.1—dc22 2007024737

A catalogue record for this book is available from the British Library.

Set in 10/12.5pt Galliard
by Graphicraft Limited, Hong Kong

1 2010

# CONTENTS

# ACKNOWLEDGMENTS

This anthology emerges from the *Light Symposium*, a conference on photography co-sponsored by the Memorial University of Newfoundland and the Art Gallery of Newfoundland and Labrador. The efforts of many members of these two institutions went into the creation of the intellectually and aesthetically satisfying atmosphere that the participants enjoyed, but special thanks are due to William Barker, Patricia Grattan, Bruce Johnson, and John Scott. Financial support for the conference from Social Sciences and Humanities Research Council of Canada is also gratefully acknowledged.

Two residences administered by the Art Gallery of Newfoundland and Labrador (and assisted by the Landfall Trust and Terra Nova National Park) provided me with time to write this introductory essay, my own essay, and to attend to the myriad details involved in assembling this volume. Special thanks in connection with this are due to Gordon Laurin and Shauna McCabe. Debbie Bula and Anupum Mehrotra, with the Philosophy Department at New York University, were stellar in helping me with a variety of administrative matters. My thanks as well to Danielle Descoteaux, Jamie Harlan, and Jeff Dean at Blackwell Publishing for a mixture of warmth and professionalism that made pulling this collection together so enjoyable.

Personal thanks are due to John Matturri for many conversations over the years, and to Gary Ostertag for planting the idea for this collection in my mind many years ago, and for his unending support and encouragement. Finally, my thanks to Christine Downie for fueling the entire project with her limitless love.

Scott Walden
New York

# LIST OF FIGURES

# CONTRIBUTORS

**Noël Carroll** is the author or editor of multiple books and dozens of articles on a wide range of humanistic and cultural topics. In 2002, Carroll was awarded a Guggenheim fellowship to explore the relationship between philosophy and dance. He is currently Andrew W. Mellon Term Professor in the Humanities at Temple University.

**Jonathan Cohen** has published numerous essays in a variety of fields, including the philosophy of mind, metaphysics, and aesthetics. He is co-editor of *Contemporary Debates in the Philosophy of Mind* (Blackwell Publishing, 2007) and *Color Ontology and Color Science* (The MIT Press, forthcoming). Cohen is Associate Professor of Philosophy and Cognitive Science at the University of California, San Diego.

**Gregory Currie** has published numerous books and articles on the arts generally, with special emphasis on cinema and narrative. His most recent works include: *Narrative Thinking* (Oxford University Press, forthcoming), *Arts and Minds* (Oxford University Press, 2005), and *Recreative Minds: Imagination in Philosophy and Psychology* (Oxford University Press, 2002). Currie is Professor of Philosophy and Dean of the Faculty of Arts at the University of Nottingham.

**Arthur Danto**'s numerous books and essays cover topics ranging from the philosophy of Hegel to debates in contemporary art. He is art critic for *The Nation* and contributing editor for several prominent periodicals, including *Artforum* and *Naked Punch Review*. Danto is Johnsonian Professor of Philosophy (Emeritus) at Columbia University.

**David Davies** works primarily in the philosophy of art, and has published articles on film, literature, and the visual arts. He has also published widely on issues in metaphysics and the philosophy of mind. His book *Art as Performance* (Blackwell, 2004) clarifies the continuities and discontinuities between traditional and contemporary art. Davies is Associate Professor in the department of Philosophy at McGill University.

**Cynthia Freeland** is the author of *But Is It Art? An Introduction to Art Theory* (Oxford University Press, 2002) and co-editor of *Philosophy and Film* (Routledge, 1995). In addition to her curatorial work and critical writing on photography, Freeland is Professor and Chairperson in the Department of Philosophy at the University of Houston.

**Dominic Lopes** has co-edited several books and published numerous essays on the philosophy of art. He is author of *Understanding Pictures* (Oxford University Press, 1996) and *Sight and Sensibility: Evaluating Pictures* (Oxford University Press, 2005). Lopes is Distinguished University Scholar and Professor of Philosophy at the University of British Columbia.

**Patrick Maynard's** numerous essays on the arts generally and photography in particular are richly informed by art-historical knowledge. He is author of *The Engine of Visualization: Thinking Through Photography* (Cornell University Press, 1997) and *Drawing Distinctions: The Varieties of Graphic Expression* (Cornell University Press, 2005). Maynard is Professor of Philosophy (Emeritus) at the University of Western Ontario.

**Aaron Meskin's** research in the philosophy of art and philosophical psychology has led to the publication of numerous essays, including 'Defining Comics?' (*Journal of Aesthetics and Art Criticism*, 2007) and 'Aesthetic Testimony: What Can We Learn From Others About Beauty and Art?' (*Philosophy and Phenomenological Research*, 2004). He is Lecturer and Director of Postgraduate Studies with the Department of Philosophy, University of Leeds.

**Barbara Savedoff** has published numerous essays on the philosophy of photography and is author of the influential *Transforming Images: How Photography Complicates the Picture* (Cornell University Press, 2000). In addition to her practice as a painter, Savedoff is Associate Professor of Philosophy, Baruch College, City University of New York.

**Roger Scruton** is a philosopher, journalist, composer, and broadcaster who has published more than 30 books of criticism, philosophy, and cultural commentary. He was Fellow of Peterhouse Cambridge and Director of Studies at Christ's College Cambridge from 1971 until 1991, and is currently Visiting Professor with the Department of Philosophy, University of Buckingham.

**Scott Walden** specializes in the theory and practice of photography. He has received multiple grants from the Canada Council for the Arts, and was awarded the 2007 Duke and Duchess of York Prize in Photography. He is currently Visiting Scholar with the Department of Philosophy, New York University.

**Kendall L. Walton** has published dozens of highly influential essays on the philosophy of art and representation, and is author of *Mimesis as Make-Believe: On the Foundations of the Representational Arts* (Harvard University Press, 1990). He has been awarded fellowships from, among other organizations, the Rockefeller Foundation, the National Endowment for the Humanities, and the American Council of Learned Societies. Walton is Charles L. Stevenson Collegiate Professor of Philosophy, University of Michigan.

# INTRODUCTION

Scott Walden

Photography received an enormous amount of critical attention during the 1970s and '80s. Roland Barthes provided a poignant meditation on the phenomenology of viewing photographs, and then a more analytical investigation into the nature of photographic meaning.[1] Susan Sontag undertook a sustained examination of the role of photography in the media, focusing especially on the limits of the medium in fostering ethical knowledge.[2] Allan Sekula worked to undermine the traditional idea that there is something especially truthful or objective about a photographic image, or that it carried a unique, context-invariant meaning.[3] And Joel Snyder argued against the modernist idea that there were principles of evaluation unique to photography, ones that set such evaluation apart from the evaluation of images generally.[4] Texts by these authors still constitute the canon in college courses devoted to photographic theory.

But much has changed since these books and articles were published. There have been developments in the philosophies of language and depiction which have advanced our understanding of text-meaning and image-meaning. Digital-imaging technology and the image-manipulation possibilities it affords have replaced the traditional negative-positive

1 Roland Barthes, *Camera Lucida: Reflections on Photography* (New York: Noonday Press, 1981); and Roland Barthes, "The Photographic Message," in *Image/Music/Text*, trans. Stephen Heath (New York: Farrar, Straus, and Giroux, 1977), and in excerpt form at pp. 521–33, in Vicki Goldberg, ed., *Photography in Print: Writings from 1816 to the Present* (New York: Simon and Schuster, 1981).

2 Susan Sontag, *On Photography* (New York: Farrar, Straus, and Giroux, 1977).

3 Allan Sekula, *Photography Against the Grain: Essays and Photo Works 1973–1983* (Halifax, NS: The Press of the Nova Scotia College of Art and Design, 1984).

4 Joel Snyder and Neil Walsh Allen, "Photography, Vision, and Representation," *Critical Inquiry* 2 (1975).

process, raising new questions about the veracity of the medium. In the artworld, photography has changed from a marginal medium fighting for institutional respect to one that not only has its own department at the Metropolitan Museum of Art, but has become the darling of the avant-garde as well. And there has been an increase in our awareness of the need for specialized attention to ethical issues arising in professions that involve human subjects such as medicine and business, a development that raises the possibility of a similar need in the professional practice of photography. Given these developments the time is right for a re-investigation of the themes the pioneering critics introduced, and for a careful examination of the new issues that have arisen.

Most of the essays presented here are thus newly written for this collection, although in three instances I have chosen to reprint already published works that bring fresh perspectives to these issues or that have been especially influential on the other works in the collection. Kendall L. Walton's first contribution, "Transparent Pictures: On the Nature of Photographic Realism," is one such reprint. Walton takes as his conceptual starting point the idea that photographs are produced by a *mechanical* process, one that bypasses the beliefs the photographer has about the scene before her. The photographer's belief that there is a tree in front of her, for example, operating in conjunction with her desire to take a picture of a tree, might cause her to point her camera straight ahead, but once she trips the shutter it is the optical-chemical (or, these days, optical-electronic) process that renders the image, not any aspect of the contents of her mind. With a handmade image such as a painting matters are different – the beliefs a painter has about the scene before him are directly involved in what gets rendered on the canvas.

Walton's second and most controversial idea is that the mechanical character of the photographic process makes photographs, quite literally, *transparent*. We see through them to their subject matter in the same way we see through windows to the things that lie on the other side. Handmade images such as paintings or drawings, because they have beliefs directly involved in their formative process, are, by contrast, opaque. We may *imagine* that they are transparent and that we see through them, but in fact we do not.

According to Walton, two additional features emerge from these twin claims of mechanicity and transparency. The first is that the transparent character of photographs places viewers in special *contact* with the things seen through them, and that from such contact arises value. If a photograph of Beethoven were discovered, we would literally see the great composer through it, and we would thereby be in special contact with him.

Such contact – and the value we associate with it – accounts for the media frenzy that most certainly would result. The second feature is that the mechanical-transparent character of the photographic process yields images that are especially helpful in enabling people to learn about the world by looking through them. This *epistemic advantage* accounts for the usefulness of photographs in journalistic, evidentiary, and scientific contexts.

Cynthia Freeland's contribution (chapter 2) focuses on Walton's contact and transparency theses. With regard to the former, Freeland investigates the extent to which photographs function like religious icons. Icons of holy figures are said to function not as representations of their subjects, but rather as *manifestations* of them and, as such, are said to afford special contact with those subjects. Furthermore, many icons are thought to have a special causal connection with their subjects, either having been rendered by someone who was actually in the presence of the holy figure or, in certain instances, having been rendered without human agency at all (by physical contact with the subject, or by divine agency). Perhaps the manifestation function of icons arises from these special causal connections, and perhaps such manifestation accounts for the sense of contact that icons are said to afford. Likewise, perhaps photographs in some sense manifest their subjects, and perhaps such manifestation arises from the mechanical character of the photographic process. If so, the analogy with icons might help us further to understand the sense of contact with the world that photographs seem to offer.

With regard to Walton's transparency thesis, Freeland notes that Walton distinguishes between seeing something directly in ordinary vision and seeing something indirectly by means of visual aids such as binoculars, telescopes, and photographs. Freeland suggests that it is typically the former kind of seeing that places us in contact with the things we see, and that the latter kind might not afford contact at all. Given this, she wonders whether there is a tension within Walton's position insofar as he is arguing that the transparency of photographs supports their capacity to convey a sense of contact with their subjects, even though the kind of seeing that occurs through them is indirect.

In chapter 3, Aaron Meskin and Jonathan Cohen refine a line of criticism of Walton's transparency thesis which they began in an earlier essay.[5] Contact with the world is an instance of seeing, they argue, only if such contact provides information about the visual properties of things (v-information) *and* information about the spatial locations of those

5 Jonathan Cohen and Aaron Meskin, "On the Epistemic Value of Photographs," *Journal of Aesthetics and Art Criticism* 62: 2 (Spring 2004): 197–210.

things in relation to the body of the viewer (e-information). While perceptual contact via a photograph might be a rich source of v-information, it is almost never a source of e-information. I can, for example, learn about the visible properties of the Eiffel Tower by looking at a photograph of it, but I cannot learn in what direction it lies relative to me by doing so (except, perhaps, in very unusual cases such as those in which my body is also depicted). Thus we do not see through photographs; they are not transparent.

Meskin and Cohen further argue that the special evidentiary status we accord individual photographs arises from the beliefs we have about photographs in general. As members of a society which regularly uses photographs in journalistic, evidentiary, and scientific contexts, we each develop the belief that photographs as a category are rich sources of v-information. Thus, when we encounter an object which we recognize as a photograph, we infer that it, as a member of this category, is a rich source of v-information. In contrast, as members of a society in which paintings and drawings are typically *not* used in contexts where v-information about things depicted is in demand, we each develop the belief that such images (again, as a category) are poor sources of such information. Thus, when we encounter an object which we recognize as a painting or a drawing – even one that aspires to photorealism – we tend to infer that it is not a rich source of v-information (even though, unbeknownst to us, it might be). Such background beliefs about these two broad categories of images, Meskin and Cohen suggest, in this way account for the special epistemic weight frequently accorded to photographs.

My own contribution (chapter 4) investigates the claims of veracity or objectivity that have been associated with photography since its invention, but that are these days regarded with suspicion. In exactly what senses might photographs be especially truthful or impartial in comparison to handmade images? Why is it that we continue to use photographic images in contexts that require these qualities (such as journalistic or evidentiary) notwithstanding the contemporary suspicions? And what bearing does the advent of digital imaging have on these issues?

I argue first of all that the notions of truth and objectivity must be detached from one another. Truth is a quality associated not with images themselves, but rather with the thoughts those images engender in the minds of their viewers. Objectivity is likewise not a quality belonging to the images themselves, but then again nor is it a quality belonging to the thoughts those images engender. Instead, objectivity is equivalent to Walton's notion of mechanicity and, as such, is a quality belonging to the *process* that begins with the original scene and ends in the formation of the image. I argue further that thoughts arising from viewing objectively formed images may or may not be true, but that *if* those thoughts are true, then the viewer can have greater *confidence* in their truth than he or she would have had had the images been subjectively formed. This loose linkage between truth and objectivity (and the tight connection between objectivity and mechanicity) opens the possibility that digital imaging leaves the veracity of thoughts formed by looking at photographic images unscathed, but takes away the viewer's confidence in the truth of such thoughts. And this would be unfortunate, as it has been recognized at least since Plato's *Meno* that it is much less valuable to have true thoughts than it is to have true thoughts *plus* grounds for confidence in their truth.

Barbara Savedoff is likewise interested in the truth or objectivity associated with photographic images, qualities she refers to under the heading of *documentary authority* (chapter 5). In an earlier work, Savedoff explained how our assumptions about the documentary authority of photographic images is a key ingredient in our appreciation of a range of important photographs from the fine-art canon.[6] Here, she applies her analysis to images belonging to the relatively unusual genres of abstract or surrealist photography. With regard to abstract photographs, Savedoff argues that our assumptions about documentary authority cause us to attempt to identify the objects that were before the camera when the photograph was taken, attempts which are in tension with the abstract qualities of the photograph itself. Such a tension has a positive effect, one that causes our appreciation of abstract photographs to differ importantly from our appreciation of abstract paintings or drawings (in which no similar assumptions about authority are operative). With regard to surrealist photographs, Savedoff argues that assumptions about documentary authority are likewise in play, although in these instances it is not *resisted* attempts at recognition that enhance the appreciation, but rather *successful* acts of recognition of familiar objects presented in uncanny ways.

Savedoff also considers a range of images that in various ways function to undermine our confidence in the documentary authority of photographic images generally, and wonders whether the recent widespread dissemination of such images will cause viewers to abandon their assumptions about the documentary authority of photographs, with the result that we will no longer be able to appreciate abstract or surrealist photographs in the traditional ways.

[6] Barbara Savedoff, *Transforming Images: How Photography Complicates the Picture.* (Ithaca, NY: Cornell University Press, 2000).

Roger Scruton's essay (chapter 6) has been the subject of heated critical attention since its initial publication in 1983. Its central thesis – that images yielded by photographic means cannot be artworks except insofar as they incorporate formative elements foreign to the photographic process – runs counter to the dramatic increase in the acceptance of photographs as artworks noted above. Scruton's central argument is straightforward:

1 An object is a work of visual art only if it is a representation.
2 An image is a representation only if it expresses the artist's thoughts or feelings about what is depicted.
3 Such expression is facilitated by the artist's control over details in an image, and the viewer's subsequent questioning why the details are arranged in the ways that they are.
4 The photographer lacks such control over details (the photographic process is, as noted, a mechanical one), and so the images produced cannot be representations, and so cannot be works of art.

Suppose, for example, that a portrait painter chooses pigments that render her sitter slightly luminescent. The attentive viewer might then ask why the artists chose to render the sitter in this way, and in answering this question might conclude that the artist regards the sitter as angelic. The image would in this way be a representation, something that conveys the artist's thoughts or feelings to the viewer. Now consider a photographic portrait. Details in a photographic portrait are the product of the mechanical operation of the camera, not the conscious control of the photographer. The viewer, knowing about this lack of control, is *not* motivated to ask why the details are as they are, and so has no means of discerning the attitudes of the photographer towards her subject. The photograph is thus not a representation, and so cannot be an artwork. Granted, the photographic image could be retouched using airbrush or (these days) digital-imaging techniques and that the control requisite for expression could thereby be introduced, but to the extent that such techniques are incorporated, the photographer becomes, essentially, a painter, and Scruton has no quarrel with the idea that *paintings* can be artworks.

One way of responding to Scruton involves denying his claim that an object can be a work of visual art only if the artist has sufficient control over its details. Examples such as Marcel Duchamp's ready-mades (in which found objects – a urinal, most infamously – are placed in galleries and declared artworks) do seem to run directly counter to this thesis. Another way would be to reject Scruton's construal of representation as being overly restrictive. Or a third way might involve granting both of these to Scruton (at least for the sake of argument) but then arguing that

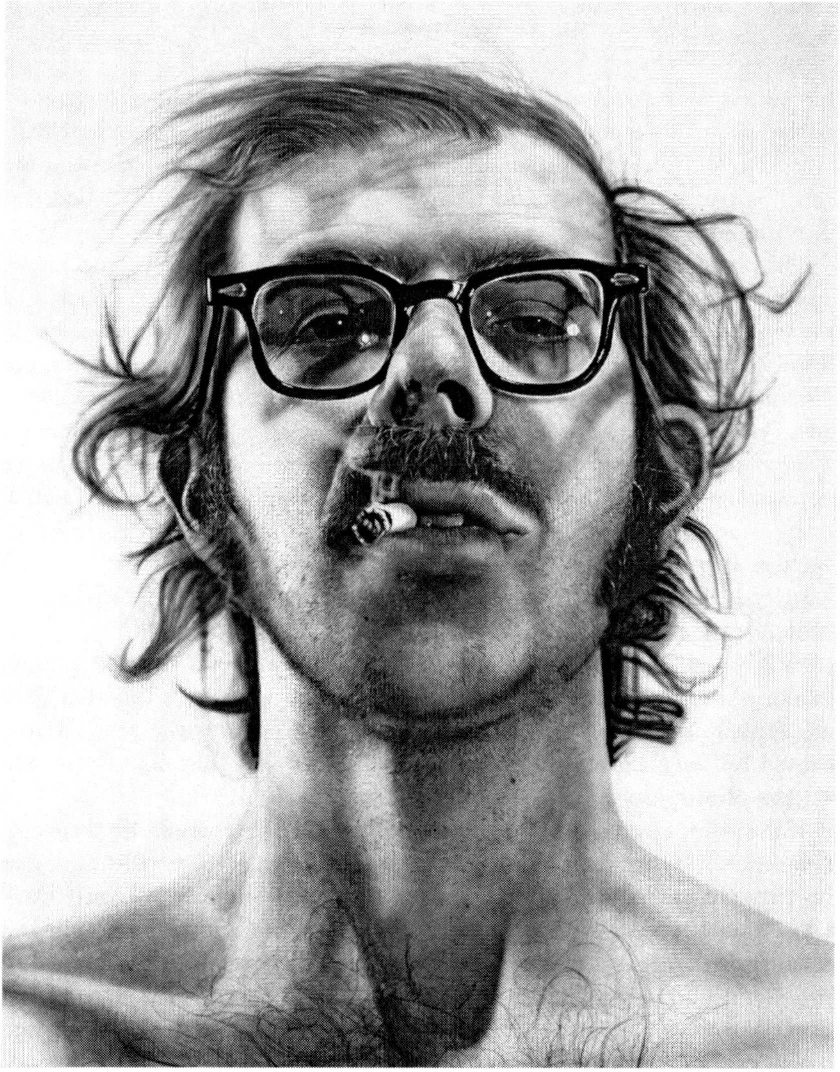

**Figure 1.3** Chuck Close, *Big Self Portrait*, 1967–8, acrylic on canvas, $107\frac{1}{2} \times 83\frac{1}{2} \times 2''$. Collection Walker Art Center, Minneapolis, Art Center Acquisition Fund, 1969.

photographers do indeed have the requisite control over details in the images they produce. David Davies takes this third approach in his contribution to our collection (chapter 7).

Davies begins by placing Scruton's discussion in historical context, noting that Rudolph Arnheim, writing almost 50 years before Scruton, considered and responded to the same sort of argument that Scruton presents (indeed, Arnheim himself is responding to Scruton-style arguments offered by both Charles Baudelaire and Lady Elizabeth Eastlake in the 1850s[7]). Arnheim agrees that there are many details in a photographic image that are beyond the control of the photographer, but points out that *how* the subject is presented – from which direction, using which camera angle, etc. – constitutes enough control over the image to enable it to express the photographer's thoughts. Davies supplements Arnheim's "response" to Scruton by carefully considering both a photograph by Henri Cartier-Bresson and that photographer's own discussion of his work. Cartier-Bresson's masterpiece, *Abruzzi, Village of Aquila* (1951) [figure 7.1], exemplifies rigorous geometrical structure, a structure which Cartier-Bresson sees as expressing the significance that he finds in the world. For Cartier-Bresson, events in the world acquire such significance by their relations to one another, and the photographer's awareness of this significance is expressed by his or her incorporation of relational geometrical structure in the photographic images he or she produces. The control over detail needed for expression is thus found not only in choice of subject matter and camera angle, as suggested by Arnheim, but by the incorporation of geometrical structure in a photographic image as well.

Patrick Maynard, like Davies, finds much of the value in many photographs in compositional matters such as geometrical form, but dramatically expands the range of such matters considered and, accordingly, augments the vocabulary used in doing so. According to Maynard (chapter 8), in creating a successful photograph the photographer uses her highly developed sense of the spatial scales, dynamics, and rhythms in the scene before her to structure the image she produces. The developed eye of the photographer might, for example, enable her to see the dynamics created by two human figures moving in opposite directions, and might therefore arrange things so that these figures are placed at opposite edges of the photograph, thereby creating a balanced tension that can serve as a backdrop for other, more localized, tensions nearer the center of the image.

7 See Charles Baudelaire, "The Salon of 1859," and Lady Elizabeth Eastlake, "A Review in *The London Quarterly Review*," in Goldberg, *Photography in Print*, pp. 123–6 and 88–99 respectively.

The sophisticated viewer, for his part, understands the image to be an artifact, and in so doing asks why objects are placed in the ways that they are, and in answering such questions both connects with the photographer insofar as he understands what she was able to see, and enhances his own powers of visual discernment in ways that will be of value on future occasions of seeing. For Maynard, the value of creating and viewing images lies both in their ability to embody the photographer's sophisticated ways of seeing *and* in their ability to further develop the ways of seeing of their attentive viewers.

Dominic Lopes is similarly interested in value, although he approaches the topic via a preliminary investigation into the nature of appreciation (chapter 9). Does adequate appreciation require true beliefs about the things being appreciated? If so, what aspects of these things must the appreciator have true beliefs about? Three options are considered:

(i) the adequate appreciator must be correct in believing that the thing being appreciated is of a certain kind, although she may have beliefs inconsistent with the actual nature of that kind;
(ii) the adequate appreciator must not have beliefs inconsistent with the actual nature of the kind to which she believes the thing being appreciated belongs, although she might be incorrect about whether that thing really belongs to that kind;
(iii) the adequate appreciator must both be correct in believing that the thing being appreciated is of a certain kind *and* not have beliefs inconsistent with the actual nature of that kind.

For example, suppose I am appreciating Andy Warhol's *Brillo Boxes*, but I am appreciating it as an instance of traditional mimetic art, not as an instance of pop art. I marvel at how realistic his depictions of actual, store-bought Brillo boxes are (although I am a bit taken aback by his choice of subject matter that goes beyond the usual landscape or portraiture). Am I appreciating *Brillo Boxes* adequately? If we take the first option, the answer is "no," since the work is an instance of pop art, not mimetic art. If we take the second option and assume that I understand mimetic art – or, at least, that I do not have beliefs that conflict with the essence of such art – then the answer is "yes," since on this option my mis-categorization is irrelevant to the quality of my appreciation. If we take the third option, then the answer is "no," since it requires satisfaction of the first.

Lopes leaves open the question which of these options best accounts for our intuitions concerning the circumstances under which someone is appreciating well. But he does note that which we choose might have significant bearing on whether, in general, we appreciate photographs

adequately. The danger lies in accepting either options (ii) or (iii) and then, in addition, accepting contemporary suspicions about the veracity of the medium. For suppose the widespread belief that photographs furnish the truth is false. If so, then appreciators of photographs typically have a belief that is inconsistent with the actual nature of photography. If this is the case, then on options (ii) or (iii) they are not appreciating photographs well. Could it be that, unbeknownst to us, there is something fundamentally wrong with our appreciation of core examples from the canon of nineteenth- and twentieth-century photography?

Kendall L. Walton's second contribution to our collection, "Landscape and Still Life: Static Representations of Static Scenes," investigates the differences in the depictive contents of still and motion-picture images.[8] Walton bases his investigation on a theory of depiction he has presented elsewhere, certain core features of which must be understood in order to follow the line of reasoning found in his essay.[9] According to Walton, the depictive content of an image is a matter of what one is prompted to *imagine* oneself seeing when one views the image. In looking at Rubens's *An Autumn Landscape with a View of Het Steen in the Early Morning* (1636?) [figure 10.1], for example, among other things I imagine that I see trees and fields, a horse-cart and a hunter, clouds in the background, buildings, etc. It is the content of such imaginings that constitute the *depictive* content of the image. Such imaginings often occur as part of larger networks of imaginings that are not unlike the networks which constitute children's games of make-believe. In the same way a group of children might agree to imagine that tree stumps in a forest are bears and that, therefore, in encountering a particular stump, they are mandated to imagine that it is a bear, in viewing the Rubens and imagining that I am seeing a cart and a hunter, I am mandated to further imagine that the cart has recently crossed the river, that the hunter has recently shot his quarry, that he will soon shoot more, etc. According to Walton's view, this network of mandated imaginings constitutes the *representational* content of the image.

8 Walton's topic is thus not photography exclusively, since many still images are non-photographic, and it is conceivable (see chapter 10) that there are motion pictures that are likewise non-photographic. It is an interesting additional question how Walton's discussion here intersects with his view – presented in his first contribution to this anthology (chapter 1) – that photographic and non-photographic images differ in terms of their transparency.

9 *Mimesis as Make-Believe: On the Foundations of the Representational Arts* (Cambridge, MA: Harvard University Press, 1990).

Furthermore, Walton's notion of imagination is quite different from imagining in our ordinary sense of the term. Ordinary imagining involves the formation of mental images. If I am asked to imagine that the Eiffel Tower is in New York I might create an image in my mind in which the tower is next to the Empire State Building, or one in which the tower is on the edge of Central Park, etc. Imagining in Walton's sense, however, requires no such mental imagery. Instead, such states are representational insofar as they have *propositional contents*, contents that can be true or false. Imaginings in Walton's sense are thus similar to beliefs. I can imagine that four is a prime number (say, as part of a mathematical investigation) or I can believe that four is a prime number (say, on the basis poor instruction) – in both cases the state would be representational insofar as it is false, but in neither case would a mental image be required.

Turning now to Walton's essay, suppose that a five-minute film is made of an unchanging scene and then projected for an audience. Suppose further that a slide is made of the same unchanging scene, and then projected for the audience, again for five minutes. Assuming both projections are in color, that they are equally sharp, that there is no image-shake in the motion-picture projection, etc., the images cast on the screen will be indiscernible. And yet the temporal depictive content of the two images may well be different. It is clear that the film depicts five minutes in the history of the unchanging scene, but what does the five-minute projection of the still image depict? Does our knowledge that the slide projection is a still photograph prompt us to imagine that we see the unchanging scene for a dimensionless instant? Does it prompt us to imagine that we see the scene for the length of time we examine the image itself? These puzzling questions arise from consideration only of the depictive content of still photographs; there remains the larger question of their representational content.

In chapter 11, Noël Carroll examines two ways in which a fiction-film audience can utilize their knowledge of the real world in the course of understanding the film they are viewing. The first, which he calls the *realistic heuristic*, involves assuming that the fictional world of the film operates as much like the real world as is possible consonant with the plot and genre-specific assumptions embodied in that particular film. For example, in viewing a western the audience knows that a hero dangling from a cliff will die if he loses his grip and falls to the ground (because in the real world people falling from great heights die), but at the same time accepts his super-human ability to haul his body to safety (because it is part of the western genre that the hero never dies).

A second way in which knowledge of the real world is brought to bear is much less direct. Fiction films can in various ways ***allude*** to aspects of the world beyond the film, including other films with which the audience can be expected to be familiar. One form such allusion takes involves using a well-known actor in a fresh role, so that the audience has the *twofold* experience of recognizing a familiar face (and thus bringing to bear their dossier of knowledge about that actor's previous roles) and yet at the same time seeing that actor as the new character embedded in the narrative of the film at hand. In his later films John Wayne takes on the personas of various new characters, but all such personas, Carroll notes, are allusively informed by the audience's knowledge of Wayne's many previous roles.

Carroll conjectures that the photographic process is an aid to such allusive techniques. Because a photographic depiction (either still or motion-picture) is always wedded in the first instance to the actual person before the camera, the audience's attention will always be directed in part to the actor himself or herself, and thus to his or her life beyond the particular film being viewed. Such divided attention will typically enrich the audience's experience of the new character, however, in much the same way that allusion to matters beyond a story presented in a work of literature – allusions to the Catholic Mass in Joyce's *Ulysses*, for example – can be used to add extra dimensions to the characters portrayed therein.

Gregory Currie, in chapter 12, likewise investigates the extent to which the photographic process engenders such twofold experience, although in Currie's case the emphasis is on the extent to which such experience is rendered dissonant – rather than enriched – by its twofold character.

Currie distinguishes between two fundamentally different ways in which things can represent. ***Representation by origin*** weds the depictive content of an image to an object or person that figured in some way in its etiology. For example, a portrait made with Queen Elizabeth as the sitter represents-by-origin Queen Elizabeth because it was she who was the sitter; likewise, a photograph made with Queen Elizabeth in front of the camera at the moment of exposure represents-by-origin Queen Elizabeth because it was she who was in front of the camera at that moment. ***Representation by use***, by way of contrast, finds some means *other* than etiological of determining depictive content – a salt-shaker, for example, might come to represent Queen Elizabeth, not by having any causal connection with her, but rather by being used (perhaps along with some other dinnerware) to demonstrate on a kitchen table her movements at a ceremony.

An image can simultaneously represent-by-origin and represent-by-use. Julia Margaret Cameron's photographic illustrations of Tennyson's Arthurian poems, in which she photographed her friends dressed in clothes appropriate to the characters in the narrative, represent-by-origin those friends, and yet at the same time represent-by-use the various Arthurian characters. One danger of such dual representation is that dissonance can arise between the two depictive contents, and Currie finds Cameron's illustrations problematic for precisely this reason. In the case of the image entitled *The May Queen* [figure 12.1], the salience of the origin-based content (her friend Emily Peacock) is not overridden by the use-based content (the May Queen) formed by the meager narrative supported by the image. Consequently, the viewer is torn between experiencing the image as being of Peacock, and experiencing it as being of the May Queen.

Such dissonance, however, need not always occur. The rich narrative frequently supported by film results in use-based contents (referring to the characters in the narrative) that are much more salient to viewers than the origin-based contents (referring to the individual actors and their lives outside of the narrative) fixed by the photographic basis of the medium. This is one of the most prominent respects in which the aesthetics of still photography can differ from that of motion-picture photography.

Given that many, if not most, photographs involve human subjects, it is surprising that there has been no extended treatment of the ethical terrain surrounding the use of the medium. In chapter 13, Arthur Danto takes a significant step in developing such a literature by focusing on the ethics of photographic portraiture. He begins by revisiting the ancient distinction between the world as it appears to us and the world as it really is. Historically, philosophers have placed dramatically greater value on the reality lying behind the appearances, and have prided themselves on their (alleged) special ability to discern it. In a reversal of this tradition, Danto argues that there is value in appearances, and especially appearances as projected by individual human beings. Part of what it is to be human, he notes, is to care about how we appear to each other – the thriving fashion, cosmetic, hairstyling, and fitness industries all stand testament to this. Given that we value our appearances, these images we project to other members of our community ought to be respected, and one facet of such respect is an obligation on the part of the portrait-maker to depict individuals in ways that convey this desired projection, or at least in ways that do not conflict with it.

The danger with photography, however, is that the camera is not unlike the traditional philosopher in that it has the ability to pierce the veil of appearances and depict the reality lying behind. High-speed shutters, for

example, enable depictions of those facial expressions that lie between the smiles, frowns, and winks that we ordinarily discern in one another, allowing for depictions of the real but unflattering arrangements of facial musculature that take place during ordinary speech (examples of this can easily be seen by pressing the pause button on one's computer while viewing footage of a person speaking). Danto refers to such appearance-piercing portraits as *stills*, and contrasts them with what he calls *natural drawings*, photographs that depict their subjects in ways consonant with normal human perception.

The discussion leads to a range of issues ripe for further investigation. Is an individual's desired appearance always to be respected, or would such a demand lead only to portraits that appeal to the vanity of their subjects? Street photography as practiced by Robert Frank, Lee Friedlander, and Garry Winogrand, or candid portraiture of friends and lovers as practiced by Nan Goldin, often depict their subjects in unflattering ways. Is such work – which includes many of the finest photographs of the previous century – to be condemned on ethical grounds?

# 1

# TRANSPARENT PICTURES: ON THE NATURE OF PHOTOGRAPHIC REALISM

Kendall L. Walton

Photography and the cinema . . . satisfy, once and for all and in its very essence, our obsession with realism.

The photographic image is the object itself.

André Bazin, "The Ontology of the Photographic Image"

Every photograph is a fake from start to finish.

Edward Steichen, "Ye Fakers"

## 1

Photographs and pictures of other kinds have various strengths and weaknesses. But photography is commonly thought to excel in one dimension especially, that of *realism*. André Bazin and many others consider photographs to be extraordinarily realistic, realistic in a way or to an extent which is beyond the reach of paintings, drawings, and other "handmade" pictures.

This attitude is encouraged by a rich assortment of familiar observations. Photographs of a crime are more likely to be admitted as evidence in court than paintings or drawings are. Some courts allow reporters to sketch their proceedings but not to photograph them. Photographs are more useful for extortion; a sketch of Mr. X in bed with Mrs. Y – even a full-color oil painting – would cause little consternation. Photographic

Reprinted with permission from *Critical Inquiry* 11/2 (December 1984): 246–77; © by the University of Chicago.

pornography is more potent than the painted variety. Published photographs of disaster victims or the private lives of public figures understandably provoke charges of invasion of privacy; similar complaints against the publication of drawings or paintings have less credibility. I expect that most of us will acknowledge that, in general, photographs and paintings (and comparable nonphotographic pictures) affect us very differently. Compare Francisco Goya's etchings *The Disasters of War* with the Civil War photographs by Mathew Brady and his associates (see, for example, figures 1.1 and 1.2). It is hard to resist describing the difference by saying that the photographs have a kind of immediacy or realism which the etchings lack. (This is not to deny that the etchings might equal or surpass the photographs in realism of some other sort, and it is certainly not to claim that the photographs are better.)

That photography is a supremely realistic medium may be the commonsense view, but – as Edward Steichen reminds us – it is by no means universal. Dissenters note how unlike reality a photograph is and how unlikely we are to confuse the one with the other. They point to "distortions" engendered by the photographic process and to the control which the photographer exercises over the finished product, the opportunities he enjoys for interpretation and falsification. Many emphasize the expressive nature of the medium, observing that photographs are inevitably colored by the photographer's personal interests, attitudes, and prejudices.[1] Whether any of these various considerations really does collide with photography's claim of extraordinary realism depends, of course, on how that claim is to be understood.

Those who find photographs especially realistic sometimes think of photography as a further advance in a direction which many picture makers have taken during the last several centuries, as a continuation or culmination of the post-Renaissance quest for realism.[2] There is some truth in this. Such earlier advances toward realism include the development of perspective and modeling techniques, the portrayal of ordinary and incidental details, attention to the effects of light, and so on. From its very beginning, photography mastered perspective (*a* system of perspective

1 Perhaps the best recent defense of this dissenting view is that of Joel Snyder and Neil Walsh Allen, "Photography, Vision, and Representation," *Critical Inquiry* 2 (Autumn, 1975): 143–69; all further references to this work, abbreviated "PVR," will be included in the text.

2 See André Bazin, "The Ontology of the Photographic Image," in *What Is Cinema?* trans. Hugh Gray, vol. 1 (Berkeley and Los Angeles, 1967), p. 12; all further references to this work, abbreviated "OPI," will be included in the text. See also Rudolf Arnheim, "Melancholy Unshaped," in *Toward a Psychology of Art: Collected Essays* (Berkeley and Los Angeles, 1967), p. 186.

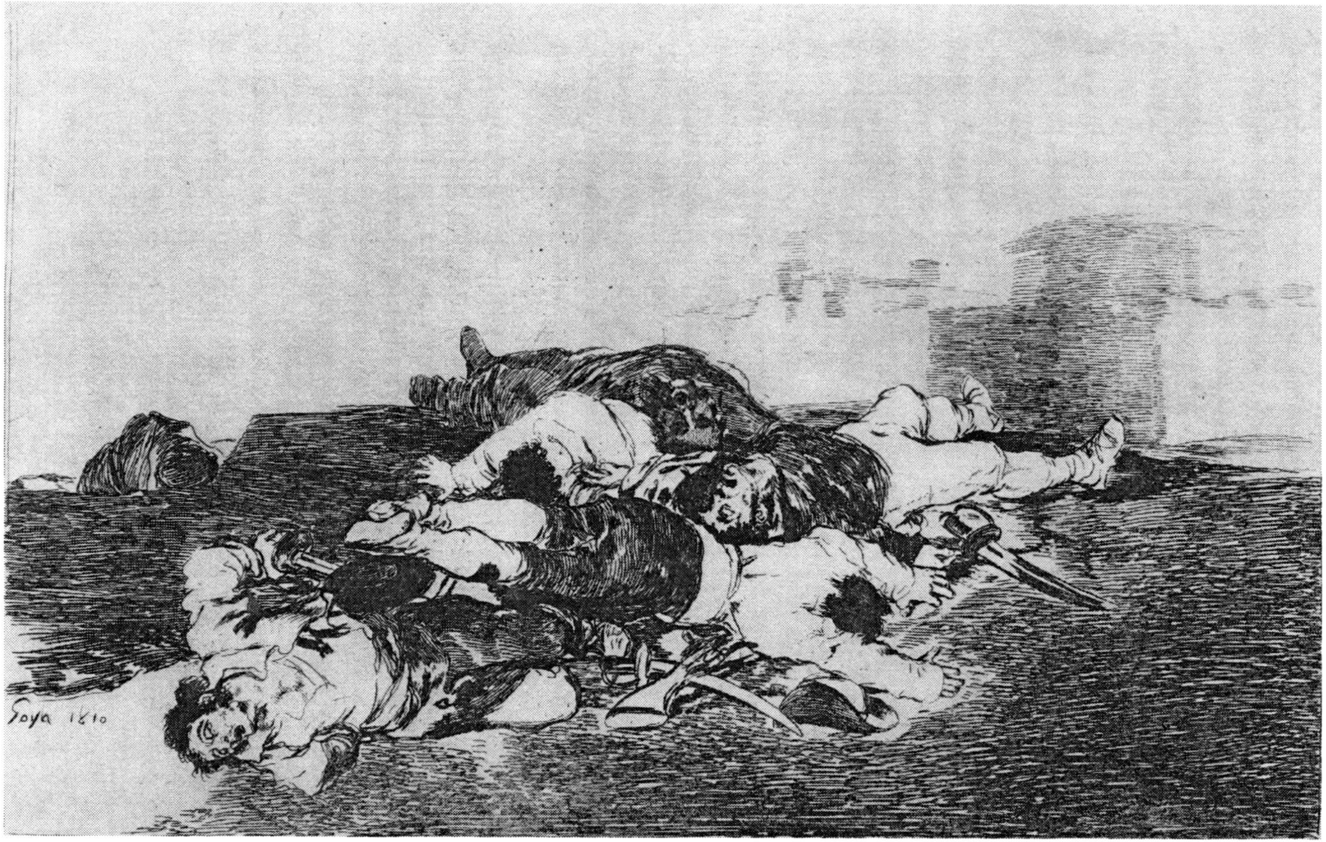


**Figure 1.1** Francisco Goya y Lucientes, *Tanto y más* (All this and more); Fatales consequencias de la sangrienta guerra en Espana con Buonaparte. Y otros caprichos enfaticos [Disasters of War], plate 22 Photograph © 2007 Museum of Fine Arts, Boston.

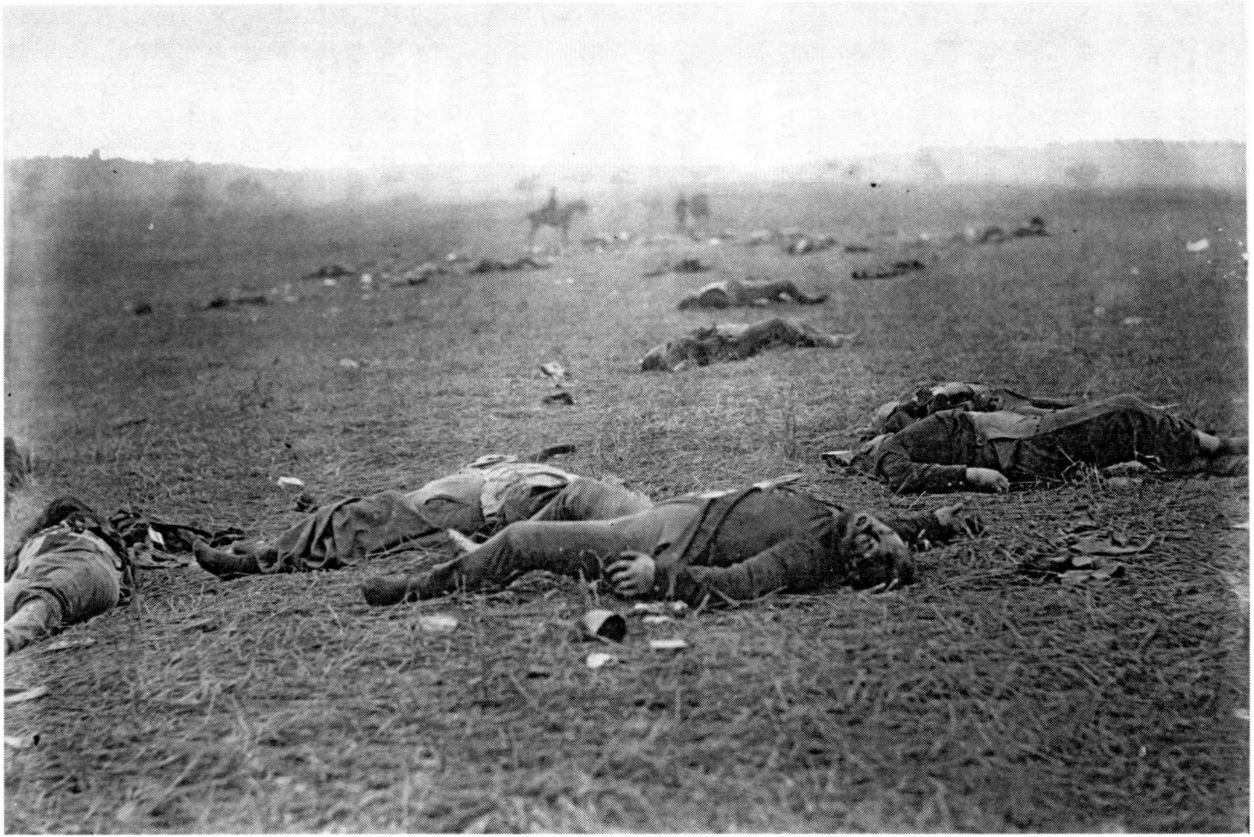

**Figure 1.2** Timothy H. O'Sullivan, *Incidents of the War. A Harvest of Death*, Gettysburg, July, 1863. Library of Congress, Prints & Photographs Division, Civil War Photographs, LC B8184 7964.

that works, anyway, if not the only one). Subtleties of shading, gradations of brightness nearly impossible to achieve with the brush, became commonplace. Photographs include as a matter of course the most mundane details of the scenes they portray – stray chickens, facial warts, clutters of dirty dishes. Photographic images easily can seem to be what painters striving for realism have always been after.

But "photographic realism" is not very special if this is all there is to it: photographs merely enjoy *more* of something which other pictures possess in smaller quantities. These differences of degree, moreover, are not differences between photographs *as such* and paintings and drawings *as such*. Paintings *can* be as realistic as the most realistic photographs, if realism resides in subtleties of shading, skillful perspective, and so forth; some indeed are virtually indistinguishable from photographs. When a painter fails to achieve such realism up to photographic standards, the difficulty is merely technological, one which, in principle, can be overcome – by more attention to details, more skill with the brush, a better grasp of the "rules of perspective." Likewise, photographs aren't necessarily very realistic in these sort of ways. Some are blurred and badly exposed. Perspective "distortions" can be introduced and subtleties of shading eliminated by choice of lens or manipulation of contrast. Photographic realism is not essentially unavailable to the painter, it seems, nor are photographs automatically endowed with it. It is just easier to achieve with the camera than with the brush.

Bazin and others see a much deeper gap between photographs and pictures of other kinds. This is evident from the marvelously exotic pronouncements they have sometimes resorted to in attempting to characterize the difference. Bazin's claim that the photographic image is identical with the object photographed is no isolated anomaly. He elaborates it at considerable length; it is echoed by Christian Metz; and it has resonances in the writings of many others.[3]

[3] Here is more from Bazin:

> Only a photographic lens can give us the kind of image of the object that is capable of satisfying the deep need man has to substitute for it something more than a mere approximation, a kind of decal or transfer. The photographic image is the object itself, the object freed from the conditions of time and space that govern it. ["OPI," p. 14]

> The photograph as such and the object in itself share a common being, after the fashion of a fingerprint. Wherefore, photography actually contributes something in the order of natural creation instead of providing a substitute for it. ["OPI," p. 15]

And see Christian Metz, *Film Language: A Semiotics of the Cinema*, trans. Michael Taylor (New York, 1974); "The cinema is the "phenomenological" art *par excellence*, the signifier is coextensive with the whole of the significate, the spectacle its own signification, thus short-circuiting the sign itself" (p. 43).

Such wild allegations might well be dismissed out of hand. It is simply and obviously false that a photographic image of Half Dome, for example, *is* Half Dome. Perhaps we shouldn't interpret Bazin's words literally.[4] But there is no readily apparent nonliteral reading of them on which they are even plausible. Is Bazin describing what seems to the viewer to be the case rather than what actually is the case? Is he saying that, in looking at photographs, one has the impression, is under an illusion, of actually seeing the world, that a photographic image of Half Dome appears to be Half Dome?

There is no such illusion. Only in the most exotic circumstances would one mistake a photograph for the objects photographed. The flatness of photographs, their frames, the walls on which they are hung are virtually always obvious and unmistakable. Still photographs of moving objects are motionless. Many photographs are black-and-white. Even photographic motion pictures in "living color" are manifestly mere projections on a flat surface and easily distinguished from "reality." Photographs look like what they are: *photographs.*

Does our experience of a photograph *approach* that of having an illusion more closely than our experiences of paintings do, even though not closely enough to qualify as an illusion? Possibly. But this is not what Bazin means. If it were, theater would qualify as even more realistic than photography. Theater comes as close or closer to providing genuine illusions than film does, it would seem. There are real flesh-and-blood

The claim that the photographic image is identical with the object photographed has resonances in Helmut Gernsheim's observation that "the camera intercepts images, the paintbrush reconstructs them" (quoted by Charles Barr, "Cinemascope: Before and After," in *Film Theory and Criticism: Introductory Readings*, ed. Gerald Mast and Marshall Cohen, 2d ed. [New York, 1979], p. 141); in Erwin Panofsky's dictum "The medium of the movies is physical reality as such" ("Style and Medium in the Motion Pictures," in *Film Theory and Criticism*, p. 263); and in the frequent characterization of photographs as "duplicates" or "doubles" or "reproductions" or "substitutes" or "surrogates" (see, e.g., Roger Scruton, "Photography and Representation," *Critical Inquiry* 7 [Spring 1981]: 577–603; repr. in this volume, chapter 6).

4 Stanley Cavell prefers not to take Bazin and Panofsky literally. The truth in what they say, he suggests, is that "a photograph is *of* the world" ("of reality or nature"), whereas "[a] painting *is* a world." In explanation, he observes that one "can always ask, of an area photographed, what lies adjacent to that area, beyond the frame. This generally makes no sense asked of a painting" (*The World Viewed: Reflections on the Ontology of Film*, enlarged ed. [Cambridge, MA, 1979], pp. 24, 16, 24, 23). But photographs typically have their own (fictional) worlds, as do paintings. And since paintings frequently portray actual scenes, they, like photographs, are often of the real world. We *can* ask, concerning a painting of an actual scene as well as a photograph, what there is in reality outside the portion depicted. Indeed we can also ask, in both cases, what the fictional world is like beyond the frame. Smoke within a frame may indicate (fictional) fire outside it.

persons on stage, and they look more like the people portrayed than do plays of light and dark on a flat screen. But Bazin regards the fact that photographs are produced "mechanically" as crucial to their special realism – and theatrical portrayals are not produced "mechanically" (see "OPI," pp. 12 and 14). (Erwin Panofsky explicitly contrasts film with theater, as well as with painting.)[5]

Bazin seems to hold that photographs enjoy their special status just by virtue of being photographs, by virtue of their mechanical origins, regardless of what they look like. "No matter how fuzzy, distorted, or discolored, no matter how lacking in documentary value the [photographic] image may be, it shares, by virtue of the very process of its becoming, the being of the model of which it is the reproduction; it is the model" ("OPI," p. 15).

To add to the confusion, let us note that claims strikingly similar to Bazin's observations about photography, and equally paradoxical, have been made concerning painting and other "handmade" representations, the very things Bazin and others mean to be distinguishing photography from!

> When we point to [a painted] image and say "this is a man" [s]trictly speaking that statement may be interpreted to mean that the image itself is a member of the class "man". . . . [A stick which a child calls a horse] becomes a horse in its own right, it belongs in the class of "gee-gees" and may even merit a proper name of its own.[6]

> [A wooden robin poised on a bird-feeding station] does not say: Such is a robin! It *is* a robin, although a somewhat incomplete one. It adds a robin to the inventory of nature, just as in Madame Tussaud's Exhibition the uniformed guards, made of wax, are . . . intended . . . to weirdly increase the staff of the institution.[7]

What, then, is special about photography?

There is one clear difference between photography and painting. A photograph is always a photograph of something which actually exists. Even when photographs portray such nonentities as werewolves and Martians, they are nonetheless photographs of actual things: actors, stage sets, costumes. Paintings needn't picture actual things. A painting of Aphrodite, executed without the use of a model, depicts nothing real.[8] But this is by no means the whole story. Those who see a sharp contrast between photographs

5 See Panofsky, "Style and Medium in the Motion Pictures," pp. 248 and 260.

6 E. H. Gombrich, "Meditations on a Hobby Horse or the Roots of Artistic Form," in "*Meditations on a Hobby Horse,*" *and Other Essays on the Theory of Art* (London, 1963), p. 2.

7 Arnheim, "The Robin and the Saint," in *Toward a Psychology of Art*, p. 325.

8 See Scruton, "Photography and Representation," p. 579, and this volume, pp. 139–40.

and paintings clearly think that it obtains no less when paintings depict actual things than when they do not, and even when viewers fully realize that they do. Let's limit our examples to pictures of this kind. The claim before us is that photographs of Abraham Lincoln, for instance, are in some fundamental manner more realistic than painted portraits of him.

I shall argue that there is indeed a fundamental difference between photographs and painted portraits of Lincoln, that photography is indeed special, and that it deserves to be called a supremely realistic medium. But the kind of realism most distinctive of photography is not an ordinary one. It has little to do either with the post-Renaissance quest for realism in painting or with standard theoretical accounts of realism. It is enormously important, however. Without a clear understanding of it, we cannot hope to explain the power and effectiveness of photography.

## 2

Painting and drawing are techniques for producing pictures. So is photography. But the special nature of photography will remain obscure unless we think of it in another way as well – as a contribution to the enterprise of seeing. The invention of the camera gave us not just a new method of making pictures and not just pictures of a new kind: it gave us a new way of seeing.

Amidst Bazin's assorted declarations about photography is a comparison of the cinema to mirrors. This points in the right direction.[9] Mirrors

[9] But Bazin was fuzzy about what direction this is. The screen, he says, puts us

> "in the presence of" the actor. It does so in the same way as a mirror – one must agree that the mirror relays the presence of the person reflected in it – but it is a mirror with a delayed reflection, the tin foil of which retains the image. . . . In the film about Manolete . . . we are present at the actual death of the famous matador. "Theater and Cinema – Part Two," *What Is Cinema?*, pp. 97–8.

Obviously, spectators of a film of a matador are not in the presence of the matador, nor does it seem to them that they are. Indeed Bazin himself apparently agrees, as he continues:

> While our emotion may not be as deep *as if* we *were* actually present in the arena at that historic moment, its nature is the same. What we *lose by way of direct witness* do we not recapture thanks to the artificial proximity provided by photographic enlargement? [Ibid., p. 98; my emphasis]

Cavell also suggests comparing photographs with mirrors (see *The World Viewed*, p. 213). F. M. Zemach discusses aids to vision more generally (see "Seeing, 'Seeing,' and Feeling," *Review of Metaphysics* 23 [Sept. 1969]: 3–24).

are aids to vision, allowing us to see things in circumstances in which we would not otherwise be able to; with their help we can see around corners. Telescopes and microscopes extend our visual powers in other ways, enabling us to see things that are too far away or too small to be seen with the naked eye. Photography is an aid to vision also, and an especially versatile one. With the assistance of the camera, we can see not only around corners and what is distant or small; we can also see into the past. We see long-deceased ancestors when we look at dusty snapshots of them. To view a screening of Frederic Wiseman's *Titicut Follies* (1967) in San Francisco in 1984 is to watch events which occurred in 1967 at the Bridgewater State Hospital for the Criminally Insane. Photographs are *transparent*. We see the world *through* them.

I must warn against watering down this suggestion, against taking it to be a colorful, or exaggerated, or not quite literal way of making a relatively mundane point. I am not saying that the person looking at the dusty photographs has the *impression* of seeing his ancestors – in fact, he doesn't have the impression of seeing them "in the flesh," with the unaided eye. I am not saying that photography *supplements* vision by helping us to discover things that we can't discover by seeing.[10] Painted portraits and linguistic reports also supplement vision in this way. Nor is my point that what we see – photographs – are *duplicates* or *doubles* or *reproductions* of objects, or *substitutes* or *surrogates* for them. My claim is that we *see*, quite literally, our dead relatives themselves when we look at photographs of them.

Does this constitute an extension of the ordinary English sense of the word "see"? I don't know; the evidence is mixed.[11] But if it is an extension, it is a very natural one. Our theory needs, in any case, a term which applies both to my "seeing" my great-grandfather when I look at his snapshot and to my seeing my father when he is in front of me. What is important is that we recognize a fundamental commonality between the two cases, a single natural kind to which both belong. We could say that

10 Siegfried Kracauer's talk of photography's *revealing* reality could be taken as making this point (see *Theory of Film: The Redemption of Physical Reality* [Fair Lawn, NJ, 1960], p. 28). And so could Arnheim's claim that "by its very nature . . . the motion picture tends to satisfy the desire for faithful reports about curious, characteristic, exciting things going on in this world of ours" (*Film as Art* [Berkeley and Los Angeles, 1957], p. 34).

11 We speak naturally enough of seeing Johnny Carson on television, of seeing Charlie Chaplin in the movies, and of hearing people over the telephone and in recordings. We may also, naturally enough, *deny* that a person has seen Johnny Carson if he has "seen" him only on television, for example.

I *perceive* my great-grandfather but do not *see* him, recognizing a mode of perception ("seeing-through-photographs") distinct from vision – if the idea that I do perceive my great-grandfather is taken seriously. Or one might make the point in some other way. I prefer the bold formulation: the viewer of a photograph sees, literally, the scene that was photographed.

Slippery slope considerations give this claim an initial plausibility. No one will deny that we see through eyeglasses, mirrors, and telescopes. How, then, would one justify denying that a security guard sees via a closed circuit television monitor a burglar breaking a window or that fans watch athletic events when they watch live television broadcasts of them? And after going this far, why not speak of watching athletic events via delayed broadcasts or of seeing the Bridgewater inmates via Wiseman's film? These last examples do introduce a new element: they have us seeing past events. But its importance isn't obvious. We also find ourselves speaking of observing through a telescope the explosion of a star which occurred millions of years ago.[12] We encounter various other differences also, of course, as we slide down the slope. The question is whether any of them is significant enough to justify digging in our heels and recognizing a basic

12 Some find the notion of seeing the past too much to swallow and dismiss talk of seeing long-concluded events through telescopes as deviant or somehow to be explained away (see Alvin I. Goldman, "Perceptual Objects," *Synthese* 35 [July 1977]: 269, and David Lewis, "Veridical Hallucination and Prosthetic Vision," *Australasian Journal of Philosophy* 58 [Sept. 1980]: 241–2). If seeing the past is allowed, one might worry that having a memory image of something will qualify as seeing it. Zemach accepts this consequence (see "Seeing, 'Seeing,' and Feeling," pp. 15–16). But it probably can be avoided, at least for most memory images. Many, if not all, memory images are based on one's own earlier beliefs about the object, in a manner relevantly similar to the way in which the visual experiences of the viewers of a painting are based on the painter's beliefs about the object. So one does not see through the memory image for the same reason that one does not see through paintings. But, if we are to speak of "seeing-through-photographs," we may have to allow that when an image of something one saw previously, but did not notice, pops into one's head, one sees it again. I do not find this result distressing. For any who do, however, or for any who reject the possibility of seeing the past, there is another way out. Suppose we agree that what I call "seeing-through-photographs" is not a mode of *perception*. We can always find a different term. The sharp break between photography and other pictures remains. We still can say that one sees present occurrences via a television monitor but not through, for instance, a system of simultaneous sketching. *This* is a significant difference. And one's access to past events via photographs of them differs in the same way from one's access to them via paintings.

theoretical distinction, one which we might describe as the difference between "seeing" (or "perceiving") things and not doing so.[13]

Mechanical aids to vision don't necessarily involve *pictures* at all. Eyeglasses, mirrors, and telescopes don't give us pictures. To think of the camera as another tool of vision is to de-emphasize its role in producing pictures. Photographs are pictures, to be sure, but not ordinary ones. They are pictures through which we see the world.

To be transparent is not necessarily to be invisible. We see photographs themselves when we see through them; indeed it is by looking at *Titicut Follies* that we see the Bridgewater inmates. There is nothing strange about this: one hears both a bell and the sounds that it makes, and one hears the one by hearing the other. (Bazin's remarkable identity claim might derive from failure to recognize that we can be seeing both the photograph and the object: *what we see* are photographs, but we do see the photographed objects; so the photographs and the objects must be somehow identical.)

I don't mind allowing that we see photographed objects only *indirectly*, though one could maintain that perception is equally indirect in many other cases as well: we see objects by seeing mirror images of them, or images produced by lenses, or light reflected or emitted from them; we hear things and events by hearing the sounds that they make. One is reminded of the familiar claim that we see *directly* only our own sense-data or images on our retinas. What I would object to is the suggestion that indirect seeing, in any of these cases, is not really *seeing*, that *all* we actually see are sense-data or images or photographs.

13 The slippery slope may make it hard to avoid sliding farther in another direction than some would like. When we look at fossils or footprints, do we see or perceive ancient marine organisms or ancient animals' feet? I repeat that my point needn't be made in terms of vision or perception. One might prefer to introduce a new notion, to speak of being "in contact with" things, for instance, when one either sees them with the naked eye or sees mirror images or photographs or fossils or footprints of them – but not when one sees drawings of them (see Patrick Maynard, "The Secular Icon: Photography and the Functions of Images," *Journal of Aesthetics and Art Criticism* 42 [Winter 1983]: 155–69). It may not be desirable for our theory to recognize, in addition, a more restricted notion of perceiving or seeing, one which better fits the cases in which we use these everyday expressions; there simply may be no such natural kind. We should be prepared for the possibility that there is no very important distinction which even approximates the difference between perceiving things, in any everyday sense, and not perceiving them – that what we need is a radical reorganization of our concepts in this area.

One can see through sense-data or mirror images without specifically noticing them (even if, in the latter case, one notices the mirror); in this sense they *can* be invisible. One may pay no attention to photographic images themselves, concentrating instead on the things photographed. But even if one does attend especially to the photographic image, one may at the same time be seeing, and attending to, the objects photographed.

Seeing is often a way of finding out about the world. This is as true of seeing through photographs as it is of seeing in other ways. But sometimes we learn little if anything about what we see, and sometimes we value the seeing quite apart from what we might learn. This is so, frequently, when we see departed loved ones through photographs. We can't expect to acquire any particularly important information by looking at photographs which we have studied many times before. But we can *see* our loved ones again, and *that* is important to us.

## 3

What about paintings? They are not transparent. We do not see Henry VIII when we look at his portrait; we see only a representation of him. There is a sharp break, a difference of kind, between painting and photography.

Granted, it is perfectly natural to say of a person contemplating the portrait that he "sees" Henry VIII. But this is not to be taken literally. It is *fictional*, not true, that the viewer sees Henry VIII.[14] It is equally natural to say that spectators of the Unicorn Tapestries see unicorns. But there are no unicorns; so they aren't really seeing any. Our use of the word "see," by itself, proves nothing.

A photograph purporting to be of the Loch Ness monster was widely published some years ago. If we think the monster really exists and was captured by the photograph, we will speak comfortably of seeing it when we look at the photograph. But the photograph turned out not to be of the monster but (as I recall) of a model, dredged up from the bottom of the lake, which was once used in making a movie about it. With this information we change our tune: what we see when we look at the photograph is not the monster but the model. This sort of seeing is like the ordinary variety in that only what exists can be seen.

[14] The reader can get a better idea of what I mean by "fictionality" from my "Fearing Fictions," *Journal of Philosophy* 75 (Jan. 1978): 5–27.

What about viewers of the movie (which, let us assume, was a straightforward work of fiction)? They may speak of seeing the monster, even if they don't believe for a moment that there is such a beast. It is fictional that they see it; they actually see, with photographic assistance, the model used in the making of the film. It is fictional also that they see Loch Ness, the lake. And since the movie was made on location at Loch Ness, they really do see it as well.

Even when one looks at photographs which are not straightforward works of fiction, it can be fictional that one sees. On seeing a photograph of a long-forgotten family reunion, I might remark that Aunt Mabel is grimacing. She is not grimacing *now* of course; perhaps she is long deceased. My use of the present tense suggests that it is *fictional* that she is grimacing (now). And it is fictional that I see her grimacing. In addition, I actually see, through the photograph, the grimace that she effected on the long-past occasion of the reunion.

We should add that it is fictional that I see Aunt Mabel *directly*, without photographic assistance. Apart from very special cases, when in looking at a picture it is fictional that one sees something, it is fictional that one sees it not through a photograph or a mirror or a telescope but with the naked eye. Fictionally one is in the presence of what one sees.

One such special case is Richard Shirley's beautiful film *Resonant* (1969), which was made by filming still photographs (of an elderly woman, her house, her belongings). Sometimes this is obvious: sometimes, for example, we see the edges of the filmed photographs. When we do, it is fictional that we see the house or whatever through the photographs. But much of *Resonant* is fascinatingly ambiguous. The photographs are not always apparent. Sometimes when they are not, it is probably best to say that fictionally we see things directly. Sometimes we have the impression of fictionally seeing things directly, only to realize later that fictionally we saw them via still photographs. Sometimes, probably, there is no fact of the matter. Throughout, the viewer *actually* sees still photographs, via the film, whether or not he realizes that he does. And he actually sees the woman and the house through the photographs which he sees through the film.

We now have uncovered a major source of the confusion which infects writings about photography and film: failure to recognize and distinguish clearly between the special kind of seeing which actually occurs and the ordinary kind of seeing which only fictionally takes place, between a viewer's *really* seeing something *through a photograph* and his *fictionally* seeing something *directly*. A vague awareness of both, stirred together in a witches' cauldron, could conceivably tempt one toward the absurdity that the viewer is really in the presence of the object.

## 4

Let's look now at some familiar challenges to the idea that photography differs essentially from painting and that there is something especially realistic about photographs. Some have merit when directed against some versions of the thesis. They are irrelevant when the thesis is cashed out in terms of transparency.

The objection that a photograph doesn't look much like the actual scene, and that the experience of looking at a photograph is not much like the experience of observing the scene in ordinary circumstances, is easily dismissed. Seeing directly and seeing with photographic assistance are different modes of perception. There is no reason to expect the experiences of seeing in the two ways to be similar. Seeing something through a microscope, or through a distorting mirror, or under water, or in peculiar lighting conditions, is not much like seeing it directly or in normal circumstances – but that is no reason to deny that seeing in these other ways is *seeing*. The point is not that "a photograph shows us . . . 'what we would have seen if we had been there ourselves.'" Joel Snyder and Neil Allen's objections to *this* view are well taken but beside the point ("PVR," p. 149, and see pp. 151–2). It may be *fictional* not that viewers of the photographs are shown what they *would* have seen but that they are actually there and see for themselves. Here, again, the confusion is caused by not distinguishing this from the fact that they actually do see via the photograph.

If the point concerned how photographs look, there would be no essential difference between photographs and paintings. For paintings can be virtually indistinguishable from photographs. Suppose we see Chuck Close's superrealist *Self-Portrait* (figure 1.3) thinking it is a photograph and learn later that it is a painting. The discovery jolts us. Our experience of the picture and our attitude toward it undergo a profound transformation, one which is much deeper and more significant than the change which occurs when we discover that what we first took to be an etching, for example, is actually a pen-and-ink drawing. It is more like discovering a guard in a wax museum to be just another wax figure. We feel somehow less "in contact with" Close when we learn that the portrayal of him is not photographic. If the painting is of a nude and if we find nudity embarrassing, our embarrassment may be relieved somewhat by realizing that the nudity was captured in paint rather than on film. My theory accounts for the jolt. At first we think we are (really) seeing the person portrayed; then we realize that we are not, that it is only fictional that

we see him. However, even after this realization it may well continue to *seem* to us as though we are really seeing the person (with photographic assistance), if the picture continues to look to us to be a photograph. (In the case of the nude, this may account for the continuation of some of our original feelings of embarrassment.)[15]

We have here a case of *genuine* illusion. It really does look to us as though we are seeing someone via the medium of photography, and at first we are fooled. This is not the sort of illusion which so often is attributed to viewers despite overwhelming evidence that it almost never occurs. It does not appear to us that we see a person directly, one standing right in front of us.

We have genuine illusions also when we do see through a photograph but what we see through it is not what it seems to be. Figure 1.4 is a photograph through which we see not people but a life-sized sculpture. Illusions of this kind are commonplace in film, and they contribute importantly to viewers' experiences. A detective in a movie surprises two thugs, pulls a gun, fires, and they drop. The viewer seems to be seeing these events via the film. He *does* see one man, an actor, approach two others, draw a gun, and pull the trigger. But he doesn't see the one *kill* the others, since what was photographed was not an actual killing – the bullets were blanks, and the blood, ketchup. Still, the scene *looks* as though it were an actual killing which was filmed. The obvious considerations against the idea that a killing occurs *in the viewer's presence* are irrelevant to the illusion I have described. The sharp edges of the illuminated rectangle, the obvious flatness of the screen, the fuzziness of some images, the lack of color do nothing to keep it from seeming to the viewer that he is seeing an actual killing *via a photographic film* of it.

There are some superrealist paintings – Douglas Bond's *Ace I* (figure 1.5), for instance – which have distinctly photographic stylistic traits but are rather obviously not photographs. Their photographic character is more pretense than illusion. It doesn't seem to the viewer that he sees through the photographs, but it may be fictional that he does. It may be fictional that *Ace I* is a photograph through which one sees a group of men walking in front of Pasadena City Hall.

The debate about whether photography is special sometimes revolves around the question of whether photographs are especially *accurate*. Some

15 Here is an analogous example: suppose a proud parent hears what he takes to be a recording of Johnny playing the piano and then learns that it is actually someone else mimicking Johnny's piano playing. He thought he was hearing Johnny play, via the recording, but he wasn't. Initially he swells with pride in little Johnny, then is deflated.

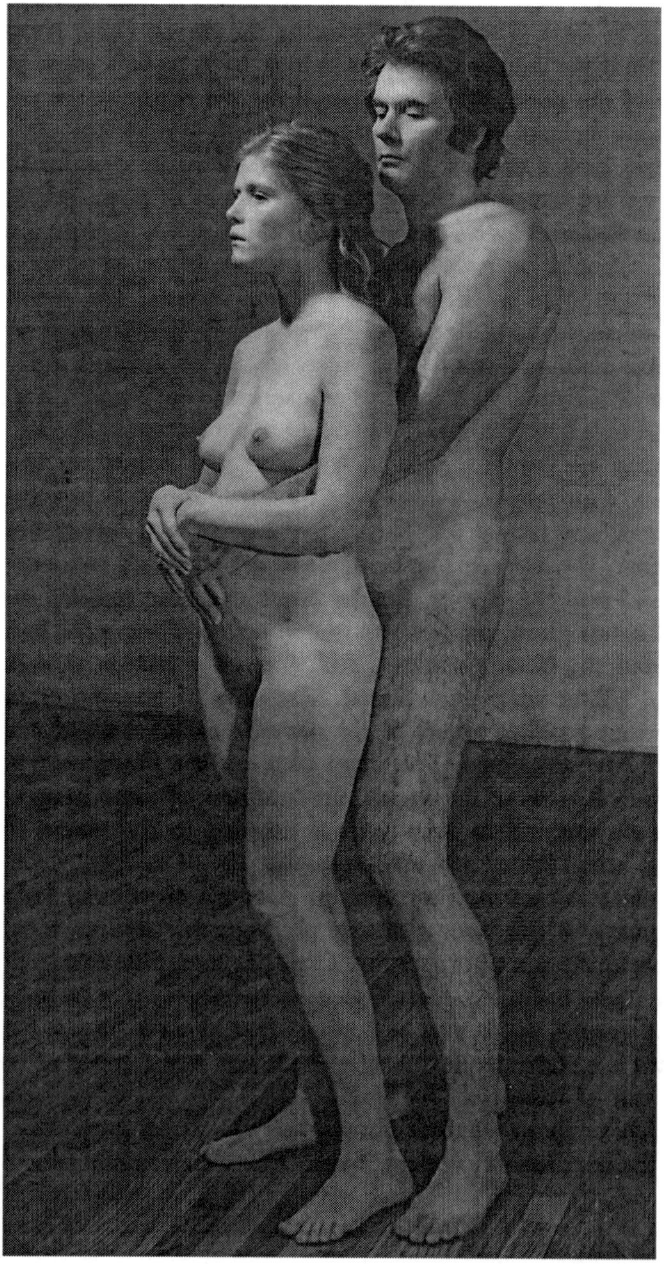

**Figure 1.4** John DeAndrea, *Man With Arms Around Woman*, vinyl polychrome, 1976. © John DeAndrea. Photograph courtesy of the artist.

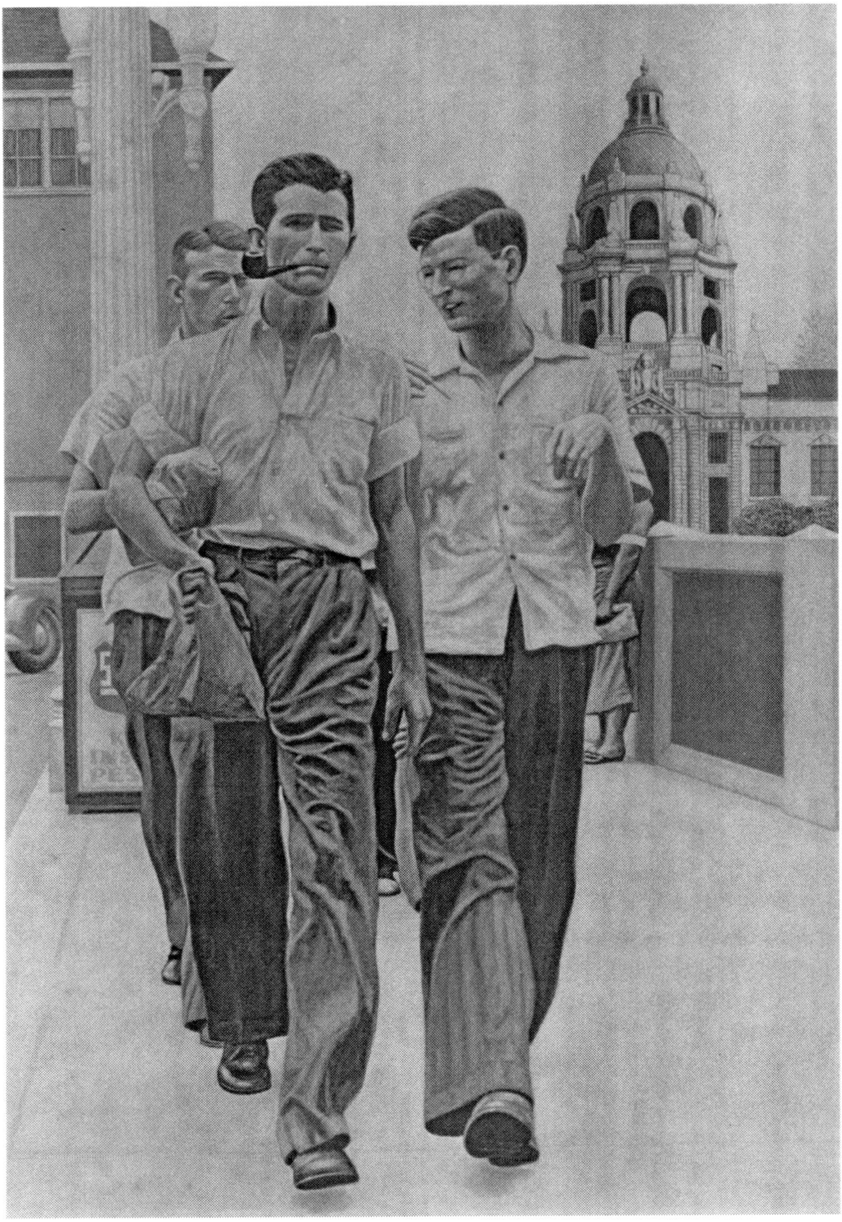

**Figure 1.5** Douglas Bond, *Ace I*, acrylic on canvas, 1967. © Douglas Bond. Photograph courtesy of the artist.

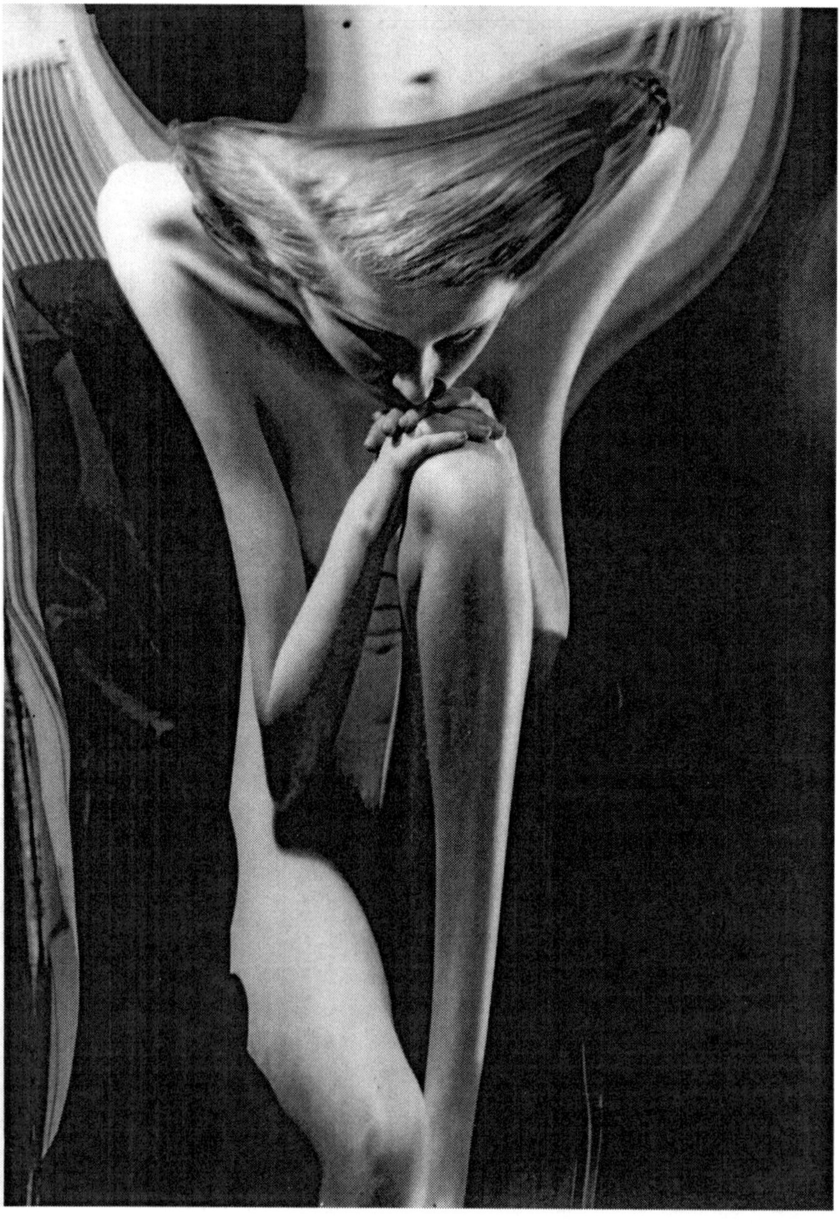

**Figure 1.6** André Kertész, *Distortion #157*, 1933. © The Estate of André Kertész. Photograph courtesy of the Estate of André Kertész.

contend that photographs regularly falsify colors and distort spatial relationships, that a photograph of a running horse will portray it either as a blur, which it is not, or as frozen, which it also is not – and of course there is the possibility of retouching in the darkroom. It remains to be seen in what sense photographs can be inaccurate. Yet misleading they certainly can be, especially to viewers unfamiliar with them or with photographs of a given kind.

But why should this matter? We can be deceived when we see things directly. If cameras can lie, so can our eyes. To see something through a distorting mirror is still to see it, even if we are misled about it. We also see through fog, through tinted windshields, and through out-of-focus microscopes. The "distortions" or "inaccuracies" of photographs are no reason to deny that we see through them (see, for example, figure 1.6).

To underscore the independence of accuracy and transparency, consider a theatrical portrayal of actual events, an acting out in a courtroom of events that led to a crime, for example. The portrayal might be perfectly accurate. Jurors might gain from it much correct information and no misinformation. Yet they certainly do not see the incident via the portrayal.

Is the difference between photographs and other pictures simply that photographs are *generally* more accurate (or less misleading), despite occasional lapses, that the photographic process is a "more reliable mechanism" than that of drawing or painting, and that therefore there is better prima facie reason to trust photographs? I doubt it. Consider a world in which mirrors are so flexible that their shapes change constantly and drastically and unpredictably.[16] There seems no reason to deny that people see through these mirrors, notwithstanding the unreliability of the mechanism. Perhaps the mechanism is not a *knowledge*-producing one.[17] If a person looks into a mirror and forms beliefs, on the basis of what he sees, about the things reflected in it and if those beliefs happen to be true, perhaps his beliefs do not constitute *knowledge*. But this does not mean that he does not *see* the reflected things.

Some objections focus on the idea that photographs owe their special status to their "mechanical," "automatic" origins, whereas paintings are "handmade." What is crucial is supposed to be the involvement of a *person* in the process. Several writers have managed to imply that people don't

16 This example is a relative of Lewis' case of the loose wire (see Lewis, "Veridical Hallucination and Prosthetic Vision," p. 244).

17 See Goldman "Discrimination and Perceptual Knowledge," *Journal of Philosophy* 73 (18 Nov. 1976): 771–91.

make photographs.[18] In any case the remarkable realism of photographs is considered to derive not from what they look like but from how they come about.

On this point I agree. Why is it that we see Lincoln when we look at photographs of him but not when we look at his painted portrait? The answer requires an account of *seeing* (or better, an account of perception in general). I would subscribe to some variety of causal theory: to see something is to have visual experiences which are caused, in a certain manner, by what is seen. Lincoln (together with other circumstances) caused his photograph and, thus, the visual experiences of those who view it. This does not yet answer our question. For Lincoln caused his portrait as well as his photograph. The difference lies in the manner of the causation.

Putting things together, we get this: part of what it is to see something is to have visual experiences which are caused by it in a purely mechanical manner. Objects cause their photographs and the visual experiences of viewers mechanically, so we see the objects through the photographs. By contrast, objects cause paintings not mechanically but in a more "human" way, a way involving the artist; so we don't see through paintings.

Objections leap to the fore. Photographs *are* made by people: "The [photographic] image is a crafted, not a natural, thing" ("PVR," p. 151). Photographers and painters just use different tools in making their pictures, it seems – one uses a camera and the other a brush. In what sense, then, are our visual experiences caused mechanically when we look at photographs and not when we look at paintings?

Objectors frequently add that photographs do not present us with things as they really are but rather with the photographer's conception or interpretation of them, that what we get from a photograph is not our own

[18] William Henry Fox Talbot, inventor of the calotype, claimed for the Lacock Abbey in Wiltshire the distinction of being the first building "that was ever yet known to have drawn its own picture" (*The Pencil of Nature* [London, 1844–6], n. to pl. 15). Bazin credits photography with "completely satisfying our appetite for illusion by a mechanical reproduction in the making of which man plays no part. . . . For the first time an image of the world is formed automatically, without the creative intervention of man" ("OPI," pp. 12, 13). "The fundamental peculiarity of the photographic medium," says Arnheim, is the fact that "the physical objects themselves print their image by means of the optical and chemical action of light" ("On the Nature of Photography," *Critical Inquiry* 1 [Sept. 1974]: 155).

view of the world but his. A photograph, no less than a painting, has a subjective point of view.[19]

All this is beside the point. The manner in which things cause my visual experiences when I see them is not one which rules out a causal role for human beings. People often *show* me things and in other ways induce me to look this way or that. They affect what I can see or how I see it – by turning the lights on or off, by blowing smoke in my eyes, by constructing and making available eyeglasses, mirrors, and telescopes. Why not say that photographers, by making photographs, show me things and also enable me to see them? Surely that does not mean that *I* don't really see them.

When I see, I may well get a sense of someone else's conception or interpretation of what I see. If you point out something to me, I know that you consider it worth pointing out. I learn by seeing, when others affect my vision, what things are objects of their fears and fetishes, what they value, and what they deplore. It may not be inappropriate to speak of seeing things "through their eyes." Yet I do see those things myself. Photography can be an enormously expressive medium – André Kertész's *Distortion #157* (figure 1.6) is certainly expressive – but this expressiveness does not render photographs opaque. If expressiveness is the mark of *art*, photography's credentials are beyond question. In *Triumph of the Will*, Leni Riefenstahl, by careful selection and editing, "interprets" for us the Nazi Party Congress of 1934; she presents it as she construes it. It does not follow that we ourselves do not see Hitler's airplane descending through the clouds, the thousands of marching troops and cheering spectators, and Hitler delivering tirades, even if the film fosters misconceptions about the things we see, inducing us to believe, for example, that the people we see were more enthusiastic about Hitler than they actually were. We can be aware, even vividly aware, of both the medium and the maker without either blocking our view of the object.

A final worry is that photography makes use of "conventions," conventions which are built into the construction of the camera and our photographic processing techniques.[20] There is nothing sacrosanct about the

19 See H. Gene Blocker, "Pictures and Photographs," *Journal of Aesthetics and Art Criticism* 36 (Winter 1977):

> Photographs most certainly do *not* escape subjectivity. . . .
> Through the selection of subject, angle, amount, and direction of light, background, sharpness of focus, and light-dark contrast – in all these ways the photographer represents the object from a subjective point of view, expressive of feeling and mood. [p. 158]

20 See ibid., p. 161, and "PVR," pp. 156 and 164–5.

system of perspective used in photography, it is argued; we just happen to have incorporated the one we did into the photographic process. Doesn't this mean that the conventions of photography get between the viewer and the objects photographed, that the viewer must know the "language" of photography and "read" its symbols, and that therefore he cannot be said to see the objects through the photographs? Not at all. We could have a convention to the effect that mirrors used in certain contexts are to be warped in a certain manner (for example, convex mirrors which enable drivers to see around dangerous corners). The convention must be understood or internalized for one to "read" properly the mirror images. Nevertheless, one sees things through the mirrors.

## 5

With these objections laid to rest, it is time to tackle directly the question of what it is about photographs that makes them transparent. The reason why we see through photographs but not paintings is related to a difference in how we acquire information from pictures of the two kinds. Suppose an explorer emerges from a central African jungle with a batch of photographic dinosaur-pictures, purportedly shot in the bush and processed straightforwardly. The pictures (together with background information) may convince us that there is a dinosaur lurking in the jungle. Alternatively, suppose that he emerges with a sheaf of dinosaur-sketches, purportedly drawn from life in the field. Again, we may be convinced of the existence of a dinosaur. Perhaps the photographs are more convincing than the drawings, but they needn't be. That is not the crucial difference between them; we *might* have better reason to trust the drawings than the photographs. The important difference is that, in the case of the sketches, we rely on the picture-maker's belief that there is a dinosaur in a way in which we don't in the case of the photographs.

The drawings indicate to us what was in the jungle by indicating what the artist *thought* was there. We have reason to believe that the artist set out to draw what he saw and that he is a competent draftsman. Since the sketches show a dinosaur, we judge that he thought he saw one. Taking him to be a reliable observer, we judge that the dinosaur he thought he saw was actually there. We trust *his* judgment – our information about the dinosaur is secondhand.

We don't need to rely on the photographer's judgment in the same way. We may infer that he believes in the dinosaur, knowing that he was looking through the viewfinder when the pictures were taken. We might even assume that it is because he believed there was a dinosaur that the photographs exist or are as they are – we may assume that he aimed the camera where he did and snapped the shutter when he did because he thought he spotted a dinosaur. But no such inferences or assumptions are required for our judgment of the dinosaur's existence. Even if we know or suspect that he didn't see the dinosaur, that he left the camera on a tripod with an automatic triggering device, for instance, we may still infer the existence of the dinosaur from the photographs. In fact, if the photographs *do* convince us that he believed in the dinosaur, they do so because they convince us that there *was* a dinosaur, not the other way around.

We do need to make certain assumptions if we are going to trust the photographs: that the camera was of a certain sort, that no monkey business was involved in the processing, and so on. These may require our accepting the say-so of the photographer; we may have to trust him. And it could be that we are being taken for a ride. It is easy to see that *this* sort of reliance on the photographer does not mean that we do not see through his photographs. In order to trust the evidence of my senses, I must always make certain assumptions about them and the circumstances in which they operate: that they are not influenced by hallucination-inducing drugs, that they are not being fed misinformation by an evil neurosurgeon, and so forth. I might rely on someone else's word in making these assumptions; I might consult a beneficent doctor. If he assures me that the system is operating normally, and it is, then I am seeing (or perceiving), notwithstanding my reliance on him.

The manner in which we trust the photographer when his photographs convince us of the existence of the dinosaur differs significantly from the manner in which we rely on the artist when we are persuaded by his sketches. Both sets of pictures have a counterfactual dependence on the scene in the jungle. In both cases, if the scene had been different – if there had been no dinosaur, for example – the pictures would have been different (and so would our visual experiences when we look at them). This is why, in both cases, given that the pictures are as they are, we can judge that the scene was as it was. But why are these counterfactuals true? A difference in the scene would have made a difference in the sketches because it would have made a difference in the artist's beliefs (and hence in the way he sketched or whether he sketched at all). But that is not why a difference in the scene would have made a difference in the photographs. *They* would have been different had the scene been different *even if* the photographer believed, and so aimed and snapped his camera, as he actually did. Suppose that the picture maker – artist or photographer – is hallucinating the dinosaur which he attempts to portray. The artist's sketches will show a dinosaur nonetheless, but the photographs will not. What the sketches show depends on what the artist thinks he sees, whether or not he is right; the actual scene in the jungle is, in *this* way, irrelevant to how his pictures turn out. But if the photographer thinks he sees a dinosaur and acts accordingly, what his photographs show is determined by what is really there before him, regardless of what he thinks. The artist draws his hallucination; the camera bypasses the photographer's hallucination and captures what is in the jungle.

A person's belief can be relevantly based on someone else's even if he doesn't realize that it is. If what convinces me of the dinosaur's existence is a painting which I take to be a photograph, I may suppose mistakenly that my belief is independent of the picture-maker's and that I see the dinosaur. My grounds for my belief do not include his belief. But still, the absence of the dinosaur would have made a difference in the picture only because it would have made a difference in the artist's belief. Unbeknown to me, my belief is (relevantly) dependent on his, and I am wrong in thinking I see the dinosaur.

Not all theories of perception postulate a strong link between perceiving and believing.[21] We needn't assume such a link. The essential difference between paintings and photographs is the difference in the manner in which they, not the beliefs of those who see them, are based on beliefs of their makers. Photographs are counterfactually dependent on the photographed scene even if the beliefs (and other intentional attitudes) of the photographer are held fixed.[22] Paintings which have a counterfactual dependence on the scene portrayed lose it when the beliefs (and other intentional attitudes) of the painter are held fixed. Both the beliefs and the visual experiences which the viewer derives from a picture are dependent on the picture-maker's beliefs in whichever manner the picture itself is. In order to see through the picture to the scene depicted, the viewer must have visual experiences which do not depend on the picture maker's beliefs in the way that paintings do. We can leave open the question of whether, to be seeing the scene, the viewer must have beliefs about it

21 See Fred I. Dretske, *Seeing and Knowing* (Chicago, 1969), chap. 2.

22 In some cases the important conditional counterfactual dependence which distinguishes opaque pictures from transparent ones may be not so much on the picture maker's *beliefs* as on his visual experience, or his thoughts, or possibly his intentions.

and what connection there may be between his visual experiences and his beliefs.[23]

A familiar pair of science fiction examples may help to convince some that I am on the right track.[24] Suppose that a neurosurgeon disconnects Helen's eyes from her optic nerves and rigs up a device whereby he can stimulate the optic nerves at will. The doctor then stimulates Helen's nerves in ways corresponding to what he sees, with the result that she has "visual" experiences like ones she would have normally if she were using her own eyes. Let us add the assumption that the doctor is conscientious about feeding Helen correct information and that she has every reason to trust him. Helen *seems* to be seeing things, and her visual experiences are caused by the things which she seems to see. But she doesn't really see them; the doctor is seeing for her. This is because her visual experiences are based on his in the way I described. It is only because differences in scenes make for differences in the doctor's beliefs that they make for differences in her visual experiences.

Contrast a patient who receives a double eye transplant or a patient who is fitted with artificial prosthetic eyes. This patient *does* see. He is not relying in the relevant manner on anyone's beliefs about the things he sees, although his visual experiences do depend on the work of the surgeon and on the donor of the transplanted eyes or the manufacturer of the prosthetic ones. In real life, cataract patients owe their visual experiences to others. All of our visual experiences depend on acts of omission by those who have refrained from altering or destroying our visual organs. Obviously these facts do not blind us.

## 6

The intuitions I have been appealing to are of a piece with those underlying H. P. Grice's distinction between *natural* and *nonnatural*

23 In special cases photographs may be causally but not counterfactually dependent on the scene. Then there may be no hope of learning about the scene from the photograph: the photograph would have been as it is even if the scene had been different. But one still *sees* the scene through the photograph. Perception is to be understood in terms of causation rather than counterfactuals, if the former doesn't reduce to the latter (see William K. Goosens, "Causal Chains and Counterfactuals," *Journal of Philosophy* 76 [Sept. 1979]: 489–95).

24 These examples are adapted from Lewis, "Veridical Hallucination and Prosthetic Vision," pp. 243–4. But Lewis does not see a sharp difference between the two cases.

meaning.[25] Spots $\text{mean}_N$ (mean naturally) measles, he says, and the ringing of the bell of a bus $\text{means}_{NN}$ (means nonnaturally) that the bus is full. Grice would say, no doubt, that if the explorer did indeed capture an actual dinosaur on film, his photographs $\text{mean}_N$ that there is a dinosaur. One characteristic of natural meaning is this: the fact that something $\text{means}_N$ that *p* entails *p*.[26] Black clouds mean ($\text{mean}_N$) rain only if they are in fact followed by rain. If the rain doesn't come, that isn't what the clouds meant. This gives us a sense in which photographs are necessarily perfectly accurate. If there was no dinosaur, then the photograph does not $\text{mean}_N$ that there was one, no matter what it looks like. One who knew enough about the camera used in making a photograph, how the film was processed, and other relevant circumstances could infer with perfect accuracy about the objects photographed. This alone does not distinguish photographs from other pictures. Presumably, if I know enough about an artist – about his beliefs, desires, attitudes, capacities, and such, or his physiological make-up – I could infer accurately, from his drawings, about what was in front of him when he drew (see "PVR," pp. 159–62). But Grice's distinction brings out a difference between the two cases. A *sketch* of a dinosaur does not *mean*$_N$ that there was a dinosaur, even if there was one. The sketch is not necessarily accurate in this way.

The essential accuracy of photographs obviously does not prevent them from being misleading. It affects instead how we describe out mistakes and how we think of them. Consider a photographic portrait of Twiggy, made with the help of a bowed mirror, which appears to show her with a huge paunch. If viewers are misled, it is not because of a divergence between what the pictures $\text{means}_N$ and reality. Their mistake is about what the picture $\text{means}_N$. It $\text{means}_N$ not that Twiggy is fat but that she is skinny, as one who knew about the mirror could ascertain.

To think of photographs as necessarily accurate is to think of them as especially close to the facts. It is not to think of them as intermediaries between us and the facts, as things that have their own meanings which may or may not correspond to the facts and which we have to decide whether or not to trust. To interpret a photograph properly *is* to get the facts.

Snyder and Allen claim that the way in which a photograph is made "has little to do with the way we normally interpret it" ("PVR," p. 159).

25 See H. P. Grice, "Meaning," *Philosophical Review* 66 (July 1557): 377–88.
26 See ibid., p. 377.

Presumably, they would say that we interpret the photograph of Twiggy as "meaning" that she is fat, regardless of the fact that it was made with a distorting mirror. There is some truth in this. We may *take* the photograph to $\text{mean}_N$ that Twiggy is fat; it may *look* to us as though it $\text{means}_N$ that: Twiggy may appear to us to be fat when we see her through the photograph. Perhaps, also, the photograph makes it *fictional* that she is fat, and it might even $\text{mean}_{NN}$ that she is. None of these facts force us to deny that the picture $\text{means}_N$ not that Twiggy is fat but that she is skinny. Photographs, as bearers of *natural* meaning, are necessarily accurate. And our realization that they are – even when we are unsure of or mistaken about *what* they $\text{mean}_N$ – profoundly affects our experience of them.

The fact that something $\text{means}_{NN}$ p does not entail *p*. It is connected instead with the notion of *someone's* meaning *p* by it. Nonnatural symbols are thought of as intermediaries which stand between us and the facts. We ascertain what the symbols mean, from which we learn what was meant by them (which needn't be the same as what the symbols mean), and we must judge whether what is meant by them is true. Our access to things via nonnatural symbols is thought of as less direct than our access via natural ones.

Drawings and paintings are sometimes nonnatural symbols – but not always. Pieter Brueghel probably did not intend viewers of *Children's Games* to learn what games were played in the sixteenth century by recognizing his intention that they do so. Still, the meaning of the picture is enough like nonnatural meaning for us to see its difference from photographs. The beliefs about children's games in the sixteenth century which the painting induces are based on the *beliefs* of the painter, if not on his communicative intentions.

## 7

The distinction between transparent and opaque pictures will provoke a variety of intriguing examples. Some of them show that this distinction does not coincide neatly with our usual differentiation between photographs and nonphotographic pictures. Some suggest that there are *degrees* of transparency, while others suggest that a picture can be transparent in certain *respects* and opaque in other respects. In some instances the question of whether a picture is transparent probably has no determinate answer.

There are pictures which are drawn or painted by people but in a mechanical manner of one sort or another. One may attach a piece of transparent paper to a window and trace the outlines of the objects seen through it. One may copy a photograph, conceivably without even recognizing what it is a photograph of, or paint over a photograph, matching the brightness of each spot of the original.[27] One might use a directional light meter and fill in the squares of a grid with shades of gray corresponding to the readings it gives of the various parts of a scene, or one might dispense with the light meter and estimate the brightnesses by eye. There are also doodles done automatically, while the doodler's mind is on other things.[28] Some such mechanically executed drawings are probably transparent.[29]

Are any photographs opaque? What about ones which are devised largely in the darkroom – by combining negatives, retouching, burning out unwanted images, manipulating exposure and contrast, using filters, and so on (see, for example, figure 1.7)? Some have maintained that such photographic constructions are essentially similar to paintings.[30] The darkroom artist exercises as much control over the finished product as painters do; his work seems no more mechanical or less human, although his tools and materials are different. The paradigms of transparent pictures would seem to be not the work of professional photographers but casual snapshots and home movies made by doting parents and wide-eyed tourists with assists from Kodak.

Photographic constructions do differ importantly from snapshots, but to lump them with paintings would be a big mistake. There is the extreme case of a "photograph" made by exposing photograhic paper, dot by dot, with a flashlight, to make a pointillist-style rendition of Lincoln, for example. *This* is drawing with a flashlight; one doesn't see Lincoln through the picture. But consider more common darkroom techniques such as combining negatives and manipulating contrast. We see a

27 It was not uncommon in the mid-nineteenth century to paint portraits over photographs (see Aaron Scharf, *Art and Photography* [Harmondsworth, 1968], p. 44).

28 I owe the last two examples, respectively, to Robert Howell and to George Wilson.

29 It is time to confess that the Chuck Close example (figure 1.3) is not as clear-cut as I implied. Close made many of his works by projecting a photograph on the canvas and painting over it. If this is how his *Self-Portrait* was executed, its opacity may be questionable. My point of course, is unaffected. If *Self-Portrait* had been painted in the usual manner, it would definitely be opaque, and the viewer who comes to believe that it was so painted after having assumed it to be a photograph experiences the jolt I described.

30 Scruton remarks that if a photographer proceeds "to paint things out or in, to touch up, alter, *or pasticher* as he pleases . . . he has now become a painter" ("Photography and Representation," pp. 593–4, and this volume, p. 156).

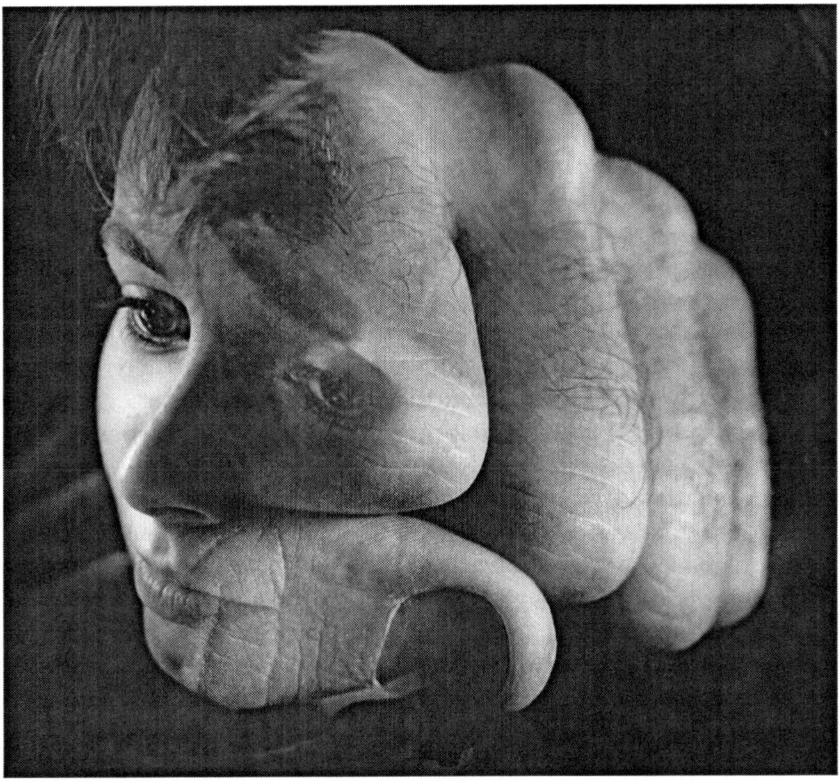

**Figure 1.7** Jerry Uelsmann, *Symbolic Mutation*, 1961. © Jerry Uelsmann. Photograph courtesy of the artist.

person through a photograph of him no matter how lightly or darkly it is printed – even if it "falsifies" the brightness of the person or the brightness relations of his parts – although we may not see the *state of affairs* of his being illuminated in a certain way. If a photograph apparently showing Deng Xiaoping conversing with Yasir Arafat was made by combining negatives of each, the viewer does not see the event of their conversing, even if they were conversing when the two photographs were taken. But he *does* see Deng, and he *does* see Arafat. Most photographic constructions are transparent in some of their parts or in certain respects. If a viewer doesn't know how a photograph was made, he won't know what he is seeing through it and what he isn't. But he will probably realize that he is seeing *some* of the things or events or states of affairs which the picture portrays, even if he does not know which ones, and this realization significantly colors his experience. His experience is not unlike that of seeing a white shape and wondering whether one is seeing a ghost.

It may *seem* to the viewer, moreover, that he is seeing everything that the photograph portrays even if he is not and even if he knows that he is not. Many photographic constructions appear to be transparent even in respects in which they are not, and this gives them a sort of realism which obviously nonphotographic pictures lack.

The viewer of Jerry Uelsmann's *Symbolic Mutation* (figure 1.7) hardly has the impression of seeing a hand fused with a face, however; it is too obvious that the picture was made from two negatives. In other cases sophisticated viewers may judge simply from the slickness of a photograph that it is likely to have been manipulated in one way or another in the darkroom, even if they don't spot the seams. As a result, their impression of seeing through the picture may be weakened. This is one reason why some filmmakers have deliberately tried to mimic the crudity of home movies, using hand-held cameras, purposefully bad focus, and so on (for example, John Cassavetes' *Shadows* [1960]). These techniques sacrifice any possibility of producing the illusion that the viewers are *face-to-face* with the characters – which is hardly a live possibility anyway – in favor of a more convincing illusion of seeing the characters *through the photographs.* This reconciles the immediacy which is claimed for such techniques – the feeling they provide of intimacy with the objects portrayed – with the obvious sense of contrivance that they engender – their calling attention to the medium. Emphasizing the medium is usually regarded as a way of distancing appreciators from the world portrayed. In this case it has just the opposite effect.

## 8

A certain conception of the nature of perception is beginning to emerge: to perceive things is to be in *contact* with them in a certain way. A mechanical connection with something, like that of photography, counts as contact, whereas a humanly mediated one, like that of painting, does not. Perceptual contact with things has rather less to do with acquiring knowledge about them than has sometimes been supposed.

We may be approaching a *necessary* condition for seeing through pictures and for perception in general, but we are far from having a sufficient condition. Imagine a machine that is sensitive to the light which emanates from a scene and that produces not pictures but accurate verbal descriptions of the scene. The machine's printouts are surely not transparent; in looking at them, one does not *see* the scene which the machine translated into words. Yet the printouts are made just as mechanically as any photographs are.

It is easy to say that the reason why we don't see through such mechanically generated descriptions is that we don't *see* them *as* the scene they describe; perhaps we are incapable of seeing them this way. If one fails to see a photograph as Dwight Eisenhower, or as a person, or as anything but a collection of blotches on a flat surface, we might deny that one sees Eisenhower through the photograph. One doesn't see Eisenhower, perhaps, unless one *notices* him, in some appropriate sense (although it isn't necessary to recognize him as Eisenhower or even as a person). But this doesn't help without an account of *seeing-as* and an explanation of why our not seeing the descriptions as the scene should make a difference. Nor will it help to declare that only *pictures*, not representations of other kinds, can be transparent. We need to know why the machine's printouts don't qualify as pictures and why nonpictures can't be transparent.

Investigating things by examining pictures of them (either photographs or drawings) is strikingly analogous to investigating them by looking at them directly and disanalogous to investigating them by examining descriptions of them. One such analogy concerns what is easy and what is difficult to ascertain and what mistakes the investigator is susceptible to. The numerals "3" and "8" are sometimes easily mistaken for each other. So when reading about a tree which is actually 85 feet high, one might easily take it to be 35 feet high. This mistake is much more likely than that of thinking it is 85.00001 rather than 85 feet high. The reverse is true when we look at the tree directly or examine a picture of it. A *house* is easily confused with a *horse* or a *hearse*, when our information comes from a verbal description, as is a *cat* with a *cot*, a *madam* with a *madman*, *intellectuality* with *ineffectuality*, and so on. When we confront things directly or via pictures, houses are more apt to be confused with barns or woodsheds, cats with puppies, and so forth.

It would be much too hasty to conclude that it is simply differences of this sort which disqualify investigating a scene through mechanically generated descriptions as seeing it. Different mistakes are likely when we see under conditions of dim illumination from those that are likely with bright illumination. (Colors are especially hard to ascertain in dim light; outlines may be easier to distinguish then than in bright light.) If there were such a thing as "seeing-through-descriptions," we should expect that the mistakes one is susceptible to when seeing in that manner would differ from those one is susceptible to when seeing in other ways. There is a deeper point to be made – one about perception in general, not just vision.

There are important correspondences between the way we perceive (whether directly or with photographic assistance) and the way the world really is (or the way we think of it as being, but I will postpone this caveat temporarily). I do not mean that the results of perception conform to facts about the world, that things have the properties we perceive them to have. Nor do I mean that our percepts or sense-data resemble what they are percepts or sense-data of. Rather, the structure of the enterprise of perceiving bears important analogies to the structure of reality. In *this* sense we perceive the world as it is.

The mistakes a perceiver is susceptible to correspond to similarities among things themselves. Things which are easily confusable perceptually, difficult to discriminate, are things which really are similar to each other in some respect, more similar than things which are less easily confusable. An 85-foot tree resembles one which is 85.00001 feet high more closely than it does a 35-foot tree. Houses are more like barns and woodsheds than horses or hearses. Things with different shades of red are more like each other (in color) than they are like green things. In fact, the degree of similarity explains the likelihood of confusion. It is because of the similarity between 85- and 85.00001-foot trees that they are difficult to distinguish. The correspondence between similarity and perceptual confusability is intrinsic, I suggest, to the notion of perception. A process of discrimination counts as perceptual only if its structure is thus analogous to the structure of the world. When we perceive, we are, in this way, intimate with what is perceived. This goes a long way toward explaining our feeling of closeness to things which we see through photographs.

We are not similarly intimate with the world when we investigate it through descriptions, even mechanically generated ones. Descriptions scramble the real similarity relations. Houses are not much like horses or hearses. The difficulty of distinguishing a house from a hearse when we are reading about it is due not to the nature of the house and hearses but to facts about the words used to describe them. So we think of the words as getting between us and what we are reading about, as blocking our view of it, in a way that photographs and sense-data do not block our view of what they are photographs or sense-data of. The structure of discrimination by means of mechanically generated descriptions does not correspond to the structure of the world and, so, does not qualify as perception.

Are things easily confusable in perception *really* similar in some respect? Scientific investigation may suggest otherwise. Perceived colors don't correlate precisely with wavelengths of reflected light. Environments which feel similarly or even indistinguishably cold may differ considerably in temperature, with compensating differences in humidity and wind One might take this to mean that the correlation between how things affect us perceptually and how things are in themselves is less than perfect. Or one might recognize properties – visible colors and perceived cold – which are distinct from wavelengths of reflected light and temperature and with respect to which the correlations do hold. In any case, we *think of* easily confusable objects as being similar, despite our awareness of the scientific facts. And perhaps it is this that is intrinsic to perception. If scientific research should uncover massive breakdowns in the presumed correlations and if, after reflecting on these results, we no longer even thought of easily confusable things as being similar, I doubt that we would or should continue to speak of *perceiving* them.

Some question the very notion of real similarity. Resemblance is only a matter of how we think of things, it is argued; similarity is relative to one's "conceptual scheme." In that case it will have to be what we think of as similarities – what similarities there are relative to one's conceptual scheme – which corresponds to difficulty of perceptual discrimination. But this will suffice. We don't think of houses as being especially similar to horses or hearses; so discrimination by means of mechanically generated descriptions is not perceptual.

Why do we regard the things we do as being similar? Sometimes, I suggest, precisely because they are easily confused (when examined in ways which otherwise count as perceptual). It is because visually discriminating among paint chips of various shades of pink is relatively difficult that we think of them as resembling each other. So facts about our discriminative capacities might be said to create similarities – similarities relative to our conceptual scheme, which on the present suggestion is the only kind that there is – thereby establishing the relevant correlations.[31]

It now looks as though mechanically generated descriptions could, in the right circumstances, be transparent. Suppose that we used description-generating devices regularly to investigate the world. Perhaps this would affect what we think of as similarities, thereby changing our conceptual

[31] This seems to turn on its head our earlier suggestion that it is similarities among things that make them difficult to discriminate perceptually. But we can have it both ways. What count as similarities for us, what respects of resemblance there are relative to our conceptual scheme, is determined (partly, anyway) by which discriminations are easy to make and which are difficult, given our usual modes of (what otherwise count as) perception. The fact that certain things are similar in these respects explains the difficulty of discriminating them.

scheme. We might recognize such properties as *apparent-via-description-generating-devices houseness* and *apparent-via-description-generating-devices hearseness* and regard these properties as analogous to visible colors, as characteristics of things themselves in virtue of which they can be alike, not just as capacities to affect us through the devices. In that case difficulty of discrimination by means of description-generating devices would be correlated with what we think of as similarities. So we might well think of ourselves as seeing through the descriptions, and – especially if there is nothing to "real" similarity among things except being thought of as similar – we might really be seeing through them. Perhaps the mechanically generated descriptions would then be transparent.

We are quickly becoming entangled in some of the deepest problems philosophy has to offer. Nevertheless, it should be clear from our recent speculations that there are fundamental differences between pictures and descriptions of a kind which plausibly allow mechanically generated pictures – photographs – to be transparent even though, apart from unusual circumstances like those just imagined, mechanically generated descriptions would not be. This challenge to the transparency of photographs is defused.

We have learned that perceptual contact with the world is to be distinguished from two different sorts of nonperceptual access to it: access mediated by intervening descriptions as well as access via another person. The common contrast between seeing something and being told about it conflates the two. When someone describes a scene to us, we are doubly removed from it; contact is broken both by the intervention of the person, the teller, and by the verbal form of the telling. Perceptual contact can itself be mediated – by mirrors or television circuits or photographs. But *this* mediation is a means of *maintaining* contact. Viewers of photographs are in perceptual contact with the world.

## 9

What is photographic realism? Transparency is not the whole story. Realism is a concept with many faces, and photography wears more than one of them. We must not forget how adept photography is at portraying subtleties of texture, shadow, and reflection; how effortlessly it captures the jumbled trivia of ordinary life; how skillfully it uses perspective. The capacity of photography as it is now practiced to "reveal reality" is especially important. Photographic evidence is often very reliable – hence its usefulness in court proceedings and extortion plots. This is no automatic consequence of the "mechanicalness" of the photographic process, however. It derives rather from the fact that our photographic equipment and procedures happen to be standardized in certain respects. (They are not standardized in all respects, of course; so we have to be selective about what conclusions we draw from photographs. We can usually say little beyond gross approximations about the absolute illumination of a scene, for example, on the basis of a photograph, since shutter speeds, film speeds, and lens apertures are so variable.)

But photography's various other talents must not be confused with or allowed to obscure its remarkable ability to put us in perceptual contact with the world, an ability which can be claimed even by a fuzzy and badly exposed snapshot depicting few details and offering little information. It is this – photography's transparency – which is most distinctively photographic and which constitutes the most important justification for speaking of "photographic realism."[32]

32 Work on this paper was aided by fellowships from the Rockefeller Foundation and the Stanford Humanities Center. I wish to thank audiences at a number of universities for helpful criticisms of earlier versions. Those whose observations had particular influence on the shape of the result include John G. Bennett, Robert Howell, David Lewis, Patrick Maynard, Christopher Peacocke, and Stephen White.

# 2

# PHOTOGRAPHS AND ICONS

Cynthia Freeland

## Photographic Realism

Many writers on art have claimed that photography is inherently realistic.[1] Since this medium operates mechanically to produce images through the use of light, chemistry, and machinery, it is alleged that photographic depiction can occur without the intervention of artistic intentions, and that the results possess unusual veracity. On this view, photographs are emanations from their subject matter or little bits of reality rather than representations of it.[2] They serve as testimonials; it is pointed out that photographs, but not paintings, are used as evidence.[3] Sonograms are the

1 See, e.g., André Bazin, *What Is Cinema?*, vol. 1, trans. Hugh Gray (Berkeley: University of California Press, 1971); Stanley Cavell, *The World Viewed: Reflections on the Ontology of Film* (Cambridge, MA: Harvard University Press, 1979); Kendall L. Walton, "Transparent Pictures: On the Nature of Photographic Realism," *Critical Inquiry* 11 (1984): 246–77 (repr. as ch. 1 in this volume); also "Looking Again Through Photographs: A Response to Edwin Martin," *Critical Inquiry* 12 (1986): 801–8. For criticism, see Edwin Martin, "On Seeing Walton's Great-Grandfather," *Critical Inquiry* 12 (1986): 796–800; also Gregory Currie, *Image and Mind: Film, Philosophy and Cognitive Science* (Cambridge, New York, and Melbourne: Cambridge University Press, 1995), esp. ch. 2, "The Imprint of Nature," pp. 48–78, and ch. 3, "Realism," pp. 79–112.

2 See Roland Barthes, *Camera Lucida: Reflections on Photography*, trans. Richard Howard (New York: Farrar, Straus and Giroux, 1985), p. x.

3 See, e.g., Walton, "Transparent Pictures," this vol., pp. 14–49. This has not always been the case: that is, paintings *were* considered evidence at times in the past; see Shearer West, *Portraiture* (Oxford: Clarendon Press, 2004), pp. 53–9 ("The Portrait as Document"). Also, John Tagg shows that complex processes were necessary to ensure the acceptance of crime-scene photographs as evidence in court cases; see his *The Burden of Representation: Essays on Photographies and Histories* (Amherst: University of Massachusetts Press, 1988), ch. 2, pp. 60–5.

first proof of a new human life and children's school pictures document their changing appearance over the years. At the other end of the spectrum, photographs of the dead at funerals show us that the deceased person existed until only recently.

But discussions of photographic realism seem to involve an important ambiguity. In one sense, to speak of a photograph's realism is to assert something about the image's *epistemic value*, implying that it has a particular kind of accuracy or that it is a truthful representation. Here the causal origin of the image is relevant, since it links photographs to other kinds of signs that show a direct causal link to their source, such as X-rays or electrocardiograms. Such signs may even be found in nature, as in the case of measles spots, teeth marks, footprints, or blood spatters at murder scenes. These indicative marks are what C. S. Peirce would call indexical signs; they may not be images at all. They will not present a "picture" directly to our eyes unless we are experts trained at interpreting them.

In this second sense, the label "realistic" characterizes the *psychological force* or emotional persuasiveness of certain images. They seem to present something directly to our eyes in a particularly vivid and lifelike way. When I view a photograph of my dead grandmother, it seems as if she is smiling directly at me. But images made in other media can be realistic in this psychological sense without being literally accurate or mechanically caused in the way photographs are. For example, the style of certain painters is said to be realistic (even photo-realistic), and some novels have a gritty realism. Fiction films like *Saving Private Ryan* or *Jurassic Park* garnered critical praise for their realistic portrayal of situations such as wartime battles or encounters with dinosaurs.

The ambiguity in the label "realistic" can be understood to reflect a fundamental difference in the way photographs and other images are commonly used. In his book *The Engine of Visualization: Thinking through Photography*, Patrick Maynard draws a distinction much like what I have in mind between the two senses of realism, but he describes it in terms of how images actually function.[4] Maynard speaks of the difference between an image's "depictive" or representational function and its "manifestation" function. I shall sometimes use his terms. I shall also speak of claims about realism in the epistemic sense of depiction as *transparency* claims, and of claims about psychological realism in the second or manifestation sense as *contact* claims.

[4] Patrick Maynard, *The Engine of Visualization: Thinking through Photography* (Ithaca and London: Cornell University Press, 1997).

Maynard traces these two functions of photographs back to sources within two distinct traditions of image-making in Europe. In the West, art associated mainly with Catholicism developed forms of ever more naturalistic, illusionistic depiction. On the other hand, in Eastern Orthodox realms, emphasis was instead placed upon icons as hieratic images revealing some holy person's manifestation.[5] Such manifestation has less to do with effecting a realistic likeness than with supplying the viewer with a sense of contact or presence with the represented subject. Insofar as a photographic image functions today to supply a similar sense of contact or manifestation, Maynard says, it "resembles an earlier and prolific, important sort of image, an icon: 'an image whose *function* is largely that of manifesting what it depicts and thereby providing realism through the sense of presence.' "[6]

Reinforcing Maynard's account of the widely divergent functions of images in East and West is the German art historian Hans Belting, who goes so far as to deny that icons are works of art in anything like the Western sense. In his monumental book *Likeness and Presence: A History of the Image before the Era of Art* (1994), he calls icons "images before the era of art."

In this essay, I shall follow up on the leads of Maynard and Belting by focusing on the twin *function* of photographic images, both of which have been linked to claims about photographic realism. In particular, I want to explore photography's manifestation function so as to reveal more about how it is related to icons as non-representational images. The manifestation function, which underlies many claims about the mysterious vivacity of photographs, is less familiar to us in contemporary aesthetics than the depictive function, and deserves separate consideration. It will turn out that the links between this manifestation function and photography's realism in the depictive sense are complex. There are some curious and

5 Ibid., pp. 238–9. This comparison between photographs and icons has been noted by others, but has not yet been as fully investigated as it can be. See, e.g., Hans Belting, *Likeness and Presence. A History of the Image before the Era of Art*, trans. Edmund Jephcott (Chicago and London, 1994), p. 53: "The analogy of today's photography seems appropriate. Priority was given not to art itself or to the artist's invention but to the utmost verisimilitude. This attitude takes us to the heart of the early use of images. The beholder was in touch with the real presence in, and the healing power of, the image. These could be guaranteed, however, only by an exact match between likeness and original, the intervention of an artist being unwanted."

6 Actually this is from one of the characters (Veronica) in the dialogue Maynard invented in "The Secular Icon: Photography and the Functions of Images," *The Journal of Aesthetics and Art Criticism* XLII: 2 (1983): 155–69: p. 165.

unexpected interactions between the way images function, how they are caused, and their (alleged) epistemic status. Understanding these links will help to clarify the two primary senses in which photographs are said to be "realistic".

## Photographs: A Brief History

To begin, it will be useful to review a small part of the history of photography and suggest some roots in earlier kinds of image-making. In the form in which they first became well-known, photographic images were daguerreotypes – images made using cameras and photographic processes, but with results chemically fixed upon metal plates rather than on coated papers. Daguerreotypy results in a unique image that is not susceptible to multiple reproduction (which is partly why it came to be replaced). Such images combine aspects of both positive and negative in one, since they must be tilted and held to the light "just so" in order for the image to appear. These tidy portable objects were typically framed in a gold-toned metal setting, padded with red velvet, and enclosed in protective leather cases. Treasured as precious items evocative of loved ones or lost family members, they achieved widespread popularity in the United States at around the time of the Civil War. It was the first historical cataclysm to be recorded in this new medium. Soldiers visited artists' studios where their likenesses were solemnly recorded and sent home to loved ones to treasure during an absence. And in turn, the soldiers' specially preserved images of wives or mothers were cherished, sometimes only to be found with their belongings after death. Such poignant revelations are a common trope of war literature and film genres. A fictional example of photographs exchanged between young lovers grounds the entire story of Charles Frazier's best-seller *Cold Mountain*, sustaining the two main characters throughout their respective tribulations.

To understand the seemingly irrational behavior of someone like the hero soldier of *Cold Mountain*, talking to the daguerreotyped image of his beloved while mired in the muck of Mississippi swamps, it is important to grasp how magical such objects seemed.

Alan Trachtenberg has written about daguerreotypes:

> No one who has not felt himself or herself spellbound by a daguerreotype portrait, drawn magnetically to the image and beyond, as if it were less an image or likeness than the thing itself, the very identity of the sitter miniaturised (*sic*) and suspended in an ambiguously monochromatic float

> or medium, can speak knowingly about this mode of photography. Only those who know by experience the sensation of succumbing to the charm of these objects can begin to understand what these objectified likenesses might have meant to their makers and possessors in the past, or the functions they performed within households and between persons, or their hold on the emotions and their influence on consciousness.[7]

Similarly, Anthony Minghella, director of the film version of *Cold Mountain*, has explained his thoughts on the use of these images as a key device:

> One of the things about the daguerreotype and the tintype is that they are distorted in the sense that the image does not absolutely capture reality – it's mediated by the chemistry of those photographs, and so it inflects the image in a very particular way. Eyes become incandescent, and the high contrast of the pictures, together with the fact that their focus and exposure is so imprecise, means that they contain the signature of the photographer in a much clearer way than modern photographs indicate. There's a more transparent indication of a mediated moment in those images than there is in modern photography, and there's also access to the look of that war, which was the first visually documented conflict.[8]

Of course, daguerreotypes were readily suited to widespread public use since they resembled other familiar forms of portraiture. John Tagg tells us: "The aura of the precious miniature passes over into the early daguerreotype."[9] The painted portrait miniature, also produced in small cases or fitted into lockets, was a very popular art form in the eighteenth and nineteenth centuries.[10] But the new processes made such imagery more affordable and hence more broadly available to the general public. Photography caught on very quickly, enabling many more people to acquire depictions of themselves than had ever before been possible. Tagg describes as an example the shift in Marseilles from around 1850, when four or five miniaturists worked in the city, to later when there were 40–50

7 Alan Trachtenberg, "Likeness as Identity: Reflections on the Daguerrean Mystique," in Graham Clarke, ed., *The Portrait in Photography* (London: Reaktion Books, and Seattle: University of Washington Press, 1992), p. 177.

8 "Interview with Anthony Minghella," by Ingrid Sischy; December, 2003: <http://www.findarticles.com/p/articles/mi_m1285/is_11_33/ai_111114552/pg_3>, accessed June 6, 2006.

9 Tagg, *The Burden of Representation*, p. 37; see also ch. 1, "A Democracy of the Image: Photographic Portraiture and Commodity Production," pp. 34–59.

10 See West, *Portraiture*, pp. 59–62 ("The Portrait as Proxy and Gift").

photographers working there, "each producing an average 1,200 plates a year. . . . By 1853, three million daguerreotypes were being made annually and there were eighty-six portrait galleries in New York City alone."[11]

Portraiture in general is thought to have originated from the desire to preserve likenesses of the dead and to facilitate contact with them. Some of the earliest portraits known to exist are funerary portraits from ancient Roman Egypt, which were probably done with the aid of wax death-masks. There is a continuous history of the painted portrait since that time, as numerous books by art historians attest; but the particular branch of art history that deserves special consideration when we are investigating the manifestation function of images is the religious icon. Like the photograph, the daguerreotype, and the portrait miniature, the icon provides an important kind of contact with its referent, the person or figure shown therein. As we shall see, there are further remarkable similarities in how icons and photographic portraits function as images.[12]

The word "icon" in English derives from the Greek term "*eikon*," designating a likeness or image. Despite this etymology, icons are not realistic or naturalistic likenesses in the sense of mirror images. They are, rather, standardized depictions of holy figures such as Jesus, Mary, and various saints. Here, for example, is a statement from an Eastern Orthodox source about Byzantine icons:

> It is important to understand that an icon does not represent, it expresses. It depicts the spiritual, not the physical. Physical characteristics are not of primary concern; it is the spiritual qualities that are the main focus in an icon. The entire icon is a symbol, not a decoration. They have never been worshipped as pieces of art. Rather, they are venerated for the divine and supernatural forces which they express.[13]

11 Tagg, *The Burden of Representation*, pp. 39, 43.

12 Charles Barber, "From Transformation to Desire: Art and Worship after Byzantine Iconoclasm," *Art Bulletin* 75 (1993): 7–16. See also Robert S. Nelson, "The Discourse of Icons, Then and Now," *Art History* 12 (1989): 144–57. Most recent is Robin Cormack, *Painting the Soul: Icons, Death Masks and Shrouds* (London: Reaktion, 1997); Robert Ousterhout and Leslie Brubaker, eds., *The Sacred Image East and West* (Urbana and Chicago: University of Illinois Press, 1995); Ernst Kitzinger, "The Cult of Images in the Age before Iconoclasm," Dumbarton Oaks Papers 8 (1954), 83–150; repr. in W. Eugene Kleinbauer, ed., *The Art of Byzantium and the Medieval West: Selected Studies by Ernst Kitzinger* (Bloomington: Indiana University Press, 1976), pp. 90–156. See also Leslie Brubaker, "Icons before Iconoclasm?" in *Morfologie sociali e culturali in Europa fra Tarda Antichità e Alto Medioevo, Settimane di Studio del Centro Italiano di Studi sull' Alto Medioevo* 45 (Spoleto, 1998), pp. 1215–54.

13 From Byzantines Net, <http://www.byzantines.net/moreinfo/iconsInTheBCC.htm>.

Icon painters or "drawers" did not usually have any freedom of expression in what they did. Typically, they were monks who had to pray before painting to achieve an attitude of appropriate submissiveness to the task. They were required to employ particular approved schemata and to use only certain materials and colors in their work. In the tradition of the East, icons do not have naturalistic coloring; for example, the space in icons is flat and the sky is rendered with gold to symbolize the heavenly realm. Body postures are stiff and people are generally shown in a full-frontal mode, and typically attenuated, putting emphasis on faces, which stare out at us with large intense eyes. These eyes crucially assist in promoting the sense of direct contact with the depicted person.

Authorities on icons defended the use of such images within the Christian Church, amid controversy arising from the Commandment that prohibits the worship of graven images or "idols," by arguing that icons are special kinds of images whose power derives from a unique relationship to their alleged source. That is, the justification of such holy images was and still is made "not through their usefulness to, or meaning for, the beholder, but through their inner relationship to their prototypes."[14] Believers assert that, "An icon . . . does not exist simply to direct our imagination during our prayers. It is a material center in which there reposes . . . a divine force, which unites itself to human art."[15] In this sense, icons function much like relics, as virtual (or in many cases literal) pieces of a lost saint or holy figure.

As noted above, Maynard contrasts the devotional Eastern uses of icons with the cooler or more depictive functions of Western painting. He too sees these images as an important source for photographs – at least in terms of some of their common functioning. Like ancient funerary portraits, photographs facilitate a sense of ongoing contact. In this way they also resemble icons, as described by the art historian Charles Barber:

> The image is not to be read in isolation; rather, it is to be interpreted with respect to the viewer's relationship with the image. . . . [T]he icon, rather than transforming spectators or acting as the site of their transformation, is not a site of identification through representation . . . but a site of desire.[16]

14 Maynard here quotes Ernst Kitzinger, "The Cult of Images in the Ages before Iconoclasm," Dumbarton Oaks Papers 8 (1954): 85–150; repr. in Kleinbauer, ed., *The Art of Byzantium*; also see Ernst Kitzinger, *Byzantine Art in the Making: Main Lines of Stylistic Development in Mediterranean Art, 3rd–7th Century* (Cambridge, MA: Harvard University Press, 1977), pp. 104–5 and 118–19.

15 Vladimir Lossky, *The Mystical Theology of the Eastern Church* (London: James Clarke, 1957), p. 189; quoted in Maynard, p. 243.

16 Barber, "From Transformation to Desire," p. 8, p. 14 (citing Mathews).

I next explore just what about icons accounts for their unusual relationship to our human desires.

## Four Key Features of Icons

A first key feature of icons is that the image on the icon is taken by believers to be an *appearance* of the holy person. As such, it is alleged to meet certain requirements of authenticity.[17] Such an image gains authority through showing a recognizably authentic appearance of the holy person or through correctly depicting specific events.[18]

Second, icons are objects of veneration. As an approved and veracious image, the icon takes on the qualities of the person depicted. The icon is treated like the saintly person him- or herself and accorded worshipful respect, since the holy person is *manifested* in the icon. People kiss the icon, bow down to it, light incense and candles before it, etc. Believers make requests of the icon and have faith that it can conduct miracles.[19] A correlate of this second feature is that icons are often regarded as having strong powers. They are paraded about the city they protect or reside in on certain special days. Icons also are said to manifest peculiar and special behaviors that are human-like, such as weeping or bleeding on specific occasions.[20]

Third, icons also are often alleged to have special causal origins. Many icons, even if painted by a human artist, were held to be directly caused by the holy person who wished to have a likeness made. Because of the emphasis on the causal role of the depicted person in the icon, there was a corresponding de-emphasis on the artistic source of the human icon painter. This was true, for example, in the case of some famous icons of Mary, which were said to have been painted originally by St Luke. It was commonly held in the medieval period, up until relatively late times (the fourteenth century), that various icons were authentic because they had been painted "from life" by St Luke, who was allegedly present at the

17 Belting comments that beauty didn't matter in an icon; rather, correctness did; see *Likeness and Presence*, p. 47.

18 According to Belting, these are events "in the history of salvation," (ibid., p. 30).

19 See ibid., p. 42. Also see <http://www.byzantines.net/moreinfo/iconsInTheBCC.htm>: "One of the most important icons transferred to Kiev was Our Lady of Vladimir. It was believed that this icon had powers that could benefit the town. It was carried onto the battlefield in the hopes of bringing additional protection, carried in processions, and called upon to bring rain to the country."

20 See "Miracles – Icons Crying, Drinking Milk, Shedding Blood, Shedding Oil," at <http://www.crystalinks.com/weepingstatues.html>.

Nativity. This was said of one of the very first icons, that of Mary in Venice, originally from Byzantium, which was supposedly posed for and approved by Mary herself. Belting explains:

> This "authentic" portrait was naturally preferred by the Virgin, as it showed her "correctly" and had been made with her cooperation; special grace thus accrued to this one painting. . . . The intervention of a painter in such a case was deemed something of an intrusion; a painter could not be expected to reproduce the model authentically. Only if one was sure that the painter had recorded the actual living model with the accuracy we today tend to attribute to a photograph, as in the case of St Luke or the painter whom the Three Kings brought with them to Bethlehem to portray the Mother and Child, could one verify the authenticity of the results.[21]

At times a miraculous or divine force was supposed to have caused an icon to come into existence on its own, using no human agency at all. Belting explains that these kinds of icons tend to be found within various cultures with traditions of sacred images said to have fallen from the sky, etc.[22] Such cult images (and after them, icons) were described as "*acheiropoietic*," i.e., not made by an artist's hand. They were simply "found" as miracles of representation or of presence, as it were.[23] *Acheiropoietic* images were provided by God and hence were exceptions to the ban on images in the Ten Commandments.

We can all no doubt think of other examples of images with a similar *acheiropoietic* origin, such as the Turin Shroud or the famous Mandylion of Christ. Another example is the image of the Virgin of Guadalupe now venerated at a shrine in Mexico City. News coverage of the Pope's visit to Latin America in July 2002 prompted considerable discussion of the newly canonized Indian saint Juan Diego's miraculous encounters with the Virgin of Guadalupe in 1531 – an encounter he proved to the Church bishop by revealing the image she miraculously imprinted upon his *tilma* or cape.[24] Other examples of *acheiropoietic* images are more mundane and controversial but still frequently occurring, such as the image of Jesus on a tortilla or in driveway oil stains, or an image of the Virgin in old panes of glass in a warehouse building.[25]

21 Belting, *Likeness and Presence*, p. 4; see also p. 53.
22 Ibid., p. 56.
23 Ibid., p. 49.
24 See the official website at <http://www.sancta.org/>.
25 See Belting, *Likeness and Presence*, p. 53; also, see "Shrine of the Miracle Tortilla," at <http://www.roadsideamerica.com/attract/NMLAKtortilla.html>.

The fourth primary feature of icons may seem paradoxical, given the beliefs summarized just above about an icon's special causal origin, but icons have also often been held to be *reproducible* in ways that transmit their authenticity and miraculous powers. In one example from 1569, numerous copies were made of an icon of the Virgin and sent all over to castles and monasteries; novices were required to pray before the copy.[26] Such reproduction is often mechanical. Thus, images were authentically reproduced by making impressions of them. And indeed, some of the images were attributed with this power themselves; i.e., they were held to have the ability to transmit copies of themselves onto fabric.[27] Maynard comments: "[T]here are legends of spontaneous occult editions of *acheiropoeitai*, and a history of mechanical, contact editions, by means which Kitzinger calls 'curiously prophetic of methods used in photography.'"[28] Even if artists were hired and employed to make the copies, the power to transmit the approved image and its miraculous abilities was attributed to the image itself (or to its prototype figure), not to the artist, who prayed to allow higher forces to operate through him.

To sum up, I have identified four key features of icons. The status of the icon as an image or likeness is unique because of (a) its subject matter, (b) the beliefs and attitudes it inspires in viewers, (c) its causal origin, and, finally, (d) its reproducibility. First, the icon is a likeness in the sense not of resembling but of being a manifestation or appearance of its prototype. I call this the icon's "authentic manifestation" aspect. Second, the icon reminds viewers of its prototype, eliciting feelings appropriate to that prototype. This is the icon's "special treatment" aspect. It serves as an aid to contemplation and a link to a higher, transcendent reality. Third, the icon has been caused to come into existence through the intentions or agency of its prototype. I call this its "causal history" aspect. Fourth and finally, the image in the icon is reproducible: its copies transmit its other powers and similarly manifest the prototype.

Let us consider the relationships among these four features of icons. From a philosopher's point of view or that of rational analysis, we would presume that it is *because* of feature (c), the particular causal origin of the icon, that conditions (a), (b), and (d) are fulfilled – that the image resembles its prototype, is treated in certain special ways, and is reproducible in a way that transmits its special powers. However, in reality, things

26 Belting, *Likeness and Presence*, pp. 485–6.

27 Ibid., p. 53.

28 Maynard, "Secular Icon," p. 166; he cites Kitzinger here as his source.

are more complicated. It seems instead that it is *because* people treat or regard an image in certain ways that they come to accept claims about that image's causal origin. Thus, believers who are convinced that an image in a tortilla or in a piece of frosted glass actually shows Jesus or the Madonna then also accept that the image has a sacred and mysterious causal origin.

We could compare the process to the reasoning in recent times about crop circles or other controversial, possibly extraterrestrial or supernatural phenomena. Some people insist that crop circles are caused by aliens from outer space, that certain footprints demonstrate the presence of Bigfoot, or that mysterious flashes of light in haunted houses manifest the existence of poltergeists. From the rational or scientific viewpoint, the signs in question are not indexical markers but, rather, evidence of clever hoaxes or somehow otherwise explainable. It seems, nevertheless, that for those who have the desire to believe in an extraterrestrial or psychic phenomena, the marks in question *are* evidence for their view – even if actual proofs of existence might still be forthcoming. As a preview, we can note that a similar duality of approaches will apply in the case of the analysis of photographs alleging to show the Loch Ness Monster, UFOs, etc. Just as with icons, believers may take the images in question to be epistemically trustworthy because they bring with them a persuasive psychological force. But of course this psychological force (or "manifestation") will not be felt by skeptics, in the case of either religious images or alleged photographs of unusual phenomena.

## Photographs as Icons

Icons are still with us today. This is obviously true in the sense that Eastern Orthodox churches still use icons and they are still commercially made available for purchase by believers. But icons have taken on new forms. An example offered by Belting shows the influence of photography in the depiction of icons of the Virgin in Argentina in the early 1970s, when she was given the features of Evita Peron.[29] Besides this, photographs have actually stood in for icons in churches as the revered images of recently recognized saints. In 1987 in Naples, a newly announced saint was celebrated with "a modern icon" over the altar in the form of his photograph.[30] Belting comments that "the cultic sphere is concerned not with

[29] Belting, *Likeness and Presence*, p. 44.
[30] Ibid., p. 11.

the *art* of memory . . . but with the *content* of memory."[31] Thus a cult image, like an icon, is not about history or the past, but about presence, "namely, the former and future presence of God in the life of humankind. . . . The image reached into the immediate experience of God in past history and likewise ahead to a promised time to come."[32]

We can see, briefly, that an image like Lincoln's photograph appears to fulfill the same four conditions that I just described as applying to icons. First, the image seems to manifest Lincoln or make him present. Walton emphasizes that when we have contact with someone through a photograph, we fictionally see that person or get "in touch" with him or her. Such contact is why we care about certain images – even if they are blurred and fuzzy. Ordinarily, fictional seeing goes along with fictional works – in the case of visual art, with such things as imaginative paintings, illustrations, and films. The people we see transparently in photographs, however, are (or were) really there. Hence, though we see them fictionally, they are not simply props in quite specialized games of make-believe. Rather, Walton writes with the sense that through photographs we can "get in touch with" a significant American hero like Lincoln, or an ancestor like his own grandfather, via their photographs. Because the US Civil War death scenes captured by the photographer Timothy O'Sullivan have more reality than the etchings in Goya's *Disasters of War* series, they are more powerful and disturbing.

Numerous testimonies from early viewers of photography reveal how these images worked to guarantee authenticity and reveal presence. Consider this example from Elizabeth Barrett:

> It is not merely the likeness which is precious in such cases – but the association, and the sense of nearness involved in the thing . . . the fact of the *very shadow of the person* lying there fixed forever! It is the very sanctification of portraits I think – and . . . I would rather have such a memorial of one I dearly loved, than the noblest Artist's work ever produced.[33]

This general idea that photographs are manifestations of their prototypes is also supported in the well-known defense of photographic realism offered by Kendall L. Walton in "Transparent Pictures: On the Nature of Photographic Realism." Walton claims: "With the assistance of the camera, we can see not only around corners and what is distant or

31 Ibid., p. 10; emphasis in original.
32 Ibid., p. 11.
33 Cited in Maynard, "Secular Icon," p. 159, n. 10.

small; we can also see into the past. We see long-deceased ancestors when we look at dusty snapshots of them."[34] This feeling of being in direct contact with the prototype of a photographic image is very important in Walton's essay, where examples of photographic portraits of people are prominent. He speaks, for example, about seeing Abraham Lincoln in photographs, as well as his dead grandfather and his Aunt Mabel. Such examples help support his claims about "contact" and make the idea of photographic "transparency" seem more plausible. In photographs, then, it seems that a real person is made present – this is not simply a likeness, but an actual appearance or an appearing-before-us. They facilitate our *contact* with people – even long-dead ones. It is this "manifestation" function of photographs that I wish to consider further here.

Patrick Maynard comments that, "testimonies about 'nearness,' 'contact,' 'emanation,' 'vestige,' 'trace,' 'co-substantiality,' and so on, register a sense that photographs of things can combine with these (depictive) characteristics a strong manifestation function as well."[35] Susan Sontag confirms this linkage when she remarks that having a photograph of Shakespeare would be like having a splinter from the True Cross.

Second, photographs are treated in specific ways, including ways that reveal love, respect, and even veneration. Walton also mentions this point: "we can *see* our loved ones again, and *that* is important to us."[36] The contemporary painter Gerhard Richter, who often works by turning photographs into paintings, has commented, in a similar vein: "Snapshots are like little devotional pieces that people have in their environment and look at."[37] In particular, photographs of the dead often receive special treatment. For example, George Santayana wrote in "The Photograph and the Mental Image":

> Photography was first employed in portraiture; that is, it was employed to preserve those mental images which we most dislike to lose, the images of familiar faces. . . . [P]hotography came as a welcome salve to keep those precious, if slightly ridiculous, things a little longer in the world. It consoled both our sorrows and our vanity, and we collected photographs like little relics and mementoes of the surfaces of our past life.[38]

34 Walton, "Transparent Pictures," p. 251 (this vol., p. 22).

35 Maynard, "Secular Icon," p. 247.

36 Walton, "Transparent Pictures," p. 253 (this vol., p. 25); emphasis in original.

37 "Gerhard Richter, The Day is Long." Interviewed by Robert Storr, *Art in America* (January 2002): 67–75: p. 121.

38 Santayana, "The Photograph and the Mental Image," in Vicki Goldberg, ed., *Photography in Print: Writings from 1816 to the Present* (New York: Simon and Schuster), p. 260.

A very common early use of the daguerreotype was to mark and in some sense "preserve" the dead body of a lost child or loved one. Sometimes the children were posed as if asleep, but, at other times, as if still alive.[39] We probably all have a treasured image of a particular lost loved one that shows their now-absent "essence," making that person once more present to us. In this regard our snapshots or old family portraits are like the portrait miniatures that served similar purposes in the early modern period. It was common for poets and writers to allude to their beloved through so-called "conversations" with these miniatures.

From a surprisingly early date, also, processes were developed to enable photographs to be recorded more or less permanently on tombstones. John Matturri reports:

> As early as 1851, Solomon Tomkins of West Cambridge, Massachusetts had obtained a patent for "securing daguerreotypes to monumental stones" and in 1855, the Scoville Manufacturing Company of New York, which three years earlier had offered a daguerreotype case specifically designed for memorial pieces, was distributing a catalog for "Monumental Daguerreotype Cases."[40]

There are many very striking daguerreotypes on gravestones of children. This practice continues even now with the use of photographs or photo-etching processes.[41] Typically, such images preserve the look of the dead person in his or her prime, although sometimes more than one portrait is included, as if to indicate several stages of the deceased person's life. In many cases couples are shown (even if only one is dead), as if to herald their future reunion in the afterlife. Photographs and photographic collages are also often displayed at funerals and memorial services, sometimes in company with a casket and sometimes along with an urn of ashes, or with no visible reminder of the corpse of the lost person at all. An ongoing relationship might also be signaled by the common practice of leaving offerings at the tomb site including not only flowers but also small notes, *ex votos*, etc. In the annual Mexican "*Dia de los Muertos*" remembrances, photographs of the dead are taken to cemeteries, where they are surrounded by candles, flowers, food, and other favorite items of the deceased.

39 Lianne McTavish, "Picturing the Dead," *Canadian Medical Association Journal* 166: 13 (2002): 1700. McTavish mentions one little girl shown as if still playing her drums!

40 John Matturri, "Traces of Mortality: The Nature of Representation in Phtographic Tombstones." Paper presented at the Annual Meeting of the Association for Gravestone Studies, Amherst College, June 1987; references omitted.

41 Now some cemeteries even provide for the use of biographical DVDs on tombstones!

Third, photographs are often taken to be "*acheiropoietic*" in some sense. This is a view often implied, sometimes even explicitly asserted, in the context of discussions of photographic realism and the associated mechanical causation. Walton writes, for example, of Abraham Lincoln's photograph: "Lincoln . . . caused his photograph, and thus the visual experiences of those who view it." It is further significant that the kind of causation is quite specific – being caused in a mechanical manner.[42]

The fourth condition, multiple reproducibility, also applies in the case of photographs (though not to daguerreotypes). Indeed, it is probable that what Walton is looking at when he speaks of looking at a photograph of Lincoln is not an original by, e.g., Matthew Brady, but a reproduction of a photograph.

## Revisiting Photographic Realism

Above, I raised the issue of the logical priority among the four conditions associated with icons: their being manifestations, eliciting special treatment, having special causation, and being reproducible. To ponder this point more might help us realize something more about the nature of photographs and their functions – and how they resemble icons. We can then revisit the issue of how claims about the two senses of photographic realism are connected. Recall that I have drawn a comparison with other sorts of (alleged) signs as well, including crop circles, footprints, and so on.

Walton's arguments for photographic realism have usually been construed as involving *epistemological* claims, and various points have been mentioned by critics to dispute this claim. Thus critics have pointed out that photographers actually *do* have the ability to manipulate the image, express an artistic vision through it, distort it through the use of various lenses and viewpoints, etc.[43] In 2004, Jonathan Cohen and Aaron Meskin

42 Walton, "Transparent Pictures," p. 261 (this vol. p. 34).

43 A different line of criticism was taken by Jonathan Cohen and Aaron Meskin in their "On the Epistemic Value of Photographs," *Journal of Aesthetics and Art Criticism* 62: 2 (2004): 197–210. They argue that we see photographs as transparent because of the familiar ways photographs work or are used in our culture. The epistemic status of photographs is variable and depends "on facts about representational practices and about our perceptual/cognitive psychology." But Cohen and Meskin go on to note that with the ongoing impact of digital technology upon the medium, our common understanding about photographs could change, so that we no longer regard them as evidence or as trustworthy. They acknowledge a similar observation by Barbara Savedoff about how our beliefs could be changed by awareness of the manipulations permitted by digital photography; see p. 19; the reference is to Barbara E. Savedoff, *Transforming Images: How Photography Complicates the Picture* (Ithaca, NY: Cornell University Press, 2000), p. 202.

again pursued this construal of Walton by arguing that we do not gain the relevant epistemic information from a photograph that we do from seeing a thing directly.[44]

What is less often noted is that Walton himself recognizes that there are two notions of realism commonly invoked in claims about photography and that, under examination, these actually break apart. In other words, he acknowledges that "contact" is *not* the same thing as veracity, and that often we don't treat photographs as information sources. This means that both his realism claim and his transparency claim are ambiguous in a very important and fundamental way.

Walton reiterated this point in a defense of the transparency thesis:

> One of the larger objectives of "Transparent Pictures" was to show that information gathering is not the only important function of perception. We sometimes have an interest in seeing things, in being in perceptual contact with them, apart from any expectations of learning about them. This interest helps to explain why we sometimes display and cherish a photograph of a loved one . . . even a fuzzy and badly exposed photograph, long after we have extracted any interesting or important information it might contain . . . We value the experience of seeing the loved one (even indirectly), the experience of being in perceptual contact with him or her, for its own sake, not just as a means of adding to our knowledge.[45]

In effect here, Walton is saying that photographs fulfill the function of images we describe as being psychologically realistic even if they are not transparent or accurate (realistic) in a depictive sense. It should not be surprising to anyone that Walton acknowledges the emotional role of photographs, since his important book *Mimesis as Make-Believe* develops a complex account of how artworks of various types function as props in imaginative games of make-believe.[46] Clearly such games reflect the many different emotional roles art can play in human lives, from early childhood onward. However, there is an unexpected tension or problem in trying to fit together Walton's transparency view of photographs with the idea that photographs can play roles in our games of make-believe. Walton argues that, strictly speaking, since photographs provide direct access to reality, they are *not* like other pictures or depictions – they are

44 Cohen and Meskin, "On the Epistemic Value of Photographs."

45 Kendall L. Walton, "On Pictures and Photographs: Objections Answered," in R. Allen and M. Smith, eds., *Film Theory and Philosophy* (Oxford: Oxford University Press, 1997), p. 72.

46 See Walton, *Mimesis as Make-Believe: On the Foundations of the Representational Arts* (Cambridge, MA: Harvard University Press, 1990).

*not* props in games of make-believe. They are, rather, instruments or tools to enlarge our visual powers, not to incite our imagination. Objects *cause* their photographs – and, hence, the visual experiences of subsequent viewers – mechanically, so that we are able literally to *see* those same objects through the photographs, just as we see stars through a telescope or cells through a microscope. Walton goes so far as to argue that a non-fiction image is not a picture, since "Pictures are fiction by definition."[47] Photographs are like other aids to vision – telescopes, microscopes, surveillance cameras, etc. This means that they are very different from other sorts of pictures. Walton writes: "To think of the camera as another tool of vision is to de-emphasize its role in producing pictures. Photographs are pictures, to be sure, but not ordinary ones. They are pictures through which we see the world."[48]

All this is one side of the story of photography – the transparency side. It seems Walton is arguing that insofar as photographs possess depictive realism, they cannot be artworks or function in an emotionally powerful way. But if we shift from this notion of realism, the epistemic one, to the psychological one, or what I call "contact," it turns out that Walton's view is more subtle and complex than is often acknowledged, since of course he does in fact recognize the strong psychological impact of photographs upon us (he mentions photographs of family members, war scenes, etc.) Part of the misunderstanding is the result of his provocative claim that we literally see dead ancestors through photos. Walton explains that there is major confusion in writings on this topic, due to:

> failure to recognize and distinguish clearly between the special kind of seeing which actually occurs and the ordinary kind of seeing which only fictionally takes place, between a viewer's *really* seeing something *through a photograph* and his *fictionally* seeing something *directly*. A vague awareness of both, stirred together in a witches' cauldron, could conceivably tempt one toward the absurdity that the viewer is really in the presence of the object.[49]

47 Ibid., p. 351. See also the discussion of this passage by Gregory Currie in his review of Walton's book in *The Journal of Philosophy* 90: 7 (1993). Pictures are depictions that authorize us to imagine what they represent. Also, personal imagining is a problem. The oscilloscope watcher who points to her screen and says "That's a loud one" is not imagining a game in which she sees noises. Rather, "What I see represents a loud noise" – and it's the same with picture viewing. A better theory is Flint Schier's: a depiction of an X is something we recognize as such by means of our capacity visually to recognize X's. Depiction is explained in terms of perceptual capacities, not imaginative ones (see Walton, *Mimeses as Make-Believe*, p. 349).

48 "Transparent Pictures," p. 252 (this vol., p. 24).

49 Ibid., p. 254 (this vol., p. 26); Walton's emphasis.

What Walton is saying, then, is that we need to distinguish a special kind of seeing that ordinarily occurs *through* photographs from an ordinary kind of seeing that only fictionally takes place. "What is literally true is that I see Aunt Mabel through the photograph of her at a long-ago family picnic. But it is fictional that I see her directly, 'without photographic assistance.'"[50] Epistemic realism is assured by the photograph's causal history, Walton thinks; but psychological realism is always a fiction and one that may be supported well by the photograph as a prop, even if the prop isn't realistic in the other sense.

Thus it turns out that in the details of his account of our psychological use of photographs (and in particular portraits), Walton actually retracts much of the force of his striking idea that we *literally* see our dead ancestors through photographs. His claim gets much weaker when we examine these details. Walton differentiates two theses: (1) that one *really* sees something *through* a photograph, and (2) that one *fictionally* sees that thing (or person) *directly*. Transparency is literal, but contact is fictional. Although I do literally see Aunt Mabel *through* the photograph, it is make-believe to imagine that I am in her presence or that I see her grimacing.

Presumably, then, many of the other sorts of things I *seem* to see through photographs are things I only see fictionally. It is fictional, for example, that Abe Lincoln is looking back at me in a particular photographic portrait, or that I can see his craggily handsome face. On the transparency claim, I literally see Lincoln. On the contact claim, I am fictionally "in touch" with him. Transparency does not support games of make-believe or emotional involvement; it is contact which serves these aims. But contact is, in a key sense, fictional – a matter of the emotional uses to which I put certain sorts of pictures. Thus for Walton, realism amounts to two quite distinct things, corresponding to the two sorts of realist claims I have distinguished. One has to do with facts about causation and epistemic value, the other has to do with facts about the psychology of image functioning.

## Conclusion

In this article I have argued that the assertion of photographic realism can mean different things. It can amount to a claim about how an image functions epistemologically or about its psychological functioning. Both sorts of claims can reflect views about the causal origin of the image, although in interestingly distinct ways. Epistemological claims reflect

50 Ibid.

assumptions about the causal history of the photographic process as relevant to what can accurately be seen in or inferred from the resulting image. The process allegedly results in an accurate and truthful rendering of the objects or actions depicted therein. Psychological claims instead place stress on the causal relationship itself: the very fact that the depicted object caused its image to appear functions to put us "in contact with" that object when we view the image.

Of course, the veridical sense of realism as transparency can be mistaken in the case of photographs as of other sorts of natural signs. Photographs can be faked just as Bigfoot tracks in the snow can, or just as crop circles might be done by hoaxers. What looks to be a photograph could be a manipulated image (even a painting), and what looks to be a huge footprint in the snow could similarly be something made by a combination of socks and fingers.

That realism can break apart into these two senses should be fairly obvious. Paintings done in the photo-realist style may *appear* as realistic as photographs; in other words, they can present people or scenes to us in vivid, lifelike ways. And conversely, photographs done in "painterly" styles (using such effects as soft focus) may seem unrealistic. That is, they may appear to have been made by hand and to reflect artistic intervention. The sense of "reality" I acquire in viewing an old photograph of my great-grandfather may, but need not, reflect the accuracy of that image. Though it seems lifelike to me, I might be mistaken, say, if the image depicts someone else or if, instead, it is a manipulated present-day image.

It is easy to see how two different sorts of claims for realism might become confused, for example, in discussions claiming that a photograph of someone results from "emanations" from that very person. Taken in the sense of transparency, this amounts to the claim that the photograph reveals its causation directly: the camera and photographic surface have captured light rays actually emanating from the person's surface. The rendering device operates like any other sort of lens in a viewing mechanism. But, taken in the sense of manifestation, realist claims concern our feeling of being in direct relation to the person or things depicted in a photograph. Such a feeling might be mediated by our awareness of the causal history of the image, but that is not what such a feeling amounts to. This is shown by the fact that such feelings may be mistaken or may be bracketed from one's knowledge of the image's causal source: thus, *Jurassic Park* seemed realistic when I saw it, although I knew that the dinosaurs shown in it were special effects creations. Similarly, we are aware that photographs are used all the time now in misleading ways, e.g., on covers of tabloids, to imply conjunctions of people, their emotional states, etc.

I have argued that beliefs in photographs' status as a means of direct contact with a depicted person are grounded less in any convictions about their special epistemic status than in attitudes and emotions that both reflect and continue traditional historical practices of making and using portraits as guarantees of presence. There are four key features that such portraits share with the religious icon: allegedly manifesting a person or revealing their essence in a moment of sustained presence; serving to elicit heightened emotions and reverent behaviors; stemming from a very particular kind of causal origin; and being reproducible, where reproductions transmit the first two properties.

I have also argued that Walton is not as staunch a defender of photographic realism as he is often taken to be. He revises his claim that we are able to see people in photographs by explaining that it is fictional that we do so in a most significant sense (that we are in their presence, that we see their facial expressions, etc.). That is, he too acknowledges a significant distinction between the two functions of photographic images in claims of realism: the epistemic and the psychological.

A final word. The most important practices and conventions that appear to ground a belief in photographic realism may reflect the desires that gave rise to the practice of portraiture in the first place: desires to sustain contact especially after death. At funerals and memorial services, as well as on gravestones and in cemeteries, and in certain religious contexts, photographs continue to serve the manifestation function that was facilitated in earlier time periods by a wide succession of types of images (icons, funeral portraits, death-masks), as well as by non-images (relics). Somehow, as Walton puts it, we do "care" about images of lost loved ones. But photographs are just one way – not the only way and not necessarily a pre-eminent way – of imagining that we are in contact with them.

# 3

# PHOTOGRAPHS AS EVIDENCE

Aaron Meskin and Jonathan Cohen

> We cannot conceive of a more impartial and truthful witness than the sun, as its light stamps and seals the similitude of the wound on the photograph put before the jury; it would be more accurate than the memory of witnesses, and as the object of all evidence is to show truth, why should not this dumb witness show it?
>
> *Franklin v. State of Georgia*, 69 Ga. 36; 1882 Ga.

## Introduction

Photographs furnish evidence. This is true in both formal and informal contexts. The use of photographs as legal evidence goes back to the very earliest days of photography, and they have been used in American trials since around the time of the Civil War. Photographs may also serve as historical evidence (for example, about the Civil War). And they serve in informal contexts as evidence about all sorts of things, such as what we and our loved ones looked like in the past.

Photographs are not, of course, the only sorts of pictures that can furnish evidence. It is not hard to think of cases in which a non-photographic picture might serve as legal evidence (perhaps of art theft?). Cave paintings serve as anthropological evidence of human habitation. And crude pictures chalked on the side of a building may serve informally as evidence of adolescent mischief. Nonetheless, photographs seem to have a distinctive epistemic status compared to other sorts of pictures. Unlike the aforementioned examples of non-photographic depictions, photographs typically provide evidence in particular about what they depict. Most significantly, the epistemically special character of photographs is revealed by this fact: we are inclined to trust them in a way that we are not inclined to trust even the most accurate of drawings and paintings.

The traditional explanation for the special epistemic status of photography is that photography is an inherently realistic medium. This certainly sounds right, but it is hard to evaluate the claim without offering a theory of what photographic realism consists in. Unfortunately, a number of the traditional accounts of photographic realism that purport to explain photography's special epistemic status rest on rather unpalatable commitments. For example, André Bazin's re-presentationalist theory[1] makes the implausible claim that "the photographic image is the object itself." And Kendall Walton's claim that photographs are "transparent"[2] – in that they literally allow us to see the objects that they depict – is both counterintuitive and (as we have argued elsewhere) simply mistaken.[3] Of course, there are also a number of less metaphysically questionable theories of photographic realism. For example, Gregory Currie offers a sophisticated similarity account of depictive and cinematic realism in his *Image and Mind*.[4] But this account offers little hope of explaining the epistemic status of photography, in part because it makes no distinction between depictive realism in general and photographic realism in particular.[5] The epistemic status of photography, then, has gone either unexplained or been explained wrongly; either way, the application of the notion of realism serves merely to label some of the distinctive features of photographic representation that need explaining. (We think much the same is true of claims about the objectivity of photographic representation.) In the rest of this essay, we offer an explanation of the epistemic status of photography – an explanation of the sort that has either gone missing or come with implausible metaphysical costs in alternative accounts.

## The Epistemic Status of Photography

What, then, does the distinctive epistemic status of photography consist in? On our view, there are two features of photography that underwrite

1 A. Bazin, *What Is Cinema?*, trans. Hugh Gray (Berkeley: University of California Press, 1967).

2 K. L. Walton, "Transparent Pictures: On the Nature of Photographic Realism," *Critical Inquiry*, 11 (1984): 246–77 (repr. as ch. 1 in this volume).

3 J. Cohen and A. Meskin, "On the Epistemic Value of Photographs," *Journal of Aesthetics and Art Criticism* 62: 2 (2004): 197–210.

4 G. Currie, *Image and Mind: Film, Philosophy and Cognitive Science* (Cambridge: Cambridge University Press, 1995).

5 Nelson Goodman's conventionalist theory is another view of pictorial realism that offers little hope of explaining the distinctive epistemic status of photography: see *Languages of Art: An Approach to a Theory of Symbols* (Indianapolis: Hackett, 1976).

its distinctive epistemic value: (1) token photographs are spatially agnostic sources of information, and (2) viewers hold background beliefs about the category of photographs that influence their attitudes towards the epistemic status of viewed token photographs. We'll unpack these claims in turn.

What do we mean by saying that photography is a spatially agnostic source of information? In order to explain this, we will first have to say a bit about what we mean by "information."

Our view of information is inspired by the account initially presented by Fred Dretske in his *Knowledge and the Flow of Information*.[6] For Dretske, information is carried when there is an objective, probabilistic, counterfactual-supporting link between two independent events.[7] So, for example, the state of a thermometer carries information about body temperature just in case there is an objective probabilistic connection between the two: the probability of the temperature being 100° conditional on the thermometer reading 100° is much higher than the probability of the temperature being 100° conditional on the thermometer not reading 100° (subject to some provisos of course). Furthermore, this probabilistic relationship must be counterfactual-supporting. In order for there to be an information-carrying relation between the thermometer's state and a person's temperature, it must be the case that (*ceteris paribus*) if the temperature were different, then the thermometer would read differently. In fact, we believe that the presence of this counterfactual relationship is generally excellent evidence for its existence.[8]

It is our contention that photographs are, in this sense, a significant source of information. In particular, photographs typically provide information about many of the visually detectable properties of the objects they depict. Consider shape and size properties. While photographs often distort and deceive with respect to this class of features, it is our contention that they nonetheless typically carry information about them. For example, if the size or shape of a depicted flower had been different, then the photographic image of it would also have been different. (A bit more precisely, if the size or shape of depicted features of the flower had been

6 F. I. Dretske, *Knowledge and the Flow of Information* (Cambridge, MA: MIT Press, 1981).

7 We do not want to commit ourselves to all the details of Dretske's development of the notion of information. In particular, we do not commit ourselves to his requirement that the probabilities in question turn out to be unity.

8 But not always – in particular, there are cases where the counterfactuals in question will come out vacuously true, but where we want to say that information is not carried. We'll consider some of these cases below.

different, then the photographic image would also have been different. Photographs do not carry information about all the visually detectable properties of the objects they depict. For example, they do not typically carry information about the hidden sides of depicted objects.) Another example of this information-carrying capacity can be seen in color photographs. These photographs typically carry information about the color of the objects they depict – if the colors of the objects had been different then the photographic image would have been different. Photographs also often carry information about many of the visual aesthetic properties of the objects they depict (hence their utility in picking travel destinations and prospective dates).[9]

It is worth emphasizing that, on our construal (viz., Dretske's construal) informational links are constituted independently of any subject's beliefs or other mental states. The state of the thermometer carries the information about the temperature of the room whether or not I (or anyone else) infer from the former to the latter, whether or not I am (or anyone else is) aware of the former, and so on. Likewise, questions about the information carried and not carried by photographs (etc.) are to be answered by considering the objective probabilistic relations they bear to various events. In particular, such questions are *not* to be answered by asking what any subjects are justified in believing on the basis of photographs, what they learn about the world from photographs, what they are prepared to infer from photographs, and the like.

Furthermore, this account of the information-carrying capacity of photographs makes no reference to the realism or objectivity of photographs, nor to their accuracy, nor (as should be clear from the prior paragraph) does it imply anything about whether or not we ordinarily make correct judgments on the basis of photographs.[10] It is also worth noting that this account allows that two photographic images that carry the same

9 More precisely, photographs carry information about the visually detectable properties of their depicta *at a time* – viz., at the time the photograph was taken. For suppose on Tuesday I paint (i.e., apply paint to) the flower I photographed on Monday; I have thereby changed the color of the flower without producing a corresponding change in the photograph. That is, the photograph on Tuesday fails to carry information about the color of the flower on Tuesday. On the other hand, the photograph on Tuesday continues to carry information about the color of the flower on Monday. We'll ignore this complication in what follows.

10 Of course, if someone should choose to use terms such as "realism" or "objectivity" to characterize the information-carrying capacity of photography, we would have no quarrel with this choice of labels.

information might look quite different (perhaps because of differences in photographic processing). As Goodman notes in a similar context, systematically replacing the colors of a picture with their complements would not thereby change the informational content of that picture.[11]

But while photographs typically carry information about many of the visual properties of the objects they depict (call this "v-information"), there is another category of information that photographs fail to provide: information about the egocentric spatial location of the objects that they depict (call this "e-information"). That is, photographs do not typically provide information about the location – with respect to viewers of that photograph – of the objects they depict. The lack of this information is made evident by the falsity of the relevant counterfactuals. Consider again that aforementioned photograph of the flower. It is not the case that if the spatial relationship between the photograph and the flower were to change then the image of the flower would change. Hence, a viewer of the photograph who carries it around with her could change her spatial relationship to the flower without any change in the photographic image. And so, the photograph (and the visual process involving looking at the photograph) fail to carry e-information about the objects it depicts.

Up to this point, we have primarily focused on the information-carrying capacity of token photographs. For ease of exposition, it may be useful to talk of the information-carrying capacities of various depictive types, including the category of photographs. We will say that a depictive type D carries information of kind K just in case tokens of type D typically carry K-information. Alternatively, we may characterize this feature of types dispositionally: D carries K-information if and only if it is disposed to have tokens that carry K-information. It will also be useful to apply the notion of information-carrying to various visual process tokens and types.[12] Thus, let us say that a visual process token carries information of a certain kind about an object just in case there is an objective probabilistic relation between the process token and the relevant features of the object. Then the visual-process token *v* of looking at a depictive token ***d*** carries K-information about an object *o* depicted in ***d*** if and only if there is an objective probabilistic relation between *v* and the K-features of *o*. Visual-process types carry K-information if and only if their tokens are typically

11 Goodman, *Languages of Art*.

12 The formulations here depart slightly from those we have adopted previously – see "On the Epistemic Value of Photographs;" we've made these modifications in order to evade some (rather technical) worries applicable to the earlier formulations.

such that they carry K-information. Accordingly, the visual-process type of looking at a depictive type D carries K-information about the objects depicted in tokens of D just in case tokens of that process type typically carry K-information about objects depicted by tokens of D.

If this analysis is right, then photographs are what we have called elsewhere "spatially agnostic informants":[13] they carry information of one sort (v-information) while failing to carry information about the egocentric locations of the objects they depict (i.e., e-information). And this begins to explain the distinctive epistemic value of photography. In the first place, photographs are a significant source of information. In this way, the type of photographs differ from many other depictive representation types that do not carry information about the visually accessible properties of the objects they depict. In the second place, the spatial agnosticism of the type of photographs, and therefore the process of looking at photographs, differentiates photographs from some other sources of visual information. For example, both ordinary vision and visual processes that use prosthetics such as telescopes and binoculars (hereafter "visual prosthetic processes") carry both v-information and e-information. This might make it seem that the process of looking at photographs is informationally impoverished in comparison with these other sources of visual information. This is correct. Ordinary vision does typically provide more information than does the process of looking at photographs. And visual prosthetic processes are also informationally richer in this way than the process of looking at photographs (i.e., the former provide both v-information and e-information about the objects they allow us to see, while the latter only provides v-information about depicted objects). Nonetheless, this feature also contributes to the special epistemic status of photography. For it is not simply that ordinary vision provides both v-information and e-information; it would not provide v-information unless it also provided e-information. The same is true of visual prosthetic processes. But photographs and the process of looking at photographs have the capacity to provide v-information without providing e-information. This makes photography a particularly valuable technology.[14]

Many things that carry v-information also carry e-information. These sources of v-information come with strings attached. They do not provide v-information in contexts in which e-information is unavailable. Yet

13 Cohen and Meskin, "On the Epistemic Value of Photographs."

14 Of course, the process of looking at photographs does provide e-information about those very photographs. But it is e-information about photographically depicted objects that is at issue. Photographs don't ordinarily depict themselves.

we often find ourselves in contexts in which we want v-information while the preconditions for the acquisition of e-information cannot be satisfied. In such cases photographs display their distinctive epistemic value. They are a relatively undemanding source of information about the visual properties of objects – a source that is available in contexts in which e-information is not.

While we believe that photography's status as a spatially agnostic source of information is a large part of the story, this cannot be the full story about the epistemic value of photography. For there are certainly other token depictions that share this feature with photographs. It is plausible that many landscape paintings and still-lifes carry information about the visually detectable properties of the objects they depict. Moreover, these pictures fail, just like photographs, to provide e-information. So these pictures are also spatially agnostic sources of information. Furthermore, it is possible to group some of these tokens together to make non-empty categories of spatially agnostic informants (e.g., consider the category of veridical still-lifes). Yet we typically treat these depictions differently from how we treat photographs. We do not typically accord the same epistemic status to still-lifes and landscape paintings that we do to photographs.

To explain this difference, we propose to appeal to a further component of our view, which involves psychological facts about viewers. First, we claim that the type of photographs is salient for subjects in a way that the type of veridical landscape paintings is not. Subjects who come into visual contact with a photograph (under ordinary viewing conditions) typically categorize that object as a photograph; in contrast, subjects who come into visual contact with veridical landscape paintings do not typically categorize them as veridical landscape paintings, but rather as paintings or landscape paintings (or, perhaps, Dutch landscape paintings). Second, it is plausible that viewers typically hold background beliefs about the depictive categories to which they assign these pictures. By and large, viewers believe that the type of photographs is one whose members carry v-information. And by and large, viewers believe that the categories to which they assign veridical paintings are ones whose members may fail to carry v-information. It is these background beliefs that explain the epistemic distinction we make between photographs and landscape paintings.[15]

[15] The explanation we are offering cites two contingent features of human psychology: (i) the saliency ordering among spatially agnostic representational types, and (ii) the background beliefs cited in such explanations. For this reason, we are committed to saying that the epistemic distinction between photographs and landscape paintings is contingent, and also a result of relational (mind-involving) facts about those types.

Our proposal explains the epistemic status of photographs in this sense: it lays out the facts about photographs and the background beliefs that people hold about the photographs they see, and shows how these facts lead subjects to treat the photographs they see as carrying evidential weight. In contrast, our account does not (and is not intended to) explain the epistemic status of photographs in the sense that it *justifies* or *provides warrant for* the evidential weight they are accorded in all cases. On the contrary, we think that some of the relevant background beliefs are false in some cases, hence that the token photographs involved in these cases don't deserve the epistemic weight they are given. (That said, we think the relevant background beliefs are true in many cases, hence that the token photographs involved in these cases do deserve the epistemic weight they are given.) Still, we think we make the extensionally correct predictions: subjects do indeed accord this (sometimes justified/warranted, sometimes unjustified/unwarranted) evidential weight to the photographs they see. Our account of the epistemic status of photographs, then, is an account of that in virtue of which photographs have the epistemic status they in fact have; it is not an attempt to say that this epistemic status is (always) deserved or justified.

## Clarifications, Objections, and Replies

While, we believe, our account resolves many outstanding puzzles about the epistemic status of photographs, it also raises a number of interesting questions of its own – questions about the details of how the view is to be understood, and questions about its applications to some difficult cases. We'll attempt to answer such questions in this section.

### *Object seeing and e-information*

In our view, spatial agnosticism is important not only for the purpose of understanding the epistemic status of photographs, but also because it can be used to draw a line between sources of v-information whose employment constitutes (object) seeing, on the one hand, and sources of v-information whose employment does not amount to (object) seeing. In particular, we contend that it is a necessary condition on a process that counts as object seeing that it carry e-information. This classification groups together processes of ordinary seeing (by means of a normal visual system), prosthetic seeing through eyeglasses, prosthetic seeing through binoculars, etc., as instances of object seeing. In contrast, we contend, looking at a photograph may be a good way of visually acquiring true beliefs about your grandmother, but it is not a way of seeing your grandmother (but see the next section for discussion of some reasons why photographs may fail to provide us with true beliefs). However, some commentators have objected that our condition on object seeing is either too strong or too weak (or both): too strong, because it seems wrongly to preclude Balint's syndrome patients from seeing (for example), and too weak because it inappropriately classifies video with binoculars and other visual prosthetics rather than with photographs. We think both of these objections are incorrect. Let us say why.

Consider the video cases first. The thought here is that our account inappropriately treats video, unlike photographs, as a visual prosthetic; but, insofar as video is something like a temporally extended sequence of photographs, an acceptable account should classify video and photographs together. Our response to this objection will be to say that, while there are different sorts of video that ought to be considered separately, our view delivers the desired verdict that all these sorts of video are (like photographs) spatially agnostic informants, hence that they do not facilitate object seeing.

First consider video that is broadcast either live or from a pre-recorded source. If a video signal is broadcast then it can be viewed by a (suitably equipped) perceiver in many different allocentric locations; hence the (fixed) depictum of the video image can be in any of many different egocentric locations with respect to the viewer without any change in the video image. This shows that (live or pre-recorded) broadcast video fails to carry information about the egocentric location of the depictum, and so counts as another spatially agnostic informant. Cases of non-broadcast video are slightly more complicated. Some security systems, for example, involve a direct video feed from a single stationary camera to a single stationary monitor. In such cases, it might happen that the camera, the monitor, and the viewer all remain fixed in allocentric space. If so, then there is a *de facto* correlation between the video image and the egocentric location of the depictum. But this *de facto* correlation doesn't make for an informational (i.e., counterfactual-supporting) link: if, contrary to fact, there were a modification in the egocentric location of the depictum (say, if, contrary to fact, someone bought a longer video cable and moved the monitor by 20 feet), the video image would remain unchanged. Here, too, then, the process type fails to carry information about the egocentric location of the depictum; hence, non-broadcast video is also a spatially agnostic informant.

Let us turn now to Balint's syndrome, a condition that often occurs in patients with bilateral damage to pareto-occipital areas of the cortex.[16] Balint's syndrome is interesting for present purposes because the visual systems of subjects with this condition can seem to be non-photographic examples of spatially agnostic (visual) informants. Patients with Balint's syndrome can have normal visual acuity and full visual field, and can report successfully the color and shapes of seen objects. However, they are afflicted by three main visual pathologies: "simultanagnosia (the inability to see more than one object at a time); optic ataxia (the fixation of gaze with severe problems in voluntarily moving fixation); and optic apraxia (the inability to reach towards the correct location of perceived objects)."[17] In addition (presumably because of the optic ataxia associated with the syndrome), such subjects are extremely poor at recognizing and reporting the geometric arrangement of objects in space or estimating distances in both 2D and 3D visual space. These facts might suggest (indeed, have suggested to more than one commentator on our earlier work) that the visual systems of Balint's syndrome patients are spatially agnostic informants; if so, our view entails that these patients fail to see objects. But this seems hard to accept; indeed, it flies in the face of the most natural way to describe the condition (viz., that subjects see only one object at a time and cannot relate to this object spatially).

We are inclined to think that Balint's sufferers do see objects (as the natural description bears out), and are therefore committed to saying that their visual systems carry e-information. But why suppose their visual systems *don't* carry e-information? Not because these subjects are unable to report on the location of objects in egocentric space: as we have emphasized, the ability to report locations in space is not required of subjects whose visual systems carry e-information. Not because they are unable to reach toward objects: nowhere have we suggested that successful performance on reaching tasks is criterial for carrying e-information. Rather, we have said, what is criterial for carrying e-information is an objective, probabilistic, counterfactual-supporting link between two independent events. As far as we can see, the obvious explicit performance measures (verbal report, reaching behavior) fail to show either that there is or that there is not the informational link in Balint's syndrome visual systems that we claim there is. The evidence considered so far leaves open the following

16 Thanks to Lynn Robertson for advice regarding our discussion of Balint's syndrome.

17 L. C. Robertson, "Binding, Spatial Attention, and Perceptual Awareness," *Nature Reviews Neuroscience*, 4 (2003): 96.

two possibilities: (1) Balint's visual systems fail to carry e-information about seen objects, and this is what leads to the difficulties with reporting or reaching toward the locations of seen objects, or (2) Balint's syndrome visual systems do carry e-information about seen objects, but the subjects fail to report on or reach correctly for seen objects because this e-information cannot be integrated with speech and motor centers. However, a number of recent experiments using implicit measures of spatial information strongly support interpretation (2). For example, Kim and Robertson found systematic effects on reaction times in spatial-alignment tests for both normal and Balint's-syndrome subjects.[18] In related work, Robertson et al. report that reading time of the words "up" or "down" increased if those words were presented in a location at odds with its meaning ("up" presented at the bottom of a rectangle, "down" presented at the top of a rectangle) relative to reading times when the same words were presented in the opposite locations (locations consonant with the word meanings);[19] similar results are reported by Humphreys and Riddoch.[20] In all these cases, the locations of distal items seems to have systematic (though implicit) effects in Balint's patients, and it is hard to see how this could be true (barring action at a distance) unless some state of (some part of) the visual system carried information about locations of distal items. For this reason, it seems reasonable to think that Balint's syndrome visual systems carry e-information, hence that they satisfy our requirement on object seeing.

Fair enough. But we can surely imagine a condition that is just like Balint's syndrome in its symptoms, but such that the visual systems of its sufferers do not carry e-information. Call this imagined condition "Shmalint's syndrome." We are committed to saying that Shamlint's patients fail to see objects, since, by stipulation, they fail to satisfy our necessary condition on object seeing. But, on the other hand, the initial reason given for holding that Balint's patients see objects seems to apply to Shmalint's

[18] M.-S. Kim and L. C. Robertson, "Implicit Representations of Space After Bilateral Parietal Lobe Damage," *Journal of Cognitive Neuroscience* 13: 8 (2001): 1080–7.

[19] L. C. Robertson, A. M. Treisman, S. R. Friedman-Hill, and M. Grabowecky, M., "The Interaction of Spatial and Object Pathways: Evidence from Balint's Syndrome," *Journal of Cognitive Neuroscience* 9 (1997): 691–700.

[20] G. W. Humphreys and M. J. Riddoch, "From *What* to *Where*: Neuropsychological evidence for implicit interactions between object- and space-based attention," *Psychological Science*, 14: 5 (2003): 487–92; cf. L. C. Robertson, *Space, Objects, Minds and Brains* (New York: Psychology Press, 2004), pp. 164–77.

patients too: the most natural way to describe the condition is to say that patients see only one object at a time but are impaired (to different extents) in relating spatially to it. We are prepared to bite the bullet here and insist that (the naive description notwithstanding) Shmalint's patients fail to see objects. It is worth bearing in mind that apparent Shmalint's patients may turn out to see objects after all: absence of evidence of e-information (e.g., absence of the sort of implicit evidence of e-information we found in Balint's patients) cannot be taken as evidence of absence of e-information. But, we claim, true Shmalint's patients – viz., patients whose visual systems, as a matter of fact, fail to carry e-information – fail to see objects. Of course, the visual systems of Shmalint's patients will carry v-information, e.g., about the color and shape of a single object in front of them. Perhaps this is enough to say that the knowledge derived therefrom counts as perceptual knowledge. Nonetheless, our contention is that, insofar as they fail to carry e-information, what these visual systems are doing falls outside what counts as object seeing.[21]

## *Questions about information*

We have argued (1) that photographs provide v-information, but (2) they do not provide e-information. Nevertheless, we would not be surprised

[21] The conclusion that Shmalint's patients fail to see objects is, as we have said, at odds with the naive description of the case, and is to that extent a counterintuitive result of our account. We are prepared to live with this counterintuitive result because, after all, Shmalint's syndrome is an extremely abstruse (not to mention fictional) condition.

However, there is another line of response for those with weaker stomachs for counterintuitive results. Namely, one might reformulate our necessary condition on seeing this way: a token process counts as seeing *x* only if properly functioning tokens of that process carry e-information about *x*. The thought, then, is that a theory of proper functioning would help us type token processes in a way that would allow a little more flexibility about cases. In particular, the contemplated revision would allow that Shmalint's sufferers see objects so long as their token visual processes turn out to be improperly functioning tokens of the type of visual process in non-Shmalint's subjects (and assuming that tokens of this type of visual process carry e-information). On the other hand, looking at photographs would still fail to carry e-information, hence would still fail to facilitate object seeing. (Presumably, if you prefer this line on Shmalint's syndrome, you would say exactly the same thing about Balint's syndrome as well.)

Of course, the price of this alternative account is the provision of an acceptable theory of proper function. We realize that many philosophers are prepared to pay this price, even though most of them regard it as large. However, given the tiny benefit to be had in the context of the present discussion – a more intuitive description of a fanciful visual pathology – it is unobvious that the price is worth paying for present purposes.

if readers were still a bit suspicious of both of these claims. With respect to (1), it is indisputable that some photographs mislead. For example, some photographs distort the shapes and sizes of the objects they depict. And photographic color is highly dependent on film processing, so processing errors may lead to inaccurate depiction of object color. Hence, one might be tempted to deny that highly distorted and poorly processed photos provide v-information. With respect to (2), some photographs seem to enable us to judge the distance between ourselves and the objects they depict. Some commentators on our earlier work have suggested that these photographs provide e-information.

We believe that both these objections are misguided. In both cases, the objections rest largely on a misunderstanding of our claims. The crucial point is that our account of information is utterly non-doxastic. That is, we do not understand the provision of information in terms of a capacity to provide true beliefs nor, in fact, do we construe information in any cognitive terms at all. We lay no claim to the term "information," however. So it may be that, in some sense or other of "information," there are photos that do not provide visual information about the objects they depict, and that there are other photos that do provide e-information about their depicta. Once the use of the term "information" is disambiguated, the truth of these claims will be clearly shown to be irrelevant to (1) and (2). Let us then turn to consideration of criticisms of our claim that photographs provide v-information.

It is certainly true that some photographs are misleading, insofar as they tend to lead viewers to form misguided beliefs about the objects they depict. In particular, many photographs mislead with respect to the visually detectable properties of the objects they depict. A photograph of a house (or horse) may make it look smaller than it really is. A photograph of your grandfather may make him look more handsome than he really was. And the poorly processed (and poorly lit) photographs of your nature hike may make the scenery look more blue than it was when you were there. But these indisputable truths are irrelevant to the question of whether such photographs provide v-information, given our technical understanding of "information." If the horse had been smaller, then the image would have been different. If your grandfather had been more handsome, then the photo would have looked different. So the requisite informational link is still present in these cases. What the cases show is that the process of forming beliefs about the visually detectable properties of objects on the basis of photographic images of them is not perfectly reliable. Providing v-information is not sufficient for producing a true belief. Who would have thought otherwise? Certainly not us.

(There may be some other sorts of photographs that do not provide v-information. For example, if there are non-depictive photographs, then such photographs do not provide v-information. But this is not damaging to any view we are propounding. Our aim has been to explain the distinctive epistemic status of photographs qua type of depictive representation. The class of photographs under consideration, then, is properly contained in the class of depictive representations. As such, non-depictive photographs lie outside the range of our explanatory target.)

What about criticisms of (2) – our claim that photographs do not provide e-information? One reason for doubting this claim might stem from the thought that photographs "can serve, along with information from other sources in an inference to egocentric information."[22] For example, consider a photograph of a well-known landmark (e.g., the Buddy Holly statue in Lubbock, Texas). If an agent is confronted with such a photograph, and she knows both her location and the location of the landmark, it may be possible for her to calculate the location of the depicted object with respect to her current location. Nonetheless, we contend that the photograph in question fails to carry e-information. After all, if the agent moves with the photograph, the egocentric location of the landmark changes, but the photographic image does not change. The photograph itself does not carry e-information.[23] (Of course, the agent may be able to recalculate the egocentric location of the depicted object after moving with the photo. But this is irrelevant to the issue at hand.[24])

A second reason for doubting our contention that photographs do not carry e-information has been suggested by Kendall L. Walton (personal correspondence), who has offered a range of cases in which it appears that photographs do, or could (under the right conditions), provide e-information. Walton first asks us to consider Polaroid photos that develop, pop out, and disintegrate rapidly. (Note that such photos would not be very useful evidentially, since any information they provide comes with significant strings attached!). He suggests that these photographs might

22 Currie, *Image and Mind*, p. 66.

23 It should be noted that Currie recognizes that – despite their occasional role in inferences of the aforementioned kind – photographs do not convey e-information (see ibid.).

24 Compare the fact that you may be able to calculate the egocentric location of someone who is speaking to you on the telephone if you happen to know where that telephone is and where you are in relation to it. Still, the sounds you hear do not carry e-information about the person to whom you are speaking. The reasoning is the same as in the photographic case.

plausibly be said to provide the spatial information that the objects they depict are in the vicinity. He also suggests that current photographs and, in particular, some photographs made before the development of the telephoto lens and space travel look to provide at least one significant piece of e-information – the information that the object depicted in the photograph occurred on the same planet as the one inhabited by the viewer of said photograph.

We contend that Walton's cases are not, in fact, ones in which photographs provide e-information – at least of the sort that we are interested in. Rather, these cases are similar to the ones that Currie describes above – they are cases in which certain photographs (and the information they do carry) may be used inferentially to form true beliefs about the egocentric location of the objects they depict.

Let us consider the disintegrating Polaroids first. While it is true that in ordinary cases one could reliably infer from such a photographic image that the object was nearby, the requisite informational link does not hold. So long as the photograph has any non-infinitesimal life-span, it is not the case that if the object were in a different egocentric location then the image would be different. For no matter how short a time that the photograph persists, it is still possible for the object or photograph to move without a change in the image. So the photograph does not carry e-information.

With respect to Walton's world-bound–photograph case, it may be instructive to consider what enables typical viewers of photographs to know that the objects depicted inhabit the same planet. Clearly what does much of the work here is the mere artifactuality of photographs. Presumably, prior to space travel it was reasonable to infer that any artifact one came across was made on the same planet that one inhabits. So, prior to space travel, it would be reasonable to believe that any photograph that one came across was made on this planet. While we now have photographs and other artifacts that are not from this planet (e.g., they are made in space), they are still relatively rare. Unless we are in a context where extra-planetary photographs are likely to be displayed (e.g., planetary geology texts), we can assume that the photographs that we are confronted with were made on this planet.

Now it does not follow that any object depicted in such a photograph inhabits this planet, not even if the photo was taken prior to the development of the telephoto lens. Earth-bound photographs can certainly represent astronomical phenomena even without telephoto lenses. But perhaps Walton's point should be understood only to apply to photographs of non-astronomical objects: "Well, think of photographs before long telephoto lenses were devised, when it is clear from qualities of the picture whether the object was photographed from a position on the same planet, or not."[25]

Nonetheless, these are still not photographs that provide e-information of any sort. Presumably one might infer from the look of a photograph that it depicts something that is on this planet. But the counterfactuals relevant for evaluating whether an informational link is present still suggest that the photograph is spatially agnostic. Perhaps what makes this case seem to be one in which e-information is carried by the photograph is that there is a *de facto* correlation between the photograph being viewed on planet P and the objects it depicts being located on planet P. But, as we pointed out above in the case of closed-circuit video, *de facto* correlations do not entail the presence of informational links. If, contrary to fact, one were able to move to another planet, the photographic image would not change.

## *Egocentric/allocentric revisited*

Our explanation of the epistemic status of photographs rests largely on the claim that photographs carry v-information without carrying e-information. But why formulate this point in terms of agnosticism about *egocentric* location (information about the location of the depictum with respect to the viewer) rather than allocentric location (information about the location of the depictum with respect to some frame of reference independent of the viewer)? When we considered this issue in an earlier essay, we decided to stick with the egocentric formulation for the reason that this allowed us to mark the distinction we wanted to make while avoiding further, controversial issues. Here is what we said then:

> [S]uppose someone wants to individuate photographs by the absolute or allocentric locations of their depicta. Then if the counterfactuals are read *de dicto*, photographs will, trivially, carry information about the allocentric location of their depicta (because the relevant counterfactuals will turn out to be vacuously true). But that would mean that a requirement stated in terms of absolute or allocentric locational information will not distinguish between the visual process of looking at photographs, on the one hand, and uncontroversial cases of prosthetic or non-prosthetic vision on the other. We suppose we could defend an allocentric/absolute formulation of our requirement if we were willing to rule out the individuative standard at issue or plump for a *de re* reading of the counterfactuals, but we'd prefer not to

[25] Walton, personal correspondence.

> take sides about such tendentious issues if we can avoid it. In contrast, (however you read the counterfactuals) individuating photographs by the allocentric location of their depicta does not make it the case that photographs carry information about the egocentric location of their depicta.[26]

We now think that this was the wrong way to approach the issue; in particular, it seems that the counterfactual question we used here as a test for the presence of an informational relation – a test that works well in a wide variety of situations – is inapplicable to cases of this sort. The relevant notion of information, which came originally from Shannon in 1948[27] (although many philosophers learned about the idea from Dretske more than 30 years later[28]), amounts to a reduction in entropy, or uncertainty. As such, if some outcome is certain, there is no entropy about that outcome that can be reduced, so nothing can carry information about that outcome. This is expressed in Shannon's setup by noting that if a random variable *p* has only a single outcome with non-zero probability, then the entropy for that variable is already zero, so can't be reduced; it follows that the maximum mutual information between *p* and any other random variable must be 0. Hence, on this setup, nothing can carry information about *p*. Dretske's (slightly different) setup gives the same result; for him, a signal *r* carries the information that *p* just in case the conditional probability of *p*, given *r*, (and *k*, the knowledge of the receiver of *r*), is 1 (but given *k* alone, less than 1).[29] But if there is no alternative outcome for *p*, then the conditional probability of *p* given *k* alone is unity; hence, on this definition, too, nothing can carry the information that *p*.[30]

Of course, informational relations support counterfactuals. For this reason, it is usually possible to test for the presence of an informational relation between *p* and *q* by asking about this counterfactual: if *q* were different, *p* would be different. However, the lesson of the foregoing is that this method will lead to errors in the case where *q* is necessary. As explained above, if *q* is necessary then nothing can (a fortiori, *p* cannot) carry information about *q*; but the standard semantics has it that the counterfactual comes out vacuously true. Consequently, the counterfactual test yields the incorrect verdict that there is an informational relation in such cases,

26 Cohen and Meskin, "On the Epistemic Value of Photographs," pp. 201–2.
27 C. Shannon, "A Mathematical Theory of Communication," *Bell System Technical Journal* 27 (1948): 379–423, 623–56.
28 Dretske, *Knowledge and the Flow of Information*.
29 Ibid., p. 65.
30 Thanks to Eric Thomson for help on the information theory.

and so cannot be trusted in these cases.[31] (The counterfactual test is, as far as we can see, safe in other cases; hence we continue to appeal to it in this essay.)

But the reason we gave, in our 2004 essay, for preferring a condition formulated in terms of egocentric rather than allocentric location turns crucially on using counterfactuals as a test for informational relations in cases where this test will go wrong. We had said that an allocentric formulation is undesirable because it makes for an informational relation (barring controversial stipulations we wanted to avoid) where none is wanted; and we said this because the allocentric formulation resulted in vacuously true counterfactuals. Now that we see that the counterfactual test delivers the wrong verdict in such cases (viz., cases where the counterfactual comes out vacuously true), and that in fact informational relations can't hold in such cases, it is clear that the allocentric formulation precludes an informational link (again, barring controversial stipulations we want to avoid making), as desired. The upshot is that our reason for preferring an egocentric formulation has evaporated.

So now we can ask again: is there any reason for preferring a condition formulated in terms of information about egocentric location (e-information) rather than information about allocentric location (a-information)?

One reason to prefer a formulation of the epistemic status of photographs in terms of e-information rather than a-information harks back to our goal of distinguishing processes that constitute object seeing from processes that provide v-information without thereby allowing for object seeing. Consider the process of ordinary, non-prosthetic object seeing; while tokens of this process type often carry a-information about seen objects, plausibly there are tokens of the same process type that do not. For example, some seen objects move in unison with the seer (e.g., a ring on one's finger or the eyeglasses perched on one's nose). As I move in allocentric space while attending to my eyeglasses, the eyeglasses change their a-location even though my visual image of the eyeglasses is unchanged. This

[31] A particularly egregious instance of the same difficulty concerns viewing photographs of oneself. If the photograph's depictum and viewer coincide, then egocentric location of the depictum with respect to the viewer is necessarily fixed at the origin. Consequently, the counterfactual ordinarily used to test for the presence of an informational relation will come out vacuously true. Again, if we took this to show that photographs of $x$ carry e-information when viewed by $x$, then our account would allow that a photograph of $x$ is transparent when viewed by $x$ (but not when viewed by $y$ when $x \neq y$). We do not accept this consequence. Rather, we take this result as another demonstration of the inapplicability of the counterfactual test for informational relations in cases where the counterfactuals are vacuously true.

suggests that some process tokens we want to count as instances of object seeing fail to carry a-information about seen objects. But recall that we hoped to distinguish the process of acquiring v-information via photographs from the process of acquiring v-information via object seeing by appeal to locational information carried by those processes. The present reflections show that, if "locational information" is understood in terms of a-information, then the process types are alike in the locational information they carry, contrary to our aim. In contrast, if "locational information" is understood in terms of e-information, then the two process types come apart, as desired.

## From *Blow-Up* to *Blow Out*: The Epistemic Status of Sound Recordings[32]

We have claimed that the distinctive epistemic status of photography lies in the fact that it is a categorially salient and spatially agnostic source of information. Let us now consider another technology – sound recording – that appears to share these features with photography. Just *because* it shares these features, our analysis predicts that sound recording should have a similar epistemic status as that of photography. And, as we argue below, this is precisely the case.

Sound recordings are significant sources of information. Of course, they do not typically provide information about the visually detectable properties of the objects they represent.[33] Rather, recordings typically provide information about the aurally detectable properties of the objects they represent (i.e., they provide what we shall call "s-information"). Evidence

32 Michelangelo Antonioni's 1966 classic, *Blow-Up*, concerns a photographer who discovers that he may have accidentally photographed a murder. Brian DePalma's 1981 thriller, *Blow Out*, inspired by Antonioni's film, concerns the accidental sound recording of what may have been the murder of a presidential candidate. Both films play on the distinctive epistemic status of spatially agnostic informants.

33 Here we are assuming that audition and sound recordings, like vision and photographs, represent individual objects. An alternative choice would be to say that audition and sound recordings represent events rather than individual objects. (We take it that the same choice is in principle available for vision and photographs, but that it has seemed less tempting for these forms of representation than for audition and sound recordings.) We are officially agnostic about this issue. Therefore, if you prefer the second way of talking, feel free to regard our talk about audition representing an object *x* as a shorthand form for talk about audition representing the event of *x*'s exemplifying some relevant property.

for this can be seen in the usual sort of counterfactuals. If the musician had played different notes on the piano (and, hence, the performance had been different), the musical recording would have sounded different. If the speaker had said different words (i.e., if the speech were different), then the recording of the lecture would have sounded different. But sound recordings, like photographs, do not provide e-information. Again, the evidence for this is to be found in the falsity of the relevant counterfactuals. It is not the case that if the Walkman-equipped listener were to change her location with respect to the (recorded) auditory object, she would hear something different.

So sound recordings are spatially agnostic informants. They provide s-information without providing e-information. And this distinguishes them from ordinary hearing – and ordinary auditory prosthetics such as hearing aids – in just the way that photographs are distinguished from ordinary seeing. For ordinary hearing also provides us with e-information. Consider ordinary conversations. As your interlocutor moves with respect to your location, what you hear is different. For example, the closer she is, the louder the sound you hear. In addition, ordinary hearing is such that the provision of s-information is tied to the provision of e-information. If you are not in a position to get e-information about an object through ordinary audition, you will typically not be able to get s-information about that object from it either. Sound recording, then, bears a relation to ordinary hearing that is analogous to the relation photographs bear to ordinary seeing. While photographs provide v-information in contexts in which e-information is unavailable, sound recordings provide s-information in contexts when e-information is unavailable.

One apparent difference between photographs and sound recordings has to do with their categorial salience. While photographs are typically categorized as photographs on the basis of purely visual cues, sound recordings do not wear their category on their sleeve, as it were. While we are almost never fooled by a photograph into thinking we are directly looking at what it depicts, sound recordings often confuse us. How many times have we thought we heard a person talking in the next room only to find out that it was merely a recording? Still, in contexts in which the category of audio recordings is salient, they are treated as having a distinctive epistemic value.

Thus, we claim that sound recordings are, like photographs, categorially salient and spatially agnostic informants; therefore, our theory predicts that sound recordings will have a special epistemic status. And, in fact, this is the case. Just as photographs serve as both formal and informal evidence, so too do sound recordings. In a legal context, the undercover agent wears a wire in order to acquire evidence about criminal misdeeds. Phone conversations are tapped for a similar purpose. Old recordings of tribal musical performances provide evidence for ethnomusicologists. And recordings of our loved ones provide informal evidence of what they sounded like.

While one might be tempted to explain the distinctive epistemic status of sound recording by reference to some auditory version of the transparency thesis (i.e., the view that sound recordings allow us to literally hear the objects recorded), we believe that there is no need to plump for such a view. It is sound recording's status as a categorially salient and spatially agnostic informant that explains its distinctive evidentiary role.[34]

[34] This work is fully collaborative; the authors are listed in reverse alphabetical order.

# 4
# TRUTH IN PHOTOGRAPHY
Scott Walden

> And while he who has true opinion about that which the other knows, he will be just as good a guide if he thinks the truth as he who knows the truth?
>
> Plato, *Meno*

Commonsense suggests there is a kinship between photographic images and truth. Several years ago the *Los Angeles Times* photojournalist Brian Walski was summarily fired after he admitted that he had used digital-imaging techniques to combine two images into a single, misleading one, which had then been printed on the front page of the newspaper. If there were not some sort of connection between photography and truth, it is hard to see what all the fuss was about. Similarly, during the Cuban Missile Crisis, it was aerial surveillance photographs that Adlai Stevenson confronted Valerian Zorin with at the infamous United Nations Security Council meeting. The ensuing debate was over the truthfulness of those photographs (Zorin insisted there were faked), an issue that would not have arisen if there had been no assumptions in play about the veracity of the medium. And even in contexts where truth is not necessarily a primary goal, photographs can have their value enhanced by their tendency to help us learn about the things depicted in them. The images made by photographers working for the US Farm Security Administration during the 1930s, for example, owe a portion of their value to their ability to help us form true beliefs about period manners of dress, architectural styles, and home furnishings.

Commonsense notwithstanding, the idea of photographic truth has received some rough treatment over the past several decades. In the 1970s Susan Sontag described photography as producing works that are "no generic exception to the usually shady commerce between art and truth." In the 1980s Allan Sekula referred to "the established myth of photographic truth." In the 1990s Fred Ritchin asserted that "[p]hotography's relationship with reality is as tenuous as that of any other medium." More recently, Vicki Goldberg has talked of "another nail in the coffin of photography's truthfulness, which has been moribund so long it's hard to mourn by now."[1] And we do not need academics or journalists to tell us that photographs can be deceptive. A modicum of experience with snapshots or photographs in advertisements is enough to convince us that having a photograph is not necessarily having the truth.

What are we to make of this apparently contradictory state of affairs? How can we reconcile the obvious utility of photographs in helping us learn about the world with their equally obvious ability to deceive? Most of the elements of an adequate answer are, I believe, already in the literature. But they are scattered in disparate areas – the philosophy of mind, aesthetics, epistemology – and need to be brought together and presented in a way that pertains especially to photography. I propose to do this here. I will begin with Jerry Fodor's characterization of visual perception as a two-stage, inferential process, add to this both Dominic Lopes's characterization of images as visual prostheses and Kendall L. Walton's construal of the photographic process as one that importantly excludes the mentation of the photographer, and then infuse the mixture with some ideas that have been part of the epistemological literature at least since Plato. The result will, I think, make it clear why the air of paradox surrounding photography and truth has emerged, but at the same time will dispel it, as learning via photographs will be seen to be simply another mode of perceptual access to the world and, as such, a mode which is frequently reliable, but occasionally not. A bonus of this new perspective leads to several implications concerning the extent to which the widespread use of digital-imaging techniques might affect our confidence in the veracity of photographs, and I have accordingly appended a coda in which I render such implications explicit.

## Limits of the Discussion

Contemporary investigations in the philosophy of mind distinguish between the *phenomenal* and the *intentional* aspects of mentation. The former include the raw feels of experience – pains and pleasures, for example – and the images that form in our minds as we experience the world in the

[1] Susan Sontag, *On Photography* (New York: Picador, 2001), p. 6; Allan Sekula, *Photography Against the Grain: Essays and Photo Works, 1973–1983* (Halifax, NS: Press of the Nova Scotia College of Art and Design, 1984), p. 5; Fred Ritchin, *In Our Own Image: The Coming Revolution in Photography* (New York: The Aperture Foundation, 1999), p. 1; Vicki Goldberg, *The New York Times*, October 21, 2001.

course of day-to-day perception. The latter, by way of contrast, have as their essence propositional contents, contents that are truth-evaluable. Paradigmatic of these are the *beliefs* that each of us has regarding the world that immediately surrounds us. Typically, each of these beliefs has a propositional content that is true, but – as famously imagined in the overture to Descartes's *Meditations* – it is possible that each has a content that is false.

The discussion that follows is limited insofar as it wholly ignores the phenomenal aspects of our mental lives. This might seem a serious omission. Clearly, a substantial part of our appreciation of photographic images is grounded in the rich phenomenology that arises as a result of viewing them, and so any comprehensive understanding of such appreciation will require discussion of this phenomenology. But the discussion that follows does not aspire to comprehensiveness; rather, it aspires only to an understanding of the medium in relation to truth. Given that it is the intentional aspects of mentation that have direct commerce with truth, it is natural to focus on the relationship between viewing photographs and the intentional states that doing so engenders. Perhaps a subsequent discussion will investigate the ways in which intentional states might inform the phenomenology of viewing photographs, but this very complex task will not be undertaken here.

The discussion will as well be limited in that I have little to say about the nature of truth itself. This too might seem a serious omission. The nature of truth is controversial, and it might be argued that truth as manifested in photography cannot be discussed intelligently until controversies surrounding the generic notion are settled.

However, such a methodological stance is needlessly stultifying. To see why, consider first of all that intentional mental states and their associated truth-evaluable propositional contents are components of a psychological theory that is central to our concept of a person. According to our commonsense understanding of ourselves, we act largely on the basis of our intentional mental states, paradigmatically on the basis of our desires and beliefs. I, for example, might travel to Paris because I desire to see the Eiffel Tower and believe I can see it if I go there. This commonsense understanding of personhood was repeatedly challenged during the previous century (behaviorism, eliminitivism, and even some proposed versions of cognitive science all questioned the idea that we typically act on the basis of our truth-evaluable intentional mental states) and yet, for all such efforts, belief-desire psychology remains as much a part of our understanding of what it is to be a person today as it was at the time of Homer. Given that it has survived such a crucible, it is a good bet that it will be with us well into the future, and such stability makes belief-desire psychology and the notion of truth embedded within it well suited to function as primitives in the current analysis. My aim will be to resolve some of the controversies surrounding photographic veracity in terms of the truth or falsity of the intentional mental states that are central to this picture. Admittedly, success at this task will not result in a net gain in our understanding of truth in general, as no one has a wholly transparent story to tell about how the propositional contents associated with intentional mental states correspond (or fail to correspond) to the physical or social facts that constitute the world. But such an analysis will, I think, constitute a significant advance in our understanding of photography, and any unanalyzed residue will at least be part of a widely accepted – perhaps indispensable – conception of what it is to be a person.

Finally, the discussion will be limited insofar as it provides an understanding only of truths about the visible properties of people and objects depicted. Such confinement to the literal might seem a serious liability, as in viewing photographs we are typically interested in truths that emerge at a broader, often figurative level. For example, in appreciating Sherrie Levine's *After Walker Evans* series (in which she re-photographed famous images by Evans and displayed the results under her name), it is not truths about the manners of dress or home furnishings of the depicted sharecroppers that are of interest. Indeed, an exclusive focus on truth in relation to such matters would be thought to miss the point of her project.

But the operative assumption here is that the best methodology for understanding our appreciation of pictures involves first developing an understanding of their most literal aspects, and then proceeding to an understanding of the more complex aspects in terms of these relatively simple ones. In this regard the study of images is not unlike the study of language, where we attempt to understand how literally construed, present-tense, declarative sentences operate before we attempt to understand more complex linguistic phenomena such as metaphor or irony. The faith is that if we can understand truth in relation to the depiction of the simple, visible properties of people and objects depicted, we can then, in terms of these and some other – as yet undetermined – principles governing the viewing of pictures, arrive at a more comprehensive understanding of the use of images in journalism, advertising, illustration, and art.[2]

[2] Although I mention this methodological analogy with the study of language, the general orientation of the discussion to follow is opposed to an understanding of images in ways akin to an understanding of language. As will emerge, truth in pictures is a quality associated with the contents of intentional states engendered in the minds of their viewers, whereas truth in language is a quality associated with the contents of the sentences themselves (although the latter typically eventuate in the formation of intentional states in the minds of hearers or readers).

## Visual Perception

Beliefs constitute our representations of the environment and function along with desires and several other types of intentional mental states to produce behavior. Typically, the contents of our beliefs are true and the ensuing behavior is successful in terms of satisfying our desires. In the example above involving my imagined trip to Paris, my belief that I could see the Eiffel Tower by going there was true, and my desire to see the tower was duly satisfied. But beliefs can also be false and when they are, the behavior they engender is almost always inappropriate. Suppose that unbeknownst to me they have moved the Eiffel Tower to London, and that my belief that I can see it by visiting Paris is therefore false. If I act on this belief my desire to see the tower will be unfulfilled, and will remain so at least until I revise my belief set so that it accurately represents the environment once again.

In this example my inappropriate behavior is essentially harmless, its costs limited to some disappointment in terms of my touristic ambitions. But often the costs of inappropriate behavior are much more severe, amounting to injury or even death – consider, for example, my false belief that there is no traffic coming as I am about to cross the street. Given this, one would expect us to have evolved with swift and highly reliable mechanisms of belief formation concerning our immediate environments. Indeed, this is what we find: our five sense modalities are not much help in forming beliefs about the past or the future, nor are they much help in forming beliefs about matters lying beyond the horizon, but they are very effective at causing us to represent quickly and accurately crucial aspects of the tiny spatial-temporal sphere in which each of us exists. As I approach the street I wish to cross, a quick glance left and right will, with a very high degree of reliability, cause me to believe that traffic is coming if it is coming, or that it is not if it is not.

Such perceptual capacities have received enormous amounts of research attention over the past 70 years. With regard to visual perception in particular, much is known about the process that begins with light being reflected from objects in the environment and ends with the formation of perceptual beliefs in the minds of persons looking at those objects. But this is not to say that there are no controversies regarding the character of the visual process; indeed, far from it. Perhaps the most divisive issues surround the question whether or to what extent visual perception is *inferential*. According to the non-inferential extreme, the process whereby perceptual beliefs are formed is wholly insulated from the large set of background beliefs a viewer brings to the occasion of viewing. On this extreme, a viewer may have a wide array of expectations concerning the character of the environment in which he or she is situated, but these will in no way influence the contents of the representations the visual system yields – each occasion of visual perception starts afresh, as it were; or, to adopt the art-historical terminology, we view the world through innocent eyes. According to the opposing, wholly inferential extreme, in practice *any* belief that the viewer brings to the occasion of viewing can act in conjunction with the character of the visual stimulus to help determine the perceptual beliefs which the visual system yields. On this extreme there is no such thing as an innocent eye – we view the world on each occasion in a knowing way, perhaps for the better, perhaps for the worse.

Jerry Fodor's highly influential construal of the visual process constitutes a compromise between these two extremes. According to Fodor, visual perception is a two-stage process. The first stage takes as inputs the visual stimulus and a *delimited* set of background beliefs and uses inferential mechanisms to generate representations of the environment. These preliminary representations, while content-bearing, are not yet beliefs, as they do not interact with desires and other mental states to produce behavior. Instead, these *proto-beliefs* function as inputs for the second stage of the visual-processing system, which uses them in conjunction with *arbitrarily many* of the background beliefs possessed by the viewer to draw inferences about the character of the environment, inferences which then constitute the fully operational perceptual beliefs that are the outputs of the visual system.[3]

Consider the familiar illusion of water pooling on the distant roadway on a sunny day. A typical viewer brings to the occasion of viewing the firm belief that water is unlikely to be on the road under such conditions, and yet the visual system persists in representing the world as though water is present. Furthermore, while the system persists in this way, the resulting representation is not fully active in the psychology of the viewer – the driver does not slow down or swerve or perform any of the other actions typical of the full-fledged belief that there is water on the road ahead. Finally, appearances notwithstanding, the viewer does not develop the perceptual belief that there is water on the road ahead. All of this can

[3] For Fodor's most comprehensive presentation of these ideas, see *The Modularity of Mind* (Cambridge, MA: The MIT Press, 1983). See also "Observation Reconsidered," in *A Theory of Content and Other Essays* (Cambridge, MA: The MIT Press, 1990). Fodor does not have a general term for the outputs of the first stage of the visual system. I offer "proto-belief," as it will prove handy in subsequent discussion.

be accounted for on Fodor's characterization. The persistence of the illusion is explained by the inability of the first stage to access the wider set of background beliefs possessed by the viewer, including, most relevantly, the belief that water is unlikely to be present under such circumstances. The relative impotence of the illusion is accounted for by assuming it is a proto-belief – a state with propositional content (that there is water on the road ahead) which is not fully functional in the viewer's psychology. And the ultimate failure to form the perceptual belief that there is water on the road is explained by the access that the second stage has to background beliefs (the beliefs that water is unlikely to be present, that this sort of illusion is common under these circumstances, etc.). Vision is at once innocent, as the unknowing eyes persist in their naive illusion, and yet knowing, as the simultaneously savvy visual system is not fooled in the end.

The division between the delimited set of background beliefs to which the first stage has access and the wider array of beliefs to which the second stage has access is non-arbitrary. The representations constituting the delimited set have contents pertaining to very general and stable characteristics of the environment, and are thus unlikely to be false (on Fodor's view, many – but not necessarily all – of these are innate[4]). The representations to which the second stage has access have contents pertaining to more specific and changeable aspects of the environment, and thus have a greater risk of being false. There is much to say about the details of this arrangement, especially about how it can maximize the chances of the system yielding true beliefs in situations where a person's expectations about the character of the environment are false. But such discussion would take us too far afield for present purposes. Here we can instead operate on the assumption that Fodor's characterization – or at least something close to it – is correct, and then investigate what implications the division between access to representations about general and stable characteristics and access to representations about particular and changeable matters might have for the formation of true perceptual beliefs when looking at pictures.

## Visual Perception and Pictures

A recent trend in the philosophical literature understands pictorial competence in terms of our capacity for visual perception generally. In the most basic terms, pictures are regarded as arrangements of marks on

[4] For further discussion, see "Observation Reconsidered," esp. pp. 247–8.

surfaces which, when presented to our visual system, cause it to operate in many ways just as it would were it confronted, not with a picture, but with what the picture is a picture of. This similarity of operation includes acts of perceptual-belief formation of the sort just described.

Suppose that I am standing on the eastern observation deck of the Empire State Building looking out over the East River, Queens, Brooklyn, and Long Island in the distance. Myriad true perceptual beliefs result: traffic is heavy inbound on the bridges, but light outbound; tugboats with barges ply the river; planes approach JFK from the south; etc. Now suppose that I am instead in a gallery many miles from New York viewing photo-realist paintings that were created from the same vantage point at the same time. The paintings are, let us suppose, by Rackstraw Downes, who creates on-site highly detailed images of urban infrastructure, frequently in New York. Under suitable conditions, the very same perceptual beliefs will result – I will likewise come to have true beliefs about the state of automobile traffic on the bridges, boat traffic on the river, and air traffic in the sky as they were at that same point in time.

As noted above, our perceptual mechanisms are ordinarily limited to the formation of beliefs about spatially and temporally proximate matters, and yet here is a familiar example of the formation of perceptual beliefs about matters spatially and temporally quite distant. How can this happen? In rough outline, the answer is that the chain of causal occurrences, which in ordinary perception begins with light reflecting from distal objects, continues through the projection of images on the retinas, and eventuates in the formation of perceptual beliefs, can easily be extended, especially in the region between the distal objects and the images cast on the retinas.

Closed-circuit television as used for security purposes is a familiar example of this. Rather than placing a guard close enough to a gate to keep an eye on it, a camera can be placed close enough and, with the aid of complex electronics, an image made to appear on a monitor which in turn can be viewed by the guard at a remote location. Monitors are designed to cast images on the viewer's retinas that are sufficiently like those that would have been cast had the viewer been seeing directly to enable the process of perceptual-belief formation to take place in (more or less) its usual way. The guard can in this way form perceptual beliefs about matters at an arbitrarily great spatial remove or, likewise, with the aid of video-recording equipment, about matters at a temporal remove as well.

From the point of view of overall function, there is nothing special about having *electronics* mediate between the original scene and the creation of an image which is then viewed by a person using his or her unaided visual system. From this functional perspective, what matters is that *some* sort of system cause the arrangement of lines and tones constituting the image to be correlated with visible features of the original scene in ways that, when viewed, cause the visual system to be stimulated much as it would have been stimulated had the viewer been looking at the original scene directly. A talented painter or sketcher, of course, constitutes an instance of such a system.

Switching back to the example involving my viewing paintings of New York while in a gallery many miles away, we can think of Downes himself in purely functional terms as operating like the closed-circuit television system insofar as his skill insures an appropriate correlation between the visible aspects of what was going on in New York when he was making his images and the arrangements of oils on the canvas. Given that he fulfills this function well, in viewing his canvases, my visual system is stimulated in ways similar enough to the ways in which it would have been stimulated had I actually been viewing the scene to cause me to form the same perceptual beliefs I would have had I been there. In this way images can dramatically extend the range of matters about which persons can form perceptual beliefs. As Dominic Lopes has noted, pictures – still or moving – can function as visual *prostheses*, extending the spatial-temporal region about which we can learn using our visual system.[5,6]

In order to properly flesh out this skeletal understanding of pictorial competence, numerous details must be attended to. To take just one example, the images cast on the retinas by pictures are typically quite different from those cast by direct looking – light reflected by oils, acrylics, or gelatin-suspended particles of silver has quite a different character than light reflected by the persons or objects depicted – and a convincing story must be told about how the visual system has come to be sufficiently flexible to allow perceptual-belief formation to take place notwithstanding such

5 See his *Understanding Pictures* (Oxford: Oxford University Press, 1996), especially pp. 191–3. Lopes does not make the point in terms of perceptual-belief formation; rather, he emphasizes the ability of pictures to enable us to *recognize* persons and objects that are distant in space or time. But I assume that belief formation is frequently consequent upon such recognition.

6 Cohen and Meskin note that, while photographic images can in this way help viewers form perceptual beliefs about visual properties of objects remote in space, they typically do not enable viewers to form beliefs about the spatial locations of those objects in relation to their bodies (ch. 3 in this volume and "On the Epistemic Value of Photographs," *Journal of Aesthetics and Art Criticism* 62: 2 [Spring 2004]). While I think they are right about this, it is worth emphasizing that the point applies to *all* informative pictures – not just to photographs. Images *generally*, if they enable viewers to form beliefs about objects remote in space (or time), do so in "spatially agnostic" (or temporally agnostic) ways.

differences.[7] But all that is required for present purposes is the general idea that in looking at pictures we can and frequently do form perceptual beliefs about matters at spatial or temporal remove.

Obviously not every instance of viewing a picture leads to the formation of beliefs. Cartoons, doodles, and sketches of imaginary scenes are typically formed with aims quite at odds with causing true beliefs to form in the minds of their viewers. Indeed, the wide variety of roles pictures have in our society suggests that the formation of beliefs about the things depicted in them is the exception rather than the rule. How can an understanding of images in terms of perceptual capacities that function to form beliefs survive this fact about the actual function of images?

An answer emerges from consideration of the two-stage inferential perceptual process sketched above. Recall that the inferences that take place in the first stage of the visual system are based on background beliefs about very general and stable characteristics of the environment, rather than on the basis of particular matters of the moment. Typically, when one is looking at a picture, one *believes* that one is looking at a picture (exceptions involve special cases in which one is, for example, viewing a *trompe l'oeil* canvas). This is a belief about a particular matter, not a belief about a general feature of the environment. As such, it is not one to which the first stage has access, and so the first stage is uninhibited from functioning in its customary manner, which is to say that it will generate proto-beliefs. But, unlike in instances of ordinary vision, these proto-beliefs will frequently not become full-fledged perceptual beliefs, as the second stage of the visual system, which does have access to the belief that it is a picture that is being viewed, is liable to block the inference. The two-stage character of the visual process in this way allows for the formation of states with propositional content, and yet at the same time accounts for the fact that frequently those states are not fully operational in the psychology of the viewer. Pictures in this way piggyback on a system the overall function of which is the formation of true beliefs about the environment.

Clearly, the belief that one is looking at a picture is an ingredient in this decision, but this cannot be all there is to the story, for frequently a person, in looking at a picture and believing that he is doing so, will

[7] The most comprehensive treatment of which I am aware is in Lopes, *Understanding Pictures*. See also Arthur Danto, "Seeing and Showing," *Journal of Aesthetics and Art Criticism* 59: 1 (Winter 2001): 1–9, and Danto's discussion of the connection between the art-historical notion of an innocent eye and a Fodor-style characterization of perception in "Animals as Art Historians," in *Beyond the Brillo Box: The Visual Arts in Post-Historical Perspective* (Berkeley, CA: University of California Press, 1992).

nonetheless form full-fledged beliefs about matters depicted. In such instances there must be extra premises being appealed to by the second stage, premises which allow inferences to beliefs to go through. Determining what these might be requires that we consider the formative conditions of pictures and, more specifically, the differences that frequently obtain between the formative conditions of handmade pictures and those of photographic ones.

## Photographs and Truth

Photographic images are a species of images generally and, as such, operate in the manner discussed in the previous section. Photographic technology is a means of marking surfaces in ways that trigger the operation of the first stage of the visual system, thus leading to the formation of proto-beliefs and subsequent evaluation on the basis of arbitrarily many background beliefs. But is there a difference in the case of photographs? Do they offer advantages over handmade images in terms of the formation of *true* perceptual beliefs, advantages which might help us understand the paradoxical attitude toward truth and photography noted at the outset? The answer is more complicated than one might expect.

An obvious first thought is that there is a direct correlation between looking at photographic images and the formation of true beliefs, and that this correlation is absent or at least less pronounced in cases of looking at handmade images. But it is surprisingly difficult to come up with a clear statement of the nature of such a correlation that is plausibly true. On a very strong interpretation, viewing photographs *always* yields true perceptual beliefs, whereas viewing handmade images sometimes yields true beliefs and sometimes yields false ones. But this is obviously false. As noted at the outset, everyone agrees that viewing photographs frequently leads to the formation of false beliefs.

On a weaker construal of the correlation, the claim is that, of all the perceptual beliefs ever formed as a result of looking at images, *more* of those formed by looking at photographic images have been true than those formed by looking at handmade images. However, obvious problems with its evaluation to one side, the claim thus construed, if true, would not necessarily reflect the substance of our intuitive sense that there is a connection between photography and truth. For, if it is true, it is likely so only because there are many more photographs than handmade images in existence (this is especially apparent if one considers all the snapshots in existence) and because there are many more people viewing them. Many

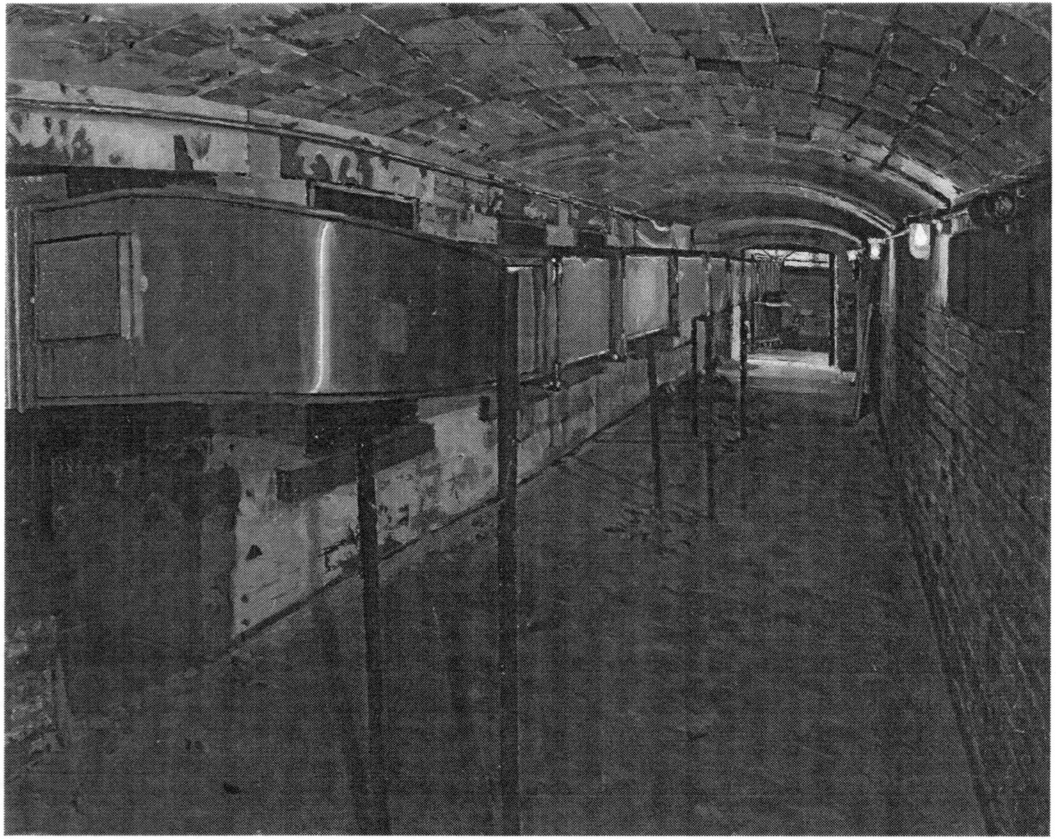

**Figure 4.1** Rackstraw Downes, *Snug Harbor, Ductwork Under the Music Hall*, 2000. © Rackstraw Downes, Courtesy Betty Cuningham Gallery, New York.

people viewing many photographs adds up to many true beliefs – and, no doubt, many false ones as well – simply as a result of arithmetic, and not as a result of anything special about the metaphysics of the photographic medium.

A more interesting interpretation of the claim construes the correlation on a per-image basis and then evaluates in terms of a counterfactual. The idea is that, for any given image of one sort, we consider the number of true beliefs that viewing it yields in the mind of a typical viewer, and then compare this number with the number that would have been formed in the mind of that same viewer had the image been of the other sort. One compares, for example, the canvas depicting the view from the Empire State Building imagined above with a photograph taken from the same vantage point, and asks whether a typical viewer would form more true perceptual beliefs by viewing the latter than the former.

A tempting first thought is that the viewer would. It seems natural to say that a highly detailed, mechanically produced photograph must yield more true beliefs than a sketchy handmade image. But it is important to be careful in evaluating the counterfactual. Notoriously, the project of determining the truth conditions for counterfactuals is unruly philosophical territory, but if there is a consensus, it is that when evaluating counterfactuals one must confine attention to "possible worlds" as similar to the actual world as is possible consonant with the changes required to make the assertion a counterfactual in the first place. In this spirit, the question is not whether the viewer would form more true beliefs by looking at a detailed photograph than a less-detailed handmade image, but rather whether he would form more true beliefs by looking at a detailed photograph than he would by looking at an *equally detailed* handmade image.

It is far from clear that the answer is yes. Consider an actual canvas, one meticulously formed by Rackstraw Downes at the Snug Harbor complex on Staten Island (see figure 4.1). In examining this image, the viewer forms myriad true beliefs about the ductwork, brickwork, flooring, and electrical systems that were before Downes when he made the picture. It is hard to imagine that a photograph made from the same vantage point – even one made with a large-format camera – would do a better job in this regard.

Overall then, given that it is difficult to know how to interpret the claim that there is a better correlation between truth and photographs than between truth and handmade images, it is best simply to remain agnostic with regard to the issue. But such agnosticism does not render futile a search for truth in photography. For, I will argue, if the substantial difference between learning about the world via photographic and handmade images cannot be found here, it can be found in the greater degree of *confidence* that typically attends beliefs created as a result of looking at the former sort of images. The central epistemic advantage associated with photographs lies at the meta-level of beliefs *about* beliefs. Second-order beliefs about first-order perceptual beliefs formed as a result of looking at photographs frequently have as their contents that those first-order beliefs are true. And, as philosophers at least since Plato have noted, while there is tremendous value in having true beliefs, there is even greater value in having true beliefs *and* having reasons to believe that those true beliefs are true.[8]

The source of confidence in the truth of beliefs is no less than the issue of justification for beliefs generally, a perennial topic in epistemology and, as such, not one that will be dealt with comprehensively here. But enough can be said by way of bringing together the idea of a two-stage visual process presented above with some reflections on photography due to Kendall L. Walton to make it plausible, I think, that we generally have better reason to accept beliefs engendered by viewing photographic images than we do those engendered by viewing handmade ones.

## Photographs, Objectivity, and Reasons to Believe

Walton's idea is one that had been noted in various nebulous ways almost since the invention of photographic technology, but which had not, so far as I am aware, been stated in a precise way until the publication of his "Transparent Pictures: On the Nature of Photographic Realism" (reprinted as chapter 1 in this volume). Consider the causal path stretching between the scene to be depicted, on the one hand, and the arrangement of lines and tones on the picture produced, on the other. In the case of a handmade image, this path includes a large number of the mental states of the image-maker, including his perceptual beliefs regarding the

8 It is worth reflecting on the source of the value that attends our capacity to reason about our beliefs. No doubt there are many such sources, but a central one has to do with the maintenance of our belief set. We can wonder whether a belief we have is true and, in consequence of this, we can think about the reasons we have for accepting it. If such reasons turn out not to be good, we can reject the belief, thus reducing the danger of acting inappropriately in our environment. Conversely, if we find upon reflection that such reasons are good, we can behave on the basis of that belief with confidence – with greater resiliency in the face of the conflicting appearances that the flux of experience characteristically provides. Other creatures, lacking this capacity for higher-order thought, either slavishly continue to act on their false beliefs, or careen from one belief to another as the limited evidence arising from particular sensory contacts dictates, in either case frequently at their peril.

scene before him. In the case of the photographic image, by way of contrast, such states might be equally present, but they stand outside of the relevant causal path (for the sake of simplicity, it helps to suppose the photographic image is produced by a Land camera). One consequence of this is that different counterfactuals are true of the two kinds of images. If the mental states of the painter had been different, then the arrangement of lines and tones on the image would have been different. But the analogous counterfactual is not true in the case of the photograph. The photographer might have been hallucinating wildly about the scene before her, and yet the image she produces – its mechanism of formation bypassing her addled mind – would remain the same.

There are several important objections that are typically raised against this construal of the difference between the two types of media: that the difference emerges only when the photographic images are produced by a Land camera, and that once the traditional negative-positive process is considered, it evaporates; that decisions by the photographer regarding what kind of film to use, what sorts of filter to place over the lens, where to point the camera, when to trip the shutter, etc. constitute kinds of mental-state involvement that undermine the distinction; and that lack of mental-state involvement is not an essential characteristic of the photographic process. Each of these objections merits careful consideration and requires convincing response. I believe I have done so elsewhere, and refer the reader who wishes to press them there.[9] Here I will assume that Walton is on the right track, and then investigate the extent to which his observations concerning the metaphysics of the two types of images may be placed into the service of the discussion at hand.

A preliminary terminological stipulation will prove helpful. The term "objective" is frequently used to denote standards or processes that in some way exclude mental states. Objective standards in educational assessment, for example, bypass the thoughts a particular teacher has about a student, and instead evaluate on the basis of standardized tests. Likewise, an objective decision-making process adopted by an individual with institutional authority is one that bypasses his or her own personal interests and operates instead on a general principle (such as the greatest good for all affected). Given such ordinary-language usage, it is natural to adopt the term as a label for the photographic process as characterized by Walton. Photography, which excludes the image-maker's mental states from the process that maps

[9] See my "Objectivity in Photography," *British Journal of Aesthetics* 45: 3 (July 2005), especially section IV on the distinction between *primary* and *secondary* modes of mental-state involvement in the process leading to the formation of an image.

features of the original scene onto features of the image, is an objective process; painting and sketching, which include the image-maker's mental states in this process, are subjective processes.[10]

Bringing Walton's idea together with the two-stage visual process characterized above, the question becomes whether objectively formed images provide better reason for accepting the proto-beliefs they engender than do subjectively formed ones. Now, strictly speaking, the processes themselves cannot provide reason; rather, it is *beliefs* viewers have about those processes that will provide reason, if available. Thus it is the background beliefs that viewers bring with them when looking at the two kinds of images that must be considered.

The contents of such beliefs, by hypothesis, are that in the case of the photograph the image was formed objectively, and that in the case of the handmade it was formed subjectively. These are both beliefs about particular matters rather than general features of the environment. As such they will not be accessible to the first stage of the visual system, and thus will not affect the production of proto-beliefs. Photographs and paintings will equally be confronted with innocent eyes, at least in the first stage of visual processing. However, the second stage *will* have such access, and while there is no reason in principle why beliefs about direct involvement of mental states (as opposed to, say, optical or chemical states) should undermine reasons for accepting generated proto-beliefs, such beliefs, operating in conjunction with other background beliefs, can yield reason for resistance.

Consider, for example, the commonly held belief that persons viewing a scene are inattentive to details of that scene unless they have special reason to be otherwise. Armed with such a belief, the viewer of a subjectively formed image will worry that the image-maker might not have noticed a particular detail in the scene – a particular graffiti-artist's tag on a lamppost, say – and that, therefore, that detail was not rendered in the image. A proto-belief produced by viewing such an image and having content to the effect that the tag was absent would consequently be treated with suspicion. No similar concerns arise in the case of an image believed to have been formed objectively. The photographer might have been as inattentive as the painter, and yet the photographic image, its formative process bypassing the photographer's inventory of mental states, would nonetheless include the detail, if it were present.

There are many other background beliefs commonly held by viewers of images that function similarly: that people creating images are

[10] There is a tendency in the literature on photography to equate objectivity and truth. The discussion here will, I hope, make it clear that, while the two notions are *de facto* importantly related, they are nonetheless conceptually quite distinct.

sometimes subject to perceptual foibles such as astigmatism or color blindness, that people creating images are subject to fatigue, that people creating images often have aims far remote from causing true beliefs to form in the minds of viewers, etc. All these are as true of the photographer as of the painter, but they will typically remain inert in the psychology of a viewer who believes that the image at which she is looking was formed objectively.

Of course there are no certainties here. Many things can go wrong. For one thing, the higher-order beliefs about the formative conditions of images might themselves be false. An individual might believe that she is viewing an objectively formed image when in fact she is not (for more on this possibility, see the discussion of digital photography below). For another, even if the higher-order beliefs concerning the objectivity of the formative process are true, the mechanism mapping features of the scene onto features of the image might do so in unexpected ways. It might, for example, map green in the scene onto magenta in the image, thereby causing an unwary viewer to accept false proto-beliefs concerning the colors of objects in the original scene. And this list of ways things can go wrong can easily be extended. Photography can fail to live up to its aura of epistemic advantage both at the level of true perceptual beliefs engendered *and* at the level of confidence in such beliefs. But it is wrong on the basis of this to careen to the conclusion that there are no epistemic advantages associated with the objective, perceptual-prosthetic technology of photography. Such technology offers *relative* epistemic advantages, perhaps in terms of the number of true beliefs engendered, and frequently in terms of confidence we have in those beliefs. And, as noted, advantages along these dimensions are of enormous value to us.[11]

## The Paradox Revisited

With these distinctions in hand we can reconsider the air of paradox surrounding photography noted at the outset. On the one hand, photographs have always been used – and will continue to be used – to help us form true beliefs about the world. On the other, experience teaches us that the beliefs so formed are frequently not true, and that our trust in them has often been misplaced. The reasons for these opposing attitudes should

[11] There are technologies which likewise act as prostheses for our other sense modalities. As Cohen and Meskin note, audio recording is one such, as it enables us to form perceptual beliefs about the audible properties of occurrences remote in space or time (see ch. 3, "Photographs as Evidence," this volume). However, they would not agree that it is the objectivity of the process that subtends such epistemic advantage (see "On the Epistemic Value of Photographs," n. 37).

now be apparent. Many pictures function as visual prostheses, enabling us to form true beliefs about occurrences that take place outside the range of our otherwise epistemically feeble perceptual capacities. As such, they have value (but not *only* as such, or *always* as such). Of this subset of pictures, smaller subsets have been formed in objective ways, and these not only enable us frequently to form true beliefs, but as well enable us to have confidence in those beliefs. As such, they have additional value (but, again, not *only* as such, or *always* as such). Given that this smaller subset is *de facto* well correlated with pictures that are photographs, photographs are frequently of special value to us. But both subjectively formed and objectively formed images remain mere extensions of our perceptual capacities and, given that our perceptual capacities are never infallible, mere extensions of them are never infallible either – beliefs formed as a result of looking at pictures will sometimes be true and sometimes be false. Furthermore, while the characteristically objective photographic process lays the ontic groundwork for increased confidence in beliefs formed as a result of looking at photographic images, such groundwork subtends an epistemic arrangement that falls short of certainty. Hence the need to be wary when it comes to beliefs formed via any sorts of pictures, photographs included.

## Digital Photography and Truth

Echoing the paradox noted at the outset, there is a paradox associated with the recent widespread adoption of digital-imaging technology in photojournalism and other activities in which the confident formation of true beliefs is a primary goal. On the one hand, the ease with which the new technology permits image manipulation should undermine our confidence in the objectivity of images formed by such means and, consequently, in the beliefs formed as a result of viewing them. On the other hand, the use of digital technology is now the norm, and yet the confidence we have in beliefs formed as a result of viewing photojournalistic images remains substantially undiminished. How can the grounds for confidence apparently be so radically undermined, and yet the confidence itself remain?

A worrisome answer is that we are simply being naive, that mere epistemic inertia lies behind our tendency to continue to believe that the images we are viewing were formed objectively and that, therefore, we can have confidence in the beliefs they engender. If this is the case, we should revise the background beliefs we bring with us in viewing such images so that they accord with our new, epistemically more treacherous, journalistic environment.

But there is reason to believe that this is not our current situation, and that various institutional pressures have had – and will continue to have – an inhibiting effect on the use of the new technology in ways that undermine photographic objectivity. We have noted that there is significant value associated, not only with the ability to form true beliefs, but as well with the ability to reason about the etiology of those beliefs in ways that give us confidence in their truth. This applies both to beliefs formed about spatially and temporally immediate aspects of our environment, as is the case in ordinary perception, and to beliefs about spatially and temporally remote aspects, as is typically the case in photojournalism. Given this, and given that digital-imaging techniques can easily be used to subvert the objectivity that subtends such confidence, it is in our collective interest to resist the implementation of such techniques, at least in certain contexts.

Examples can be found which suggest that we have indeed developed institutional structures that express such collective interest by punishing severely photographers who avail themselves of objectivity-undermining techniques. Consider the example of Brian Walski noted at the outset. Photojournalists regularly use digital-imaging techniques to sharpen or make "gamma" or color-balance adjustments to their images. But these function merely to compensate for various psychophysical idiosyncracies of human perception (without them, images look fuzzy, dull, or tinted) and do not undermine the objectivity of those aspects of the formative process subtending rationale for confidence in beliefs we form regarding things that matter to us. Walski, however, in combining two images to create a third, caused viewers of the resultant image to form false beliefs about the direction in which a soldier's gun was pointed relative to a group of civilians, one of whom was carrying an infant – certainly an occurrence of interest and concern to those perusing the newspaper. Furthermore, in doing so he rendered false viewers' background beliefs about the objectivity of the formative process and (again, unbeknownst to the viewers) thereby removed grounds for their confidence in the perceptual beliefs they formed. In doing so, he damaged a valuable process. The reaction on the part of the newspaper's administration, justifiably concerned about such damage, was swift and severe. Immediately upon the discovery of the manipulation, the newspaper published an editor's note explaining what had happened, displaying the original and composite images, and announcing Walski's dismissal.[12] Walski's hitherto highly successful career as a photojournalist was ruined.

[12] *Los Angles Times*, April 2, 2003. The newspaper withheld permission for the reproduction of these images, but they are easily located on the internet.

It is worth emphasizing that it was not the particular false beliefs that viewers of the image formed that merited the punishment, nor was it the single instance of undermining the grounds for confidence in those particular beliefs. Both of these occurrences were unfortunate, but taken together they would probably not justify terminating a career. Rather, it was the threat that this isolated action posed for the *general practice* of confidently forming true beliefs when viewing photographs presented in journalistic contexts that constituted the rationale for the severe punishment. If Walski's example were to be widely discovered and yet not visibly punished, confidence that viewers of photojournalistic images have in their background beliefs about the objectivity of the formative process would be eroded and, eventually, those background beliefs would be rejected. The result would be a loss of confidence in perceptual beliefs formed as a result of looking at pictures in newspapers and, consequently, the loss of a general practice which is of tremendous value to us.[13]

In closing I note that there are many uses of photography remote from those that have the confident formation of true beliefs as their primary goal. Photography as used in various artistic practices constitutes a source of many such examples. If the *only* reason for maintaining the objectivity of the photographic process arises from its role in relation to the confident formation of true beliefs, we can assume that there will be no institutional pressures to maintain objectivity in such contexts. It is an open question whether, absent such pressures, photographers working in such contexts will abandon objectivity and, if so, whether this will be harmful to the communicative practices in which they engage. This question merits sustained investigation.[14,15]

13 I note once again that the claim is not that learning about the world via photographs guarantees the formation of true beliefs or confidence in them. As has been noted at least since Hume, perceptual beliefs are *never* attended by complete confidence. Perceptual beliefs formed via photographs, as a species of perceptual beliefs in general, thus likewise never deserve unreserved confidence. But we are nonetheless better off – perhaps in terms of truth and frequently in terms of confidence – learning about the world via photographs than we are learning about the world via subjectively formed images. The advantage is a relative one.

14 For excellent examples of such investigation, see Barbara Savedoff, *Transforming Images: How Photography Complicates the Picture* (Ithaca, NY: The Cornell University Press, 2000), pp. 202–9, and Savedoff's contribution to this volume.

15 The participants at the 2004 American Society for Aesthetics Meeting (Eastern Division) made a variety of helpful suggestions from which this essay has benefited. My thoughts on this topic have benefited as well from numerous conversations with John Matturri.

# 5

# DOCUMENTARY AUTHORITY AND THE ART OF PHOTOGRAPHY

Barbara Savedoff

Photographers and theorists have long claimed a special objectivity or documentary authority for the photographic process, contrasting it with the presumably more subjective and manipulable media of drawing and painting.[1] Whether such special objectivity indeed exists, and if so, how to characterize it, has occupied much of the philosophical writing on photography. But this issue has been no less a topic of interest for artistic exploration. Much recent art, in particular, has exploited or challenged notions of photographic objectivity and authority, and has questioned the line drawn between images produced by the camera, and those produced "by hand."

These challenges come at a time when the very nature of photography is changing. With the advent and growing prevalence of digital photography, the opportunities for alteration and invention have been greatly expanded. The notion of a special authority now seems chained to the photography of the past, as digital tools move contemporary photography closer to the subjectivity of drawing and painting.

In this essay, I will discuss the photograph's documentary authority, as it has been commonly conceived, and the critical role it has played in our use of photographs and in their interest as works of art. I will argue that this authority is the distinctive factor that has separated photography from other

1 Portions of this paper were first published as "Abstract Photography: Identifying the Subject," *Exposure* 37: 2 (2004): 25–34.

I would like to express my thanks to the people who have commented on this and earlier versions of this paper, particularly Carl Chiarenza and George McKnight. Also, I would like to thank Scott Walden and Susan Feagin for their comments and good counsel. This paper was supported, in part, by a grant from the Professional Staff Congress of the City University of New York.

kinds of images, and that it has been key to our appreciation of photographic art. I will also, however, look at ways in which this authority has been undermined within the framework of art, and challenged in ways particularly relevant to the shifting conditions and conventions of the digital age.

## Photographic Authority

The notion that the photographic image has a special authority, objectivity, or transparency has been put forward, in different forms, by numerous theorists. André Bazin, Siegfried Kracauer, Rudolf Arnheim, Susan Sontag, and Kendall L. Walton are but a few. That we have, at least traditionally, ascribed to the photograph a special documentary authority or objectivity can be appreciated by considering any of a broad range of examples: the special weight of photographic evidence in trials, the efficacy of photographs in blackmail, their role in scientific and historical research, their use by insurance companies, and for passports and identity cards. This authority is not only evident in the way we use photographs; it also can be seen in the distinctive power photographs have as works of art.

Consider Arnold Newman's 1962 portrait of Marilyn Monroe. The photograph makes Monroe vividly present – we feel confronted by the person herself in all of her troubling complexity. This is the opposite of her glamour shots, which present a façade of carefree sensuality. Newman's portrait has a great sad beauty, but its intensity comes, at least in part, from its documentary power, from our feeling that it reveals something about this unhappy person whose life is about to end so tragically.

Or consider Ansel Adams's *Moon and Half Dome*, 1960. The beauty of the composition only partly explains its power. The knowledge of its being a photograph, a document of the world, plays a great part in our appreciation of it, and the way we look at it. I am not suggesting that we look through the photograph to the object – the famous granite formation – as we might look at a good travel postcard. Rather, I am suggesting that our appreciation of the dramatic compositional values are not isolated, but informed by our knowledge that we are looking at a photograph, a captured bit of our world. Consider for a moment if the moon, the profile of the cliff, or the shadow, had been "photo shopped." The composition would still be beautiful, but the type of interest we take in the image would change – it would be a delight in the creative composition of the artist, rather than a delight in the majesty of nature conveyed and interpreted through the camera.

The comical photograph of a bride and groom taken by an anonymous photographer also relies on documentary authority for its impact (see figure 5.1). An unexpected gust has blown the bride's veil so that it envelops the face of the groom, while her sash and the corner of her dress flap across his legs. The groom's ensnarement might seem somewhat ominous were it not for the bride's bemused reaction and the groom's awkward gesture and his laughing face, barely visible through the white veil. The comic effect is enhanced by the fact that the sash and veil seem to take the place of arms entangling the groom, since the bride's arms are not visible in all the waves of cloth. If this image were a drawing, it would retain its humor, though it might seem contrived and exaggerated. As a photograph, however, the humor is bolstered by the realization that the image is of something that really occurred, by a delight in the happy accident, and in the camera's ability to capture the image of a moment.

Finally, consider Margaret Bourke-White's *Louisville Flood Victims*, 1937 (figure 5.2). The photograph shows Louisville residents, all African American, waiting in a breadline in front of a billboard proclaiming the "World's Highest Standard of Living." The billboard shows a smiling, white, middle-class family out for a drive, as seen through the windshield of their sedan. Next to the car the billboard proudly states: "There's no way like the American Way." The giant billboard overpowers the figures in the breadline, and the car, with its cheerful, oblivious occupants, seems about to drive over the flood victims who are waiting so patiently for food.[2] In this image, Bourke-White exposes the gap between propaganda and reality, between black and white, between those who enjoy the "world's highest standard of living," and the vulnerability of those suffering in need.

It is critical to the impact of Bourke-White's image that it is recording a bit of the world. It moves us to know that the breadline really did pass in front of this billboard, that the irony presented was found and not constructed. The photograph reveals the cruel complacency of the billboard's message, but it does so without seeming polemical, for it simply records what was there to be seen. If Bourke-White had somehow assembled this image, through montage or other means, it would not have had the same penetrating effect.

## Appearance and Authority

The images discussed above support the notion that photographs have a special documentary authority, one which plays a significant role in their

2 William Kunstler makes this point in his essay in Marvin Heiferman and Carole Kismaric, eds., *Talking Pictures: People Speak about the Photographs that Speak to Them* (San Francisco: Chronicle Books, 1994), p. 45.

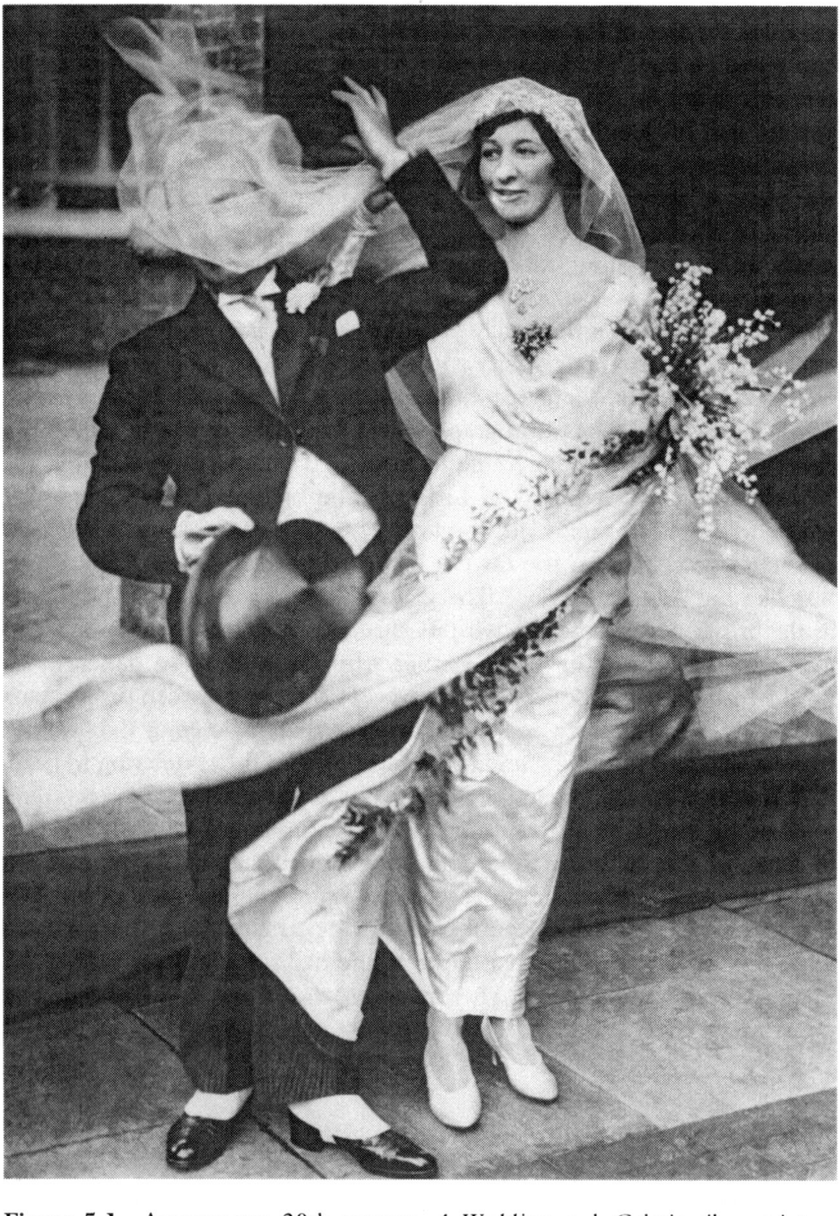

**Figure 5.1** Anonymous, 20th century, *A Wedding*, n.d. Gelatin-silver print, $14\frac{3}{16} \times 10\frac{1}{16}''$ (SC2006.58). The Museum of Modern Art, New York, NY, USA. Digital Image © The Museum of Modern Art/Licensed by SCALA/Art Resource, New York.

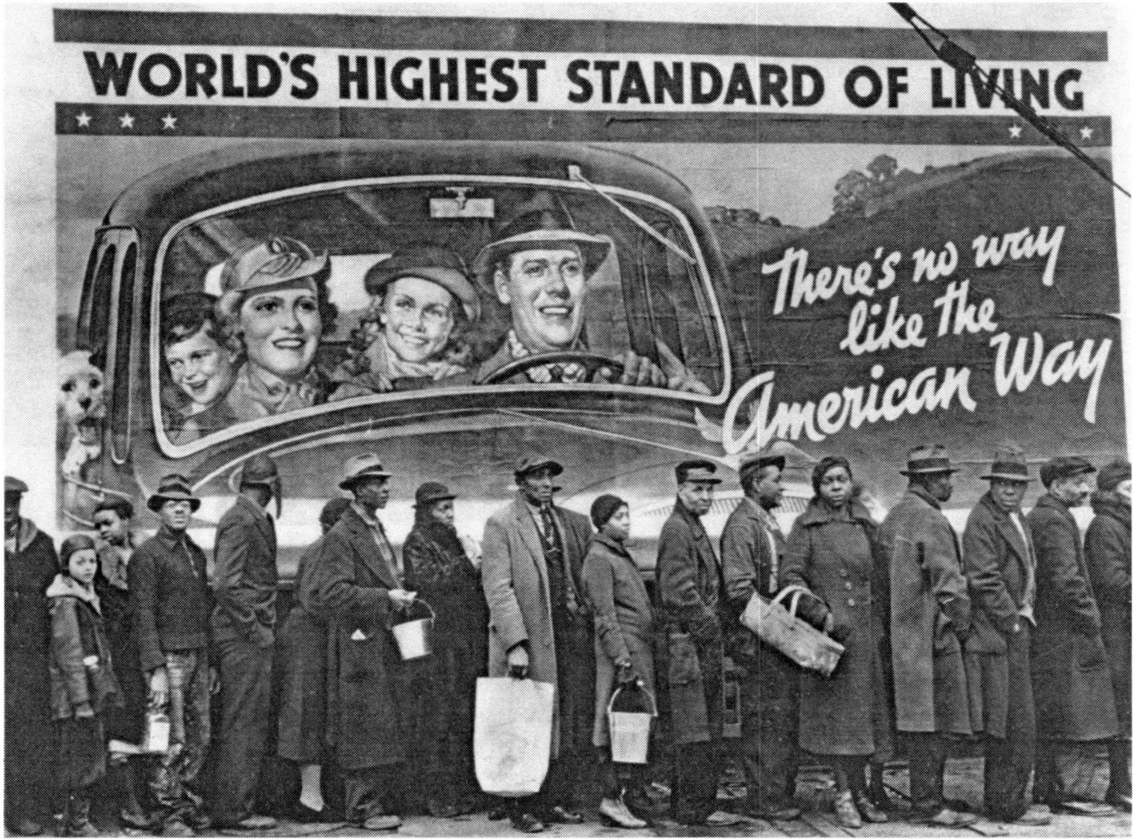


**Figure 5.2** Margaret Bourke-White, *Louisville Flood Victims*, 1937. Time & Life Pictures/Getty Images.

aesthetic impact. But what of all the strange and wonderful photographic images that seem to contradict this notion – the difficult, surreal, or abstract images that are valued precisely because of the interesting ways in which they stray from conventional documentary realism? I will argue that the power and interest of these photographs also rests on the notion of documentary authority.

The "authority" of the photograph, as I am using the term here, resides in the idea that the photograph gives evidence of what exists in front of the camera. Because of the causal relation that typically obtains between a photograph and the photographed object, we see the photograph of a woman as evidence of the existence of that woman – the photograph is not just a record of the photographer's imagination. This idea of authority is not to be confused with the idea that the photograph accurately duplicates appearances – the woman may look very different in the photograph, or the image may be blurred, and yet the photograph provides evidence that even a more accurately detailed painting could not provide.

Though documentary authority and accurate duplication of appearances are two different things, the two are often intertwined in our thinking about photography. We think of photographs as documenting the existence of things in the world, and this leads us to think of them as documenting the *appearance* of things in the world. The tendency to take this step is understandable, given the high degree of accuracy possible in conveying those appearances, and given our most common uses of photographs as identification, documentation, record, and memento. However, this tendency to think of photographs as faithful records of appearance can come into conflict with what we see in a photograph. Things look different in photographs than they do in person. A photograph is a two-dimensional, bounded, still image, often in black and white, and the choice of lens, exposure, angle, and contrast, among other things, all have profound effects on the results. Through photography, appearances can be radically transformed.

This conflict between how we habitually think about photographs, as objective records of appearances, and the actual transformations of photography, far from being a problem, actually opens up a fertile area for photographic art. The transformations of photography are not easily dismissed as the product of creative license or imaginative fantasy. They are fascinating and compelling precisely because we think of photographs as recording the appearances of our world. Photographs show us our world made strange.

For example, consider Edward Weston's *Cabbage Leaf*, 1931. Weston's lighting and his carefully chosen angle and framing create a graceful, fluid, sensuous, and richly sculpted object – one that defies our expectations for cabbage leaves. We can, of course, imagine a painter presenting a cabbage leaf in much the same way, and we might find it interesting to see the leaf painted as a sensuous or elegant object. But in such a case, we would not necessarily have any sense that the painter was revealing something about the leaf itself. With the photograph, however, there is astonishment that a cabbage leaf can look this way. We seem to see the actual leaf, or at least its appearance, transformed.

The combination of the documentary authority of the photograph along with its actual transformations also contributes to another phenomenon – we are not only fascinated by images of "the world made strange," we feel driven to untangle any ambiguities or identify any puzzling elements that are presented. If it were not for the transformations of photography, there would not be so many visual ambiguities, so many baffling elements encountered. And if it were not for the documentary aura, we wouldn't feel so compelled to resolve these ambiguities or puzzles of identity.

For example, Cartier-Bresson's *Valencia, Spain*, 1933 (figure 5.3) shows a puzzling and seemingly incongruous space. On the right of the photograph we see the right side of a wooden gate to a bullring, cropped by its proximity to the camera. A man with round glasses looks through a small rectangular window in the gate, his right lens a white disk reflecting the sunlight. Close behind the man is a brick wall. On the left of the image, in the distance beyond the edge of the gate, we see a boy in shadow.

Both the man and the boy are located behind the gate, yet one is in light, the other in shadow; one occupies a seemingly shallow space, the other a much deeper space. Because the right side of the composition is so shallow and light, while the left side recedes into shadow, because we have no sense of an architectural structure which encompasses both sides of the image or any demonstration of a unified space that holds man, gate, boy, and wall, the photograph seems a collage of space. It seems a collage, but because *Valencia* is a straight photograph, we assume that it shows us a unified space, a real scene. As a result, we become engaged in making sense of that space and figuring out the relations between its various parts, confident that it is possible to do so.

However, if we could imagine *Valencia* as a painting, or if we consider the spatial ambiguities and paradoxes that can be found in paintings and drawings, such as those by Magritte or Escher, or even Manet, our confidence in resolving ambiguity or confusion disappears – for we do not necessarily bring to paintings and drawings an expectation that they faithfully model appearances in the world.

It is in the light of this analysis that I will consider the ways in which we view abstract and surreal works in photography and in painting. My

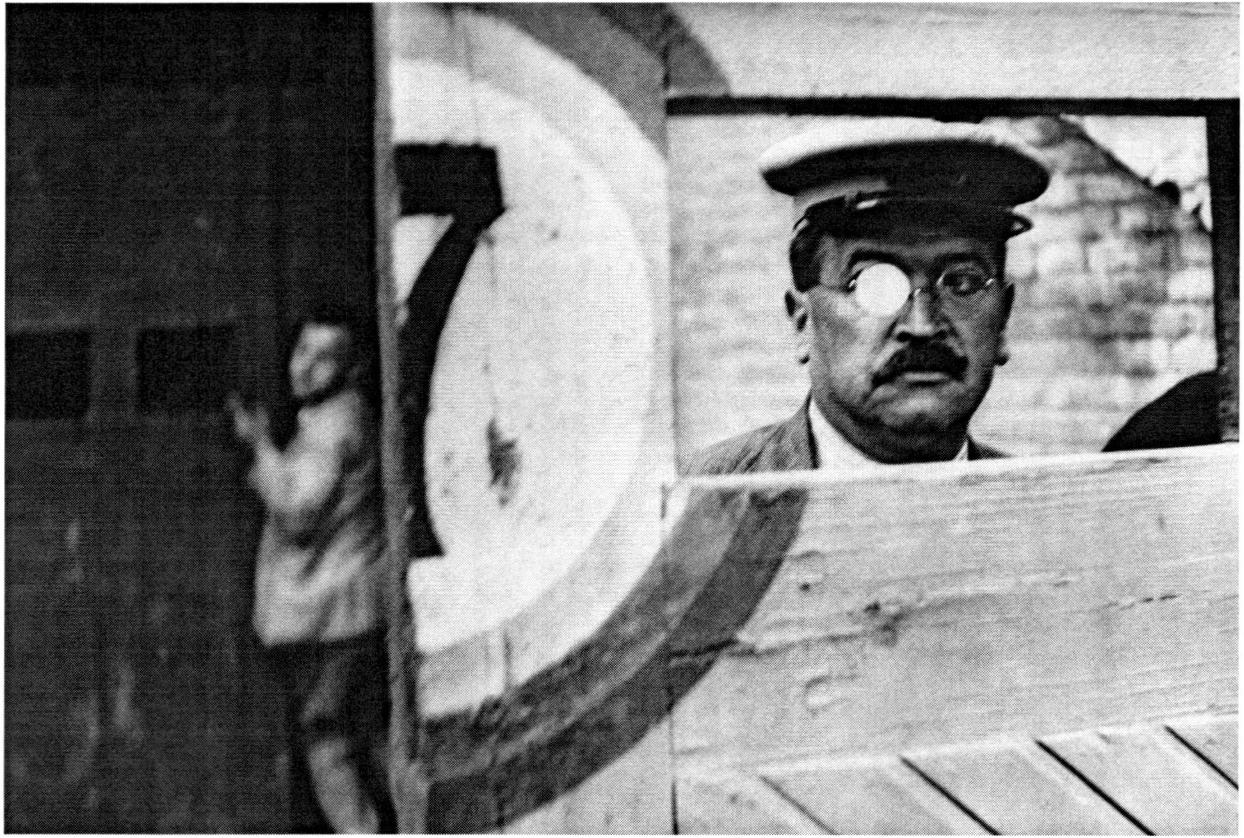

**Figure 5.3** Henri Cartier-Bresson, *Valencia*, Spain, 1933. Gelatin-silver print. Henri Cartier-Bresson/Magnum Photos, Inc., New York.

claim is that the documentary authority of the photograph, combined with its transformations, accounts for the peculiar interest of abstract and surreal photographs – an interest quite different from that of paintings of those same genres.[3] In photography, the appreciation for the abstract or surreal composition coexists with and is enhanced by a sometimes frustrated drive to identify and untangle the real-world elements that make up the image.[4]

## Abstract Photography/Abstract Painting

"Abstract painting" is a term that is used to embrace quite a wide range of styles – everything from Cubist deconstructions of objects to the nonfigurative works of Color Field painting, and beyond. The term "abstract photography" is less commonly employed, and its scope less clear. For the most part, the term is used to refer to photographs, such as those of Minor White and Aaron Siskind, which, through close-up, cropping, and other means, emphasize formal composition, line, and texture, over the presentation of any readily recognizable object. Though we find similar interests and even similar images in abstract painting and abstract photography, our knowledge of each medium, of the way in which images are generated in painting and in photography, influences the type of interest we take in the abstract images of each art form.

For instance, in the abstract paintings of the 1940s and '50s, the composition grows out of gesture and the build-up of paint. We see the way the forms and lines of the paintings are constructed by drip, brush, or palette knife in the works of Jackson Pollock, Franz Kline, or Clyfford Still, and this plays an important role in how we read the compositions. A Pollock seems inseparable from the gesture of its making; and without its worked surface, a Still might seem aimless and insubstantial – the gesture gives sense to the form. With photography, however, our attention shifts. The photographs of White and Siskind, as well as the abstract-tending images of Paul Strand, Imogen Cunningham, and Edward and Brett Weston, to name a few, also have an emphasis on line, form, texture, and color (the interplay of black and white); but in the case of these

3 For a more extensive discussion of how the documentary authority of the photograph combined with its transformation of appearances helps to explain our interest in the fortuitous and the ambiguous, see my *Transforming Images: How Photography Complicates the Picture* (Ithaca: Cornell, 2000), ch. 2.

4 As will be discussed below (in the section "Subjects that Resist Identification"), this kind of frustration can be an aesthetic virtue.

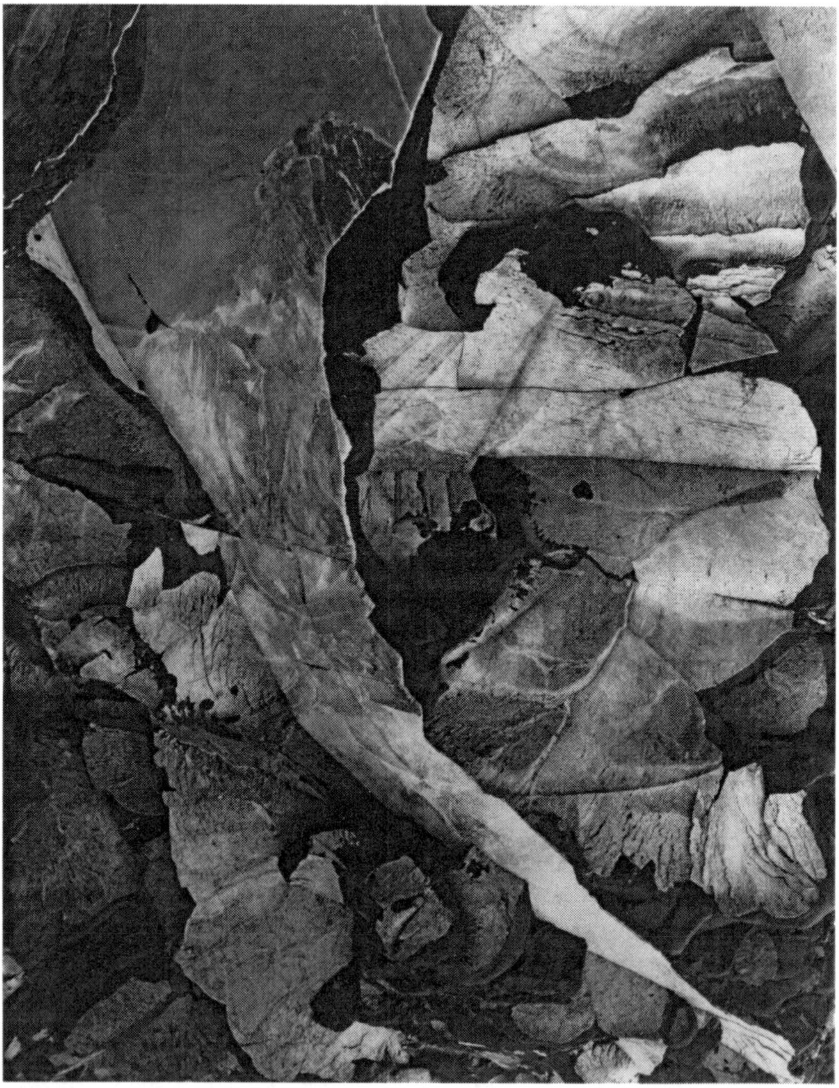

**Figure 5.4** Minor White, *Capitol Reef*, Utah, 1962. Gelatin-silver print. Reproduction courtesy the Minor White Archive, Princeton University Art Museum. Copyright Trustees of Princeton University. All rights reserved.

photographs, the abstract compositions are grounded by bits of the world: rocks, windows, walls, plants. And this grounding of the abstract pattern in the world of objects becomes a major focus of interest.

Photography allows us to explore the visual world. In our most typical encounters, we examine photographs to see what they show and what they can reveal to us about the world. Basic to this task is the task of identification. (This is not to say that we are only interested in identification, but that identification or its attempt almost always underlies our response.) Before anything else, when we look at a photograph we want to know what (in the world) it shows. Often this can be, at least on the surface, unproblematic, as in the typical family snapshot; but sometimes this task can be more challenging, as with *Valencia* and Cunningham's *Leaf Pattern*, 1929, and sometimes it can be downright baffling, as with, for example, White's *Capitol Reef, Utah*, 1962 (figure 5.4).

The drive to identify the subject of a photograph does not disappear when confronted with hard-to-identify or abstract works; in fact, the more difficult and challenging the identification, the more we may find ourselves concentrating our efforts on it. This marks an important distinction between how we respond to abstraction in painting and in photography. Whereas with abstract painting it is often misguided to ask "what is this?" (in the sense of identifying a real-world subject), with photography the question always has its place. For, with rare exception, all photographs taken with a camera (and even some without) are of something, except perhaps for the more arcane experiments with lenses, mirrors, and light, such as Alvin Langdon Coburn's Vortographs. Part of the initial interest in an abstract photograph (or photogram) might be this puzzle of identification.

For example, Siskind's *Chicago*, 1949 (figure 5.5), and Kline's *Mahoning*, 1956, both present strong, simple formal compositions, contrasts in black and white, but in both cases, formal description is only a part of understanding the work. In the case of Kline's painting, layering and gesture are critical elements. In the case of Siskind's photograph, it is identification which is crucial. In looking at *Chicago* we quickly recognize that it shows part of a sign, perhaps a segment of lettering turned on its side, so that the image has a dual nature or identity: cropped sign/abstract form. We also have the scraped and punctured, but primarily flat, surface of the presented sign contrasting with the shallow depth and smooth surface of the photograph. If Siskind had created his images without a camera, there would not be these contrasts and tensions. And there would not be the joy of discovering compelling abstract composition in the world of the everyday object.

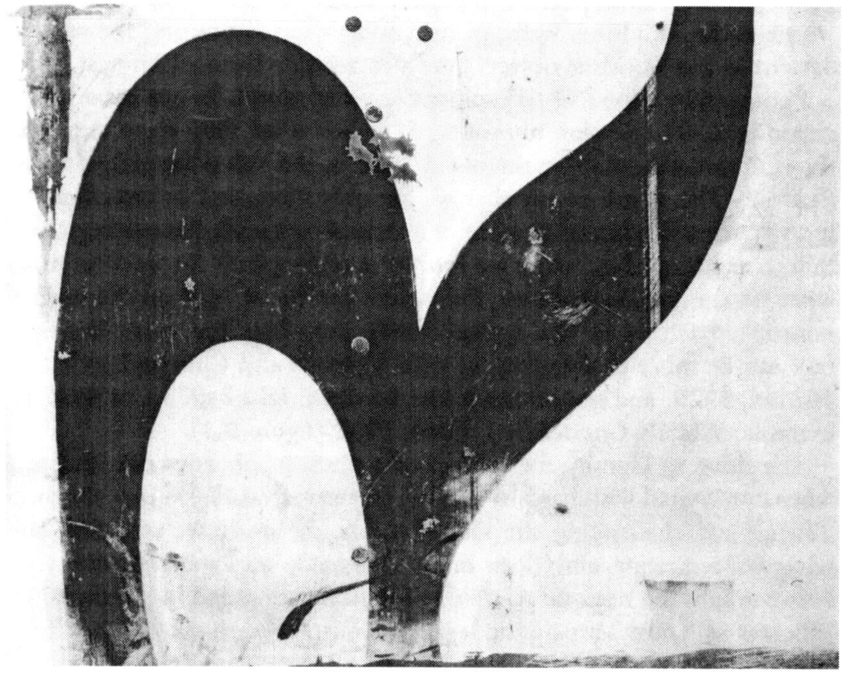

**Figure 5.5** Aaron Siskind, *Chicago*, 1949. Gelatin-silver print. © The Aaron Siskind Foundation, courtesy George Eastman House, Rochester, New York.

It is worth emphasizing that this is *not* just the kind of thing we find in painted abstractions of objects, say in a Picasso still life. In the case of painting, the forms *refer* to objects – bottles, tables, and bowls. In the case of photographs, the forms *are* the objects (or more precisely, the forms are those of the objects before the lens): the image is both record of the object *and* abstraction.[5] There is a sense in which we see the object transformed.

[5] Siegfried Kracauer admires what he calls the "ambiguity" of abstract photographs: on the one hand, they record existent objects; on the other, they affect us as free composition. I would argue, however, that this way of putting it is misleading – that photographic compositions almost never affect us as truly free. Even as we admire the abstract composition, we are always to some degree aware of the grounding of that composition in the world of actually existent object. See Kracauer, "Photography," in Alan Trachtenberg, ed., *Classic Essays of Photography* (New Haven: Leet's Island Books, 1980), pp. 245–468. The discussion of abstraction is on p. 262.

## Surrealism

Though they aim at different effects, both abstract photography and surrealist photography concern themselves with the transformation of ordinary objects. In photography, then, we can see a connection between abstraction and surrealism that is not easily found in painting. In fact in painting, the two tendencies are more often opposed. Surrealists like Magritte, Dali, and de Chirico adopt a realist style, and de-emphasize any attention to paint and surface, whereas abstract expressionists like Still and Pollock are largely about surface, paint, and gesture. The abstract painters of the 1960s and later had even less to do with surrealism. Abstract painting, as it moves away from the representation of objects, and even of three-dimensional space, has little to do with paintings that seek to present a world of paradox or strange transformations.[6]

Abstract photography, on the other hand, has a natural affinity for surrealism, since it too involves transforming our world. In the case of abstraction, a rock, a shadow, a plant, or a little piece of wall, becomes a pattern, an abstract form. In the case of surrealism, however, the transformation is for supernatural or paradoxical effect.

Images by photographers as diverse as Eugène Atget, Bill Brandt, and Robert Frank have a surreal aspect: in Atget's *Magasin, avenue des Gobelins*, 1925, the shop window mannequins seem weirdly animate; in Frank's *Chicago*, 1955–7, the sousaphone player seems to have the bell of his horn where his head should be; in Brandt's image, *East Sussex*, 1957, a monumental ear seems to loom in front of the rugged coastal scene. In these images, ordinary objects and scenes of the world are transformed by framing and two-dimensionality, and through black-and-white imagery into images of the strange, the paradoxical, and the uncanny. Even when the object is not ordinary, as in Clarence John Laughlin's *Our Festering Hands Ruin All . . .*, 1949 (figure 5.6) the constructed figure is transformed through (straight) photography. Laughlin shows a draped figure, a piece of gnarled wood emerging from the cloak, as though it were a hand. We respond to the figure in the photograph very differently from how we would respond in person. In the photograph, the wood becomes a hand in a way that can only be suggested in person and only illustrated by painting. (When double exposure, photomontage, or other special effects are used by photographers, the documentary authority is compromised

[6] This is not to say that paintings never combine the two tendencies. Some of Joan Miro's paintings, for instance, might be seen as both surreal and abstract.

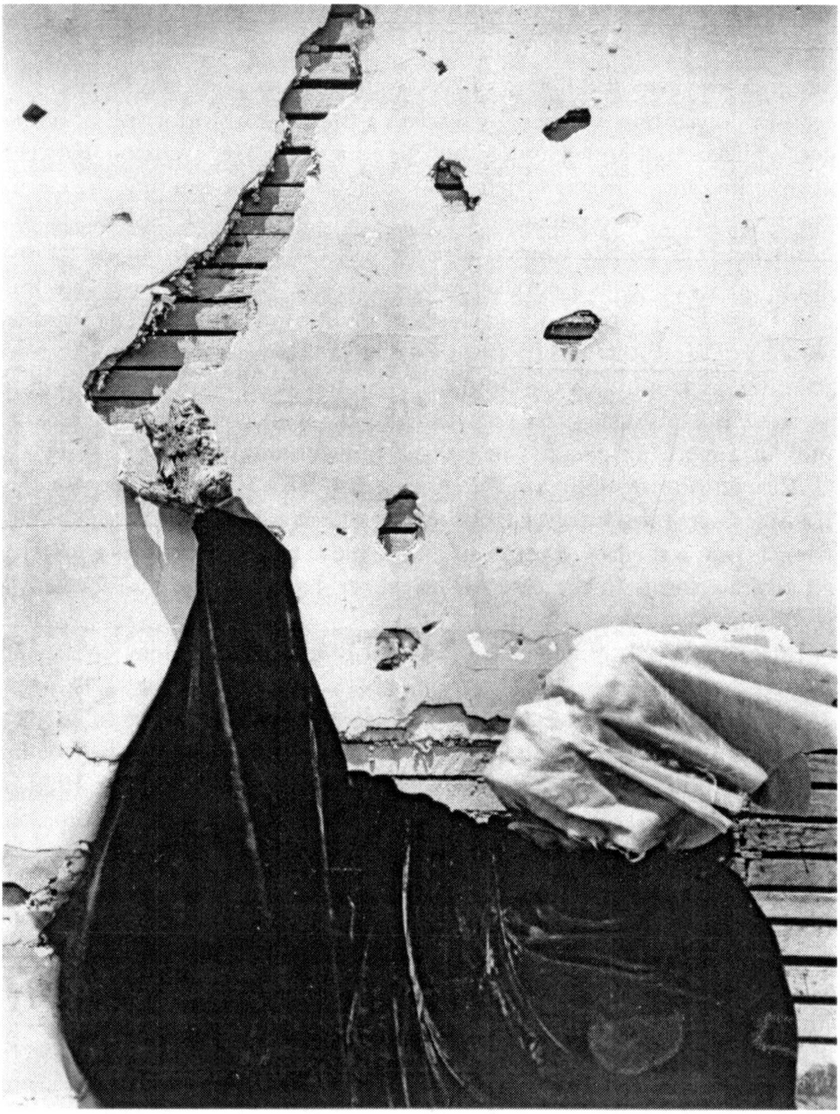

**Figure 5.6** Clarence John Laughlin, *Our Festering Hands Ruin All . . .*, 1949. Gelatin-silver print. © The Historic New Orleans Collection.

and the images tend to read more like illustrations of the artist's vision – more like paintings.)

The difference in effect between surreal painting and surreal photography is most strikingly borne out by Magritte's photographic studies, which are often much more intriguing in their effects than are the corresponding paintings. For example, his photograph *God on the Eighth Day*, 1937, shows an image very similar to his painting *The Therapist*, 1937.[7] Both show a seated figure whose torso and head have been replaced by space. In *The Therapist*, the head and torso have been replaced by a birdcage with two birds. A cloth is draped over the cage, and a hat perched atop it. In the photographic study, the effect of empty space is achieved by propping a painting (a crudely painted landscape) on the man's lap, hiding his head and body. The edges of the painting are disguised by the blanket draped over them, and a hat rests on top. The photograph creates the illusion of a missing torso, but at the same time it records an actual person. In the photograph, we find ourselves facing an image that is both "real" and unlike reality, and this paradox engages us more than the mere illustration of an idea, no matter how provocative.

With both surrealism and abstraction, objects are transformed by the camera, objects whose identities are made problematic, either through an emphasis on form and line or an emphasis on the strange and paradoxical (or both). So we should not be surprised to find photographers who work with both surrealism and abstraction and produce images that can be seen as both abstract and surreal. (Laughlin's *The Language of Light*, 1952 – an image of light filtering through a curtain – fits this bill, as do many of Man Ray's rayographs.)

## Subjects that Resist Identification

But what of abstract photographs that frustrate our attempts at identification – that we know show us a bit of the world – but a bit we cannot recognize or make sense of?

If with Siskind's photographs we see a bit of the world, a wall, a sign, transformed to abstract composition, what can we say of White's *Capitol Reef* (see figure 5.4), where identification is so thwarted that it is hard

[7] These examples are reproduced in my *Transforming Images*, pp. 96–7. (Also reproduced there, on p. 205, is the Pedro Meyer image that will be discussed below in the final section "The Digital Challenge.")

to say what it is that grounds the abstract composition? John Szarkowski says of this image:

> [I]n spite of the immaculately precise photographic description, one cannot be quite sure what objects are being described: stone, ice, ancient bones, desiccated leaves, fossilized wood – or what? Nor can we be confident of our own vantage point: Does this landscape lie at our feet, or a thousand yards beneath our plane, or in the wall before us? Nevertheless, it is clear that we are being shown a true and terrifying fact of nature: the irreversible and unreconcilable conflict that shapes the surface of our world.[8]

Though we might not be able to tell exactly what is being transformed, "stone, or ice, or ancient bones," the fact that we see this as a straight photograph means that we are drawn into a project of identification. We are continually pulled back into an examination and re-examination of the image in an effort to make sense of its forms (until we might begin to see it as a revelation of something new – as though it were a landscape of the moon). The beauty of the abstract composition is still tethered by the world; the difficulty of identification just draws us that much deeper into the photograph.

With Brett Weston's *Shattered Plastic*, and Frederick Sommer's *Smoke on Cellophane #1*, 1961, we are given the identity of the subject, but the effect is much the same as with *Capitol Reef*. Even as we admire the delicate feathering of Weston's image, we struggle to reconcile that image with its identification as plastic, and we try to see through to the plastic at the same time we appreciate the abstract composition. As we attempt to reconcile the "feathers" of the Weston and the biomorphic shapes of the Sommer with their titles, our concentration on each image is sharpened, and our appreciation of the formal composition both challenged and enriched by the difficulties and revelations attending the identification of its subject.

## Abstract Constructions

Even when the object to be photographed has been especially constructed for the photograph, the image can be understood as transforming a bit of the world into pattern and form. For example, Carl Chiarenza's photographs of collages present us with abstract compositions, but also with

[8] John Szarkowski, *Looking at Photographs* (New York: MOMA, 1973), p. 174.

records of material, and this adds a layer of complexity that would be absent from a similar composition achieved by pen or brush, or even by the collage itself.

Consider *Untitled Triptych 195/190/188*, 1994 (figure 5.7) with its "landscape" of wonderful textures, rough and crinkly, luminous lights and deep blacks. The delight is in its contrasts of textures and tones, but we cannot help straining to identify whether it is patterned paper that is employed here or crinkled foil that is used there. Nor can we help wondering about the materials which are less easily recognized. Chiarenza states:

> [T]he problem in the case of my work is to hold the viewer's attention beyond the initial frustration of not knowing, or being unable to decipher, "what it is"; the problem is to get the viewer to release the commonly but falsely held belief in the photograph as a window; to get the viewer to go through the window in a state of openness to a new experience, not a representation of one that has already occurred.[9]

But even when we realize we are looking at collage constructions in the photographs, we are looking through a window of sorts – that is what makes Chiarenza's photograph distinct from the collage which serves as its subject. Chiarenza uses the collage as a starting point for the image – whose final form will depend on lighting, angle, cropping, contrast, etc. – so that the collage, as presented, does not exist in the world. Moreover, in taking a photograph, Chiarenza undermines our identification of materials. When presented with a collage directly, we can more readily identify edges and layers, and recognize different materials. In a photograph, these recognitions and identifications are problematized in such a way that the forms are freed to take on other identities – torn paper can become a riverbed, a cloud, a landscape. The abstract collage itself, unphotographed, can also take on these references, but not as identities.

In other words, in looking at the abstract collage itself, we might see a reference to mountains, but we never think that the forms actually are other than they are – we never think that they actually are mountains rather than paper. In collage, confusions of identity are usually less radical – mistaking cloth for paper, or a painted element for a collaged item. Once a collage or construction is photographed, however, we can and do often have radical confusions and rich ambiguities – and not just with abstract work.

9 Carl Chiarenza, unpublished manuscript for lecture, 1994. Quoted in *Carl Chiarenza: Passages and Transformations,* exhibition pamphlet, George Eastman House (Rochester, NY, 1995).

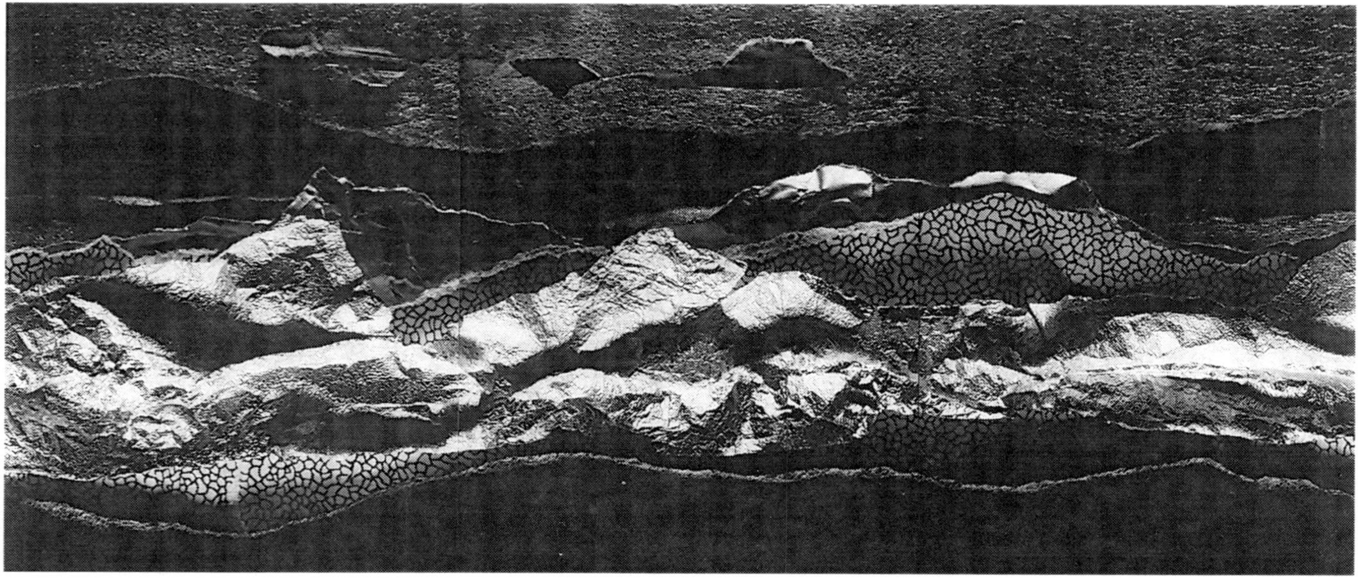

**Figure 5.7** Carl Chiarenza, *Untitled Triptych 195/190/188*, 1994. Three selenium-toned gelatin-silver prints, image approximately 18 × 42 inches. © Carl Chiarenza.

## Other Identities

Confusions of identity are also found in the work of Vik Muniz. Muniz makes photographs that create the illusion that we are looking at something other than what they actually show. A photograph of a cloud turns out to be really a photograph of cotton, a photograph of the moon landing turns out to be the photograph of a sketch.

Muniz's "Sugar Children" series is a series of black-and-white photographic images showing the children whose parents and grandparents work on the sugar plantations on the island of Saint Kitts (figure 5.8). But these photographs are not of the children themselves; they are of sugar – sugar which has been used to "draw" the portraits – using Polaroid images as models. What we identify as a rather grainy photograph of a young girl is actually a photograph of sugar grains, meticulously arranged on black paper – a photorealist drawing in sugar. This sugar drawing itself does not pose a puzzle, for it presents a young girl in the same way a charcoal drawing or a watercolor might. But once the drawing is photographed, medium is obscured, and a different kind of genesis and identity are assumed for the image – assumptions which are subverted by Muniz's process. Muniz undermines our assumptions about photography by undermining our attempts to identify the subject.

## Undermining Photographic Authority

While surreal and abstract images challenge our assumption of the photograph's fidelity to appearances, they still very much rely for their impact on our assumption of documentary authority, for it is these assumptions which make the transformed appearances intriguing, that draw us into a project of discovery, making sense of the unorthodox images as documents of "what is."

Muniz takes the disruption of expectations one step further, for with Muniz we have not simply an object made to look mysteriously different, but a radical misidentification of what we see: a hand-made representation (in sugar or syrup, no less) is taken for the thing itself. A sugar-grain portrait is confused for a person. We are led to ask how a photograph of sugar grains can look so much like the photograph of a girl; and to wonder how it is that a photograph can ever be thought of as having greater documentary authority than a drawing, if we cannot tell the difference between the photograph of a girl and the photograph of a representation of a girl. Muniz's work provides a profound challenge to documentary authority.

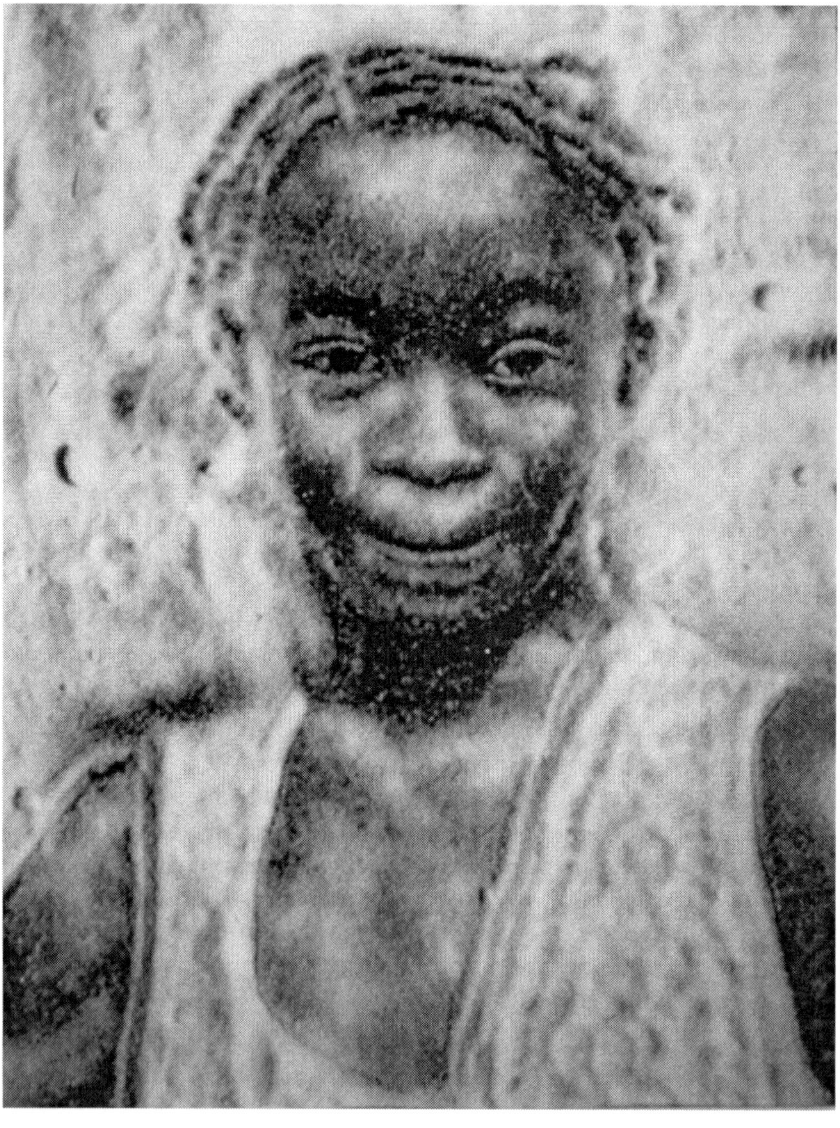

**Figure 5.8** Vik Muniz, *Valentina, the Fastest*, (from Sugar Children) 1996. Gelatin-silver print, 14 × 11″. © Vik Muniz/Licensed by VAGA, New York, Courtesy Brent Sikkema NYC.

For other challenges to documentary authority, we may look to painters – in particular, the painters of the photorealist movement. One effect of photorealism was to begin to disentangle the two notions of documentary authority and accurate duplication of appearances, and to question photography's special claims with respect to them.

The photorealist paintings of Richard Estes, Chuck Close, and others separate the look of the photograph from its ontology, thereby raising questions about the source of photographic authority as well as its ultimate legitimacy. Photorealist paintings have the look of photographs, but at the same time, when seen in person, they are easily identifiable as paintings. On the one hand, they can be seen as borrowing, for painting, the documentary authority of photography; on the other, they can be seen as challenging that authority by divorcing the "look" from its causal underpinnings.

Close's early portraits, such as *Robert* (1973–4), present an especially interesting case. With most photorealist paintings, size is important, but with Close's portraits, its impact is singular. Close's giant portraits are Brobdingnagian in their effects, making ordinary people appear grotesque, and every pore, blemish, crease, monumental.

The size of the image also emphasizes the photographic distortions that may be noticeable, but regularly ignored, in snapshot-size images. For instance, the flattening of the face typical of photographic portraits is unmistakable when reproduced on such a gigantic scale, making us acutely aware of the perceptual peculiarities of the photograph.

Close's characteristic grid, used to transfer the image to canvas, also contributes to our awareness. The grid gives evidence of the painstaking accuracy of the image, its fidelity to the source photograph, but it also belies the hand-made nature of the image, and thus its inherent "subjectivity."

This subjectivity is intensified in Close's later paintings. Whereas in the early portraits each grid cell functioned as a half-tone dot, or even a pixel, in the more recent ones the cells are like tiny gestural paintings, their exuberant subjectivity colliding with the sense of authority borrowed by the photographically derived image.

## Compound Images

Close's photographs, such as his *Self-Portrait/Composite/Sixteen Parts*, 1987 (figure 5.9) also provide a challenge to the notion of photographic authority. This imposing self-portrait is pieced together from sixteen oversize (23″ × 19″) black-and-white Polaroids. (Close stares at the viewer

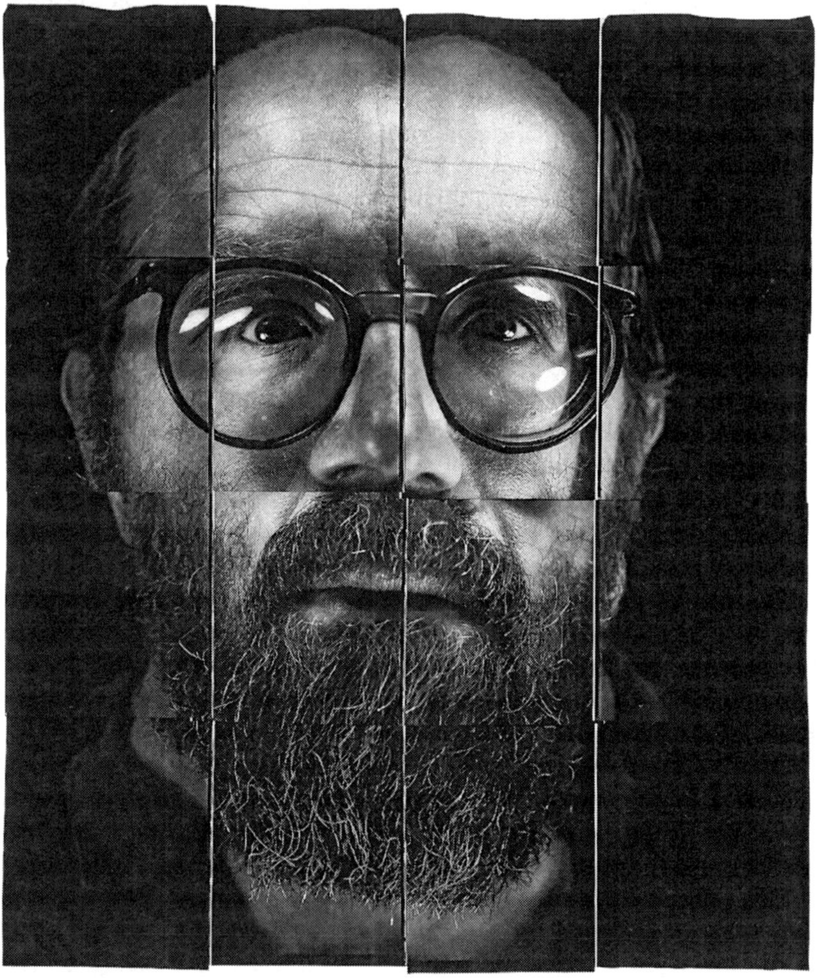

**Figure 5.9** Chuck Close, *Self Portrait/Composite/Sixteen Parts*, 1987. Silver-gelatin transfer print, 233.7 × 193 (92 × 76). Courtesy Pace/MacGill Gallery, New York. Copyright Chuck Close.

through glasses, each lens of which is as big as the viewer's head.) As with his paintings, size, distortion, and grid are important – but here they take on new functions. Now size not only magnifies any photographic distortion, it also intensifies the authority, for we are dealing with Polaroids, not enlarged prints. The size of each component means enormous detail and resolution.

The use of large-scale Polaroids enhances the idea of authoritative documentation, both because of the extraordinary resolution of the images, but also because the medium does not admit of alteration in the same way that more conventional photographic processes do. But when the segments are pieced together, with lines and features not quite matching, the idea that we have "the thing itself" is destroyed. Instead we have a process of approximation, zeroing in, piecing together.

The grid also takes on new import. Instead of a lightly drawn, finely divided grid, we are presented with a mosaic of sixteen large component images, fitting together – but not exactly. The very visible seams contradict the presence of the image, forcefully reminding us that we are looking at a surface. But more than that, the seams and the mismatch leave us with the feeling that the composition is provisional, only one of many possible constructions. They also leave us with the feeling that we are looking at a process, a temporal record, a series in time.

Compound images do not necessarily imply provisionality. Consider the digital images collected by Viking Orbiter 2 that are pieced together to provide a comprehensive record in *The Southern Latitudes of Mars at the Time of the Spring Equinox*, 1977. We are shown a photograph of Mars, but the image is not of a piece – it is constructed of many component images that were transmitted back to NASA and fitted together. We have a picture constructed of "straight" images, precisely located. Though we do not have an impress, or trace, of the whole – only of the various parts, recorded at different moments – our faith in the documentary authority of the whole is preserved by the scientific context, and by the meticulousness evident in the finished image. However, once compound images leave this atmosphere of scientific precision, they can become vulnerable to doubts and uncertainty.

The patchwork imaging of the Orbiter is echoed by the photo-collages of David Hockney, such as his *Pearblossom Highway 11–18 April 1986, #2*. But in Hockney's work, the scientific exactitude and regularity of the Orbiter collage has been exchanged for a crazy quilt of irregular spacing and angles. Hockney's image brings together hundreds of color prints, which pieced together show a highway in the California desert, littered with trash and road signs, and flanked by stumpy cacti. The camera is positioned so that the yellow line of the highway runs vertically up the image, disappearing in the bright-blue distance. There is a sometimes marked, sometimes slight, overlap in the way the pieces fit together, creating a "jumpy" effect. Furthermore, the images were taken over a period of time, so there are differences in light, color, sky, and there are dislocations of objects and lines. Hockney's work is made up of photographs, each of which we take to document a particular space and time. But taken together, they create a fictional space and scene – one which never existed in quite that way.

Close's self-portrait presents the same paradox: the authority of the part is at odds with the uncertain, provisional nature of the whole, but the tension is more subtle and perhaps more powerful than with the Hockney. More subtle, because the units are much larger, the mismatch of boundaries less extreme, the wholeness of the individual face serves to assure us of a certain fidelity. And yet, the vivid presence of the Polaroid images pointedly forces the issue of authority and makes us less certain of our response.

Another group of composite images bears mention here – simpler in construction, but more peculiar in effect. Svetlana Kopystiansky's 1990s landscape images seem off-kilter at first glance, and, as we look more closely, the reason becomes obvious. Each work combines a photograph with an art postcard (such as a Corot landscape). The two are connected in a way that is far from seamless, yet which provides for an odd continuity. These works vividly illustrate the difference between how we look at photographs and how we look at paintings. The juxtaposition and connection of the two images creates an identity crisis that calls into play and reveals two very different habits of viewing at war with each other.[10] But insofar as the photograph becomes an extension of the fictional space of the postcard, its documentary authority is punctured.

## The Digital Challenge

The challenges to photographic authority posed by the "photo-mosaics" of Hockney and Close parallel the broader challenges posed by digital imagery. The fluidity in the arrangement of pixels in a digital photograph, while expanding pictorial possibilities, threatens to destroy any illusion of documentary authority. Others, most notably Fred Ritchin,[11] have noted the impact of digital imagery on our use of photographs in the journ-

[10] True, Kopystiansky uses a photograph of a painting, not an actual painting, but I have argued elsewhere (*Transforming Images*, ch. 4) that photographic reproductions, despite the many important ways in which they diverge from the original paintings they present, function somewhat transparently. We tend to look at them in the same way we look at paintings.

[11] Fred Ritchin, *In our Own Image: The Coming Revolution in Photography* (New York: Aperture, 1990).

alistic and legal spheres; in this section I will discuss the impact for the aesthetics of photography.

Pedro Meyer's *Mexican Migrant Workers/Highway in California*, 1986/90, shows migrant workers stooped over their crops in front of a billboard advertising "free luxury service from your motel" to Caesars. Next to the message, the billboard shows a man dressed as a Roman soldier holding open the door to a well-appointed van. The juxtaposition is jarring: the billboard's promise of luxury seems cruelly out of place as it hovers over the migrant laborers, and in this context the Roman soldier looks more like an overseer than an attendant.

Meyer's image has an irony similar to that found in Bourke-White's photograph of flood victims discussed earlier, but there is an important difference. Whereas Bourke-White came upon the flood victims actually standing in front of a billboard touting the world's highest standard of living, Meyer's image is in reality the digital combination of two different photographs. The migrant workers never picked crops in front of that particular billboard; the juxtaposition was created by Meyer. Meyer's image is vivid and provocative, but the irony presented is an artificial construction, an irony of idea, not one of circumstance. Our knowledge of this makes the irony less penetrating, less compelling.

But what of Bourke-White's image of flood victims? As digital tools allow for more and more resonant juxtapositions to be constructed rather than found, as we become accustomed to seamless assemblages and montages, might we become less able to appreciate the profundity, the powerful testimony, of the straight image? As the prevalence of digital imagery changes our assumptions about the photographs we encounter, we may find these changes informing not only our encounters with contemporary photographs, but also encounters with photographs of the past. This is a problem that has the potential to affect all manner of photographs, not just those that fall within the realm of social commentary.

As we have seen, the drive to identify the subject of a photograph, and the exploitation, complication, and hindrance of this drive, are all threads that run through much work in photography – abstract, surrealist, and conceptual. As a result, these movements are much more closely allied, and the boundaries more malleable, than in painting.

However, with the advent of digital imagery and manipulation, we may begin to see less interest in this aspect of photography, as the connection between the photograph and the world is made more tenuous by widespread digitization. The drive to identify may weaken in the face of the possibility of digital manipulation, and we may find our understanding and treatment of photography moving closer to that of painting.

Consider Andreas Gursky's wall-sized image *Rhine II*, 1999, which shows horizontal swaths of gray, green, and silver that are at the same time the elements of a riverscape. Abstraction and representation are delicately balanced. Does our response to this image change when we discover that Gursky manipulated the image, digitally removing buildings from the river's banks? Certainly this information does not change how the image looks – the beauty and calm of its colors and proportions remain the same. But once we know the striking abstraction was not wrested from the world, but rather crafted on the computer, the coincidence of abstract image and representational landscape might seem less intriguing, less revealing, more contrived – more "painterly."

However, the question is not just whether we view a digitally altered photographic abstraction differently from a straight abstraction: this question would be no different from asking whether we view conventionally altered abstraction differently. Rather, the question is whether and how digital culture might affect the way we view *all* photographs, altered or straight. All photographs are at issue, because we cannot necessarily tell, by just looking, whether an image is (digitally) altered or not. And although the assumption has generally been that an image is straight unless otherwise noted (or unless the alteration is obvious), this assumption may change as digitally altered images become more and more prevalent.

Photographers have always had the ability to manipulate their images, to create fictions. But conventional alteration – cropping, retouching, combination printing – took place in a world dominated by straight photographs. For every doctored image in a tabloid or retouched image in an advertisement, there were thousands of straight images: family snapshots, IDs, newspaper photos. The widespread availability and increasing use of digital alteration, however is shifting the balance.

Digital manipulation is relatively fast and easy for anyone with the appropriate software, and the alterations are virtually limitless. Features can be reshaped, repositioned, or removed at will; images from different sources can be combined or blended, and the alterations can be virtually undetectable when handled skillfully. As a result, not only are we finding ourselves surrounded more and more by images that have been altered in some way, but it is also becoming impossible to tell which images are straight and which have been altered. As the number of digitized and altered images continues to grow, as more and more people play around with their snapshots on their home computers, our expectations when confronted with a photograph are bound to change.

In a world where digital manipulation – digital collage – has become the norm, we may simply come to assume that a photograph has been altered if it is at all challenging to read it as straight. In such a world we might not feel compelled to untangle the spatial ambiguities or confusions of an image such as *Valencia* – we would simply assume that we are dealing with a composite. The quest to make sense of the image as a unified space would thus be undermined and much of its interest lost.

Similar losses may await photographs of all kinds. The idea of a "decisive moment" may lose its hold in a world where happy coincidence and fortuitous accident can be digitally simulated. We may still be amused by the photograph of the windswept bride and groom, but the image may be less engaging once we have become used to images skillfully counterfeiting spontaneity and chance, digitally manufacturing the potent, or simply comic, vision of a moment. In a world where digital manipulation is the norm, we may still admire *Cabbage Leaf* for its beauty, but that beauty may be less intriguing and paradoxical, since its silken textures and sensuous curves would be seen against a backdrop of digitally reworked images. Such a context could make it difficult to see the image as surprising, and as a revelation by the camera of something unexpected about our world. And as we become more and more conditioned by digital manipulation, we may still admire *Capitol Reef* for its striking composition, but the mystery of its identity may no longer be compelling, for we will no longer assume that photographs correspond to something in the real world. This is not to say that such an image would hold no interest for us – but the interest would no longer be a fascination with the defamiliarization of objects in our world. (Perhaps what would interest us instead would be the apparent reality, palpability, of what we perceive to be a fictional construction.)

Of course it may be objected that these considerations show only that *contemporary* work faces a changed world, where the drive to identify has been muted by expectations of alteration, but that our appreciation for work from the past remains untouched. However, we may find that digital culture is changing even the way we are able to look at photographs from the past. Those who grow up in an age where the photographic image is seen as fluid and manipulable may be unable to appreciate the documentary aura surrounding traditional photographs. Future generations may come to see the transformations of photography as constructions or fictions, rather than as revealing something uncanny about our world.

# 6

# PHOTOGRAPHY AND REPRESENTATION

## Roger Scruton

Critics and philosophers have occasionally been troubled by the question whether the cinema is an independent art form – independent, that is, of the theatre, from which it borrows so many conventions.[1] This question can be traced back to a more basic one, the question whether photography is capable of representing anything. I shall argue that it is not and that, insofar as there is representation in film, its origin is not photographic. A film is a photograph of a dramatic representation; it is not, because it cannot be, a photographic representation. It follows that if there is such a thing as a cinematic masterpiece it will be so because – like *Wild Strawberries* and *La Règle du jeu* – it is in the first place a dramatic masterpiece.

It seems odd to say that photography is not a mode of representation. For a photograph has in common with a painting the property by which the painting represents the world, the property of sharing, in some sense, the appearance of its subject. Indeed, it is sometimes thought that since a photograph more effectively shares the appearance of its subject than a typical painting, photography is a better mode of representation. Photography might even be thought to have *replaced* painting as a mode of visual representation. Painters have felt that if the aim of painting is really to reproduce the appearances of things, then painting must give way to whatever means are available to reproduce an appearance more accurately. It has therefore been said that painting aims to record the appearances of things only so as to capture the experience of observing them (the

[1] See for example, the discussions in Allardyce Nicoll, *Film and Theatre* (London, 1936; New York, 1972).

Reprinted with permission from Roger Scruton, *The Aesthetic Understanding: Essays in the Philosophy of Art and Culture* (London and New York: Methuen)

*impression*) and that the accurate copying of appearances will normally be at variance with this aim. Here we have the seeds of expressionism and the origin of the view (a view which not only is mistaken but which has also proved disastrous for the history of modern art) that painting is somehow purer when it is abstract and closer to its essence as an art.

Let us first dismiss the word "representation." Of course this word can be applied to photography. We wish to know whether there is some feature, suitably called representation, common to painting and photography. And we wish to know whether that feature has in each case a comparable aesthetic value, so that we can speak not only of representation but also of representational art. (There is an important feature – sound – in common to music and to fountains, but only the first of these is properly described as an *art* of sound.)

## 1

In order to understand what I mean by saying that photography is not a representational art, it is important to separate painting and photography as much as possible, so as to discuss not actual painting and actual photography but an ideal form of each, an ideal which represents the essential differences between them. Ideal photography differs from actual photography as indeed ideal painting differs from actual painting. Actual photography is the result of the attempt by photographers to pollute the ideal of their craft with the aims and methods of painting.

By an "ideal" I mean a logical ideal. The ideal of photography is not an ideal at which photography aims or ought to aim. On the contrary, it is a logical fiction, designed merely to capture what is distinctive in the photographic relation and in our interest in it. It will be clear from this discussion that there need be no such thing as an ideal photograph in my sense, and the reader should not be deterred if I begin by describing photography in terms that seem to be exaggerated or false.

The ideal painting stands in a certain "intentional" relation to a subject.[2] In other words, if a painting represents a subject, it does not follow that the subject exists nor, if it does exist, that the painting represents the subject as it is. Moreover, if $x$ is a painting of a man, it does not

[2] See Franz Clemens Brentano, *Psychology from an Empirical Standpoint*, ed. Linda McAlister (London and New York, 1973); Roderick M. Chisholm, *Perceiving* (London and Ithaca, NY, 1957), chapter 11; and G. E. M. Anscombe, "The Intentionality of Sensation," in R. J. Butler (ed.), *Analytical Philosophy*, Second Series (Oxford, 1965).

follow that there is some *particular* man of which *x* is the painting. Furthermore, the painting stands in this intentional relation to its subject because of a representational act, the artist's act, and in characterizing the relation between a painting and its subject we are also describing the artist's intention. The successful realization of that intention lies in the creation of an appearance, an appearance which in some way leads the spectator to recognize the subject.

The ideal photograph also stands in a certain relation to a subject: a photograph is a photograph *of* something. But the relation is here causal and not intentional.[3] In other words, if a photograph is a photograph of a subject, it follows that the subject exists, and if *x* is a photograph of a man, there is a particular man of whom *x* is the photograph. It also follows, though for different reasons, that the subject is, roughly, as it appears in the photograph. In characterizing the relation between the ideal photograph and its subject, one is characterizing not an intention but a causal process, and while there is, as a rule, an intentional act involved, this is not an essential part of the photographic relation. The ideal photograph also yields an appearance, but the appearance is not interesting as the realization of an intention but rather as a record of how an actual object looked.

Since the end point of the two processes is, or can be, so similar, it is tempting to think that the intentionality of the one relation and the causality of the other are quite irrelevant to the standing of the finished product. In both cases, it seems, the important part of representation lies in the fact that the spectator can see the subject *in* the picture. The appreciation of photographs and the appreciation of paintings both involve the exercise of the capacity to "see as," in the quite special sense in which one may see *x* as *y* without believing or being tempted to believe that *x* is *y*.

## 2

Now, it would be a simple matter to define "representation" so that "*x* represents *y*" is true only if *x* expresses a thought about *y*, or if *x* is designed to remind one of *y*, or whatever, in which case a relation that was *merely* causal (a relation that was not characterized in terms of any thought, intention, or other mental act) would never be sufficient for representation. We need to be clear, however, why we should wish to define representation

[3] I think that in this area nonextensionality (intensionality) and intentionality should be sharply distinguished, so that the claim is not affected by any argument to the effect that causal relations are non-extensional.

in one way rather than in another. What hangs on the decision? In particular, why should it matter that the relation between a painting and its subject is an intentional relation while the photographic relation is merely causal? I shall therefore begin by considering our experience of painting and the effect on that experience of the intentionality of the relation between a painting and its subject.

When I appreciate a painting as a representation, I see it as what it represents, but I do not take it for what it represents. Nor do I necessarily believe that what is represented in the painting exists nor, if it does exist, that it has the appearance of the object that I see *in* the painting. Suppose that a certain painting represents a warrior. I may in fact see it not as a warrior but as a god. Here, three "objects" of interest may be distinguished:

1 The intentional object of sight: a god (defined by my experience).
2 The represented object: a warrior (defined, to put it rather crudely, by the painter's intention).[4]
3 The material object of sight: the painting.[5]

The distinction between 1 and 2 is not as clear-cut as it might seem: it would become so only if we could separate the "pure appearance" of the painting from the sense of intention with which it is endowed. We cannot do this, not only because we can never separate our experience of human activity from our understanding of intention but also because in the case of a picture we are dealing with an object that is manifestly the expression of thought. Hence we will look for clues as to how the painting is intended to be seen and – such being the nature of "seeing as" – our sense of what is intended will determine our experience of what is there.

The "inference" view of perception, the view that there are certain things that we *basically* see (sense-data, etc) from which we then *infer* the existence of other things, is wrong both as a matter of philosophical psychology, since there is no criterion for distinguishing datum and inference, and as a matter of epistemology, since it is only if we sometimes have knowledge of the "inferred" entities that we can have knowledge of the experience.[6] The point applies also to intention: we do not

4 I pass over the problem here of selecting and describing the appropriate intention.

5 For the material/intentional distinction, I rely on Anscombe.

6 The most famous arguments for this conclusion occur in Kant's *Critique of Pure Reason* (in particular in the "Transcendental Deduction") and in Wittgenstein's *Philosophical Investigations*, part I.

see the gestures and movements of another man and then infer from them the existence of intentions; rather, we see the gestures as intentional, and that is the correct description of what we see. But of course we cannot choose to see just what we will as a manifestation of intention. Our ability to see intention depends on our ability to interpret an activity as characteristically human, and here, in the case of representational art, it involves our understanding the dimensions and conventions of the medium. Art manifests the "common knowledge" of a culture;[7] as E. H. Gombrich has made clear, to understand art is to be familiar with the constraints imposed by the medium and to be able to separate that which is due to the medium from that which is due to the man. Such facts lead us to speak of understanding or misunderstanding representational painting.

Although there is not space to discuss fully the concept of "understanding" that is involved here, it is worth mentioning the following point: to understand a painting involves understanding thoughts. These thoughts are, in a sense, communicated by the painting. They underlie the painter's intention, and at the same time they inform our way of seeing the canvas. Such thoughts determine the perception of the man who sees with understanding, and it is at least partly in terms of our apprehension of thoughts that we must describe what we see in the picture. We see not only a man on a horse but a man of a certain character and bearing. And *what* we see is determined not by independent properties of the subject but by our understanding of the painting. It is the way the eyes are painted that gives that sense of authority, the particular lie of the arm that reveals the arrogant character, and so on. In other words, properties of the medium influence not only what is seen in the picture but also the way it is seen. Moreover, they present to us a vision that we attribute not to ourselves but to another man; we think of ourselves as sharing in the vision of the artist, and the omnipresence of intention changes our experience from something private into something shared. The picture presents us not merely with the perception of a man but with a thought about him, a thought embodied in perceptual form.[8] And here, just as in the case of language, thought has that character of objectivity and publicity upon which Frege

7 The importance of "common knowledge," its complexity as a phenomenon, and its natural co-existence with conventions has been recognized in the philosophy of language; see especially the interesting discussion in David K. Lewis, *Convention: a Philosophical Study* (Cambridge, MA, 1969; Oxford, 1972).

8 I have discussed elsewhere what I mean by the "embodiment" of thought in perception; see my *Art and Imagination*: A *Study in the Philosophy of Mind* (London, 1974), chapters 7 and 8.

commented.[9] It is precisely when we have the communication of thoughts about a subject that the concept of representation becomes applicable; and therefore literature and painting are representational in the same sense.

## 3

The ideal painting has no particular need for an identity of appearance with its subject. In order to present a visual account of the Duke of Wellington, it is not necessary for an artist to strive to present an exact copy of the Duke's appearance.[10] Indeed, it is tempting here to dispense with the notion of appearance altogether, to construe the painting as a conventional or even quasi-linguistic act which stands in a semantic relation – a relation of reference – to its subject, and which presents a visual appearance only as a means of fulfilling a referential function. Such a view would explain, perhaps better than all rival theories of representation, the role of intention in our understanding of art.[11]

I do not know how far those philosophers influenced by Gombrich's arguments – arguments emphasizing the place of convention in our understanding of visual art – would wish to take the analogy with language. I do not know, for example, whether a convention according to which colours were to be represented by their complements – a red object by a patch of green, a yellow object by a patch of blue – would be conceivable for such philosophers, conceivable, that is, as a mode of pictorial representation. It is undeniable, however, that such a painting would convey to someone who understood the convention as much information about its subject as another painting in which the colours copy the original. More bizarre conventions could also be imagined: a painting could be constructed entirely out of dashes and circles, arranged according to the grammar of a visual code. Given the right conventions, such a painting would count, according to the reference theory, as an extremely faithful representation of its subject. It would be read as a kind of scrambled message which had to be decoded in order to permit an understanding of what it says.

9 G. Frege, *Translations from the Philosophical Writings*, ed. Peter Geach and Max Black (Oxford, 1980), p. 79.

10 There is a problem here about "identity of appearance" on which I touch again, pp. 154–5.

11 Nelson Goodman, the most important exponent of a semantic theory of art, manages to reconcile his approach with a view of photographs as representational; see his *Languages of Art: An Approach to a Theory of Symbols* (London, 1969), p. 9n.

However, we cannot treat the visual connection between a painting and its subject as an entirely accidental matter, accidental, that is, to any process of representation that the painting may display. For we cannot deny that representational painting interests us primarily because of the visual connection with its subject. We are interested in the visual relation between painting and subject because it is by means of this relation that the painting represents. The artist presents us with a way of seeing (and not just any way of thinking of) his subject. (Hence the revolutionary character of such painters as Caravaggio and de la Tour.) It is this visual relation which seems to require elucidation. We cannot explain pictorial representation independently of the visual aspect of paintings and still expect our explanation to cast light upon the problem of the visual relation between a picture and its subject-matter. And yet it is that relation which is understood by the appreciative spectator.

That objection is of course not conclusive. It also seems to assume that a semantic theory of art (a theory which sees representation in terms of reference) must necessarily also be a linguistic theory. Surely there could be relations of reference that do not reflect the conventions of language, even relations that need to be understood in essentially visual terms. Let us, then, consider what such a conception of reference might be like.

It is no accident that language has a grammar. The existence of grammar is a necessary part of language and part of the all-important connection between language and truth. But there is a further significance in grammar, at least as grammar is now conceived. For the contemporary logician, grammar is primarily a "generative" function, a means of building complex sentences from the finite number of linguistic parts. Taken in conjunction with a theory of interpretation, a proper grammar will explain how speakers of a language understand an indefinite number of sentences on the basis of understanding only a finite number of words.[12] In this way we can show how the truth or falsehood of a sentence depends upon the reference of its parts, and the concept of reference in language becomes inextricably bound up with the idea that from the references of words we may derive the truth conditions of sentences. This "generative connection" between reference and truth is part of the intuitive understanding of reference which is common to all speakers of a language.

It is here, I think, that we find a striking difference between language and painting. While there may be repertoires and conventions in painting,

12 I draw here on the now familiar arguments given by Donald Davidson in "Truth and Meaning," which originate with Frege and which were given full mathematical elaboration in Alfred Tarski's theory of truth.

there is nothing approaching grammar as we understand it. For one thing, the requirement of finitude is not obviously met. It is clearly true that we understand the representational meaning of, say, a Carpaccio through understanding the representational meaning of its parts. But the parts themselves are understood in *precisely the same way*; that is, they too have parts, each of which is potentially divisible into significant components, and so on ad infinitum. Moreover, there seems to be no way in which we can divide the painting into grammatically significant parts – no way in which we can provide a syntax which isolates those parts of the painting that have a particular semantic role. For in advance of seeing the painting, we have no rule which will decide the point, and thus the idea of syntactic or semantic rules becomes inapplicable. The means whereby we understand the total representation are identical with the means whereby we understand the parts. Understanding is not secured either by rules or by conventions but seems to be, on the contrary, a natural function of the normal eye. As we see the meaning of the painting, so do we see the meaning of its parts. This contrasts sharply with the case of reference in language, where we *construct* the meaning of the sentence from the reference of its parts, and where the parts themselves have reference in a way that is ultimately conventional.

There seems to be no justification, then, for thinking of representation in terms of reference. We could, however, insist that the relation of a painting to its subject is one of reference only by removing from "reference" that feature which leads us to think that an account of reference is also an account of understanding. To speak of the connection between a word and a thing as one of reference is to show how we understand the word, for it is to show how the truth conditions of sentences containing the word are determined. If we speak of reference in describing paintings, therefore, we should not think that we thereby cast any light on the *understanding* of representation. What representation is, how we understand it, and how it affects us – those questions seem to remain as obscure as ever. The only thing that remains to support the invocation of reference is the fact that paintings may be true or false. It is that fact which we must now consider.

## 4

The fact that a painting may be true or false plays a vital role in visual appreciation. We could not explain realism, for example, either in painting or in literature, unless we invoked the concept of truth. Again we must emphasize information (and therefore the concept of reference) in our understanding of the painter's art; or at least we are obliged to find some feature of the painting that can be substituted for reference and which will show how the connection with truth is established.

Such a feature, as a matter of fact, has already been described: we may describe realism in terms of what we see *in* the painting. We therefore analyse truth not in terms of a relation between the painting and the world but in terms of a relation between what we see in the painting and the world. Goya's portrait of the Duke of Wellington is realistic because the figure we see in the painting resembles the Duke of Wellington.[13] The truth of the painting amounts to the truth of the viewer's perception; in other words, the "intentional object of sight" corresponds to the nature of the subject. Those thoughts which animate our perception when we see the realistic painting with understanding are true thoughts.[14] Truth is not a property of the painting in the direct way in which it is the property of a sentence, and the possibility of predicating the truth of a painting does not open the way to a semantic theory of art any more than it opens the way to a semantic theory of, for example, clouds, or of any other phenomenon in which aspects may be seen.

Although distinctions may be made between true and false pictures, an aesthetic appreciation remains in one sense indifferent to the truth of its object. A person who has an aesthetic interest in the *Odyssey* is not concerned with the literal truth of the narrative. Certainly it is important to him that the *Odyssey* be lifelike, but the existence of Odysseus and the reality of the scenes described are matters of aesthetic indifference. Indeed, it is characteristic of aesthetic interest that most of its objects in representation are imaginary. For unless it were possible to represent imaginary things, representation could hardly be very important to us. It is important because it enables the presentation of scenes and characters toward which we have only contemplative attitudes: scenes and characters which, being unreal, allow our practical natures to remain unengaged.

If the concept of representation is to be of aesthetic importance, it must be possible to describe an aesthetic interest in representation. Only if there is such a thing as aesthetic interest which has representation as its object can there be representational art (as opposed to art that happens to be representational). It is commonly said that an aesthetic interest in something is an interest in it for its own sake: the object is not treated as a surrogate for another; it is *itself* the principal object of attention. It

13 That is, provided the painting is independently *of* the Duke of Wellington.

14 See n. 8, above.

follows that an aesthetic interest in the representational properties of a picture must also involve a kind of interest in the picture and not merely in the thing represented.[15]

Now, *one* difference between an aesthetic interest in a picture, and an interest in the picture as a surrogate for its subject, lies in the kind of reason that might be given for the interest. (And to give the reasons for an interest is to give an account of its intentional object and therefore of the interest itself.) If I ask a man why he is looking at a picture, there are several kinds of reply that he might give. In one case his reasons will be reasons for an interest only in the things depicted: they will describe properties of the subject which make it interesting. Here the interest in the picture is derivative: it lies in the fact that the picture reveals properties of its subject. The picture is being treated as a means of access to the subject, and it is therefore dispensable to the extent that there is a better means to hand (say, the subject itself). With that case one may contrast two others. First, there is the case where the man's reasons refer only to properties of the picture – to pictorial properties, such as colour, shape, and line – and do not mention the subject. For such a man the picture has interest as an abstract composition, and its representational nature is wholly irrelevant to him. Second, there is the case where the reasons for the interest are reasons for an interest in the *picture* (in the way it looks) even though they make essential reference to the subject and can be understood as reasons only by someone who understands the reference to the subject. For example, the observer may refer to a particular gesture of a certain figure, and a particular way of painting that gesture, as revelatory of the subject's character (for example, the barmaid's hands on the counter in Manet's *Bar aux Folies-Bergère*). Clearly, that is a reason not only for an interest in the subject but also (and primarily) for an interest in the picture, since it gives a reason for an interest in something which can be understood only by looking at the picture. Such an interest leads naturally to another, to an interest in the use of the medium – in the way the painting presents its subject and therefore in the way in which the subject is seen by the painter. Here it could not be said that the painting is being treated as a surrogate for its subject: it is *itself* the object of interest and irreplaceable by the thing depicted. The interest is not in representation for the sake of its subject but in representation for its own sake. And it is such an interest that forms the core of the aesthetic experience of pictorial art, and which – if analysed more fully –

15 Hence the tradition in philosophy, which begins with Kant, according to which representation constitutes a threat to the autonomy of art.

would explain not only the value of that experience but also the nature and value of the art which is its object. We see at once that such an interest is not, and cannot be, an interest in the literal truth of the picture.

## 5

If I were to describe, then, *what I see* in a picture, I would be bound not merely to describe the visual properties of the subject but also to provide an interpretation of the subject, a way of seeing it. The description under which the subject is seen is given by the total thought in terms of which I understand the picture. In the case of portraiture, this interpretive thought need not be a thought about the momentary appearance of the subject: it need not be the thought "He looked like that." The thought may relate to the subject not as he appeared at any one moment but as he was or, rather, as the artist saw him to be. The appearance may be presented only because it embodies the reality, in which case it will be the reality that is understood (or misunderstood) by the spectator.

One of the most important differences between photography and portraiture as traditionally practised lies in the relation of each to time. It is characteristic of photography that, being understood in terms of a causal relation to its subject, it is thought of as revealing something momentary about its subject – how the subject looked at a particular moment. And that sense of the moment is seldom lost in photography, for reasons that will shortly be apparent. Portrait painting, however, aims to capture the sense of time and to represent its subject as extended in time, even in the process of displaying a particular moment of its existence. Portraiture is not an art of the momentary, and its aim is not merely to capture fleeting appearances. The aim of painting is to give insight, and the creation of an appearance is important mainly as the expression of thought. While a causal relation is a relation between events, there is no such narrow restriction on the subject-matter of a thought. This perhaps partially explains the frequently made comment that the true art of portraiture died with the advent of photography and that representational art, insofar as it still pursues an ideal of realism, is unable to capture, as the realist ought to capture, the sense of the passage of time.[16]

[16] I am thinking of recent exercises in "photographic" realism by such painters as Ken Danby and Alex Colville. More traditional styles of realism have also emerged in open opposition to both the clinical lines of the photographic school and the contentless images of abstract expressionism. Witness here the paintings of David Inshaw and Robert Lowe.

Of course a photographer can aim to capture that fleeting appearance which gives the most reliable indication of his subject's character. He may attempt to find in the momentary some *sign* of what is permanent. But there is a great difference between an image which is a sign of something permanent and an image which is an expression of it. To express the permanent is to give voice to a thought about its nature. To give a sign of the permanent is to create something from which its properties may be inferred. A man may remain silent when asked to defend his friend, and from that silence I infer his friend's guilt. Yet the man has certainly not expressed the thought that his friend is guilty. Similarly a photograph may give signs of what is permanent despite the fact that it is incapable of expressing it.

## 6

The ideal photograph, as I mentioned earlier, stands in a causal relation to its subject and "represents" its subject by reproducing its appearance. In understanding something as an ideal photograph, we understand it as exemplifying this causal process, a process which originates in the subject "represented" and which has as its end point the production of a copy of an appearance. By a "copy" of an appearance I mean an object such that what is seen in it by a man with normal eyes and understanding (the intentional object of sight) resembles as nearly as possible what is seen when such a man observes the subject itself from a certain angle at a certain point in its history. A person studying an ideal photograph is given a very good idea of *how something looked*. The result is that, from studying a photograph he may come to know how something looked in the way that he might know it if he had actually seen it.

With an ideal photograph it is neither necessary nor even possible that the photographer's intention should enter as a serious factor in determining how the picture is seen. It is recognized at once for what it is – not as an interpretation of reality but as a presentation of how something looked. In some sense, looking at a photograph is a substitute for looking at the thing itself. Consider, for example, the most "realistic" of all photographic media, the television. It seems scarcely more contentious to say that I saw someone on the television – that is, that in watching the television I saw *him* – than to say that I saw him in a mirror. Television is like a mirror: it does not so much destroy as embellish that elaborate causal chain which is the natural process of visual perception.

Of course it is not necessary to define the subject of a photograph in terms of this causal process, for the subject could be identified in some other way. But the fact remains that when we say that *x* is a photograph of *y* we are referring to this causal relation, and it is in terms of the causal relation that the subject of a photograph is normally understood. Let us at least say that the subject is so defined for my logical ideal of photography: that premise is all that my argument requires.

It follows, first, that the subject of the ideal photograph must exist; secondly, that it must appear roughly as it appears in the photograph; and thirdly, that its appearance in the photograph is its appearance at a particular moment of its existence.

The first of those features is an immediate consequence of the fact that the relation between a photograph and its subject is a causal relation. If *a* is the cause of *b*, then the existence of *b* is sufficient for the existence of *a*. The photograph lacks that quality of "intentional inexistence" which is characteristic of painting. The ideal photograph, therefore, is incapable of representing anything unreal; if a photograph is a photograph of a man, then there is some particular man of whom it is a photograph.

Of course I may take a photograph of a draped nude and call it *Venus*, but insofar as this can be understood as an exercise in fiction, it should not be thought of as a photographic representation of Venus but rather as the photograph of a representation of Venus. In other words, the process of fictional representation occurs not in the photograph but in the subject: it is the *subject* which represents Venus; the photograph does no more than disseminate its visual character to other eyes. This is not to say that the model is (unknown to herself) acting Venus. It is not she who is representing Venus but the photographer, who uses her in his representation. But the representational act, the act which embodies the representational thought, is completed before the photograph is ever taken. As we shall see, this fictional incompetence of photography is of great importance in our understanding of the cinema; but it also severely limits the aesthetic significance of "representation" in photography. As we saw earlier, representation in art has a special significance precisely because of the possibility that we can understand it – in the sense of understanding its content – while being indifferent to, or unconcerned with, its literal truth. That is why fictional representation is not merely an important form of representational art but in fact the primary form of it, the form through which the aesthetic understanding finds its principal mode of expression.

One may wish to argue that my example is a special one, that there are other ways of creating fictional representations which are essentially photographic. In other words, it is not necessary for the photographer to create an independent representation in order for his photograph to be fictional. Suppose he were to take a photograph of a drunken tramp and label it *Silenus*. Would that not be a fictional photograph, comparable, indeed, to a painting of Silenus in which a drunken tramp was used as a model?

This example, which I owe to Richard Wollheim, is an interesting one, but it does not, I think, establish what it claims. Consider a parallel case: finding a drunken tramp in the street I point to him and say "Silenus." It is arguable that my gesture makes the tramp into a representation; but if it does, it is because I am inviting you to think of him in that way. I have expressed a representational thought: imagine this person as Silenus. And I have completed the thought by an act of ostension toward its dozing subject. The act of ostension might on some other occasion be accomplished by a camera (or a frame, or a mirror, or any other device which isolates what it shows).

The camera, then, is being used not to represent something but to point to it. The subject, once located, plays its own special part in an independent process of representation. The camera is not essential to that process: a gesturing finger would have served just as well. If the example shows that photographs can be representations, then it shows the same of fingers. To accept that conclusion is to fail to distinguish between what is accidental and what is essential in the expression of a representational thought. It is to open the way toward the theory that everything which plays a part in the expression of thought is itself a representation. Such a view does not account for the aesthetic significance of representations. It also, however, and far more seriously, implies that there is no distinction between representational and nonrepresentational art. The concept of representation that I am assuming makes such a distinction, and it makes it for very good reasons. I am not tempted by such dubious examples to abandon it. One might put the point by saying that a painting, like a sentence, is a *complete* expression of the thought which it contains. Painting is a sufficient vehicle of representational thought, and there may be no better way of expressing what a painting says. That is why representation can be thought of as an intrinsic property of a painting and not just as a property of some process of which the painting forms a part.

Consider also the second feature mentioned above: the subject of an ideal photograph must appear roughly as it appears in the photograph. By its very nature, photography can "represent" only through resemblance. It is only because the photograph acts as a visual reminder of its subject that we are tempted to say that it represents its subject. If it were not for this resemblance, it would be impossible to see from the photograph how the subject appeared, except by means of scientific knowledge that would be irrelevant to any interest in the visual aspect of the photograph. Contrast here the case of an electron microscope, which punches out on a ticker tape a codified indication of a crystal's atomic structure. Is that a representation of the atomic structure? If it is, then why not say that any causal relation which enables us to infer the nature of the cause from the properties of its effect provides us with a representation of the cause in the effect? Such a concept of representation would be uninteresting indeed. It is impossible, therefore, that the ideal photograph should represent an object except by showing how it appeared at a certain moment in its history and still *represent* it in the way ideal photography represents anything. How indeed could we make sense of an ideal photograph representing its subject *as* other than it appeared? We could do so only if we could also say that a photograph sometimes represents its subject as it appears; that is, if we could say that representation here is "representation as." But consider this sentence: *x* is an ideal photograph of *y* as *z*. It seems that we have no means of filling out the description "*z*," no means, that is, of filling it out by reference only to the photographic process and not, say, to some independent act of representation that precedes or follows it. One might say that the medium in photography has lost all importance: it can present us with what we see, but it cannot tell us how to see it.

We *must* be aware of the three features mentioned above if we are to appreciate the characteristic effects of photography. In looking at an ideal photograph, we know that we are seeing something which actually occurred and seeing it as it appeared. Typically, therefore, our attitude toward photography will be one of curiosity, not curiosity about the photograph but rather about its subject. The photograph addresses itself to our desire for knowledge of the world, knowledge of how things look or seem. The photograph is a means to the end of seeing its subject; in painting, on the other hand, the subject is the means to the end of its own representation. The photograph is transparent to its subject, and if it holds our interest it does so because it acts as a surrogate for the thing which it shows. Thus if one finds a photograph beautiful, it is because one finds something beautiful in its subject. A painting may be beautiful, on the other hand, even when it represents an ugly thing.

## 7

Someone might accept the general difference I have indicated between an aesthetic interest and an attitude of curiosity, and accept too the implication that something is a representation only if it is capable of carrying a reference to its subject without merely standing as a surrogate for it. He still might argue, however, that it is possible to be interested in a photograph *as* a photograph and find it, and not just its subject, beautiful.

But what is it to be interested in a photograph as a photograph? Of course one might have a purely abstract aesthetic interest in a photograph – an interest in the photograph as a construction of lines and shapes (as one is intended to appreciate Man Ray's Rayogrammes, for example). One can have a purely abstract aesthetic interest in anything; photography is only a representational art if our interest in a photograph as a photographic "representation" is a type of aesthetic interest.

Let us return to the previous discussion of representation in painting. It appears that there is a prima facie contradiction between saying that I am interested in a thing for its own sake and saying that I am interested in it as a representation of something else. In attempting to reconcile these two interests, it is necessary first to restrict the place of truth in aesthetic interest. Truth is aesthetically relevant only insofar as it may be construed as truth to the situation presented rather than "truth to the facts." From the point of view of aesthetic interest, it is always irrelevant that there should be a particular object which is the object represented or, if there is such an object, that it should exist as portrayed. That is not to say, of course, that an aesthetic interest does not require things to be in general roughly as they are shown; but that is another matter.

As I have already said, this conflicts with the typical way in which we are interested in photographs. Knowing what we know about photographs, it is at least natural that we should be interested in them both because they are true to the facts and because they tell us useful things about their subject-matter. It seems, therefore, that the emotional or "aesthetic" qualities of a photograph tend to derive directly from the qualities of what it "represents": if the photograph is sad, it is usually because its subject is sad; if the photograph is touching, it is because its subject is touching, and so on. It is worth reflecting on why there could not be a photograph of a martyrdom that was other than horrifying. One's curiosity here would be no different from one's curiosity in the act itself. Hence it would be as difficult (and perhaps also as corrupt) to have an aesthetic interest in the photograph as it would be in the real situation. By contrast, a painting of a martyrdom may be serene, as is Mantegna's great *Crucifixion* in the Louvre. The painting has emotional qualities in defiance of the qualities of its subject. In the case of a photograph – say of the victim of some accident – one's attitude is determined by the knowledge that this is how things are. One's attitude is made practical by the knowledge of the causal relation between photograph and object. This is not to deny that one might be interested in a photograph for its own sake and at the same time maintain a proper distance from its subject, even when it depicts a scene of agony or death. But the real question is, Can we have such an interest in a photograph without having the same interest in its subject? Can I have an aesthetic interest in the photograph of a dying soldier which is not also an aesthetic interest in the soldier's death? Or, rather, can I maintain that separation of interests and still be interested in the "representational" aspect of the photograph? If we are distanced from the photograph only because we are distanced from its subject, then the important distinction that I wish to emphasize, between interest in the representation and interest in the subject, has still not been made. It seems necessary to show that photography *can* – by itself – create that sharp separation of interests which is everywhere apparent in serious painting. Consider too the photographs of old London. How is it possible to detach one's interest in their beauty from an interest in the beauty of London as it was? Regret is here the appropriate reaction to the photograph (as it is not – or at least not normally – an appropriate reaction to a Canaletto). "That is how it looked!" is the central index of one's emotion.

Consider, then, the reasons that may be given in answer to the question, "Why are you looking at that?" With a photograph, one mentions the features of the subject; with a painting, one mentions only the observable aspect captured in the picture. This essentially is what distinguishes an interest in a representation as a surrogate from an interest in a representation for its own sake. Suppose now that someone wishes to argue that it is *not* inevitable that we treat photographs, even ideal photographs, as I have described. Let us see what the consequences of such a position might be.

## 8

Imagine that we treat photographs as representations in just the same way that we treat paintings, so that their representational natures are themselves the objects of an aesthetic interest. What are the consequences if we study photography in such a way that it does not matter whether its subject actually existed or actually looked like the thing we see in the picture? Here we are interested not in the subject but in its manner of presentation. If there *can* be such an interest in a photograph, it suggests that a photograph may sometimes be the expression of a representational thought and not merely a simulacrum of its subject.

An interest in an object for its own sake, in the object as a whole, must encompass an interest in detail. For if there is nothing *for* which one contemplates an object, as has frequently been argued, there is no way of determining in advance of looking at it which features are, and which are not, relevant to one's interest.[17] It is for this reason that we cannot rest satisfied with nature but must have works of art as the objects of aesthetic judgment. Art provides a medium transparent to human intention, a medium for which the question, Why? can be asked of every observable feature, even if it may sometimes prove impossible to answer. Art is an expression of precisely the same rational impulses that find an outlet in aesthetic interest; it is therefore the only object which satisfies that interest completely.

The photographer, then, who aims for an aesthetically significant representation must also aim to control detail: "detail" being here understood in the wide sense of "any observable fact or feature." But here lies a fresh difficulty. The causal process of which the photographer is a victim puts almost every detail outside of his control. Even if he does, say, intentionally arrange each fold of his subject's dress and meticulously construct, as studio photographers once used to do, the appropriate scenario, that would still hardly be relevant, since there seem to be few ways in which such intentions can be revealed in the photograph. For one thing, we lack all except the grossest features of style in photography; and yet it is style that persuades us that the question, Why this and not that? admits such fruitful exploration in the case of painting. Style enables us to answer that question by referring solely to aspects of the painting rather than to features which are aesthetically irrelevant, or in no way *manifest* in what is seen.[18] The search for meaning in a photograph is therefore curtailed or thwarted: there is no point in an interest in detail since there is nothing that detail can show. Detail, like the photograph itself, is transparent to its subject. If the photograph is interesting, it is only because what it portrays is interesting, and not because of the manner in which the portrayal is effected.

Let us assume, however, that the photographer could intentionally exert over his image just the kind of control that is exercised in the other representational arts. The question is, How far can this control be extended? Certainly there will be an infinite number of things that lie outside his

17 See for example, Stuart Hampshire, "Logic and Appreciation," in William Elton (ed.), *Aesthetics and Language* (Oxford, 1954; New Jersey, 1970).

18 See Richard Wollheim's interesting discussion "Style now," in Bernard William Smith (ed.), *Concerning Contemporary Art* (Oxford and New York, 1975).

control. Dust on a sleeve, freckles on a face, wrinkles on a hand: such minutiae will always depend initially upon the prior situation of the subject. When the photographer sees the photographic plate, he may still wish to assert his control, choosing just this colour here, just that number of wrinkles or that texture of skin. He can proceed to paint things out or in, to touch up, alter, or *pasticher* as he pleases. But of course he has now become a painter, precisely through taking representation seriously. The photograph has been reduced to a kind of frame around which he paints, a frame that imposes upon him largely unnecessary constraints.[19]

In other words, when the photographer strives towards representational art, he inevitably seems to move away from that ideal of photography which I have been describing toward the ideal of painting. This can be seen most clearly if we consider exactly what has to be the case if photography is to be a wholly representational art – if it is to manifest all those aspects of representation that distinguish it from mere copying and which endow it with its unique aesthetic appeal. No one could deny that from its origins photography has set itself artistic ideals and attempted to establish itself as a representational art. The culmination of that process – which can be seen in such photographs as Henry Peach Robinson's "Autumn" – is to be found in the techniques of photo-montage used by the surrealists and futurists (and in particular, by such artists as László Moholy-Nagy and Hannah Höch). Here our interest in the result can be entirely indifferent to the existence and nature of the original subject. But that is precisely because the photographic figures have been so cut up and rearranged in the final product that it could not be said in any normal sense to be a *photograph* of its subject. Suppose that I were to take figures from a photograph of, say, Jane, Philip, and Paul, and, having cut them out, I were to arrange them in a montage, touching them up and adjusting them until the final result is to my mind satisfactory. It could very well be said that the final result represents, say, a lovers' quarrel; but it is not a photograph of one. It represents a quarrel because it stands in precisely the same intentional relation to a quarrel that a painting might have exhibited. Indeed, it is, to all intents and purposes, a painting, except that it happens to have employed photographic techniques in the derivation of its figures. Insofar as the figures can still be considered to be photographs, they are photographs of Jane, Philip, and Paul and not photographs of a lovers' quarrel. (Of course the fact of their *being* photographs might

19 This argument is hinted at in B. Croce, *Estetica,* 10th edn (Bari, 1958), p. 20.

be aesthetically important. Some ironical comment, for example, may be intended in using figures cut from a medium of mass production.)

The history of the art of photography is the history of successive attempts to break the causal chain by which the photographer is imprisoned, to impose a human intention between subject and appearance, so that the subject can be both defined by that intention and seen in terms of it.[20] It is the history of an attempt to turn a mere simulacrum into the expression of a representational thought, an attempt to discover through techniques (from the combination print to the soft-focus lens) what was in fact already known.[21] Occasionally, it is true, photographers have attempted to create entirely fictional scenes through photography and have arranged their models and surroundings, as one might on the stage, in order to produce a narrative scene with a representational meaning. But, as I have argued, the resulting photograph would not be a representation. The process of representation was effected even before the photograph was taken. A photograph of a representation is no more a representation than a picture of a man is a man.

## 9

It might be felt that I have begged the question in allowing only one way in which photography may acquire representational meaning, a way which inevitably leads photography to subject itself to the aims of painting. One may argue that a photographer does not choose his subject at random, nor is he indifferent to the point of view from which he photographs it or to the composition in which it is set. The act of photography may be just as circumscribed by aesthetic intentions as the act of painting. A photograph will be designed to show its subject in a particular light and from a particular point of view, and by so doing it may reveal things about it that we do not normally observe and, perhaps, that we might not have observed but for the photograph. Such an enterprise leads to effects which are wholly proper to the art of photography, which therefore has its own peculiar way of showing the world. Why is that not enough to give to photography the status of a representational art?

20 See for example, Aaron Scharf, *Creative Photography* (London, 1975) and Rudolf Arnheim, *Film as Art* (California, 1957; London, 1958).

21 See especially Henry Peach Robinson, *The Elements of a Pictorial Photograph* (London, 1896).

I do not think that such an objection need cause me to revise my argument. For exactly the same might be said of a mirror. When I see someone in a mirror I see *him*, not his representation. This remains so even if the mirror is a distorting mirror and even if the mirror is placed where it is intentionally. This intention might even be similar to the intention in photography: to give a unique and remarkable view of an object, a view which reveals a "truth" about it that might otherwise have gone unobserved. One could even imagine an art of mirrors, an art which involves holding a mirror aloft in such a way that what is seen in the mirror is rendered by that process interesting or beautiful.

This art of mirrors may, like the art of photography, sometimes involve representation. It may, for example, involve a representation of Venus or of Silenus in the manner of the two types of "fictional" photographs considered earlier. But representation will not be a property of the *mirror*. It is impossible that I could, simply by holding a mirror before someone, make him into a representation of himself. For after all, whether I look at him or at the mirror, in either case it is *him* that I see. If the mirror is to become the expression of a representational thought, it too must be denatured; like the photomontage, it must be freed from the causal chain which links it to its subject. One can perhaps begin to see the truth in Oliver Wendell Holmes's description of the daguerreotype as a "mirror with a memory."[22] It was just such a mirror that led to the downfall of Lord Lambton.

It does not matter, therefore, how many aesthetic intentions underlie the act of photography. It does not matter that the subject, its environment, activity, or light are all consciously arranged. The real question is, What has to be done to make the resulting image into a representation? There are images which are representations (paintings) and images which are not (mirrors). To which class does the photograph belong? I have argued that it naturally belongs to the latter class. Photography can be *made* to belong to the former class by being made into the principal vehicle of the representational thought. But one must then so interfere with the relation between the photograph and its subject that it ceases to be a *photograph* of its subject. Is that not enough to show that it is not just my ideal of photography which fails to be a mode of representation, but also that representation can never be achieved through photography alone?

[22] Holmes, quoted in Beaumont Newhall, *History of Photography* (New York, 1964; London, 1972), p. 22.

A final comparison: I mark out a certain spot from which a particular view of a street may be obtained. I then place a frame before that spot. I move the frame so that, from the chosen spot, only certain parts of the street are visible, others are cut off. I do this with all the skill available to me, so that what is seen in the frame is as pleasing as it might be: the buildings within the frame seem to harmonize, the ugly tower that dominates the street is cut off from view, the centre of the composition is the little lane between two classical façades which might otherwise have gone unnoticed, and so on. There I have described an activity which is as circumscribed by aesthetic intentions as anything within the experience of the normal photographer. But how could it be argued that what I see in the frame is not the street itself but a representation of it? The very suggestion is absurd.

## 10

Here one might object that representation is not, after all, an intrinsic property either of a painting or of a description. Representation is a relation; an object can be described as a representation only if one person uses it to represent something to another. On this view, there is no such thing as "being a representation;" there is only "having a representational use." And if this were the case, my arguments would be in vain. Photographs are as much, and as little, representations as paintings, as gestures, as mirrors, as labels, and as anything else that can play its part in the process of communication.

The objection is more serious, and reflects a well-known dispute in the theory of meaning. Meaning, some say, is a property of a sentence; others, for instance, H. Paul Grice, argue that meaning is primarily a relation between utterance and speaker.[23] Now, even for Grice, there remains a distinction between utterances which are articulate and utterances which are not. Sentences are to be distinguished from nods of the head in that they participate in and exemplify a grammar, and through that grammar they can be understood independently of the context of their use. By being articulate, the sentence can stand alone as the principal expression of a thought. There arises a kind of interest in the sentence (and in its content) which is independent of any direct involvement in the act of communication. Meaning can be read *in* the sentence and need not be inferred from surrounding circumstances.

[23] "Meaning," *Philosophical Review*, LXVI (1957), pp. 377–88.

Similarly, painting, being fully articulate, can attract attention as the principal expression of a process of thought. It can be understood in isolation from the special circumstances of its creation, because each and every feature of a painting can be both the upshot of an intentional act and at the same time the creation of an intentional object. The interest in the intentional object becomes an interest in the thought which it conveys. A painter can fill his canvas with meaning in just the way that a writer may fill his prose. This is what makes painting and literature into representational arts: they are arts which can be appreciated as they are in themselves and at the same time understood in terms of a descriptive thought which they articulate.

In photography we may have the deliberate creation of an image. Moreover, I may use a photograph as a representation: I may use a photograph of Lenin as a representation of him, in the way that I might have used a clenched fist or a potato or a photograph of Hitler. The question is, What makes the image *itself* into the principal vehicle of representational thought? I wish to argue that an image can be deliberate without being properly articulate. The image becomes articulate when (a) the maker of the image can seriously address himself to the task of communicating thought through the image alone, and (b) when the spectator can see and understand the image in terms of the process of thought which it expresses. To satisfy (a) we require a painterly approach to detail; to satisfy (b) we must distract the spectator's attention from the causal relation which is the distinguishing feature of photography. Either way, the persistence of that relation – in other words, the persistence of the *photographic* image – can only hinder representation. It can contribute nothing to its achievement. This is perhaps what James Joyce meant when he wrote the following in his Paris notebooks of 1904:

> Question: Can a photograph be a work of art? Answer: A photograph is a disposition of sensible matter and may be so disposed for an aesthetic end, but it is not a human disposition of sensible matter. Therefore it is not a work of art.

If Joyce meant by "work of art" what I mean by "representation," then he was clearly getting at the same point. The property of representation, as I have characterized it, is the upshot of a complex pattern of intentional activity and the object of highly specialized responses. How can a photograph acquire that property? My answer is that it can do so only by changing in precisely those respects which distinguish photography from painting. For it is only if photography changes in those respects that the photographer can seriously address himself to the thoughts and responses of his spectators. It is only then, therefore, that the photograph becomes a proper *vehicle* of representational thought.

## 11

Photography is not representation; nor is it representation when used in the cinema. A film is a photograph of a dramatic representation, and whatever representational properties belong to it belong by virtue of the representation that is effected in the dramatic action, that is, by virtue of the words and activities of the actors in the film. *Ivan the Terrible* represents the life of Ivan, not because the camera was directed at *him*, but because it was directed at an actor who *played the part of* Ivan. Certainly the camera has its role in presenting the action, much as the apparatus of production has its role on the stage. It directs the audience's attention to this or that feature and creates, too, its own peculiar effects of atmosphere. Proper use of the camera may create an interest in situations that could not be portrayed on the stage. Hence photography permits the extension of dramatic representation into areas where previously it would not have been possible, just as music, which is not a representational art, enabled Wagner to create for the first time a theatrical representation of a cosmic theme.[24] (Consider, for example, the camera in Bergman's *Persona*, where it is used to create a dramatic situation between two characters, one of whom never speaks. Such mastery is perhaps rare, but it has existed as an ideal since the earliest days of cinema.) Nonetheless, the process of photography does not, because it cannot, *create* the representation. Thus documentary films are in no sense representations of their subject-matter. (Which is not to say that they cannot involve the realization of elaborate aesthetic ideas: it is hardly necessary to mention Leni Riefenstahl's film of the Berlin Olympics.) A cinematic record of an occurrence is not a representation of it, any more than a recording of a concert is a representation of its sound. As all must agree, representation in the cinema involves an *action*, in just the way that a play involves an action. The action is understood when the audience realizes that the figure photographed is attempting to portray adventures, actions, and feelings which are not his own, and yet which are nevertheless the proper subject-matter of aesthetic interest. It follows that the fundamental constraints which the

[24] See "Representation in Music" in my collection *The Aesthetic Understanding: Essays in the Philosophy of Art and Culture* (London: Methuen, 1983).

cinema must obey as an art form – those constraints which are integral to its very nature as a representational art – are dramatic ones, involving the representation of character and action. ("Dramatic" here does not mean "theatrical", but is applied in the sense which Henry James gave to it when he spoke of the novel as a form of dramatic art.) To succeed as cinema, a film must have true characters, and it must be true to them; the director can no more sentimentalize with impunity than can the novelist or the playwright. The true source of the badness of most cinema lies, of course, in the fact that the gorgeous irrelevancies of photography obscure the sentimentality of the dramatic aim.

Photography, far from making dramatic representation more easy, in fact makes it more difficult. Indeed, the possibility of dramatic success in the cinema is a remote one, for which there are two reasons. The first, and somewhat shallow, reason is that the film director is photographing something which either is or purports to be a part of the actual world. It follows that he can only with the greatest difficulty convey to his audience an appropriate sense of detail. Typically the audience is given no criterion of relevance, no criterion which settles what must be attended to. Was the audience meant to notice the man on the street corner, the movement of the eyebrow, the colour of the macintosh, the make of the car? In every cinematographic image, countless such questions remain unanswered. There are various reasons for this. For one thing, a film is fixed with respect to all its details; although it is a dramatic representation, it cannot exist in more than one performance. Therefore features of interpretation cannot be separated from features of the action: there is no such distinction. It is only in understanding the representation as a whole that I come to see what I should be attending to. Furthermore, the cameraman operates under a permanent difficulty in making any visual comment on the action. The difficulty can be solved, but its solution is perforce crude in comparison with the simpler devices of the stage; crude because it must both create irrelevancies and at the same time persuade us to ignore them. (Consider, for example, the ritualized expressionism of *Der blaue Engel* or *The Cabinet of Doctor Caligari*. Even Fritz Lang's *Siegfried* contains reminiscences of this *comedia dell'arte* mannerism, whereby the actor attempts to divert the audience's attention from the infinite irrelevance of detail, toward the dramatic meaning of the whole. Of course more recent directors have emancipated themselves from the theatrical constraints of expressionism; as a result they have at least felt happy to ignore the problem, even if they could not solve it.)

In the theatre the situation is different. The necessary limitations of the stage and the conventions of stage performance, which derive from the fact that the play exists independently of its performance, provide a strong representational medium through which the dramatic action is filtered. Someone with a knowledge of the conventions will see at once what is relevant and what is not. Symbolism in the theatre is therefore clear and immediate, whereas on the screen it is too often vague, portentous, and psychologically remote. Consider, for example, *L'Eclisse*, where the camera, striving again and again to make a comment, succeeds only in inflating the importance of the material surroundings out of all proportion to the sentiments of the characters. The effect is to render the image all-engrossing, while at the same time impoverishing the psychology.

It is for this reason that what often passes for photographic comment in the cinema ought more properly to be described as photographic effect. The camera may create an atmosphere – it may be an instrument of expression – but it is unable to make any precise or cogent analysis of what it shows. Consider the techniques of montage, used to such effect by the Russians. Eisenstein argues that there is a precise parallel between the technique of montage and the sequential structure of verse.[25] For example, each image that Milton presents in the following passage corresponds to a precise and unambiguous shot:

> . . . at last
> Farr in th'Horizon to the North appeer'd
> From skirt to skirt a fierie Region, stretcht
> In battailous aspect, and neerer view
> Bristl'd with upright beams innumerable
> Of rigid Spears, and Helmets throng'd, and Shields
> Various, with boastful Argument portraid,
> The banded Powers of *Satan* hasting on
> With furious expedition . . .

(One may note the cinematographic device "and neerer view" and the very Eisensteinian quality of the image that follows it.) The contention is that for each of Milton's images one may find a cinematic shot that somehow "says the same thing;" the total montage would form a dramatic unity in precisely the same sense, and for the same reason, as Milton's lines. The director will be doing something analogous to the poet: he will be focusing attention on carefully chosen details with a view to creating a unified expression of the prevailing mood.

[25] See Sergei Eisenstein, "Word and Image," *The Film Sense* (London, 1943; New York, 1969).

It should be noted, however, that each shot in the montage will also present infinitely many details that are *not* designed as objects of attention. The shot corresponding to "Helmets throng'd" will capture that idea among others, but it will also say much more that is irrelevant. It will not be able to avoid showing the *kind* of helmet, for example, the material, size, and shape of it. By so concretizing the thought, the camera leaves nothing to the imagination. As a result the detail that really matters – the thronging of Satanic helmets – is in danger of being lost. It was for this reason that Eisenstein developed techniques of contrast and composition in order to control more effectively the attention of his audience. It is a testimony to his genius that the poetry of *Ivan the Terrible* has rarely been rediscovered by subsequent directors. Even in Eisenstein, however, comment comes primarily through drama rather than through image. The whole effort of photography lies in expression and effect. And interestingly enough the clearest examples of photographic comment in the cinema come when once again the causal relation between image and subject is replaced by an intentional one. Consider the following sequence from *The Battleship Potemkin*:

1 Title: "And the rebel battleship answered the brutality of the tyrant with a shell upon the town."
2 A slowly and deliberately turning gun-turret.
3 Title: "Objective – the Odessa Theatre."
4 Marble group at the top of the theatre building.
5 Title: "On the general's headquarters."
6 Shot from the gun.
7 Two very short shots of a marble figure of Cupid above the gates of the building.
8 A mighty explosion; the gates totter.
9 Three short shots: a stone lion asleep;
a stone lion with open eyes;
a rampant stone lion.
10 New explosion, shattering the gates.[26]

Here we have one of Eisenstein's most striking visual metaphors. A stone lion rises to its feet and roars. This amazing image (impossible, incidentally, outside the limitations of the silent screen) acts as a powerful comment on the impotence of imperial splendour precisely because it startles us into a recognition of the underlying thought. But we know that this

[26] Discussed by V. I. Pudovkin, *Writings*, trans. I. Montagu (London, 1954), p. 88.

cannot be a photograph of a stone lion roaring. It is, rather, the intentional juxtaposition of unconnected images; it is the intention that we see and which determines our understanding of the sequence. It is of course lamentable that such art should have subjected itself to the inane myth-making revealed in the titles to this script; that does not alter the fact that, if there is art here, it is an art which is essentially photographic.

The second and deeper point I wish to mention is extremely difficult to express in terms that would be acceptable to the contemporary analytical philosopher. I shall try not to be too deterred by that.[27] Photography, precisely because it does not represent but at best can only distort, remains inescapably wedded to the creation of illusions, to the creation of lifelike *semblances* of things in the world. Such an art, like the art of the waxworks, is an art that provides a ready gratification for fantasy, and in so doing defeats the aims of artistic expression. A dramatic art can be significant only if it is, at some level, realistic; but to be realistic it must first forbid expression to those habits of unseriousness and wish fulfilment that play such an important part in our lives. Unless it can do that, the greatest effects of drama – such as we observe in the tragedies of the Greeks, of Racine, and of Shakespeare – will be denied to it. Art is fundamentally serious; it cannot rest content with the gratification of fantasy, nor can it dwell on what fascinates us while avoiding altogether the question of its meaning. As Freud put it in another context, art provides the path from fantasy back to reality. By creating a representation of something unreal, it persuades us to consider again those aspects of reality which, in the urgency of everyday existence, we have such strong motives for avoiding.[28] Convention in art, as Freud saw, is the great destroyer of fantasies. It prevents the ready *realization* of scenes that fascinate us, and substitutes for the creation of mere semblance the elaboration of reflective thought.

The cinema has been devoted from its outset to the creation of fantasies. It has created worlds so utterly like our own in their smallest details that we are lulled into an acceptance of their reality, and persuaded to overlook all that is banal, grotesque, or vulgar in the situations which they represent. The cinema has proved too persuasive at the level of mere

27 The point is made at greater length, and more rigorously, in my "Fantasy, Imagination and the Screen," in my *The Aesthetic of Understanding*, ch. 10.

28 See *The Standard Edition of the Complete Psychological Works of Sigmund Freud*, ed. James Strachey, 24 vols. (London, 1953–74; New York, 1976), IX, p. 153; XI, p. 50; XII, p. 224; XIII, pp. 187–8; XIV, pp. 375–7; XX, p. 64.

realization and so has had little motive to explore the significance of its subject. It is entirely beguiling in its immediacy, so that even serious critics of literature can be duped into thinking that a film like *Sunset Boulevard* expresses an aesthetic idea, instead of simply preying on the stereotyped fantasies of its audience.

Moreover, the cinema, like the waxworks, provides us with a ready means of realizing situations which fascinate us. It can address itself to our fantasy directly, without depending upon any intermediate process of thought. This is surely what distinguishes the scenes of violence which are so popular in the cinema from the conventionalized death throes of the theatre. And surely it is this too which makes photography incapable of being an erotic art, in that it presents us with the object of lust rather than a symbol of it: it therefore gratifies the fantasy of desire long before it has succeeded in understanding or expressing the fact of it. The medium of photography, one might say, is inherently pornographic.[29]

[29] I have benefited greatly from discussions with Richard Wollheim, Mark Platts, John Casey, Peter Suschitzky, and Ruby Meager, as well as from the criticisms of Robert A. Sharpe and Rickie Dammann, my fellow symposiasts at a conference organized in Bristol by Stephan Körner, to whom I am grateful for the opportunity to reflect on the nature of photography.

# 7

# HOW PHOTOGRAPHS "SIGNIFY": CARTIER-BRESSON'S "REPLY" TO SCRUTON

David Davies

## I

In an infamous passage in Book X of *The Republic*, Plato argues that artistic representations of the world can have no value for us because, like mirrors, they merely capture the appearances of things. Even if we don't buy into the Platonic metaphysics whereby the things reflected in mirrors or represented in paintings are themselves merely pale imitations of those truly real entities that are the proper objects of knowledge, the charge that artistic representations lack value requires an answer. An answer doesn't seem hard to come by, however. Here is a simple model of how representational artworks can be of value to us.

1 In the process whereby a representational artwork comes into existence, the agency of the artist mediates between the world and the artistic representation of the world such that the latter embodies the artist's way of thinking about the things portrayed.
2 Artistic representations do not merely reflect the world from a particular physical perspective. They also embody a cognitive perspective on the world, or upon the subject represented, the perspective of a particular conscious intelligence.

Given this simple model of artistic representation, however, it is easy to understand why, from its very inception, the artistic pretensions of photography have been subject to challenge. The charge is that the process whereby a photographic image is produced by the world is "causal" or "mechanical," and does not accord a significant role to the formative intelligence of the artist in the generation of the image. Because of this, it is said, photographic representations lack the cognitive dimension that allows us to take a legitimate artistic interest in representation in the plastic arts. Perhaps the most sophisticated version of this argument is contained in Roger Scruton's paper, "Photography and Representation" (reprinted as chapter 6 in this volume) – of which more below.

## II

The reflections of Henri Cartier-Bresson on photography would seem an unlikely place in which to seek a response to this sort of reasoning. For Cartier-Bresson, usually characterized as a "documentary" photographer or as a "photojournalist," has always insisted on his conception of photography as "reportage." And the ability of the photographic image to "report" on the world seems tied to its ability to provide a record that is unbiased by the mediating influence of the image-maker. Furthermore, Cartier-Bresson's own "philosophy of photography,"[1] which views the camera as "a sketch book, an instrument of intuition and spontaneity" and the photographer as one who seizes upon "the decisive moment" to capture her subject, might be thought to deny the moment of cognitive "reflection" to which the foregoing defense of representational art appeals. But I think the following brief passage from Cartier-Bresson does suggest an answer to those critics of photography to whose arguments I have just alluded. For reasons that will soon be apparent, I shall quote the passage in the original language:

> Pour "signifier" le monde, il faut se sentir impliqué dans ce que l'on découpe à travers le viseur. Cette attitude exige de la concentration, de la sensibilité, un sens de la géométrie. C'est par une économie de moyens et surtout un oubli de soi-même que l'on arrive à la simplicité d'expression. . . .
>
> Photographier: c'est dans un même instant et en une fraction de seconde reconnaître un fait et l'organisation rigoureuse des formes perçues visuellement qui expriment et signifient ce fait.[2]

1 Henri Cartier-Bresson, *The Mind's Eye* (New York: Aperture, 1999), p. 15.

2 This passage, originally part of a reflection titled "L'imaginaire d'après nature" and written in 1976, appeared in French in the 1996 collection of the same name (Paris: Editions Fata Morgana) and in English in Cartier-Bresson's 1999. The English translation, apparently by Cartier-Bresson himself, reads as follows: "In order to 'give a meaning' to the world, one has to feel oneself involved in what one frames through the viewfinder. This attitude requires concentration, a discipline of mind, sensitivity, and a sense of geometry – it is by great economy of means that one arrives at simplicity of expression. . . . To take photographs means to recognize – simultaneously and within a fraction of a second – both the fact itself and the rigorous organisation of visually perceived forms that give it meaning" (*The Mind's Eye*, pp. 15–16).

At first glance, what is at issue here is how the photographer can "capture" facts in the world – how she can employ the camera to "report" on those facts. What is puzzling, therefore, is the role accorded to "a sense of geometry" ("un sens de la géométrie") and to the ability to recognise "the rigourous organisation of visually perceived forms" ("l'organisation rigoureuse des formes perçues visuellement"). For unless one holds to an implausibly Platonic conception of the phenomenal world, it is unclear how capturing facts about that world requires that one "get the geometry right." One might try to link the required "sense of geometry" to another of Cartier-Bresson's requirements for photographic "reportage" – the loss of self-awareness – "un oubli de soi-même."[3] The "sense of geometry," it might be said, is necessary in order to produce the loss of self-awareness required for effective "reportage" – it is because the photographer is herself responsive to the formal properties of what is seen in the viewfinder that she attains the required state of self-forgetfulness. Such a reading might also fit with the "surrealist" or Buddhist interpretations of Cartier-Bresson advanced by some commentators. Such interpretations highlight biographical facts about Cartier-Bresson – his interest in Buddhism and his association, in the early 1930s, with André Breton, for example – in drawing comparisons between his photographic technique and either Zen practice in archery or the "automatic writing" advocated by Breton.[4]

I shall return to these matters later, after offering my own reading of Cartier-Bresson's remarks. But we may immediately note two difficulties with the proposed reading of the reference to "a sense of geometry." First, it leaves us still lacking an explanation as to how a loss of self-awareness, so conceived, bears upon the ability of the photographer to " 'signifie[ ]' le monde" in the images she produces. Second, Cartier-Bresson's text suggests that the engagement of the photographer's "sense of geometry,"

[3] Curiously, the 1999 English translation (apparently by Cartier-Bresson himself) of this 1976 text, "The Mind's Eye," omits any reference to the "oubli de soi-même" identified as the principal requirement for simplicity of expression. As noted in the previous footnote, the sentence in question is translated: "it is by great economy of means that one arrives at simplicity of expression" (ibid., pp. 15–16).

[4] For example, Yves Bonnefoy, "Foreword," in *Henri Cartier-Bresson: Photographer* (Paris: Delpire, 1979), and Gérard Macé, "Preface: The Lightest Baggage," in Cartier-Bresson, *The Mind's Eye*, pp. 8–11, profess the influence of Buddhist thinking on Cartier-Bresson, while Colin Westerbeck and Joel Meyerowitz, *Bystander: A History of Street Photography* (Boston: Little Brown, 1994), pp. 153–9 and Ian Walker, *City Gorged with Dreams: Surrealism and Documentary Photography in Interwar Paris* (Manchester: Manchester University Press, 2002) suggest that Breton influenced Cartier-Bresson's conception of photography. I thank Scott Walden for drawing my attention to the possibility of a surrealist reading of the passage from Cartier-Bresson cited above.

and her consequent ability to "'signifie[ ]' le monde," depend upon her ability to forget herself, rather than vice versa. It is the formal properties of the image that somehow "expriment et signifient ce fait," not the disengaged nature of the photographer's attention to that fact, as the second part of the quotation makes clear.

To get a clearer sense of what Cartier-Bresson is saying, we need to grasp what he has in mind in characterizing the photographer as one whose aim is "'signifier' le monde," or about the manner in which formal properties of what is imaged "expriment et signifient" the facts that the photographer strives to capture. First, "signifier" doesn't have the English sense of "signify" where this is equivalent to "denote," or to "represent" in a denotational sense. The object of the verb "signifier" is normally that which is *meant* by an expression or gesture, or (a secondary sense) that which a speaker (or a gesture of a speaker) "makes known" or "makes apparent."[5] Second, the use of "scare quotes" around "signifier" warns us that this is not a standard use of the French term. This suggests that we should translate the proposed goal of photography – "'signifier' le monde" – as something like "to 'give a meaning' to the world,"[6] or perhaps "to make the world apparent."

The latter reading, with its implication that a photograph "uncovers" or "reveals" the world, accords most closely with the idea of photography as "reportage," but leaves quite mysterious the role ascribed to form and geometry in the "revealing of facts." The former reading seems even less promising, in that it is more enigmatic, and no less pregnant with the question how formal or geometrical properties can play a necessary role in conferring a meaning on the world as represented in a photograph. Nevertheless, I think the first reading – that the photographer "gives a meaning" to the world – is a crucial part of what Cartier-Bresson is saying, and that, once understood, this is in fact quite compatible with the second reading – that the photographer "makes the world apparent" – if we take what is made apparent to be a meaning that the world can be taken to have.

## III

On the reading I shall elaborate and defend, Cartier-Bresson can indeed be interpreted as offering an answer to one of the more-developed

5 See, for example, *Le Petit Robert* (Paris: SNL, 1981), p. 1814.

6 As noted above in note 2, this is how "pour 'signifier' le monde" is rendered in the 1999 English translation – apparently by Cartier-Bresson himself – of "The Mind's Eye."

variants on the traditional challenge to the artistic pretensions of photography cited above. So read, Cartier-Bresson's remarks supplement and support one of the most forthright defenses of photography against this challenge. First, let me sketch the case against photography, as presented by Scruton in his essay "Photography and Representation."

Scruton argues that, even if certain photographs have interesting *formal* properties, there can be no representational properties of photographs that have an artistic value analogous to that which inheres in the representational properties of works in the plastic arts. The argument is sometimes opaque, both in its detail and in its intended conclusion,[7] and there is arguably an inconsistency in the relationship that is claimed to hold between two distinct theses advanced by Scruton concerning photographs:

(T1) There can be no photographic representations.
(T2) We cannot take an aesthetic or properly artistic interest in the "content" of a photographic image, where such an interest requires that we take the image to "embod[y] in perceptual form" a thought about its subject.

What is puzzling is that, in places, Scruton takes our inability to take a properly artistic interest in the "content" of a photographic image (T2) as the reason for denying that photographs "represent" their subjects in the artistically relevant sense (T1): "It is precisely when we have the communication of thoughts about a subject that the concept of representation becomes applicable; and therefore literature and painting are representational in the same sense."[8] However, when considering the possibility that (T2) is false – that we *can* regard a photographic image as embodying the photographer's thought about the subject, in virtue of the way in which he or she has chosen to shoot the subject and to compose the picture – Scruton offers what appear to be quite independent grounds for denying the status of representation to the photographic image. He argues that a photograph no more *represents* what is imaged in it than does a mirror or, indeed, an empty frame held up to nature.[9]

7 For a rather different reading of Scruton's argument, see Dominic Lopes, "The Aesthetics of Photographic Transparency," *Mind* 112 (2003): 433–48.

8 Roger Scruton, "Photography and Representation," in *The Aesthetic Understanding* (London: Methuen, 1983). Repr. in Alex Neill and Aaron Ridley, *Arguing about Art* (New York: McGraw-Hill, 1995), pp. 89–113: p. 93. Also repr. in this volume, as chapter 6. All references are to the Neill and Ridley reprint, with page numbers for this volume in parenthesis.

9 Ibid., pp. 106–7 (143).

Rather than enter further into Scruton exegesis or into the semantics of the term "representation," however, I shall extract what I take to be the most interesting and challenging line of reasoning from his paper, namely that which is offered in support of (T2).[10] This line of reasoning begins by marking what is taken to be a fundamental difference between the images produced by painters and those produced by photographers. In the case of paintings, what an image is *of* depends crucially upon the successful realization of the representational intentions of its maker. On the other hand, it may be said, what is imaged in a photograph is entirely a function of the causal process that produced the image – the image is *of* whatever generated the pattern of light rays responsible for producing its monochromatic or polychromatic array.

This difference might seem to have little bearing on the status of photographic images as representations or as art. For, it might be said, the taking of a photograph is just as intentional an activity as the painting of a picture. However, Scruton argues, the intentional activity that enters into the taking of photographs does not bear in any essential way upon what we *see* in a photograph, or the interest we take in a photograph, whereas such intentions do enter into our commerce with paintings in a way that is crucial to the capacity of the latter to function as properly artistic representations.[11] First, so he claims, the way we look at paintings is deeply informed by our awareness that they are the products of representational acts on the part of their makers. We take it that the manifest properties of the image are ones that were intentionally conferred upon it by the artist, and we may therefore regard the painted canvas as an expression of thought about its subject. This enters into our engagement with a picture in two ways. First, we do not look *through* the canvas to what it represents, but rather take its representational content to be determinable

10 There is also reason to think that this best represents Scruton's considered position, given the overall shape of his argument and his suggestion, in the introduction to his paper, that the issue is not merely whether we can *call* photographs "representations," but "whether there is some feature, suitably called representation, common to painting and photography . . . [and] whether that feature has in each case a comparable aesthetic value, so that we can speak not only of representation but also of representational art" (ibid., p. 89 [139]).

11 Expressed in terms of Scott Walden's very helpful distinction, Scruton claims that (a) while mental states may be secondarily involved in the production of photographic images, they are not primarily involved, and that (b) primary involvement is a necessary condition for properly artistic representation in an image: see Scott Walden, "Objectivity in Photography," *British Journal of Aesthetics* 45: 3 (2005): 258–72. The Arnheimian response to Scruton outlined below grants the former, but denies the latter, claim.

only by scrupulous attention to the painted surface itself. Second, we attend to *how* the subject has been rendered, and thereby treat the painting as "a thought [about its subject] embodied in perceptual form."[12]

This is crucial, for Scruton, to the properly aesthetic/artistic interest that we take in the representational content of a painting, and thus to the artistic value of representation in such works. For, he argues, an aesthetic interest in something must be an interest in it "for its own sake," and an aesthetic interest in a representational painting must be an interest in inherent properties of *the representation*, rather than an ulterior interest in the thing represented. The representational content of a painting enters into our assessment of its artistic value because a properly artistic interest in a representational painting is always an interest in *how* the representation renders the subject in two distinct senses:[13] first, it is an interest in the thought expressed about the subject – what we may term the "thought-content" of the representation; and second it is an interest in the manner in which this thought-content has been expressed through the manipulation of the medium – what we may term the "contentful articulation of the representational medium."

However, according to Scruton, no such account can be given of our engagement with a photographic image, for the latter can at best be viewed as a "sign" of the way the photographer thinks about her subject, and never as the *artistic expression* of that thought.[14] For, so he claims, there are two crucial differences between painting and photography in this respect, both of which derive from the essentially causal nature of the process whereby photographic images are generated. First, because we know that what is imaged in a photograph must have existed in front of the camera when the image was generated, our attitude to photographs is "made practical,"[15] in that we are led to look through the image to its subject and to take an interest both in the existence of the subject and in the truths about it revealed by the photograph. Photographs therefore serve not as things in which we are interested for their own sakes, but rather as entities in which we have an ulterior interest parasitic upon our interest in their subjects.

Even if this is true, it might seem to be no more than an interesting fact about human psychology, and therefore no obstacle to the claim that

12 Scruton, "Photography and Representation," p. 93 (142).

13 Only the first of these senses is explicit in Scruton's essay, although I think he would also endorse the second, which seems to further strengthen his argument.

14 Scruton, "Photography and Representation," p. 98 (149).

15 Ibid., p. 103 (153).

we *can*, if we wish, take a properly aesthetic interest in how the subject is represented in a photograph. But, so Scruton further charges, such an interest is impossible because we cannot *see* how the subject is represented (in either of the above senses) by looking more closely at the photograph. In the case of paintings, our attention to the finer details of the picture is rewarded by a greater appreciation of how the subject has been represented, both in terms of thought-content and in terms of medium articulation. This is possible because, assuming the competence of the artist, we are able to refer every detail of the painting to the intentional activity of the artist. In virtue of this, Scruton maintains, painting provides us with "a medium transparent to human intention":[16] the content of the artist's thinking about the subject can be seen in the ways in which pigment has been applied to the painted surface. But this is what we lack in the case of the photographic image, since so many of the details are determined by *the world*, given the causal process whereby the image is produced. While the photographer is able to arrange details of the subject, and indeed to choose what to photograph and the perspective from which the photograph is taken, none of this, according to Scruton, can be determined by the receiver who more closely scrutinizes the image. At best, as noted above, the viewer can take the image as a sign from which certain representational intentions might be inferred. In photography, the medium "has lost all its importance: it can present us with what we see, but it cannot tell us how to see it."[17]

## IV

To see how we might read Cartier-Bresson as providing an answer to this argument, we must consider what might be regarded as the most comprehensive "response" to Scruton to be found in the literature, a "response" composed some 50 years before Scruton's article appeared! In papers written in the early 1930s defending the idea of photographic and cinematic art, Rudolph Arnheim is responding to earlier and less sophisticated versions of the kind of challenge mounted by Scruton. His concern is with those who argue that:

> "Film cannot be art, for it does nothing but reproduce reality mechanically." Those who defend this point of view are reasoning from the analogy of painting. In painting, the way from reality to the picture lies via

16 Ibid., p. 104 (155).
17 Ibid., p. 101 (152).

> the artist's eye and nervous system, his hand and, finally, the brush that puts strokes on canvas. The process is not mechanical as that of photography, in which the light rays reflected from the object are collected by a system of lenses and are then directed onto a sensitive plate where they produce chemical changes.[18]

But the main thrust of his reasoning seems equally apt as a response to Scruton's arguments, and indeed some passages read as if they were written precisely to counter the latter.

For Arnheim, art is a matter of expression. But what is expressed by an artwork is not to be thought of as a feeling, but, rather, as a way of thinking about the subject imaged in a work.[19] Thus, "expression," as understood by Arnheim, is analogous to "artistic representation," as understood by Scruton, in that both involve an image's embodiment of a thought about its subject in perceptual form. Arnheim's claim that photographic and cinematic media are genuinely "expressive" is therefore a direct challenge to Scruton's claim that photography cannot be a genuinely representational art form. Furthermore, as we shall see, Arnheim offers responses to both of the arguments marshaled by Scruton in defense of his position – that (a) our interest in a photograph is always in the subject causally responsible for the image rather than in the manner in which the subject is depicted, and that (b) we cannot determine the thought-content of a photograph by attending closely to details of the image.

There are two steps to Arnheim's argument.[20] First, he identifies a number of respects in which a photographic image necessarily departs from being a "mechanical reproduction/recording" of reality. Then he argues that photographic art is possible precisely in virtue of these departures from mechanical reproduction, which furnish the photographer with the resources that make expressive use of the medium possible. To understand the argument, we must first clarify what is meant by a "mechanical reproduction" of reality. Noël Carroll, in a critical discussion of Arnheim, attributes to the latter the thesis that a "mechanical recording" of an aspect

18 Rudolf Arnheim, *Film as Art* (Berkeley: University of California Press, 1957), p. 8. Arnheim doesn't identify who he has in mind, but for a lively critical discussion of earlier proponents of such arguments, such as P. H. Emerson, see Patrick Maynard, *The Engine of Visualization: Thinking Through Photography* (Ithaca: Cornell University Press, 1997), pp. 269–77, 290–3. See also Noël Carroll, *Philosophical Problems of Classical Film Theory* (Princeton: Princeton University Press, 1988), pp. 20–9.

19 Rudolf Arnheim, *Art and Visual Perception* (Berkeley: University of California Press, 1954), ch. X.

20 Given the theme of this essay, I shall restrict myself to Arnheim's argument as it applies to photography, passing over its extension to cinema.

of reality is one that is unimaginative, or that stresses quantitative aspects of the subject, or that focuses on those aspects of things of which people are normally aware in ordinary perception.[21] Arnheim is then taken to be arguing that photography can function as an expressive medium through eschewing the mechanical, so construed: expression depends upon photographing things from unusual perspectives, or focusing on unfamiliar aspects of things.[22] Carroll responds that photographs that focus on the ordinary or the quantitative can be expressive of precisely that fact.[23]

Carroll rightly notes a lack of consistency in Arnheim's talk of "mechanical recording,"[24] but defends his interpretation of this term by contrasting it with what he sees as the only alternative, an alternative he takes to be incoherent even if it most often seems to be what Arnheim is saying. The alternative reading is that a "mechanical recording" would capture the way in which things are normally perceived, in the sense that it would reproduce the way a subject would look to a normal perceiver under normal conditions of observation. Such a reading is incoherent, according to Carroll, because there could not be a photographic or cinematic recording of anyone's perceptions: "Arnheim cannot mean that art must diverge from the mechanical recording of normal perception – no one can mechanically copy my perceptions. My percepts, for example, make no imprint on celluloid."[25]

What Carroll misses, here, I think, is that there is another sense in which it might be held that photographs merely record or reproduce "what we perceive," and it is this that Arnheim is trying to capture in much of his talk of "merely mechanical recording," where he seeks to contrast *any* photographic image with a "merely mechanical recording."[26] His claim

21 Carroll, *Philosophical Problems*, p. 76.
22 Ibid., pp. 36ff., 77.
23 Ibid., p. 78.
24 Ibid., pp. 31–2.
25 Ibid., p. 76.
26 I say in *much* of his talk, because it is undeniable that Arnheim sometimes uses "mechanical" in the sense specified by Carroll – for example, in his discussion of "the projection of solids upon a plane surface" and of the "absence of the space-time continuum." But, in the discussion of other characteristic features of the photographic medium – "reduction of depth," "delimitation of the image," and "absence of the non-visual world of the senses" – the claim is clearly that photography is by its very nature non-mechanical, rather than something that can be pursued in a more or less mechanical manner. Matters are complicated, however, because, as noted below, Arnheim also believes that it is by offering images that are non-mechanical (in Carroll's sense) that the photographer can make salient to the viewer her expressive exploitation of the non-mechanical (in my sense) nature of the photographic medium.

is that a photographic or cinematic image is by its very nature non-mechanical in that it fails, in certain systematic ways, to record or reproduce *what is given to* normal perceptual experience, the optical and other information about the world whose processing by the visual and nervous system issues in such experience. Consider Arnheim's summary of the argument in Part 1 of *Film as Art*, where the purportedly "mechanical" nature of photographic imaging is critically assessed. What has been established, Arnheim claims, is that "the images we receive of the physical world differ from those on the movie screen."[27] In a later summary of the overall argument for the expressive potential of photography, Arnheim puts this in the following way:

> Challenged by the favorite argument of people who dislike film – that it is nothing but the mechanical reproduction and therefore not art – we have examined in detail the various aspects of filmic representation and have found that even at the most elementary level there are significant divergences between the image that the camera makes of reality and that which the human eye sees.[28]

Arnheim's talk of "the images we receive of the physical world" is unhelpful, since what we receive is not images but information. But correcting for this misspeaking, we can characterize a "merely mechanical recording," for Arnheim, as one which preserves and makes available to us all of the information about a given scene whose processing by the visual and nervous system results in perceptual experience of that scene. If photographs were indeed such recordings, then, in looking at a photograph, we might hope to replicate the visual experience obtainable by directly observing the photographed scene, just as we may imagine that, in listening to a sound recording of a concert, we are replicating the acoustic experience of those who directly heard the concert. But, if photographs are mechanical recordings so understood, then a photograph of a subject can no more embody a thought about that subject than can the subject itself when standardly perceived. Arnheim's claim is that, of necessity, photographs can preserve only some of the visually processable information issuing from a scene, and that it is in many cases up to the photographer to decide *which* information is preserved in a given photographic image.

A couple of examples will help to bring this out. First, as a projection of a three-dimensional reality onto a two-dimensional plane, a photographic

27 Arnheim, *Film as Art*, p. 34.
28 Ibid., p. 127.

image of X necessarily fails to reproduce many of the depth-cues available in the ordinary perception of X, and, as a result, certain phenomena in ordinary perception that are a function of depth-perception are not preserved – in particular, constancy of shape and size over distance and the sense of an object continuing when it is overlapped by another object in the visual field. Furthermore, while the perspective and angle from which a scene is viewed in ordinary perception rarely admits of an explanation in terms of purposes and intentions, the manner in which a subject is presented in a photograph is almost always to be referred to a choice on the part of the photographer who is showing us the scene from this perspective for a reason. Second, in the kinds of photographs of concern to Arnheim and in much "art" photography, we confront a monochromatic image of a polychromatic scene. Third, any photographic image strictly delimits the pictured space, whereas in ordinary perception we receive information concerning things in peripheral vision and are able to take in the surrounding circumstances at will through controlled eye and body movement. And fourth, our perceptual experience depends not only upon visual cues but also upon other sensory stimuli. We perceptually encounter the world as embodied perceivers, but the information that informs such aspects of ordinary perception cannot be preserved in a photographic image.

Arnheim's second claim is that photography can serve as an expressive medium precisely because the images produced by those who work in this medium necessarily depart from being mechanical recordings of reality.[29] All of those respects in which a photograph fails as a mechanical recording require that the photographer make certain choices, and, by making those choices apparent to the viewer, she can make manifest in the image the thought thereby embodied about the subject of the photograph. For example, by choosing a particular angle from which to photograph a subject, the photographer leads the receiver who studies the image to ascribe intentions underlying such a choice.[30] Again, Arnheim compares the abilities of the painter and the photographer to "convey [their] artistic intention"[31] by the use of lighting and the distribution of color and monochromatic masses. And, in choosing how to delimit the image, the photographer has "the greatest possible control of his audience's attention."[32] By skillfully manipulating those features of the photographic image

[29] Ibid., pp. 9, 35.
[30] Ibid., pp. 47ff.
[31] Ibid., p. 66.
[32] Ibid., p. 85.

that necessarily distinguish it from a "mechanical recording" of its subject, therefore, the photographer, like the painter, is able to produce an image which "embodies thought about its subject" in such a way as to engage the viewer in a detailed scrutiny of the image. Such scrutiny attends to the image itself, rather than using it merely as a means of access to its subject, and enables the viewer to appreciate how the subject has been represented in both of the above senses. Thus, contrary to Scruton's charge, photography, no less than painting, can serve as a "medium transparent to human intention."

## V

In his detailed and very interesting discussion of photographic and cinematic expression, Arnheim offers many examples of ways in which the choices photographers have to make in respect of the non-mechanical aspects of the photographic image can serve expressive purposes. But *how* are the photographer's choices made salient to the viewer? It is in answer to *this* question that Arnheim prescribes photographing things from unusual perspectives, and focusing on unfamiliar aspects of things.[33] While "mechanical reproduction" is not, *pace* Carroll, to be identified with the unimaginative, the quantitative, and the customary, it is, according to Arnheim, through the imaginative, exaggerated, or unfamiliar manner in which the photographer presents her subject that she can make salient the expressive choices involved in the taking of her photographic images. Carroll is surely right in questioning this constructive thesis on Arnheim's part, but then an alternative account of expressive salience is called for. Here, I think, is where Cartier-Bresson's claim that the photographer must exercise a sense of geometry can supplement Arnheim's answer to the Scrutonian arguments.[34]

First, we may note, given our earlier discussion, that Cartier-Bresson's talk of photographs " 'giving a meaning to' the world" is talk about what

[33] To create a work of art, the photographer must "consciously stress the peculiarities of his medium" (ibid., p. 35).

[34] This is not to say that Arnheim is unaware of the significance of "geometry" and "composition." Discussing the composition of a shot in a film by Alexander Room, for example, Arnheim asserts that this "guides the spectator's attention, gives him directions, indicates the interpretation he is to put upon objects," and speaks of how "a connection is established by means of perspective between two features of a situation" (ibid., pp. 49, 51). But he also ties this to the use of the exaggerated and the unusual.

Arnheim terms "expression" and what Scruton terms the "aesthetic/artistic" value of a representation. In all three cases, what is at issue is the ability of a photograph to "embody a thought in perceptual form" in a manner analogous to representational paintings. That Cartier-Bresson is concerned with the ability to articulate and communicate such "thoughts" through photography, and that he believes this ability to depend crucially upon the "geometry" or composition of a photograph, is clear from many of his observations in "The Decisive Moment" and "The Mind's Eye." Take, for example, the following passage – which follows the remarks about what is necessary "pour 'signifier' le monde" – quoted earlier in French but now given in Cartier-Bresson's English translation: "To take photographs means to recognize – simultaneously and within a fraction of a second – both the fact itself and the rigorous organization of visually perceived forms that give it meaning."[35] The photographer presents, in her photographs, facts grasped as contentful, where the content is given through the "geometry" of the image. In "The Decisive Moment," he puts this point as follows: "To me, photography is the simultaneous recognition, in a fraction of a second, of the significance of an event as well as of a precise organization of forms which give that event its proper expression."[36] Furthermore, the photographer uses her images to communicate the significances that she finds expressed in the organization of forms captured in them. The objective is "to depict the content of some event which is in the process of unfolding and to communicate impressions."[37]

Cartier-Bresson insists, throughout "The Decisive Moment," that it is only through the "geometrical" or compositional aspects of the image that the significance of events can be visually apprehended and communicated. "If a photograph is to communicate its subject in all its intensity, the relationship of form must be rigorously established . . ." ". . . for me, content cannot be separated from form. By form, I mean a rigorous organization of the interplay of surfaces, lines, and values. It is in this organization alone that our conceptions and emotions become concrete and communicable."[38] The integral relationship, for Cartier-Bresson, between the meaning to be communicated through a photograph and its "form" or "composition" is even more unequivocally asserted in his claim that "one does not add composition as though it were an afterthought superimposed on the basic subject material, since it is impossible to

35 Cartier-Bresson, *The Mind's Eye*, p. 16.
36 Ibid., p. 42.
37 Ibid., p. 24.
38 Ibid., pp. 32, 42.

separate content from form."[39] The claim, I take it, is that the "thought" about the subject of a photograph which the latter "embodies in perceptual form" is expressed through the compositional relationships between the elements that make up the image: only through the organization of those elements is that thought expressed, and only through the viewer's apprehension of that organization can the thought be communicated.

However, as Cartier-Bresson repeatedly insists, composition, for him, is not the result of prior rational reflection upon different ways in which elements might be organized for expressive purpose. Rather, where the world to which "meaning" is to be given is "the world of real things," rather than the artificial world of the studio, it is the photographer's "eye," her intuitions and instincts, working in unison with her sensitivity to the meanings and interest of events in the world, that enables her to compose expressive images – photography of this sort requires "putting one's head, one's eye, and one's heart on the same axis":[40]

> Composition must be one of our constant preoccupations, but at the moment of shooting it can stem only from our intuition, for we are out to capture the fugitive moment, and all the interrelationships involved are on the move. . . . In a photograph, composition is the result of a simultaneous coalition, the organic coordination of elements seen by the eye. . . . Visual organization can stem only from a developed instinct.[41]

It is only when the photographer sees the finished picture that she can analyze it in terms of the compositional features in virtue of which it expresses what it does: "Any geometrical analysis, any reducing of the picture to a schema, can be done only (because of its nature) after the photograph has been taken, developed, and printed."[42]

The role which Cartier-Bresson accords to "intuition" or "instinct" in the generation of expressive images, however, might be thought to undermine my contention that his talk of the essential "geometry" of the image can supplement Arnheim's answer to Scruton. For it might seem that, where the act of composition is assigned to the workings of instinct rather than reason, we cannot take the photographer to be consciously employing geometrical properties of the image in the interests of perceptually embodying her thoughts about the subject, and thus we

39 Ibid., p. 32.
40 Ibid., pp. 32, 16.
41 Ibid., p. 34.
42 Ibid.

cannot rightly see in the resulting image those "choices" of the photographer whereby she presents her subject in a certain way. Indeed, those who have urged a "surrealist" interpretation of Cartier-Bresson's practice might maintain that he repudiates any aim at conscious design, and holds only that the photographer should be open to whatever chance or unconscious processes might produce a geometrically interesting image.[43]

But this objection rests upon a failure to distinguish two senses in which the photographer can be said to "consciously employ geometrical properties of the image" for expressive purposes – what we might term "reflective composition" and "intuitive composition." It is clear from the passages cited above that Cartier-Bresson takes the photographer's aim to be expression in Arnheim's sense, and that the taking of an image is guided by the recognition of a "meaning" of an event which is both expressed by and communicable through the organization of elements captured in the image. Given that the act of (intuitively) composing the image is so guided, we can rightly read it as expressive in virtue of the choices made by the photographer in taking *that* image with *that* composition. While the composition is not the result of conscious *reflection* of the kind that might engage a photographer working in a studio, this reflects the circumstances under which the photographer is working, and in no way impugns the expressive function of her images.[44] Indeed, there is no reason why we could not extend Cartier-Bresson's account to allow for reflective composition of the image when permitted by the context or dictated by the disposition of the photographer.[45]

The "sense of geometry" taken by Cartier-Bresson to be essential for the expression and communication, through a photographic image, of the apprehended significance of an event bears directly upon the obstacles cited by Scruton in arguing against the idea that expression so conceived can occur in the photographic medium. First, as a direct or indirect function of the distribution of lines and masses in the image, the geometry of a photograph directs attention to the image itself, preventing the receiver from treating it as a transparent window upon its subject. This applies also to those geometrical properties of the image that depend upon its

43 I am grateful to Scott Walden for raising this difficulty.

44 For a more detailed and illuminating discussion of the role of the photographer's "eye" in the composition of her photographs, see Patrick Maynard's contribution to this volume (chapter 8).

45 For a similar response to this kind of worry about how we should reconcile Cartier-Bresson's talk of "geometry" and "composition" with his insistence on the instinctive nature of his photographic practice, see Bonnefoy, "Foreword."

being a representation of a three-dimensional space, for the appreciation of these geometrical properties depends not merely upon our awareness of properties of the three-dimensional space, but also upon our awareness of the manner in which that space is articulated in the two-dimensional image.

Second, the geometrical properties of the image immediately refer the viewer to the intentional agency of the photographer and to the expressive purposes that are manifest in the pictorial composition. They indicate how the photographer intended the photograph to be viewed, the path that the eye is intended to follow, the way that the subject is meant to be looked at. Thus the "geometry" of a photograph serves both as the necessary stimulus to a detailed scrutiny of the image for its intentional content, and as a necessary guide to the viewer in her engagement in this scrutiny which leads her to see the subject in a particular way in attending to the details of the image.

To see how geometry can guide us in such scrutiny, consider one of the most obviously "geometric" of Cartier-Bresson's photographs, taken in Abruzzi in Italy in 1952 (figure 7.1). The "geometry" of the image is striking and complex. It incorporates both properties that belong to the image as a two-dimensional design (as is readily apparent if one inverts the image), and properties that it possesses as a representation of a three-dimensional space (the receding and returning cobbled street to the right and centre and the narrowing and descending stairway in the bottom left of the image). The descending railings in the bottom right-hand corner lead the eye to the two figures on the staircase, and then, via the diagonal fence running from the left-hand side of the image, to the huddled groups of figures in the square in the background. However, as we look into the square, the curving arch above the figures leads us back towards our starting point, until we encounter the group of figures in front of the church on the right, and the child whose arms mirror the curve of the arch and also the curve of the hitherto-unnoticed thinner archway that spans the two women in the stairwell. We now see the two curves for what they are, a sort of structural canopy over the stairwell that leads our eyes to the face of the church itself, with its Latin inscription, "Pray for us," familiar from the Catholic services that we take to be central to the life of the people portrayed. We see the figures as enacting their lives in a kind of passive acceptance of a divine will that shelters and structures their existence, lives punctuated by practices and rituals into which the children before the door of the church are already being admitted. The "thought embodied in perceptual form" in this photograph is graspable only through a careful attention to the details of the image, an attention which

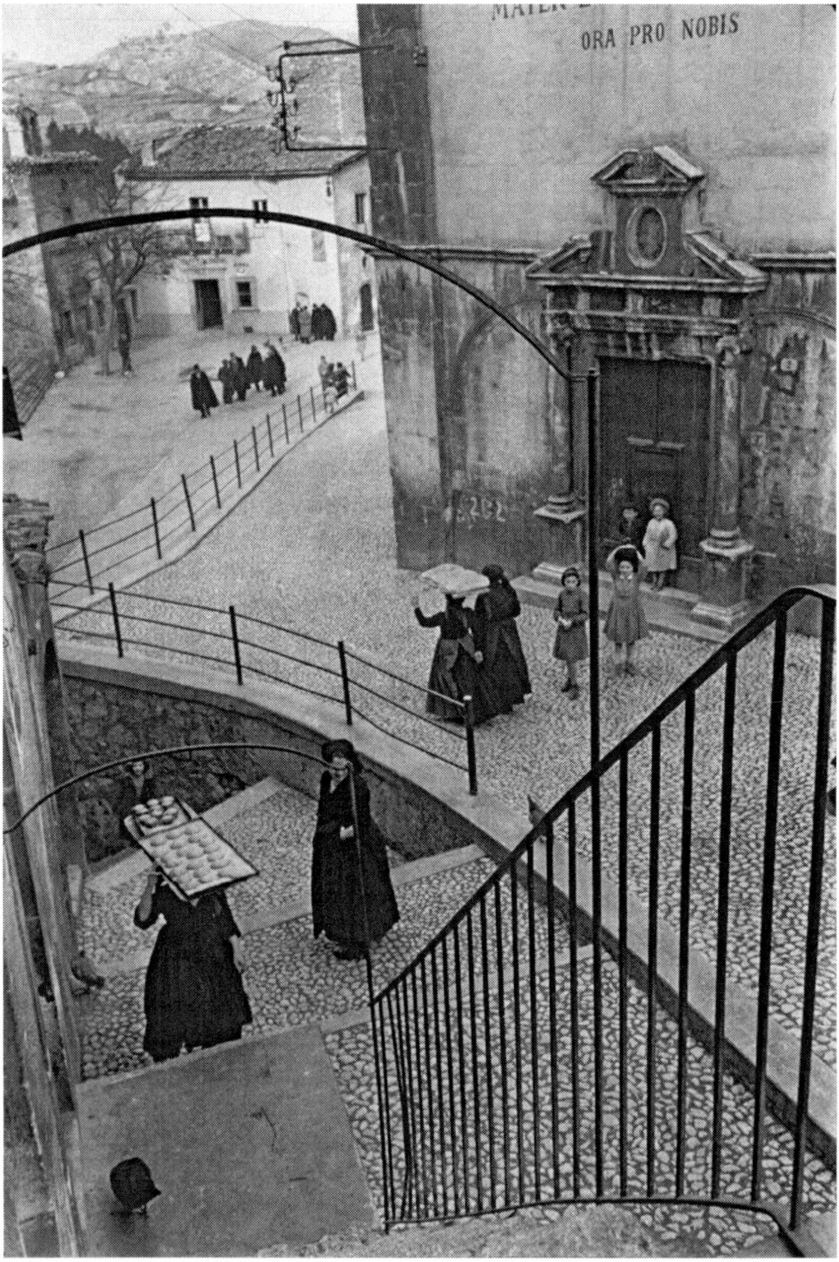


**Figure 7.1** Henri Cartier-Bresson, *Abruzzi, Village of Aquila*, 1951. Magnum Photos.

is guided by the arrangement of lines and structures that make up its "geometry." In attending to these details, however, we never look *through* the image to the scene causally responsible for it, but always refer these details, in our looking, to an act of composing an image that expresses a significance apprehended in that scene. Cartier-Bresson's "sense of geometry" plays an essential part in the apprehension of a significance in the imaged scene expressed and communicable through the composition of the image – the "geometry" through which the image "gives a meaning" to the world depicted.[46]

Let me counter one possible objection to this reading of Cartier-Bresson, insofar as it is offered as a response to Scruton. It might be argued that, even if viewers of photographs can be guided in a principled way in the ascription of representational content to photographs, the "thought about the subject" that is referred to the photograph is not *seen* in the photograph in the way that, in the case of a painting, we have the embodiment of a thought in perceptual form. Rather, it might be said, that the subject is being represented in a certain way is something *inferred* on the basis of what can be seen in the photograph. Thus, to refer back to a distinction drawn by Scruton, photographs may function as *signs* of thoughts but not as objects expressive of those thoughts.

This distinction seems to me to be ill-motivated, however. For the process of interpreting the expressive content of a *painting* is surely both perceptual *and* inferential, and requires that we relate observable details of the painting to a presumed history of making, in a given art-historical context, where manipulating pigment on canvas in a particular way can be taken to embody a particular way of thinking about the subject. What is crucial for the "aesthetic" nature of our appreciative engagement with a painting is not that it be free of inferential activity, but that our inferences always be grounded in and further inform our perceptions of the details of the painting. But this is surely precisely what is going on

[46] For a similar strategy in explaining how geometry "signifies" in Cartier-Bresson's photographs, see Bonnefoy's discussion of the picture *Athens 1953*: "Here is a juxtaposition of old age and youth, deformity and beauty, everyday life and dream, which immediately conveys that organic relationship between every thing and every other of which Cartier-Bresson is the poet. But how is this relationship shown? By the quite formal tension which has for a second united the principal signifiers, the statues and the women beneath; form thus plays the role of the syntax that makes a sentence readable" (ibid.). Or consider the role played by the almost perfectly triangular composition in bringing into dialogue the two male figures lying on the grass, one contemplative and withdrawn and the other sprawling and insensitive to what goes on around him, in his *Marseilles 1932*.

in the above reading of Cartier-Bresson's photograph. The latter, I conclude, functions as an "expressive" object, in Arnheim's sense, no less than representational paintings do. That the medium is film rather than pigment, and that the distribution of illumination on the negative is caused by physical processes in the world rather than by the intentional manipulation of brushes, does not preclude artistic representation or expression: it simply offers a different form for such expression to take. And that the subject of a photograph, in the bare sense, is an existent that stands in a causal relation to the image rather than an intentional object of the painter's devising, real or invented, does not entail that our interest in a photograph must be in its bare subject. What is represented in a photograph can be seen-in the image, no less than what is seen-in a painting, and our appreciative interest in each can be in *how* a subject has been presented, in both senses, rather than merely in the subject itself.[47]

47 An earlier version of this essay was presented at a symposium on the philosophy of photography at the annual meeting of the Canadian Philosophical Association, 2002. I would like to thank my fellow symposiasts, Karen Bardsley, Sherri Irvin, and Dom Lopes, and members of the audience, for helpful feedback. I would also like to thank Scott Walden and Berys Gaut for reading and providing very constructive criticisms of later drafts.

# 8

# SCALES OF SPACE AND TIME IN PHOTOGRAPHY: "PERCEPTION POINTS TWO WAYS"

Patrick Maynard

A question fundamental to the philosophy of any art is how it be can be so meaningful to us. Two extremes of explanation posit entirely autonomous sources of value for works of art or, in polar opposition, attempt to reduce artistic value to non-artistic significances.[1] Varieties of neither view seeming satisfactory; philosophers are in a familiar position, explaining how artistic meaningfulness can be inextricable from, yet also irreducible to, basic life values. This essay attempts such a philosophical reconciliation for the familiar street-photography snapshot, leaving open generalization to other kinds of photography, depiction, and art.[2] Since evaluative

[1] The most discussed example of the former is Clive Bell, but Oscar Wilde is also notable. For relevant excerpts from both, see Susan Feagin and Patrick Maynard, eds., *Aesthetics* (Oxford: Oxford University Press, 1997). Examples of the opposite view abound, in theories such as Tolstoy's (also in *Aesthetics*), popular attitudes, cultural policies. For a recent, best-selling, example, see Steven Pinker, *How the Mind Works* (New York: W. W. Norton & Co., 1997). The "*irreducible* . . . as well as *inextricable*" idea – but as applied to the historical "conditions of emergence" of artworks – is due to Michael Podro, *The Critical Historians of Art* (London: Yale University Press, 1982), p. xviii.

[2] This essay may be read as an investigation of ideas, including the following, from Ben Lifson's essay, "Garry Winogrand's Art of the Actual," in Garry Winogrand, *The Man in the Crowd: The Uneasy Streets of Garry Winogrand* (San Francisco: Fraenkel Gallery, 1999): "The figure group is the main building block of a Winogrand picture. It gives the picture its major shape; . . . orders, clarifies and stills but does not rectify the disorder" (p. 159), "He taught us to see . . . the world we create by acting together in public space"

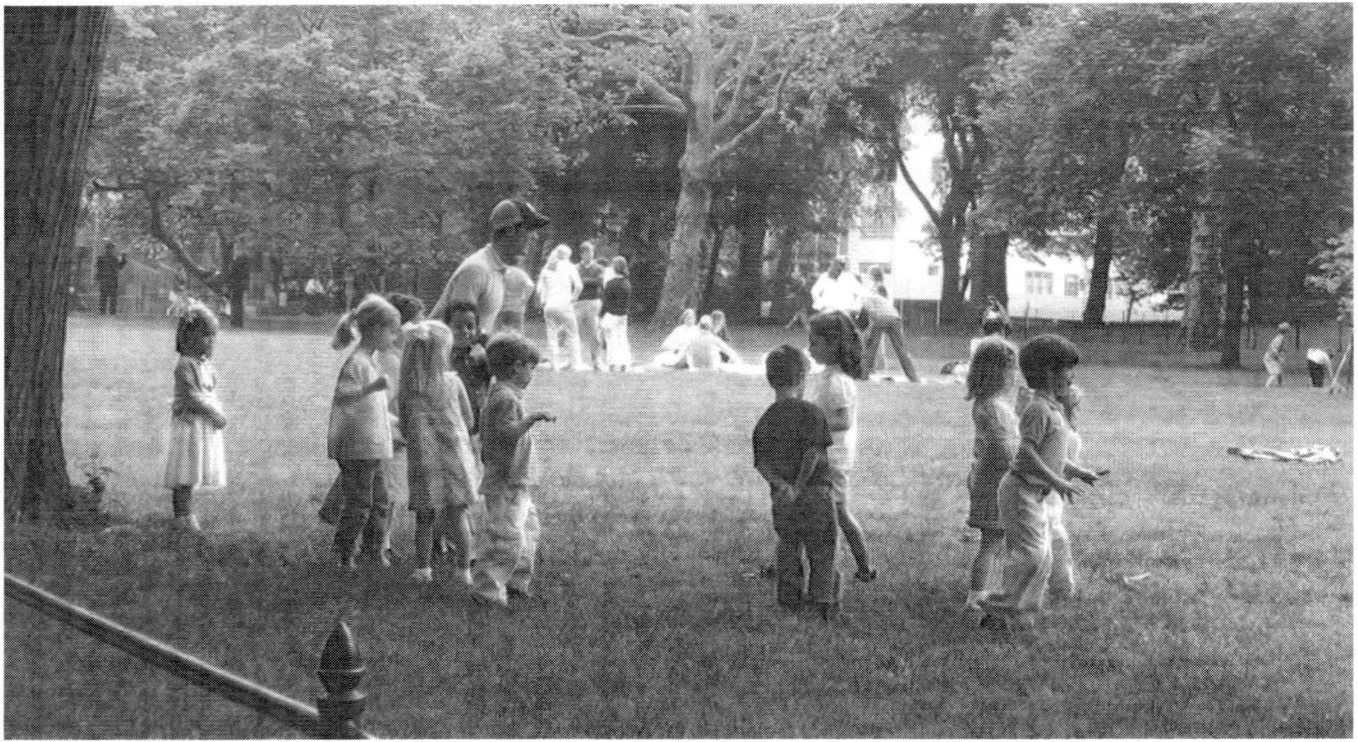

**Figure 8.1** Patrick Maynard, *Unsure*, 2005.

argument presupposes adequate description, the first part of the essay develops some descriptive conceptions with which the second part can address our central value issue, by means of two arguments that emphasize pictorial composition.

## Space and Time Scales

Several space and time conceptions background our common idea of photographs as presenting "a piece of time and space." We tend to think of photographs as made at specific times, based on brief exposures – "instants" – also as formed from three-dimensional situations, according to perspective. We know of important exceptions to all this: that many photos are not taken instantaneously, that the process of producing them has multiple stages, that familiar photo techniques strongly suppress perspective effects. Nevertheless, the majority of photographs that we treat as depictions of things and situations (especially snapshots) do feature perspective, along with camera positions and angles that crucially affect them. Also, they are of short exposure: thus Robert Doisneau's title for a career collection of street photography, "Three Seconds of Eternity." For purposes of discussion, figure 8.1, taken in Central Park in Manhattan one June morning, is a modest example. Let's describe it in terms of space and time.

### *Perspective: spaces and substances*

The perspective nature of such a picture shows in several ways, according to that system's defining properties. We note occlusions (overlap) of objects, setting one behind another, also foreshortening of side planes. Camera perspective, which shares occlusion and foreshortening with other representational systems, is distinguished from all others by its set of "gradients" (grades or rates of change) that are interrelated into depth. Best known is perspective's diminution of areas: objects providing smaller images the farther off they are. This correlates with grades of distinctness and of

(p. 154), "He handled the camera . . . to express not what he saw but his transformation of it into a new, aesthetic, and imaginative world" (p. 158) – "his vision of a world containing elements of regeneration" (p. 157). In addition, the following statements by Winogrand quoted by Lifson might be kept in mind: "You're talking about *meaning*. I want to talk about the *picture*" (p. 157), "Every photograph is a contention between form and content" (p. 157), "Our aspirations and successes have become cheap and petty. . . . They all deal in illusions and fantasies. . . . We have not loved life" (pp. 154f).

textural coarseness. Crucial for our sense of depth-space as continuous here are effects along the foreshortened plane of the ground, which provides a continuous "floor" for the scene. Textural gradients across the lush spring grass are strong and detail drops off with distance. A related perspective characteristic is the horizon. First, we sense that there is one, which we can roughly place, and judge relative heights of objects by their "horizon ratios" – that is, according to their being below or at the horizon, and, if above, by what proportions of their heights. For example, the capped "counselor" overseeing the foreground children's games is, even while leaning, a head above the horizon (which is at eye-level of the man seen behind him). All the children's forms in the picture are entirely below the horizon, while the metal rail and finial at bottom left are even lower. Comparison of all these factors, along with verticals on the distant buildings, produces the impression that we face a level field, our view tipped slightly right. Thus, in picture as in park, we not only see a scene, we see it by means of the perspectival factors just listed – and can be aware of this fact. There is a further point to make: "we face," "our view": as the psychologist J. J. Gibson remarked, this perceptual information "points two ways," since it also provides us with a strong sense of a point of view on the scene. "To perceive the world is to co-perceive oneself" – that's how we locate our own bodies. Gibson continued: "The awareness of the world and of one's complementary relations to the world are not separable."[3]

## *Perspective in perspective: spatial scales*

Regarding a picture such as figure 8.1 as a flat design, we have, by means of perspective, briefly considered space. But we have not put perspective sufficiently "in perspective," so that we can understand what sort of system this is. Also, except for relative sizes, we've neglected the compositionally crucial matter of the placement of designed shapes on the picture surface – crucial, because although many images feature little or even no depth relationships, all must distribute their forms over surfaces, indicating two-dimensional relationships. Most naturally we would describe these two-dimensional relationships simply in terms of directions – left/right,

[3] J. J. Gibson, *The Ecological Approach to Visual Perception* (Boston: Houghton Mifflin, 1979), p. 141: quoted by Sheena Rogers, "Truth and Meaning in Pictorial Space," in H. Hecht et al., eds., *Looking into Pictures: An Interdisciplinary Approach to Pictorial Space* (Cambridge, MA: MIT Press, 2003), p. 302. Rogers's paper presents a clear account of horizon ratios, however, given our topic, it is appropriate to warn readers of her misrepresentation of Walton's views, in passing, which does not affect her own thesis.

up/down – along with the relative distances. For example, the image of the little girl, left, is closer to that of the counselor than is that of the jumping boy, right, and the images depict this, too: the girl is depicted as being about twice as close. The space between the images of the framing oak, left, and that of the little girl is only slightly less than the space between hers and the main group's images, which is about the same as that between the jumping boy's group's image and that of the walking girl – which is, in turn, about half that between the latter group and the leader's – and we judge the depicted intervals that way, too. When we add the perspective depth-planes mentioned earlier, the spatial situation becomes complex. The distance between the image of the counselor and that of the standing adult group behind is less than that between the former and the image of the little girl left, whereas, thanks to perspective diminution function, the depicted distances are quite the opposite.

Such spatial judgments may be understood in a still wider "perspective," by means of a classification of different kinds of spatial scales. With both perspective depth and placement on the surface, we've already considered what might be loosely called some "***interval*** scales" – that is, one thing's being closer to another than to a third (although that will need refining). Such scaling presupposes another scale we had begun: that of what are termed the "***ordinal***" relationships of left/right, up/down, front/back in depth, which hold for groups, such as children and leaf masses, as well as for the individual substances. In depth, some standard groupings are of people in foreground, middle-ground, background. The foreground figures are presented frieze-like, by a series of silhouettes. Then there is a gap in people-populations until we get to the older social groups in middle distance, also presented in roughly orthogonal line-up. In background we see a pair of black shapes bracketing the little girl, left, and the children, right. Further on is a sense of people in vista, along another path, in a playground left, then of buildings beyond. The overall result is a set of distinct depth-planes, along a common "floor."

Let's now generalize these scales. Choosing a criterion of identity (persons or groups), we get "***nominal***" counts of them, by the rule that each is assigned a distinct number: eleven children and one adult in foreground, eleven adults behind.[4] Next we have the spatially ordinal arrangements just mentioned, giving sequences of things counted. But here ties are allowed, as in races. For example, there is a child behind the jumping boy, who might get the same ordinal arrangement as he, though – counting

4 What is here called "nominal" is not really a scale, since it isn't ordered on a number line.

children – she is nominally distinct. There are ambiguous cases, such as where to order the counselor in the front frieze. Next we have the interval assignments of close and far, which may also be shared. Each of these assignments presupposes the previous one: we cannot order things if we cannot count them, and we cannot compare their distances apart unless we can order them.

Besides the three scales, nominal, ordinal, interval, is a fourth: "*absolute*." To see what that adds to interval, consider how, to enlarge this picture, we would have to multiply measurements in all directions by a common factor, since adding the same amount to each thing's image within it, even while preserving the interval order, would distort their size proportions. The concept of absolute scaling helps us better understand camera perspective, which is marked out in contrast with other representational systems by featuring a zero point: the camera's position. Since absolute scales involve multiplications, going over the earlier-mentioned perspective diminution with depth function, we can say, roughly, that a thing's image diminishes at a rate inverse to its recession.[5] Thus, if a figure is to be represented as twice as far off, its image height and width must diminish by about half. Suppose that the counselor in our picture were only slightly taller than both the man in the center of the group by the central plane tree and the dark figure behind the little girl, left: assigning the dark figure's image a height of one unit, the others would be, roughly, two and five and half. Thus if the counselor is, say, 16 paces away, the group behind would be 45 paces off, and the dark figure around 90.

## *Time scales*

We can confirm the generality of this group of scales – nominal, ordinal, interval, absolute – by familiar facts about our experience of time. Time is a series, thus an ordinal, conception: a linear one of before and after, presupposing nominal distinctions of events. Simultaneity of events is crucial to it. Yet ordinality, including simultaneity, is refined by an all-important interval conception of time into spans. Here we must be careful. This picture's exposure would be what we call "instantaneous" – a fraction of a second. That was a crucial fact in taking it: timed for the running counselor still to be with the group of children and before his younger (also blue-shirted) version, right, cleared the other group. But that has no automatic temporal implication for how we experience the

[5] More accurately, it diminishes with tangent of the visual angle. I am grateful to Keith Niall for this correction.

picture. To be sure, simultaneity, like perspective, frames the scene, but photographs differ as to what, if any, meaning that has. There are other notable dimensions of the picture, having to do with calendars. It is early summer; it seems present, yet over the years the clothing will date it, as a stronger sense of the past appears. This invokes our famously paradoxical sense of time, as an ordinal and interval series, marked with that curiously moving absolute cursor, "now." The often noted poignancy of old photographs might be that in seeing them we detect a time of having been as being subjectively experienced as such a "now," implying that our (present!) "now" may sometime be detected the same way – vanished like the horizons of our childhoods, which we took for granted in those springtimes.[6]

## *Space bands: personal, action, vista*

By now it is clear that our consideration of scales of space and time is firmly set in the human scale of perceptual experience. That allows us, in our theorizing about perception, to do as we do in perception itself: to make a second "pass" over the question of depth spaces in the picture, giving more emphasis to human measure. This, increasingly, will be the direction of this essay, as first the viewer, then the maker are brought into the picture – as must be, if our theme is the meaning and value we find in such photographs.

To begin, we had considered foreground, middle-ground, background. But, as James Cutting points out, there is a more significant psychophysical classification to be made in terms of three space bands in perception: personal space, action space, vista space – the trio "hither, thither and yon(der)" – not determined by perspective optics or vision alone, but also by our bodies.[7] "To perceive the world is to co-perceive oneself," indeed, and as a *body* of certain kind, not just an eye, as many accounts of perspective have it. Personal space extends about as far as we can reach, perhaps after taking a step – or others might easily touch us. This is a very significant, intimate space, perceptually a range in which binocular disparity and abrupt changes in parallax, as we or objects move, provide strong three-dimensional experiences. Personal space also corresponds to

6 For a fuller consideration of different kinds of time in photography, see Patrick Maynard, "The Time It Takes," in Jan Baetens, ed., *The Graphic Novel* (Leuven: Leuven University Press, 2001), pp. 191–210.

7 James Cutting's papers (notably "Reconceiving Perceptual Space," in Hecht, *Looking into Pictures*) on this and related subjects are available in pdf form on his personal website: <http://people.psych.cornell.edu/~jec7/>.

that of intimate conversation (even whisper), recognition of subtle facial expression and quick action. The low railing in the picture is its only element that is near personal space for the viewer. Like most pictures, ours centrally concerns action space, against a backdrop of vista space, literally over-looking the implied personal space. Action space runs out from the margin of personal space to about the approximate depth of effective binocular vision, which would perhaps just reach the group of older people, center.[8] Theirs is a distance at which we might hope to hail someone by shouting, also close to the distance that we might try to throw or kick something – or be alert regarding something projected toward us. Facial features are increasingly indistinct across that span, as we communicate increasingly by broad gestures. By the perspective rough inverse function, at that distance some differences in ratios of image-size differences draw close together, and accordingly need more effort to discern. By contrast, the children's group, in central action space, is causally and perceptually immediate for us. We could interact easily with people in this space – "be there in a flash." We can comprehend facial and bodily attitudes, also hear voices. This is a distance at which we can take in a whole situation – perhaps even better than the participants – against a vista backdrop: the classic position of spectators.

Psycho-physical spaces need to be appreciated for the depicted subjects, too. The counselor and his arc of children share personal spaces, while part of the isolation of the little girl, left, is that (besides their backs being turned) that group is out of her personal space – which, because she is a smaller person, is a smaller space. That she is out of ours, too, and with an intervening barrier, has meaning.

## *Space as place*

Finally, stage-like, as noted, our scene is closed by a backdrop of vista space, which though not without depth is perceptually flattened, beyond physical interaction, perceptually indistinct, relatively static and helping (with the framing tree, left) to close a rough but real subjectual spatial experience of a place, a site.[9] As Cutting has emphasized, we often misjudge vista space, compress it, increasingly so with distance. Thus the composition of this photograph, in friezes suggesting personal space,

8 As "effective" signals, there is no sharp line here; also, evidence varies. Readers may enjoy working this out for their own vision.

9 The term "subjectual" as simply implying a standpoint, less misleading than "subjective," is due to Peter Railton, "Subjective and Objective," *Ratio* 8 (1995): 259–76.

showing near and distant action space, then vista space, with the grassy gradient floor sweeping through them, corresponds to the three subjectual bands of our perceptual, cognitive, social, and causally interactive relationships. Such fitting to our perceptual structures can itself be satisfying. No wonder it is standard to several pictorial traditions.

## *Space as shapes*

Whatever the physical optics of the picture, our ability to comprehend its overall space depends on abilities to recognize substances and thereby to scale their images. We just noted how this scaling ability is shaped by our own bodies. Far from "hawk-eyed" we: even the red-tailed hawks famously perched a few blocks away from this green have more acute powers of vista-space estimation. Let's now refine our comments regarding this substance-identifying recognitional ability, which allows us to scale at least personal and action spaces, by thinking about individual objects' *shapes*. In pictures, as in real environments, we tend strongly toward substance identification by characteristic shape and attitude – as we know from drawing. Although a snapshot, for the most part the children in figure 8.1 do not look "frozen." Beginning with the little girl, left, most of those in the foreground provide clear silhouettes, whose contours define them in stances, attitudes, with gestures that we would understand if they were taken separately from the scene: in other words, they work pretty well as "drawings" of the individual figures. Remarkable in this respect is the descriptive profile of the girl with a pony-tail and bell-shaped translucent (pink) top. "Good drawing" applies as well to the figure-groupings, including that of three people standing in the distance. Again, it is satisfying to find how easily we grasp the attitudes of that central group, human bodies perpetually exchanging messages in recognizable shapes of form and behavior. In contrast is the icon of a man in black with one arm up, below a squiggle of black branch in the left distance, a portentous hieroglyph.

## *Topological shapes*

Shape and figure recognition entail another essential spatial category, often neglected in accounts of pictorial space: topology.[10] Regarding identification of substances, photography is notorious for obscuring a basic topological characteristic, continuity – also an associated one, contact. We have seen that the most basic spatial scale is the nominal, for which we

[10] With apologies, the term "topology" in used here in a very loose, unmathematical, sense.

use cardinal numbers – e.g., counting children in the game. This most meaningful category is also too often taken for granted. Yet it presupposes the even more basic spatial perceptual ability of grasping the integrity of entities, which, ironically, is often compromised by that powerful depth-ordinal indicator, occlusion. Wherever one figure occludes another, two opposed topological problems arise: separating occluder and occluded, and rejoining parts of occluded figures. Photography is well known for ambiguities of "false attachment." For example, what might appear to be a (pink) ribbon behind the little girl's head is the skirt of a woman pushing a stroller in vista. A second common figure problem is due to interruption. All is legible where the girl strides back toward the main group, past the boy with arms behind his back. Although only her right foot projects past his leg, we have no tendency to assign it to him. Furthermore, as in good drawing, we easily relate that shape to her body and action. The counselor's heel, visible left of pony-tail, is clear enough to detach from the boy behind her and stay with the adult, strengthening the diagonal of his running form. The weakest "drawing" in the picture is in the two figures behind the jumping boy, but not due to false attachment. One girl barely gets in her side-silhouette, feet together in bobby-socks, while the other is so occluded that posture and action are almost indecipherable. Here, that time-ordinal, simultaneity, intrudes. Waiting for the jumping boy to pass her would have cost the legible shape of the girl walking back – crucial, we shall see, to the whole composition.[11] Maybe Cartier-Bresson would have gotten it all.

## Inextricable but Irreducible: Artistic Values in Snapshot Art

Our consideration of scales of space and time has worked steadily from optical and numerical facts, through psychophysical matters relative to human subjects, thus to issues of undeniable meaning, including the integrity of bodies and groups. These descriptions are prelude to the main project of placing of artistic values among these and other life values generally.

[11] Putting these considerations together with our initial ones concerning space as recession, we come upon an interesting paradox. Occlusion of figures, the most forceful ordinal depth indicator for human vision, sets one behind another in transitive sequence. Yet how can we tell that one figure occludes another unless we already take the latter as behind the former? Perhaps a topological-continuity hypothesis precedes tentative occlusion assignments, which then allow the latter to confirm the order.

But has the value project become more complicated by the descriptive one? In seeing how different kinds of space and time apprehensions cooperate in our perception of scenes, and how these carry over to perception of photographs and other pictures, have we put at risk the basic task of understanding photography as art? That is, are we not suggesting that photographs are mainly substitutes for actual views (which is indeed how people describe them), and therefore that their values are entirely derivative?

My reply to this has two parts, beginning with what is usually called "composition." Composition arguments in defense of photographic artistry are standard, yet they seem always to be rather vague and general.[12] Let us see if we can be more explicit about what composition is and how it matters to us.

## A: Composition

### *Negative space*

After subject matter, composition is probably the most noticed aspect of pictures. Perhaps excessively, we tend to understand composition in terms of spatial categories like those just reviewed. For example, our picture's composition might be considered a loose ellipse within a rectangle, which contains triangles and rectangles. In taking, it was centered on a negative space. Cropping has displaced that center only slightly downward from the horizon, but still within the large negative space between two groups of children, and symmetrically flanked by a pair of negative spaces between them and the next children. Negative spaces are not only two-dimensional. That central gap is within a three-dimensionally rounded "bubble" of space that we can imagine, defined by the chest of the counselor, the curve made by the dark opening in the trees, and the curved back of the jumping boy, who corresponds to him. The center of this bubble is just off the left shoulder of the boy with crossed arms, and the girl walks into it. This bubble is also a sort of "lens" through which we see the three groups beyond. And it places the little girl, left, in a further isolation of being well "outside the bubble," her contrast with the walking girl heightened.

12 A quick sampling of compositional arguments may be had from essays by Stieglitz, Weston, and Anonymous in Alan Trachtenberg, ed., *Classic Essays in Photography* (New Haven: Leete's Island Books, 1980) and Robert Adams, "Beauty in Photography," in *Beauty in Photography: Essays in Defense of Traditional Values* (New York, Aperture Foundation, 1996).

A similar isolating feature of implied spaces is the little girl's framing by the negative space between the two black vista figures with their crooked branch, and the two railing finials, just into action space (one cropped from figure 8.1, since the oak trunk takes care of the left-hand side of her enclosure). This framing works as both a two-dimensional form on the picture surface and a depth-enclosure within which the girl stands, occupied by nothing else but lawn. That is a third way in which she is isolated, a second that we may call "compositionally."

Regarding our artistic value question, skeptics may insist that all this about composition applies as well to the actual scene – indeed that much of it was likely seen there by the photographer, which is how it got into the picture. The first reply is that much was indeed sensed in the real scene, but the scene looked at *pictorially* (even, as Edward Weston said, "photographically"): that is, in terms of how it would appear in a photograph.[13] But that must be only part of the reply, since it is important not entirely to separate pictorial seeing from environmental seeing, as activity and as value. Nonetheless, the point remains that there are things, such as the spatial forms described, that most people would be unlikely to notice, looking upon the children playing. Let's investigate this more closely.

Most people taking pictures focus on what most sighted creatures do: the states and movements of things of interest. One looks at the field, sea, sky, mist, but – at least with foveal vision – most often one looks to see bounded substances. Since many people simply point their cameras at these things, hoping that what they see will show up in the result, they hardly attend to positive shapes, much less to the negative intervals and shaped spaces we've been considering. Yet, as studio teachers insist, we must attend, if we expect to make *pictures* – not just pictures of things – for, whether or not we notice such spaces, we are still aware of them, and can be made more so.[14] Teachers employ techniques for developing

[13] Thus the bootlessness of Roger Scruton's anti-compositional suggestion in "Photography and Representation," section 9 (ch. 6 in this volume), that an aesthetically controlled cropping-frame providing "a particular view of a street" would be equivalent to a photograph, achieving an aesthetic view of the street, but not a representation of it. Besides the impossibility of making a view of a changing scene indistinguishable from a still photograph, the hopeless effort would be in trying to make a view of a scene the illusion of a photograph (and one could try the same with a painting), thus the argument runs backwards.

[14] The case of drawing is complicated because drawings of things are made according to drawing rules – usually unconscious – for constructing them. Simply put, there are many things people are well aware that they cannot draw, lacking procedures to do so. (For a systematically argued, illustrated account of the necessity and nature of such rules see John Willats, *Making Sense of Children's Drawings* [New Jersey: Lawrence Erlbaum, 2005]).

such attention to shapes, including those of negative spaces, against the difficulty that, since (with important exceptions of doorways, windows, etc.), not being substances with repeated shapes, it is not easy to state rules for noticing them.

What to do with these shapes, once noticed? Two problems regularly attending elementary statements of negative-spaces rules are vagueness and flatness. We are vaguely enjoined to make negative spaces "balance" the positive ones, while it is unclear what such balance is and why it is good. Perhaps better advice would be that, in taking a photograph, one is giving directions to produce a pattern on a rectangular surface; therefore, that one should attempt to make that pattern – including its positive and negative forms – interesting. The flatness difficulty is that, as noted, negative spaces may include three-dimensionally shaped spaces that we imagine seeing in the depicted scene, not just patterns on the surface that do the depicting. We have seen how negative spaces can be scaled the way substances are, also that topological ideas of separation, contact, containment apply to them. Thus, visual imaginations stimulated, we may also see behind the bubble containing the walking girl an undulating negative shape in the opening in the view of trees in vista, half dark with the gesturing plane-tree in its midst (figure 8.2), then half light, cut by darker silhouettes.

## *Dynamics*

Compositionally, the most serious shortcoming of our spatially based account so far is its neglect of dynamics, our sense not only of movements but of perceptual forces. Artistically, that would be disastrous, since perhaps the simplest statement of what it is that people who do not understand visual arts artistically fail to grasp is perceptual "dynamics."

Although drawing rules apply significantly to photography, an advantage of photography is that people can make recognizable pictures of things without them, but – as shows up in snapshots – that does little for their compositions. Beginning-photography teachers attempt to frame rules of composition, including "the rule of thirds": to position main subjects asymmetrically, at the four intersections of two pairs of lines that trisect the format, vertically and horizontally. This rule (built into digital-editing programs) tends to be object-based. Besides its figure 8.1 violation, it is violated in perhaps the most famous photo of children playing, by Henri Cartier-Bresson (Seville, 1933). Study of a hundred or so pictures by Bresson – among photographers most famous for instinctive geometry of composition – reveals general non-compliance with the rule of thirds. The thirds we do find in Bresson are in a coincidence of long vertical forms with width-thirds divisions. Bresson puts main subject matter into one of the nine divisions, often the center – violating the anti-symmetry purpose of the "rule" – as in the famous 1952 picture of the boy Michel Gabriel with wine bottles. As mentioned, figure 8.1 locates the horizon at a height-thirds division.

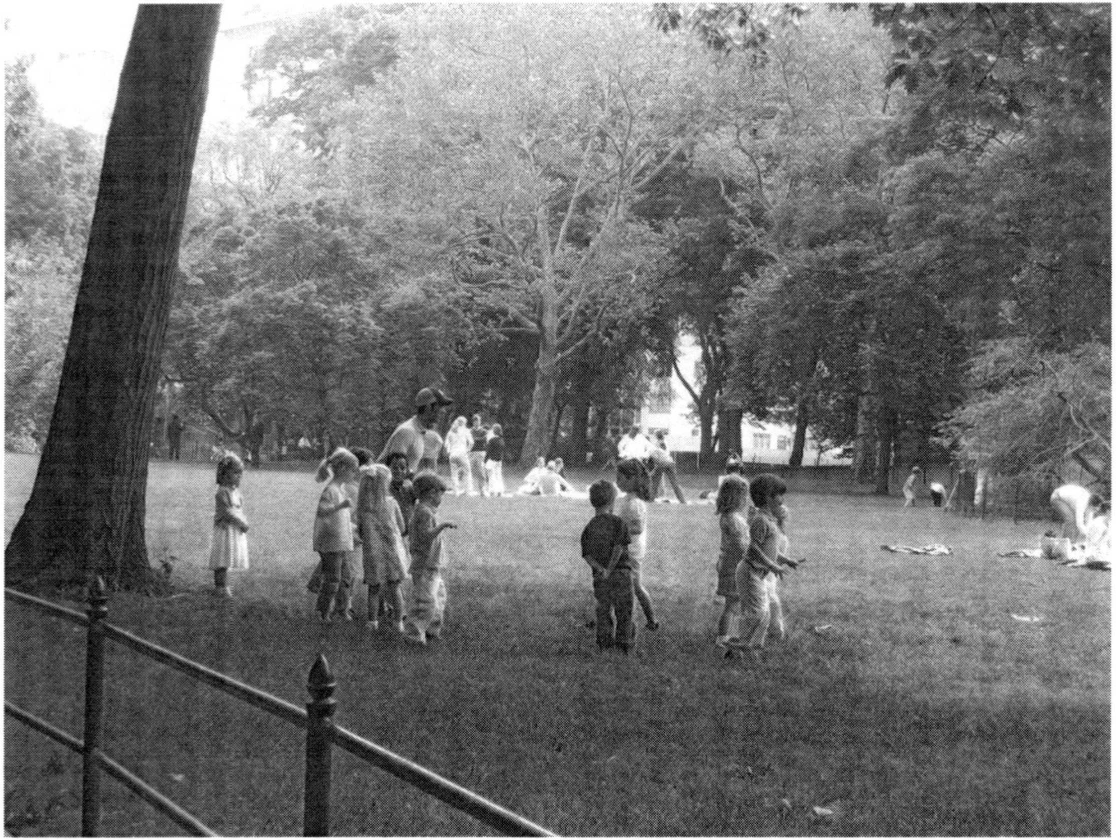

**Figure 8.2** Patrick Maynard, *Unsure* (uncropped).

Thus, more even than main shapes, we need to consider the main dynamics of a composition. In our example, one is a pull between the walking-girl group and the jumping-boy group. The two children left counteract the other group in their direction of regard, the girl opposing and the boy crossing the thrust of the right-hand group.[15] A related dynamic is in the surrounding bubble. The jumping boy not only defines its right margin, we may imagine it pressing against his back. A very important dynamic element in pictures is a shearing sense, whereby one shape seems to slide past another. Painters call this "shifting." This happens between the walking girl and the boy turning in front of her, in a torque between their forms, especially their heads. Thus the dynamic generators in this picture seem to emerge from the two groups right, not from the little girl left, who might be its main subject. Covering the jumping-boy group, the walking-girl group also pulls against the main group of children across the picture's central negative space, as, by mirror symmetry, the little girl and the walking one come into opposed relation. We count at least four dynamic relationships, and it would be interesting to see how these interact, art being, like perception itself, a thing of relationships of relationships. So is life.

## *Rhythm and repetition*

Typically interacting with dynamics in pictures are rhythms in repetitions of units, often in terms of symmetry patterns. Across the front of the central frieze of children, with arms to body (a) or open (b), we have a rhythm: a, b, a, b (space) a, b – with sub-rhythms. In the (a) group, the girl with a bow also leans in the same attitude as the turning boy, whose clasped hands behind his back link to their opposite gesture of the little-girl-left's hands clasped before her, while in the distance the blonde girl's older version leans her way, too. Counselor and jumping boy are strongly related, and the trees lean with them. Next, a boy in the right distance echoes the crouch of the jumper, as an extended right leg in the older-group frieze repeats the scissor shape of the walking girl's step, in parallel with a diagonal branch above – and a vista figure seems to pick up their stride. Once we attend to the middle frieze, we notice four pyramids of groups: high, low (sitting and center), high, low.

[15] The sense of shift, across the space separating, is increased by a higher crop of the picture, placing the horizon near its midline. Then the dark parting of the trees, with aligned verticals and bright walls beyond, carries the sense of a negative-space vertical crack through the picture.

## B: Artists' Actions

By attention to a simple snapshot example, I hope that we understand better how one kind of photographic vision, while being inextricable from normal vision, is still irreducible to it, since it not only derives from, but is capable of developing, redirecting, and transforming that normal vision, toward richer meanings.

Proof of this would have to be found in changes in picture viewers' perceptual experiences, something impossible to provide here. Some confirmation lies in the very production of such photographs: that photographers would have to be able to see their environments in such ways in order to produce them. Yet that claim is likely to elicit another familiar challenge. A question likely to arise from accounts of the sorts just given regards what of this is accidental and what put there by the photographer. Certainly some of it is put there – at least made more evident there – by the actions of cropping for just those effects. But how much was put there in the snapshot, how can we tell?

Using our descriptive vocabulary, let's begin with skepticism concerning the space scales, dynamics, and rhythms described. As it takes study to see the things I have described in the photograph, isn't it implausible that a snapshooter could be aware of all that in the time required to take it? Therefore, if such are, as argued, valued aspects of the picture, isn't it unclear how much of what is artistically interesting could have been put there by the photographer?

We can meet this objection in terms of some elementary facts of vision. Photographic seeing is a development of environmental seeing, which itself works through patterns, indeed the anticipation of shifting patterns. We recognize this from driving in traffic or from making our way through busy streets, as well as from many other situations, notably including sports. Although our normal powers here are great, we do in sports single out "physical genius": for example Wayne Gretzky's "capacity to pick up on subtle patterns that others generally miss," for – talk of dynamics – as described by that hockey star, "the whole sport is angles and caroms, forgetting the straight direction capacity to pick up on subtle patterns the puck is going, calculating where it will be diverted, factoring in all the interruptions."[16]

As observed earlier with perspective gradients, individual substance recognitions are embedded in these changing pattern recognitions. Something similar is at work in our comprehension of the massing and movement

[16] See Malcolm Gladwell, "The Physical Genius," *The New Yorker* (June 2, 1999).

of leaves in the trees here without being able to distinguish individual leaves (figure 8.2), rather as we see movements across patterns of countless water waves. Tacitly, much of our sense perception works from pattern recognition. Indeed, changes of pattern – even patterns of change in patterns – are often perceptually most salient. In the simplest tune, we hear not the individual vibrations but their (several) frequencies, with attention not only to changes but to patterns in these changes. In the same way, with practice, not only may the spacings, dynamics, and rhythms in a camera viewfinder be responded to directly, they may be tracked and anticipated. An example crucial to this picture: one need not estimate the size of the negative space behind the jumping-boy group if one looks straight for the purpose of that space, which lies less in geometrical proportions than in the dynamics described. This must be combined with subject-matter recognition, which anticipates the pattern development. For example, the little girl, left, literally was not going anywhere. Again, all this is routine for visual perception, as foveal vision is backgrounded by a larger field, which, toward its peripheries, gives way to motion, not form, detection. Neither is visual art strictly foveal.

Even if that suffices as a general account, how could we tell about photographers' vision in specific cases? For example, how likely is it that the photographer could have been aware of the contours of even half the figures in the foreground group while grasping an overall composition? Well, this picture was taken not far from the Metropolitan Museum of Art, where the girl turning back may be compared with Balthus's "Nude Before a Mirror," the treed park screening a busy road with facing townhouses loosely with Monet's "Parc Monceau" (with Boulevard de Courcelles, not Fifth Avenue) – composed vertically on thirds – and the whole with figure-friezes such as Puvis de Chavannes' "Patriotic Games" (thirds again, both ways, centered on a negative space flanked by two narrower equal ones).[17] For quick grasp of the expression of figures seen from behind, there is also some evidence in drawings by the photographer (figure 8.3). Years of looking at such pictures, of drawing and photographing, make it at least plausible that the photographer habitually looks at scenes this way, even when not making pictures – a situation normal to many specialist disciplines. Thus, regarding specific attributions of perceptions, a reply to skepticism takes the shape of most of the arguments in this paper: reference to well-known, everyday facts about perception. Meyer Schapiro

[17] Also, the trees, right, screen the Frick Collection. Inspiration for the central negative space motif was Cézanne, as discussed in Patrick Maynard, *Drawing Distinctions: The Varieties of Graphic Expression* (Ithaca, NY: Cornell University Press, 2005).

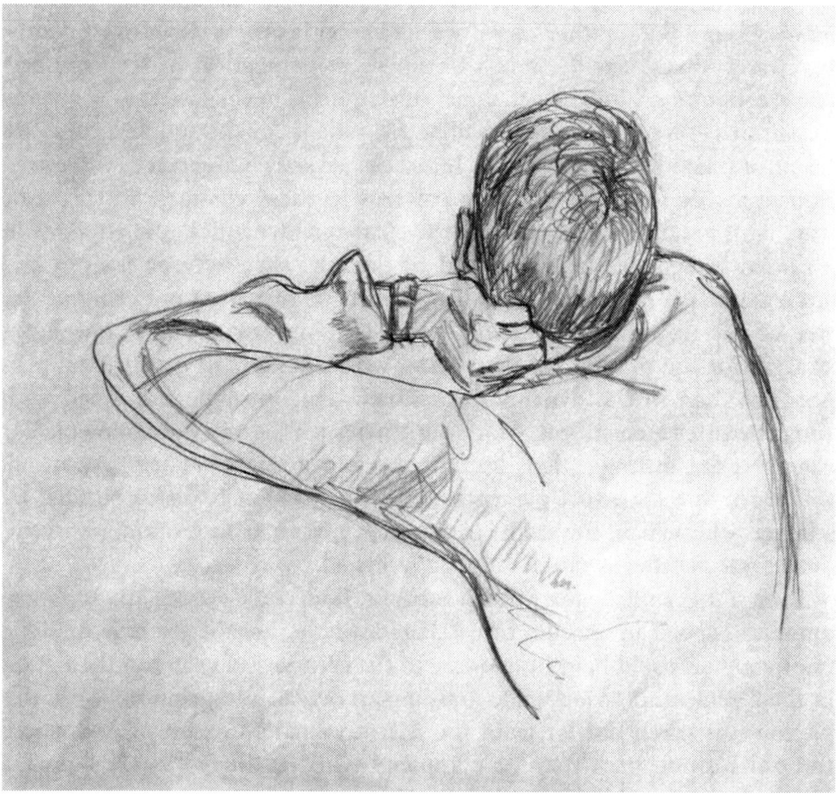

**Figure 8.3** Patrick Maynard, *Robert*, 2005.

reminded us that aesthetic perception, like all perception, is hypothetical and invites comparisons with others' experiences.[18] As with any other kind of perception, to test a hypothesis about a photograph, we should use normal means of seeking invariants. We would consult our experience of snapshots of like situations, to see how readily the compositional features described are to be found among them. We would also look at other works by the photographer. That is how we come better to understand individual pictures by Cartier-Bresson, Frank, Friedlander, Weegee, Winogrand – to tell Bresson from Erwitt and appreciate the difference. But such is only common sense and normal practice, a development of our ability to tell an alligator from a crocodile.

[18] See the extract from Meyer Schapiro, "On Perfection and Coherence in Art," in Feagin and Maynard, *Aesthetics*, pp. 348f.

## *Artworks as works*

Although the fine-art status of photography is not our topic here, reference to photographers' actions, as parts of arguments from composition, are standard to defenses of photographic art, as in writings by such outstanding modern photographers as Alfred Stieglitz, Weston, Paul Strand.[19] Yet when Weston, in an essay titled "Seeing Photographically," argues that what had been called the photographer's "power of selection and rejection" ranges over "an infinite number of varied compositions [even] with a single stationary object,"[20] it isn't clear what that implies for our topic. Whether or not a photograph may be art, the question remains what such an "infinity" implies, for the value of seeing photographically, through composition and factors particular to photography. Suppose a composition that works (perhaps along the lines indicated above): still, the question arises, what value is added to perception when we recognize the photographer's role in producing (or "selecting") it? Why should it matter?

Rather than requiring aesthetic theorizing, once again our answer may lie in common facts about perception. As the very word tells us (twice), artworks are *artifacts*, not just outcomes – that is, things intentionally made by people – and "artifact" itself is a basic perceptual classification. Kant remarks in *Critique of Judgment* (sec. 43), that when we spot a plank lying in a bog, it stands out as such, as a product of art – as something made: "its producing cause had an end in view." When we perceive something as made thus, we look at it differently from how we do when we consider it as natural or as accidental. If an anthropologist tells us that the interesting flint we picked up is a Paleolithic hand axe, this will reorganize our perception of it – we will look at it differently: as a core, not a flake, its narrower edge now appearing blade-like, its broader side like a hand-grip, and so forth.[21] Besides what Kant suggests, to perceive some wood or stone is thus to take it not only as made *on* purpose but made *for* a use or purpose. The "why" of the wood is that we conjecture further purposes.

Photographs are artifacts. But when they are perceived as such, as they normally are, there is a crucial, more specific perceptual point to add. When, as with depictions, an artifact's main purpose is not to be wielded, but to be looked at in certain ways, that not only affects but specifies our

[19] In Trachtenberg, *Classic Essays in Photography*: see also the essay by "Anonymous," pp. 134–40.

[20] Edward Weston, "Seeing Photographically," repr. in Trachtenberg, *Classic Essays in Photography*, pp. 170–5.

[21] This point is derived from Michael Tomasello, *The Cultural Origins of Human Cognition* (Cambridge, MA: Harvard University Press, 1999), p. 84. Tomasello's views on artifacts' cultural "affordances" are in strong agreement with those expressed here.

perception of it in its aspects, parts, details. Understood simply as artifacts, things put there on purpose, we relevantly ask *why*, with respect to perception, the maker put a certain kind of mark at a certain place on the surface.[22] In other words, as with any artifact, we want to know, "what's that for?" This is a matter of degree. Looking at our example as a snapshot, it is clear that one would not ask purpose questions to the extent that one could if it were a drawing or painting. "Why do the two running males (in the original) have blue tops, two standing females pink ones, but the little girl left a blue, not a pink, top?," would be a meaningful question with this as a painting, less so as a snapshot. However, unless the photograph is largely accidental, it is meaningful, to ask questions such as, "Why is there a big negative space right in the middle?," "Why are the counselor's back and head aligned with the dark curve of the vista trees?," shading off into "Why is there a triangle of six people (three standing, three sitting) in the central negative space?" A partial answer to the last is that jamming an available white wedge into the central negative space pushes it apart – but not a complete answer, for I'll next suggest that it is a significant value of such photographs, not a fault, that the artist cannot be expected to have done so much as a painter, regarding composition.

To conclude the present argument: as appreciation develops, we may come to see the compositional elements described as having been purposely placed, pushed, contrasted, combined, and so forth, and this affects the way they appear to us and what we look for in the picture. For example, we might see the figure of the little girl not only as isolated, but as having been pictorially isolated, by several graphic means. This, too, becomes an artistic variable, for photographers not only vary in their compositional actions, but in the extent to which they make them visible. That, for certain purposes, such factors do not matter or matter

22 The following considerations seem relevant to challenges to photographic arts by Scruton, "Photography and Representation," section 8 (ch. 6 this volume), bearing on "intention" in photographs and explanations of why something is in a picture – and include, perhaps, a rejection of his composition argument in section 9. Since the time of Elizabeth Eastlake, photo-art "naysayers," while allowing for photographic representational powers, have faulted its mechanical causality for limiting photographers' formative contributions. Scruton is unusual in denying photo representation, as well, but that is because he takes a formative view of representation. His argument rests on an exclusive "or" "mechanism or photographer" formative conception, already rejected by Siegfried Kracauer (*vide*, Trachtenberg, *Classic Essays in Photography*, p. 268) and rejected here. Thereby Scruton prevents himself from applying his perceptive section 2 observations about pictorial perception to photographic pictures.

much does not affect the fact that sometimes they do, and matter a great deal, especially for art.[23]

Given these considerations, especially since our central example is a kind of snapshot, it is important to emphasize the limits of photographers' actions. It is crucial to street photography that many relevant aspects, rather than being produced by the photographer, have been allowed to happen. The particular moment caught may contain chance features, showing, for example, the grace of human form and movement. There may be a sort of "crystallization," whereby strong forms will tend to draw random shapes to them – like three sitting, three standing; parallel diagonals of legs and branch; the shape of the finial resembling that of the pink smock it points to; and so forth. Also, letting things happen with the natural rhythms of groups of people can be something done. Successful fishers are not criticized for not having placed the fish on their hooks or in their nets.

Finally, a strong sense of cooperation between artist and events is not only important to photography, but normal to many arts – indeed to humans interacting with natural environments. All the trees in our picture were planted and cultivated by gardeners, yet grown and shaped by nature, as the trunk of the central plane (*planatus x accrifolia*) curves back against the prevailing winds, limbs expressively gesturing above the standing trio. This point about interaction opens perhaps philosophically the most meaningful issue. There is often a value in such pictures that even the things done by the photographer should be partly the result

[23] Carelessness about these matters underlies another recent formative "naysayer" challenge to photographic art, which has affected practice and criticism, that modern exhibits of "vernacular" photographs have constituted "a shattering experience for the advocate of photography's claims as an art form," and the idea that "in the hands of a great talent, and by dint of long study and extraordinary effort, photography can overcome its mechanical nature and ascend to the level of art," since such photos, put beside canonic art-photography works, often prove their "aesthetic peers": see Janet Malcolm, *Diana and Nikon: Essays on Photography* (1980: expanded edn, New York: Aperture, 1997). (For a broader, more systematic and researched version, see Ulrich F. Keller, "The Myth of Art Photography: A Sociological Analysis," *History of Photography* 8 (Oct.–Dec. 1984): 249–75 and "The Myth of Art Photography: An Iconographic Analysis," *History of Photography* (Jan.–Mar., 1985): 1–38.) The argument seems fallacious because, in the most influential cases of such exhibits, one begins with "canonic" photos and seeks vernacular ones that look like them. But selecting vernacular cases with the canonic ones in mind, the former may look interesting in ways established by the canonic ones. Worse, the canonic pictures are also presented singly, instead of as parts of the photographers' work. This will affect the way a picture appears, something particularly true of photographs. Photographers, unlike novelists, playwrights, and film directors, rarely make an artistic impression by single works.

of seeing what was there to be seen – including the spatial rhythms and dynamics considered. This suggests that such factors are present to us, in inexhaustibly many aspects, much of the time. Insofar as these aspects are meaningful, that implies something important: that there are great resources of meaning freely available to sense experience. Yet, considered in terms of perception, there is still an important aspect of pictorial experience not available in nature.[24]

## *"To co-perceive"*

From the point in the compositional argument where photographers' actions were introduced, another response to the question of the autonomy of artistic meaningfulness has been developing. Having just considered how awareness of the picture's being composed by a photographer might affect our perception of it, a further point, essential to all representational arts, can now briefly be indicated.[25] In some cases of attending to the composition of a photograph, it is appropriate to speak, to use an ordinary phrase, of how the photographer saw it. What does this mean? As observed above, in actual environments one not only sees a scene but sees it by means of visual cues such as the perspectival that we considered, and we can be aware of this. This holds for pictures as well, but, given that pictures are normally understood as artifacts, something additional obtains, not found in nature. We can not only see depictions according to such cues and composition and be aware of that, but, recognized as pictorial artifacts – as arranged for the purpose of our perceptual experience – we can experience these elements as purposive: in terms of what they are *for*. Then, not only do we experience, say, a photograph as something made (which is the usual point of compositional arguments), but as made in order to shape perception. That is our "awareness of the world" through another's awareness of it: not simply according to an optical point of view, but via another's mental actions – which is the meaning of

24 For an interesting, brief account of some of these values, see Adams, *Beauty in Photography*, where he holds that form is beautiful because it "helps us meet our worst fear, . . . that life may be chaos and that therefore our suffering is without meaning" (p. 25); that "the shapes nearest shapeless" (p. 27) and everyday details (pp. 28, 79) are best for that, both as encompassing more and as giving the sense that it is our reality that is being formed; that the reassurance is greater if redone in fresh ways and with apparent (though not actual) ease, producing the impression "that Beauty is commonplace" (p. 30), since we are lucky (p. 28).

25 I argue the thesis sketched here at more length in *Drawing Distinctions*, ch. 14.

"a way of seeing." This can carry the intellectual, psychological, moral, and other values that we ascribe to mental actions generally. Here, clearly, perception of representational arts could not be reduced to normal perceptual experiences of environments; indeed, here depictions, including many photographs, fully become works of art.[26] "The awareness of the world and of one's complementary relations to the world are not separable," Gibson remarked: "to perceive the world is to co-perceive oneself." Depiction allows us to co-perceive another self, as well, as it points more than two ways.

In conclusion, it may seem paradoxical that stages in this defense of our interest in a certain kind of photography as not reducible to interest in non-pictorial experience should have depended on general principles of perception. However all arts involve a carrying-through of activities well begun in non-artistic experience. Artists typically fix on some aspects of those activities – often very simple, limited ones – and show us how, in terms of an artistic medium, the movements begun there may be carried forward, to greater fulfillment, in a variety of ways. What of aesthetic or artistic vision: are not these, at least to some extent, distinct from other experiences? They are, but due to a feature that is, again, quite general to mental processes: reciprocity. The media that artists use become means by which artists and audience experience. This does not imply that such are the only means by which we experience – a fallacy of aestheticism.

Thus, without resort to ideas such as pure form or aesthetic disinterest, we have been able to see how one kind of photographic vision, while inextricable from normal vision, is not reducible to it, since it is capable of developing normal vision toward increased meaning. That this may be interpreted to imply either that photographic vision is a heightening of aspects of normal vision, or that "practical" vision is the inchoate beginning of artistic vision, perhaps leaves the matter where it should be.[27]

[26] Much design of artifacts, from tools to architecture, is, and is perceived as, done in order to shape perceptual experience – which is partly why there are arts of design – but the situation with regard to ways of seeing subject matter still constitutes a difference.

[27] This essay includes thoughts and expressions of Hugo du Coudray. Its "substantive aesthetics" method was also developed in discussion with Lisa Pelot, and partly accommodates patient criticisms by Keith Niall. It is dedicated to Nora Maynard, who made visits to my childhood playground possible, and who regularly runs the beautiful six-mile loop of her park.

# 9

# TRUE APPRECIATION

Dominic McIver Lopes

"I appreciate fine cooking" – that is, I enjoy it. "I appreciate your point" – that is, I see what you are saying and see that it is warranted, perhaps also true. Thus appreciation has a cognitive element – sizing something up – as well as an affective element – a response of liking or disliking.[1] The cognitive element is a good place to look for the beginnings of a theory of appreciation: we may ask what epistemic standards appreciation must live up to. Here are two answers. A familiar answer demands that an appreciator take the object of appreciation to be what it is. An unfamiliar answer says that when something is appreciated as something of a kind, appreciation must not get wrong the nature of the kind. If appreciation need not live up to both standards, then the unfamiliar standard has greater claim upon appreciators. This thesis has surprising implications for appreciations that spring from misunderstandings of appreciative kinds. Photography is an excellent case in point, if, as many claim, lots of people misunderstand what it is.

## Appreciation, Judgment, and Belief

Were there a compendium of theories of appreciation, we might look them up, work out what epistemic standards each implies, and test the standards to see which is best. However, nobody has a theory of appreciation. The first step in building one up is to fix in place the correct epistemic standard. To do this, we need some very broad idea of what the standard governs.

[1] Paul Ziff, "Reasons in Art Criticism," in *Philosophic Turnings* (Ithaca: Cornell University Press, 1966), pp. 49–54.

It is better, at the beginning, to err on the side of breadth. Thus prudence advises against assuming that appreciation only targets artworks or that appreciation is always aesthetic – whatever "aesthetic" means. For one thing, an independently worked-up theory of appreciation might one day come in handy as part of a theory of art or the aesthetic. For another, there is so little consensus around theories of art or the aesthetic that qualifying appreciation as artistic or aesthetic gains us little but controversy. Of course, nothing is wrong with considering cases where appreciation targets artworks or aesthetic objects. Appreciating them leaves room for appreciating sports, nature, food, and much else besides.

Assume appreciation to be a process made up of a series of states of mind and typically leading to the state of mind traditionally named "judgment" – that is, an evaluation, an ascription of value. The assumption that appreciation is governed by an epistemic standard implies that at least some of the states it involves are truth-apt. If appreciation involves beliefs, non-cognitivism about appreciation is false.

However, appreciation is not judgment, so the claim that appreciation involves beliefs is consistent with the proposition that judgment, which is the outcome of appreciation, is not truth-apt. For this reason, a non-cognitivist about judgment may – and should – accept variants upon Arthur Danto's and Kendall L. Walton's indiscernibility arguments, which show that some beliefs about a work's context are required for its appreciation.[2] Arguments such as these will prove useful in justifying the choice of an epistemic standard on appreciation. Accepting that there is such a standard and thus that appreciation involves belief is consistent with non-cognitivsm about judgment.

So read no further if you are a non-cognitivist about appreciation, for your view is just assumed to be false. Read on if you are a non-cognitivist about judgment, for nothing that follows is inconsistent with your view.

Since appreciation is a process, indeed often an activity, it can go well or poorly. Call it "adequate" to the extent that it goes well and "inadequate" to the extent that it goes poorly (adequate appreciation is a matter of degree). The plan is to find out what it is for appreciation to be adequate or inadequate by fixing on the epistemic quality of some of the beliefs that appreciation involves.

[2] Arthur Danto, "The Artworld," *Journal of Philosophy* 61 (1964): 571–84; Kendall L. Walton, "Categories of Art," *Philosophical Review* 79 (1970): 334–67.

## Two Principles

Appreciation involves belief and its adequacy is in part a matter of the quality of that belief. This proposition is widely accepted, and there is a widely accepted standard for measuring the quality of appreciative belief. Nobody considers alternative standards, though one is worth considering.

Allen Carlson and Malcolm Budd contend that no appreciation of a natural phenomenon is adequate unless the phenomenon is appreciated as the phenomenon that it is. Budd writes:

> [I]f you aesthetically appreciate a natural object as an instance of natural kind K and it is not of kind K, then your appreciation is, in that respect, malfounded, and an awareness of your mistake undermines *that* aspect of your appreciation . . . you must reject as mistaken the enjoyment or excitement you felt that arise from that misapprehension.[3]

Some elements of this statement are best put aside for now. One is that Budd and Carlson talk of *aesthetic* appreciation, though they do not deny that the same goes for appreciation across the board. Another is that Budd recommends that one reject as mistaken the fruits of inadequate appreciation – though it is unclear what it is to reject pleasure as mistaken. We may leave open what the practical implications are of inadequate appreciation. Finally, both Budd and Carlson are concerned with appreciating natural phenomena under natural-kind concepts, though they take what they say to apply a standard that covers appreciating all phenomena under any concepts. Setting these matters aside, we are left with the

Carlson–Budd Principle: an appreciation of O as a K is adequate only if O is a K.

To appreciate O adequately, you must classify O as belonging to a kind that it does in fact belong to. In addition, the classification of O as a K must play an active role in the appreciation in the sense that the appreciation would not be what it is were it not for your classifying O as a K. The appreciation must counterfactually depend on the classification.

Budd and Carlson are scientific cognitivists about nature appreciation. They think that nature appreciation must be informed by what science

[3] Malcolm Budd *The Aesthetic Appreciation of Nature* (Oxford: Oxford University Press, 2002), p. 23; see also Allen Carlson "Nature, Aesthetic Judgement, and Objectivity," *Journal of Aesthetics and Art Criticism* 40 (1981): 15–27.

can tell us about natural objects. Given that thought, there is something odd about the Carlson–Budd principle. It is no part of science, at least as philosophers mostly understand it, that O, for any O, is a K. Science is not a scheme for classifying everything in the universe into kinds; it is a system of laws. That is, it consists in propositions about the Ks, not the Os.

An alternative to the Carlson–Budd principle is the

True Appreciation Principle: an appreciation of O as a K is adequate only as far as it does not depend counterfactually on any belief that is inconsistent with the truth about the nature of Ks.

This principle says that the adequacy of an appreciation is diminished when several conditions are met. First, the appreciation counterfactually depends on a belief: it would not go as it does were it not for the belief. Second, the belief is inconsistent with some truth about the Ks. Third, the relevant truth about the Ks is a truth about the nature of Ks.

Both principles are modest. They both state only very weak necessary conditions on adequate appreciation. Neither is a theory of adequate appreciation, for neither says that your appreciation is adequate if it meets the weak epistemic standard alone, and neither ventures additional conditions jointly sufficient for adequate appreciation. Moreover, both allow that almost every appreciation is adequate at some level of description. Suppose that you inadequately appreciate O as a K because O is not a K. The appreciation is inadequate by the Carlson–Budd principle. But there is very likely some K* such that the Ks are K*s, you appreciate O as a K* and O is a K*. Your inadequate appreciation of O as a K is an adequate appreciation of O as a K*. Similarly, suppose that you inadequately appreciate O as a K because you have a false belief about the nature of the Ks. The appreciation is inadequate by the true appreciation principle. Nevertheless, chances are good that there is some K* such that the Ks are K*s, you appreciate O as a K*, and your appreciation of O as a K* counterfactually depends on no beliefs inconsistent with the nature of K*s. Again, your inadequate appreciation of O as a K is an adequate appreciation of O as a K*. Neither principle is terribly demanding.

Although the Carlson–Budd principle and the true appreciation principle set standards for adequate appreciation, they are independent. The Carlson–Budd principle holds that one adequately appreciates something as a K only if it is a K. The true appreciation principle holds that one adequately appreciates something as a K only so far as one is free of beliefs inconsistent with the nature of Ks. Either requirement can be met without meeting the other.

That leaves us four options: (1) assert both, (2) assert the Carlson–Budd principle and deny the true appreciation principle, (3) deny the Carlson–Budd principle and assert the true appreciation principle, or (4) deny both. Denying both betrays the assumption that some epistemic standard governs appreciation. To choose between the remaining options, it would help to know what is at stake.

## Punks, Parks, and Whales

Some appreciations are adequate according to the true appreciation principle and inadequate according to the Carlson–Budd principle.

Turner hears Avril Lavigne's music as punk – as raw and unproduced. So hearing it, he believes that it is punk. His belief about the music is false: the music is a packaged pop imitation of 1970s punk. But so what? Believing what he does, he gets to enjoy the music, and that matters. Believing the truth would cut him off from a source of pleasure, insight, and community.

Central Park is beloved of New Yorkers, who view it as the last trace of the natural state of Manhattan and so a bucolic refuge from bustle of the city that engulfs it. They are wrong, of course. The park is an artifact: a meticulously planned and maintained work of landscape architecture. Before Olmstead built the park, the land housed squatter camps and factories, and, before that, it was a dingy, malarial swamp, barely fit to graze cattle. But what follows from this? The boys at the deli have good reason to shrug off this recitation of facts. Historical truth deprives them of the pleasures of the park as they know it.

Thinking like this is not unique to teenagers and urbanites. Noël Carroll reports: "[I] may be excited by the grandeur of a blue whale. I may be moved by its size, its force, the amount of water it displaces, etc., but I may think that it is a fish."[4] The mistake is not exactly simple. The blue whale is grand indeed when compared to fish, for it is two to four orders of magnitude larger and stronger than them. It is not grander than other sea mammals to the same degree. Thus one might find the blue whale especially grand because one believes it is a fish. That is a benefit of believing it to be a fish.

Do not dismiss these cases as aberrant. Many more are easy to think up. Consider theistic appreciation of nature as a divine invention, animal appreciation rooted in anthropomorphism, or art appreciation framed by romantic ideas about creativity.

4 Noël Carroll "On Being Moved by Nature: Between Religion and Natural History," in *Beyond Aesthetics* (Cambridge: Cambridge University Press, 2001), p. 379.

The Carlson–Budd principle pronounces that Turner, Noël, and the boys at the deli appreciate inadequately. Avril Lavigne is not punk (she is faux punk). Central Park is not the last vestige of the original state of Manhattan, and the blue whale is not a fish. Moreover, these mistaken classifications are not inert: in each case, the appreciation counterfactually depends on the classification. Turner would not judge Avril Lavigne's music to be raw and unproduced if he believed the truth about its packaging – instead, he would judge it a disappointing sell out. The boys at the deli would not judge Central Park to be a refreshing escape from the human sphere if they believed it to fake nature – they might despise it, or come to like it for different reasons. Noël's comparing the blue whale to other mammals would diminish the blue whale's grandeur in his eyes.

By contrast, the true appreciation principle leaves Turner, Noël, and the boys at the deli in peace. That Turner falsely believes that Avril Lavigne's music is punk does not imply that he has any beliefs inconsistent with the nature of punk. On the contrary, his appreciation of Avril Lavigne may counterfactually depend on a rich knowledge of the nature of punk as a rebellion against commercial music. In the same way, the boys at the deli believe Central Park is "nature," but although it is not "nature," they may know what "nature" is. Their appreciation of the park may in fact depend counterfactually on true beliefs about the nature of "nature." Finally, believing, falsely, that the blue whale is a fish, Noël appreciates it as a fish, though he knows perfectly well that no fish are mammals. Notice that his appreciation would be different if he believed that fish are mammals – the blue whale would lose its grandeur. So Turner, Noël, and the boys at the deli do not appreciate inadequately.

True appreciators – those whose appreciations conform to the true appreciation principle – need not have true beliefs about what kinds the objects of their appreciations belong to. They may falsely believe that a creature is a fish, when in fact it is a mammal, that a play is a comedy, when in fact it is a tragedy, that an image is a photograph, when in fact it is a painting – and their appreciations are no less adequate. The true appreciation principle does not mandate finding out whether O is in fact a K as part of appreciating it adequately.

## An Image of Photography

It might seem that the Carlson–Budd principle frequently condemns appreciations as inadequate. That is a cost it has, and it is a cost we want it to have if we are to hold appreciation to an epistemic standard. It might also seem that the true appreciation principle impeaches no appreciations. Unless it does, it sets an empty standard.

Photography is a new art form and, like anything new, it is liable to be misunderstood. In addition, new art forms run a special risk of misunderstanding when they arise out of traditional art forms. Photography arose from painting and its early practitioners mimicked painting. Finally, photography is a new technology as well as a new art form, and new technologies are prone to misunderstanding, especially when they are hyped as something revolutionary, as happened with photography. We should therefore expect some misunderstanding of photography. In fact, it has been misunderstood in a way that plays a profound role in the way we appreciate it as art.

Barbara Savedoff's book, *Transforming Images*, is a penetrating analysis of what we appreciate in photography, what we believe about photography, and the way our beliefs underlie our appreciations. According to Savedoff, we appreciate photographs for their power to transform, "to make even the most familiar objects appear strange."[5] An example is an arresting photograph of J. P. Morgan, whose hat seems to stand in for his head (see figure 9.1). Savedoff observes that this photograph "seems to reveal something strange and unsettling about the way the world looks, and we are startled to find a gap between what the photograph compels us to see and what we know to be true."[6] Of course, Daumier might have drawn something much the same, but it could not have the same force, since only the photograph compels us to see the scene as strange but real, and strange because it is real. Nor is the photograph of Morgan one of a kind. Savedoff shows how photographs of the classic era from the turn of the century to the 1960s are compelling because they " 'document' an unfamiliar world that is at the same time *our* world, transformed."[7]

Photographs are compelling only because they "have our confidence in their veracity."[8] This confidence stems from the conflation of two beliefs. One is that photographs ***document*** their subject: they are the result of a causal, mechanical process originating in the subject. The other is that they ***duplicate*** their subject: they accurately record how it looks. These two beliefs get run together in our thinking about photographs: we conflate

5 Barbara Savedoff *Transforming Images: How Photography Complicates the Picture* (Ithaca: Cornell University Press, 2000), p. 2.

6 Ibid., p. 88.

7 Ibid., p. 128.

8 Ibid., p. 108.

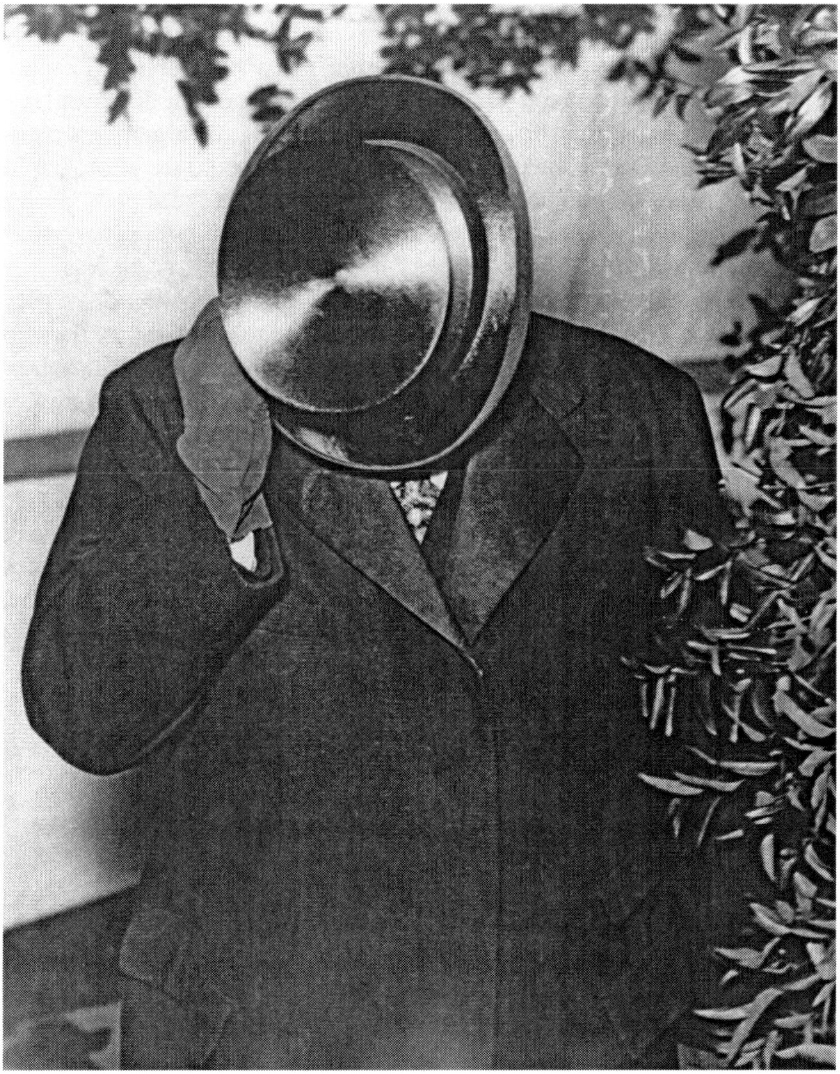

**Figure 9.1** Photographer unknown, *J. P. Morgan at Society Wedding Dodging the Camera*, 1937. Gelatin-silver print, 20 × 16″. The Museum of Modern Art, New York. Digital Image © The Museum of Modern Art/Licensed by SCALA/Art Resource, NY.

perfect copying with mechanical copying, and "this conflation allows our faith in the documentary character of photography to be inappropriately transferred to the way things appear within the photograph."[9] That we do not think this way about painting explains why painting does not have this power to transform the appearance of things. If photographers regularly used gum-bicarbonate painting techniques, we would see photographs differently, more like paintings.[10] However, we do in fact "read photographs as documenting the world," so "photography cannot simply adopt painting's critical principles."[11]

Here is another way to make the point. There is a phenomenon of trick photography. Trick photographs show things as looking the way they do not look and thereby evoke a (delightfully) surprised response. What explains this response is that trick photographs violate the expectation that photographs accurately record the way things look. Notice that there is no trick painting. Paintings may show things as looking the way they do not look but they do not thereby evoke any response of surprise. The reason is that nobody expects paintings accurately to record appearances. There can be no trick painting without such an expectation. There are trick photographs because we have confidence in the veracity of photography.

Savedoff is neutral on whether we are right or wrong to have confidence in the veracity of photographs. She writes:

> [P]erhaps photographs cannot be correctly understood as possessing a special documentary status; nevertheless, that is how they are experienced. . . . And insofar as [this] is necessary to a well-grounded evaluation and understanding of the photographs that we have been considering, it must be reflected in the critical principles we bring to bear.[12]

Again, "whether it is warranted or not, we tend to see photographs as objective records of the world, and this tendency has a far-reaching influence on interpretation and evaluation."[13] Is this a fair description of photographic appreciation? It certainly rings true of a large number of photographs, which we would not find very interesting were it not for their perceived transformative effects. Moreover, it speaks for the dominant tradition of photographic theory, clarifying and systematizing the views

9 Ibid., p. 193.
10 Ibid., p. 115.
11 Ibid., p. 149.
12 Ibid., p. 128.
13 Ibid., p. 49.

of theorists such as Arnheim, Barthes, Bazin, and Sontag.[14] The theorists include philosophers. Roger Scruton writes: "[I]t is in terms of the causal relation that the subject of a photograph is normally understood . . . it follows . . . that it must appear roughly as it appears in the photograph."[15] These theorists may or may not have the truth about photography, but we have every reason to believe that they have the truth about how we think about photography.

If Savedoff is right that photographic appreciation depends on a belief that photographs deserve the special confidence that we have in them, then, to that extent, photographic appreciation is inadequate by the true appreciation principle. While many photographs are reliable sources of information about their subjects, they do not deserve the special confidence we have in them, because documentation does not imply duplication. The belief that it does is inconsistent with the truth about the nature of photography.

## The Argument from Objectivity

The Carlson–Budd principle and the true appreciation principle pronounce contrary verdicts on our cases. According to the Carlson–Budd principle, Turner, Noël, and the boys at the deli appreciate inadequately, but our appreciations of photographs as photographs are adequate, since photographs are photographs. According to the true appreciation principle, if Savedoff is right, then our appreciations of photographs as photographs are inadequate: although photographs are photographs, our appreciation of them counterfactually depends on beliefs inconsistent with the true nature of photography. The good news is that Turner, Noël, and the boys at the deli appreciate adequately, since their appreciations counterfactually depend on no beliefs inconsistent with the nature of punk, whales, and nature. As long as intuitions are divided, neither principle is more plausible.

The argument for the Carlson–Budd principle is an argument from objectivity. In this argument, the Carlson–Budd principle is offered as a solution to a problem. If the problem is real, the Carlson–Budd principle solves it, but the true appreciation principle solves it too.

14 Ibid., pp. 48–9; see also Rudolf Arnheim, "The Two Authenticities of the Photographic Media," *Journal of Aesthetics and Art Criticism* 51 (1993): 537–40.

15 Roger Scruton, "Photography and Representation," in *The Aesthetic Understanding* (London: Methuen, 1983); see this volume, ch. 6, p. 150.

The argument from objectivity is adapted (without his endorsement) from Kendall L. Walton's "Categories of Art." Walton shows that the aesthetic properties a work seems to have depend on the non-aesthetic properties it seems to have relative to perceptually distinguishable categories. In the now famous example, *Guernica* looks "violent, dynamic, vital, disturbing" when viewed as a painting, but it would look "cold, stark, lifeless, or serene and restful, or perhaps bland, dull, boring" when viewed as a guernica – a category of works that implement the 2D pattern of *Guernica* in degrees of bas-relief.[16]

Walton individuates categories such as paintings, guernicas, and classical sonatas by appeal to which non-aesthetic properties of works in the categories are "standard," "contra-standard," and "variable." A property is standard for a category just in case its *absence* would (tend to) disqualify a work from the category. It is contra-standard for a category just in case its *presence* would (tend to) disqualify a work from the category. A property is variable for a category just in case neither its absence nor its presence would (tend to) disqualify a work from the category. In painting, flatness is standard, having moving parts is contra-standard, and having red patches is variable.

Categories are individuated by sets of properties, so there are many, many categories. Here is where our troubles begin. If the aesthetic properties a work seems to have depend on the category in which it is perceived, then works may seem to have different aesthetic properties when viewed in different categories. For any work and any aesthetic property, F, there is some category of art in which it appears F. However, Walton objects, category-relative perceptions of works do not allow ascriptions of aesthetic properties to be mistaken often enough.[17] For any such ascription, there is some category in which the ascription is true.

The solution is to claim that it is correct to perceive a work in certain categories and incorrect to perceive it in others. Some ascriptions are mistaken: those that depend on perceiving the work in an incorrect category.

The argument easily carries over to appreciation. Suppose that the kinds that figure in appreciation are individuated at least as finely as Walton's categories (maybe they are Walton's categories). If any given item may be appreciated as K, for any K, then for any ascription, p, there is some K such that p is not mistaken when the item is appreciated as a K. Our ascriptions are not mistaken often enough. The solution enlists the Carlson–Budd principle to restrict adequate appreciation: one adequately

[16] Walton, "Categories of Art," p. 347.

[17] Ibid., p. 355.

appreciates something as a K only if it is a K. Ascriptions are mistaken when they issue from inadequate appreciations. Inadequate appreciation is common, so our ascriptions are often mistaken.

This solution succeeds in its aim: it explains why ascriptions are often mistaken. However, there is another solution. Note that Walton does *not* object that category-relative interpretations *never* allow ascriptions to be mistaken. His use of the weaker "often enough" hints at a recognition that there is already room for error in category-relative appreciation.

Munro judges that a dog is rather too short for its breed. Posh objects that the dog is a shetland sheepdog, not a collie, and Munro must be viewing it as a collie because, although it is short for a collie, it is a good height for a shetland sheepdog. "No," replies Munro, "it's too short for a sheltie." Munro's ascription is mistaken if Posh is right and the dog is the ideal height for a shetland sheepdog. Alternatively, Posh's ascription is mistaken if the dog is short for a shetland sheepdog and she is viewing it as one.

Rosalind remarks that *Guernica* is restful. You might think that she takes her philosophy a little too seriously, for she is appreciating *Guernica* as a guernica. However, she reads your mind and, realizing that *you* take philosophy too seriously, hastens to add, "and I mean that it's restful *as a painting*." Rosalind is obviously mistaken. *Guernica* is not restful when appreciated as a painting.

There is more than one way to explain these mistakes. Perhaps Munro lacks the concept of height and Rosalind lacks that of restfulness, or perhaps they misuse English vocabulary. Those are not the only explanations, however. Stipulate that Munro and Rosalind have the concepts in question and know the English words that name them. They can still be mistaken. After all, Munro may have a wrong idea about shetland sheepdogs and Rosalind may have a wrong idea about painting. Munro may falsely believe that the mean height of a shetland sheepdog is 50 centimeters and Rosalind may falsely believe that most paintings look like Jackson Pollock's drips.

Another solution to the objectivity problem enlists the true appreciation principle: one adequately appreciates something as a K only as far as one's appreciation counterfactually depends on no beliefs inconsistent with the nature of Ks. Ascriptions are mistaken when they issue from appreciations that are inadequate by this standard. Inadequate appreciation is common, because beliefs inconsistent with the truth about what things are are also common, so our ascriptions are often mistaken.

Both solutions to the objectivity problem are successful insofar as both explain why ascriptions that issue from appreciations are sometimes mistaken – more often than never and perhaps quite often. This much is news, since the Carlson–Budd principle is widely accepted as the sole solution to the objectivity problem. However, each principle implies that a different set of ascriptions are mistaken, for each proposes that different sets of appreciations are inadequate. Your intuitions may go with the Carlson–Budd principle or they may go with the true appreciation principle. That is, your intuitions may go with the photography fans or with Turner, Noël, and the boys at the deli. The argument from objectivity cannot decide between these conflicting intuitions.

One way to resolve the conflict is to uphold both sets of intuitions by denying both the true appreciation principle and the Carlson–Budd principle. That resolution denies that the objectivity problem is real. It is the non-cognitivist solution.

Another option is to assert the true appreciation principle and the Carlson–Budd principle together. This option will appeal to those whose intuitions go against the fans of photography as well as Turner, Noël, and the boys at the deli. Perhaps there is reason to uphold intuitions as severe as these. The reason cannot be that both principles are needed to solve the objectivity problem. Only one principle is needed to do that job.

## The Ontology of Appreciation

The argument from objectivity does recommend accepting the Carlson–Budd principle if the true appreciation principle is untenable. It is untenable if any appreciation that fails to meet it also fails to meet the Carlson–Budd principle or if it is empty, setting a standard on appreciation that is always met.

One objection builds upon a view about what it is to have true beliefs about the nature of the Ks. On this view, having true beliefs about the nature of the Ks entails being able to tell Ks from non-Ks. One cannot have all true beliefs about what it is to be a K and yet fail to recognize Ks. If this is correct, the generous account of Turner, Noël, and the boys at the deli is incoherent. We said that, in each case, an appreciator wrongly takes a work to be a K and also has true beliefs about the nature of the Ks. If having these true beliefs entails being able to tell Ks from non-Ks, then the appreciators do not in fact appreciate what they do as Ks. And if we have no reason to doubt appreciators' reports that they take something to be a K, then they must not have true beliefs about the nature of the Ks. That explains their misidentification of a non-K as a K: they do not know what Ks are.

If this line of thought is correct, then Turner, Noël, and the boys at the deli appreciate inadequately. In effect, anyone who fails the standard of the true appreciation principle also fails the standard of the Carlson–Budd principle. The two principles do not issue contrary verdicts. The choice between them is now clear: choose the Carlson–Budd principle. Whereas both principles condemn Turner, Noël, and the boys at the deli, the Carlson–Budd principle does not condemn appreciations of photographs and the argument from objectivity warrants only one standard.

One difficulty with this objection is that the true appreciation principle does not require that adequate appreciators have true constitutive beliefs about the nature of Ks. It says only that appreciation is adequate only as far as it counterfactually depends on no beliefs inconsistent with the truth about the nature of Ks. An appreciation is no less adequate for depending on no beliefs whatsoever about the nature of Ks. The point is not academic: some appreciations are so thin as not to depend on any such beliefs.

More importantly, the objection sets the bar too high for classification. In general, having all true beliefs about the nature of Ks does not imply an infallible ability to classify Ks. I know that water is $H_2O$ and yet I sometimes mistake non-water for water. You may know that to be a wolf is to be a member of a certain biological lineage and yet you may mistake swamp wolf for a member of *Canis lupus*. The point is pressing when it comes to artifacts which are members of historical kinds. Perceptually indiscernible objects may belong to different kinds just because they were made in different circumstances.[18] Danto's indiscernibles dramatize a more widespread phenomenon: not every feature that makes a K a K is an intrinsic, perceptible feature of Ks. Mimickry may be deliberate. This explains why Turner, Noël, and the boys at the deli make the mistakes that they make. Avril Lavigne sounds like punk, the blue whale resembles a fish, and Central Park looks like a natural landscape.

(Needless to say, this is consistent with the fact that misclassifications are sometimes due to false beliefs about the nature of the kind into which an item is misclassified. You misclassify "Pressure Drop" by Toots and the Maytals as polka because you falsely believe that to be a polka is to have a reggae beat.)

A second objection raises the question of what concepts we should attribute to appreciators. Suppose that any case where your appreciating O might be said to depend counterfactually on beliefs inconsistent with

[18] Danto, "The Artworld."

the nature of the Ks is in fact a case where you are appreciating O as a K*, where K* is the kind whose nature fits the relevant beliefs. Suppose that "fauxtographs" have the very features that we wrongly attribute to photographs. Unlike photographs, fauxtographs really do deserve our confidence in their veracity. Thus to appreciate an image as something that deserves confidence in its veracity is just to appreciate it as a fauxtograph.

It follows that our appreciation of photographs is exactly like Turner's appreciation of Avril Lavigne, the boys' appreciation of Central Park, and Noël's appreciation of the blue whale: in each case, a K is appreciated as a K*. The true appreciation principle is trivial, for the condition it imposes on adequate appreciation is always satisfied. If the true appreciation principle is trivial, however, then only the Carlson–Budd principle solves the objectivity problem, and that gives us good reason to accept it.

The objection assumes that to appreciate a work is to appreciate it as *whatever* kind has the nature that fits the appreciation. Only given this assumption can we say that to appreciate an image as something that deserves confidence in its veracity is just to appreciate it as a fauxtograph. However, the assumption is false.

I might believe that conifers are by nature evergreens. You know better: there are deciduous conifers. Nevertheless, you and I share a concept of conifers. We do so because we defer to the tree experts about the nature of conifers. Indeed, our deferring to the experts explains why I can misclassify some trees and why I can either have false beliefs about the nature of conifers or else have beliefs that are inconsistent with the truth about the nature of conifers. Were it not for deference (or something like it), I could never misclassify or make mistakes about the nature of things. What look to you like misclassifications of conifers are in fact classifications of shconifers, about whose nature the classifier cannot be wrong.

What goes for trees also goes for art forms. Turner defers to the experts about the nature of punk. You and I defer to the experts, unless we are the experts, about the nature of photography. Our concept of photography is a concept of a kind whose nature is known by the experts. It is not a concept of *whatever* kind fits our appreciations. The objection gives us too much power over our appreciative concepts.

That is not to say that we have no power over our appreciative concepts. I am free to stipulate that I appreciate photographs as fauxtographs, knowing full well that photography is not fauxtography and that there are no fauxtographs. However, such a stipulation falls short of what the objection requires: that when we appreciate photographs as we do – taking ourselves to appreciate them as photographs – in fact we appreciate them as fauxtographs.

A final objection trades on the proposition that there are no truths about the nature of photography or other appreciative kinds. If there are no such truths, then all beliefs are consistent with the truth about the nature of Ks. Applying the reasoning to the case of photography, if there is nothing about photographs that makes photography the kind that it is, then photographic appreciations never depend counterfactually on beliefs that are inconsistent with the nature of photographs. The true appreciation principle is satisfied trivially and we should prefer the Carlson–Budd principle for solving the objectivity problem.

Tony is listening to an ordinary waltz, which he says he appreciates as a waltz. He is clearly enjoying the music, humming and tapping along with it, when he exclaims, "Blimey, what an innovation!" Puzzled, you ask him what he has in mind. "It's a waltz in 3/4 time!" If this is not an inadequate appreciation of a waltz as a waltz, then it is hard to know what is. It is not inadequate in the sense that Tony fails to enjoy the music. He may enjoy it a great deal. It is inadequate in the sense that appreciation is an activity and although Tony is engaging in the activity, he is not doing it very well.

What explains the inadequacy? One option is that Tony does not understand time signatures. That is easy enough to dismiss: ask him to tap the beat of "Money" and he taps you some flawless 7 time, or ask him to tap the beat of an "old school" waltz and he taps some common time. What else is there? He believes falsely that the work is in 3 time? No, it really is a waltz. The explanation must be that he has a false belief about the nature of waltzes. It is only in light of this belief that he finds the music innovative.

If this explanation is right, then the waltz is a kind whose instances are all in 3 time. Adequately appreciating a waltz as a waltz means hearing it in a way that is controlled by the fact that waltzes are in 3 time. That is, it means hearing the waltz as something in 3 time. Tony's misapprehension breeds misappreciation. If he is to do better, one of his beliefs about waltzes must be revised. Which one? His belief about what makes a waltz a waltz: its time signature.

The case of Tony is a template from which it is easy to stamp out examples of equally inadequate appreciation. Tenille complains that the pinotage she is tasting is too bold for a pinotage – she believes that the pinot noir is overpowered by the varieties with which it has been blended (cabernet sauvignon, she speculates). Pinotage is not a blend, however, and Tenille's false belief that it is a blend of pinot noir leads her to think about the wine in the wrong way. Tenille is right: the wine is bigger than a pinot noir. As a pinotage, however, it is not too big. She fails to appreciate it adequately as a pinotage.

Biting the bullet is an option. Tony and Tenille are adequate appreciators, because there are no intrinsic features that make a waltz a waltz or a pinotage a pinotage (or a photograph a photograph). Perhaps being a waltz or a pinotage (or a photograph) is merely a matter of origins.

The bullet is a hard one. If being a photograph is merely a matter of origins, then it is presumably a matter of origins in a practice of making photographs. Photographs are those items made by photographers as part of their practice as photographers. No additional conditions require that a photograph have this or that intrinsic feature. So nothing stops a photographer working within her practice from making a photograph that has all the intrinsic features of a painting – or a Petrarchan sonnet. To block that result, you might think that the practice includes rules limiting what counts as a photograph. An item, say the rules, must have such-and-such intrinsic features if it is to count, within the practice, as a photograph. It must be an image, perhaps. One that has been made by means of a camera, no doubt. In that case, however, being a photograph is not merely a matter of origins: some intrinsic features of photographs are part of what makes them photographs.

The true appreciation principle is not untenable. It remains a live option, in competition with the Carlson–Budd principle as a solution to the problem of objectivity and hence as an epistemic standard on appreciation.

## Accounting Intuitions

Accept the true appreciation principle. What price is paid? Tony's appreciation of the waltz, Tenille's appreciation of the pinotage, and our appreciation of photographs are all inadequate. At the same time, Turner's appreciation of the Avril Lavigne, the boys' appreciation of Central Park, and Noël's appreciation of the blue whale are all adequate. Denying the true appreciation principle converts our credits to debits and our debits to credits. The next step is to see which method of accounting yields the higher balance. The complication is that those who side with Turner, Noël, and the boys at the deli discount the cost of ruling against the fans of photography and those who side with the fans of photography discount the cost of ruling against Turner, Noël, and the boys at the deli. The only effective way to settle the dispute is to see whether intuitions apparently favoring one principle or the other can be explained way. Explaining them away tips the balance sheet.

The true appreciation principle leaves Turner, Noël, and the boys at the deli in peace; it is the choice of those who believe that their appreciations are adequate. Perhaps, however, anyone who sides with Turner, Noël, and the boys at the deli will accept another explanation of why they should be left in peace. Turner, Noël, and the boys at the deli are *blameless* in appreciating as they do. Although their appreciations involve false beliefs, those beliefs are warranted, and warranted beliefs are blameless even when false. Turner has good reason to believe that Avril Lavigne's music is punk: after all, she mimics punk and he is not in a good position to see through the trick. Likewise, whales have many of the superficial characteristics of fish – and Noël is no biologist. It is urban lore that Central Park is the last trace of the natural state of Manhattan Island. Thus, Turner, Noël, and the boys at the deli appreciate inadequately, just as the Carlson–Budd principle predicts, but the inadequacy is blameless.

This does not go far enough to appease those who side with Turner, Noël, and the boys at the deli. The true appreciation principle does not merely imply that Turner, Noël, and the boys at the deli are blameless in their classifications. It says, more strongly, that their misclassifications and the false beliefs that they imply are irrelevant to the adequacy of their appreciations. The claim that Turner, Noël, and the boys at the deli misclassify things blamelessly rests on their not being in a position to classify correctly. Were Turner older, Noël better schooled in biology, and the boys at the deli well informed about the picturesque, then their misclassifications would be culpable. Not even this is allowed by the true appreciation principle. Mere misclassification is never relevant to the adequacy of appreciation.

Suppose that Turner learns that Avril Lavigne's music is a packaged pop imitation of punk. So what? He may opt to hear it as punk. Hearing it as punk, he has access to a source of pleasure, insight, and community.

Everybody knows that the blue whale is not a fish. If you want to experience its grandeur, however, appreciate it as a fish.

Central Park is beloved of New Yorkers. Those who know their history know that it is a meticulously planned and maintained work of landscape architecture. However, the park loses its charm when seen as an artifact. For this reason, historically informed New Yorkers may continue to appreciate it as the last trace of the original, bucolic state of their city.

These descriptions are less bizarre than they may seem at first. The deliberate and knowing appreciation of non-Ks as Ks is widespread. It is widespread because it is a freedom that delivers important appreciative goods that would otherwise lie beyond reach. For example, we regularly appreciate picturesque landscapes as paintings, and we do the same thing with dance performances, appreciating them as two-dimensional images.

Some paintings we regularly appreciate as little pieces of theatre, and others we appreciate as photographs. Some photographs we appreciate as paintings. In each of these cases, we appreciate what we believe to be a K* as a K. In some of these cases, part of full appreciation of the K* as a K* involves appreciating it as a K.

There are additional cases where we misclassify and also have a false belief about the nature of the appreciative category, but where it is reasonable to expect that we will only correct the latter. Greco-Roman sculpture was painted – indeed, rather garishly. The discovery during the renaissance of ancient marbles that had lost their paint over time established the false image we have of Greco-Roman sculpture as unpainted marble and bronze. It also established the norm for modern sculpture, which copied its norms and aims from norms and aims that were thought to be embodied in Greco-Roman sculpture. As a result, our appreciation of a Polykleitos as Greco-Roman sculpture counterfactually depends upon a false belief that Greco-Roman sculpture is naked marble, and it is to that extent inadequate. We can do better. Armed with better knowledge of the ancient world, we can appreciate the Polykleitos as Greco-Roman sculpture, deploying a conception of Greco-Roman sculpture that fits the truth about its paint job. Alternatively, we can appreciate it as belonging to the kind whose norms and aims were established in the renaissance. It does not belong to that kind, so we make an error in classification. In fact, we mostly opt for the latter. We would lose too much, no matter what the gain, by opting for the former.

The Carlson–Budd principle would put a stop to all these appreciations. Only the true appreciation principle accommodates them.

Moreover, the fact that we may deliberately and profitably appreciate a non-K as a K suggests how to explain away the intuitions that side with the fans of photography. If Savedoff is right, we falsely believe that photographs deserve confidence in their veracity. The true appreciation principle implies that our appreciations are inadequate insofar as they rest on this false belief. However, we need not appreciate photographs as photographs. If we profit from appreciating photographs as fauxtographs, then we have reason to appreciate them as fauxtographs, knowing all the while that they are not fauxtographs. The appreciations are adequate.

Both the true appreciation principle and the Carlson–Budd principle grant us the freedom of some false belief. Having these false beliefs does no harm to the quality of appreciation. Since they disagree about which false beliefs we are free to have and since we are not free to have them all, we must choose. The true appreciation principle is viable in so far as it survives objections. In addition, it vindicates intuitions about Turner,

Noël, and the boys at the deli, while it explains away intuitions about photographic appreciation.

## Fakes and Severity

The argument from objectivity warrants either the true appreciation principle or the Carlson–Budd principle and not both. It asks us to choose, and we should choose the principle that best fits our intuitions, either by capturing them or by explaining them away. But maybe some intuitions favor the severe option, conjoining the principles. The intuitions concern fakes.

This painting looks like a Vermeer, but suppose that it was actually painted by Han van Meegeren in 1938. If you appreciate it as a Vermeer, your appreciation will go one way and if you appreciate it as a van Meegeren, it will go another. For example, you might issue different judgments – it is a success, in the former case, or it is a travesty, in the latter case. The so-called problem of forgery arises at this point: the problem is how two indiscernible objects can give rise to different appreciations in the same context. However, that problem is not a problem for either the true appreciation principle or the Carlson–Budd principle. Both principles build in a difference between appreciating O as a K and as a K* – between appreciating a Vermeerish-looking painting as a Vermeer or as a van Meegeren. Put another way, the difference in appreciation by itself makes neither appreciation inadequate. Even so, many people intuit that the appreciation of the painting as a Vermeer is inadequate if it is a van Meegeren and that the appreciation of the painting as a van Meegeren is inadequate if it is a Vermeer. The Carlson–Budd principle captures that intuition.

However, intuitions about fakes do not by themselves favor the Carlson–Budd principle over the true appreciation principle. On the contrary, they lend some support to the true appreciation principle. Fakes are disturbing, to those who are disturbed, in two ways. It is obviously vexing that one might appreciate a fake as a Vermeer and so overvalue it, as it is vexing that one might appreciate a Vermeer as a fake and thereby undervalue it. It is also vexing that one might, by taking van Meegerens to be Vermeers, come to have the wrong idea about Vermeers. Scholars report that van Meegeren was able to pull of his stunt partly because he achieved some success with one or two fakes, which changed the experts' idea of what a Vermeer is, and each new fake was easier to sneak into the reconfigured canon. The former vexation depends on the latter. No minds worried about overvaluing fakes are put at ease by the observation that to appreciate a

Vermeer as a Vermeer is to appreciate it as belonging to that category of painting polluted by van Meegerens. Such minds will see in this more, not less, reason to worry. They will insist that the true appreciation principle applies.

So if intuitions about fakes support the Carlson–Budd principle, then they also support the true appreciation principle. The intuitions support the severe option. The result is that Turner, and Noël, and the boys at the deli appreciate inadequately, and so do those fans of photography who have confidence in its veracity. Moreover, since the intuitions endorse both principles, there is no chance that one principle can explain away the intuitions in favor of the other.

Nevertheless, it is probably premature to settle upon the severe option. Not everybody shares the intuition that there is a difference between appreciating a painting as a Vermeer and as a van Meegeren (because they look so much alike). Grant the moral and legal difference; the appreciative difference is controversial.[19] Thus not everybody shares the intuition that one appreciation is better than the other. Indeed, it may be prior acceptance of the Carlson–Budd principle that is driving the intuition. The matter cannot be settled until we know more about appreciation than the epistemic standards that govern it. A non-cognitivist may deny that adequate appreciation is diminished by false belief. She may deny the true appreciation principle and the Carlson–Budd principle. But if non-cognitivism is false, then one or both principles are true. If only one is true and the arguments given above are correct, then the true appreciation principle is true. If both are true then the true appreciation principle is true. However, the principle is only a first step towards a theory of appreciation, for it sets only a weak epistemic standard upon appreciation. Even as a start, it is a big step, for it compels us to take a second look at photography. Nobody knows whether that is worthwhile.[20]

19 Denis Dutton, *The Forger's Art: Forgery and the Philosophy of Art* (Berkeley: University of California Press, 1983).

20 I am grateful for discussion of this essay to audiences at the 2005 Aesthetics Anarchy, the University of British Columbia, Kansas State University, Sheffield University, Cambridge University, Warwick University, and McGill University. Scott Anderson, Rob Hopkins, Hugh Hunter, Bence Nanay, Doug Patterson, Jeff Speaks, Dustin Stokes, and Scott Walden made some especially helpful suggestions.

# 10

# LANDSCAPE AND STILL LIFE: STATIC REPRESENTATIONS OF STATIC SCENES

Kendall L. Walton

When a person views Rubens's *Autumn Landscape* (figure 10.1):

(a) She sees the picture, the pattern of colored marks on the picture surface.
(b) She imagines seeing the depicted scene: trees and fields, a horse cart and a hunter, clouds in the background, buildings on the left, etc.
(c) She imagines her actual perceiving of the picture surface to be a perceiving of the trees and fields, clouds, horse cart, etc.[1]

These imaginings are not undertaken deliberately, of course. The viewer doesn't decide to imagine seeing trees and fields, etc., set out to imagine them, and then do it. The marks on the canvas are such as to trigger the imaginings more or less automatically. She might, however, choose which part of the picture to look at when, knowing that this will affect what imaginings she will find herself engaged in as a result.

The imagination-imbued visual experience I just described is necessary for seeing the painting as a picture of trees and fields and buildings, etc., for seeing them "in" the visual design (as Richard Wollheim would put it). But the viewer is likely to engage in further, more detailed imaginings as well, as her eyes scan the picture surface. She may imagine surveying the scene for an extended period of time, noticing first this, then that, looking for this or that, etc. A typical viewer, leisurely contemplating this picture in a typical manner, might describe her experience as follows:

1 These three points are the key elements in an account of the nature of picture perception which I have developed and defended elsewhere. Cf. especially Walton, *Mimesis as Make-Believe: On the Foundations of the Representational Arts* (Cambridge, MA: Harvard University Press, 1990). My claims in the present essay could probably be reformulated to accommodate different ways of understanding picture perception.

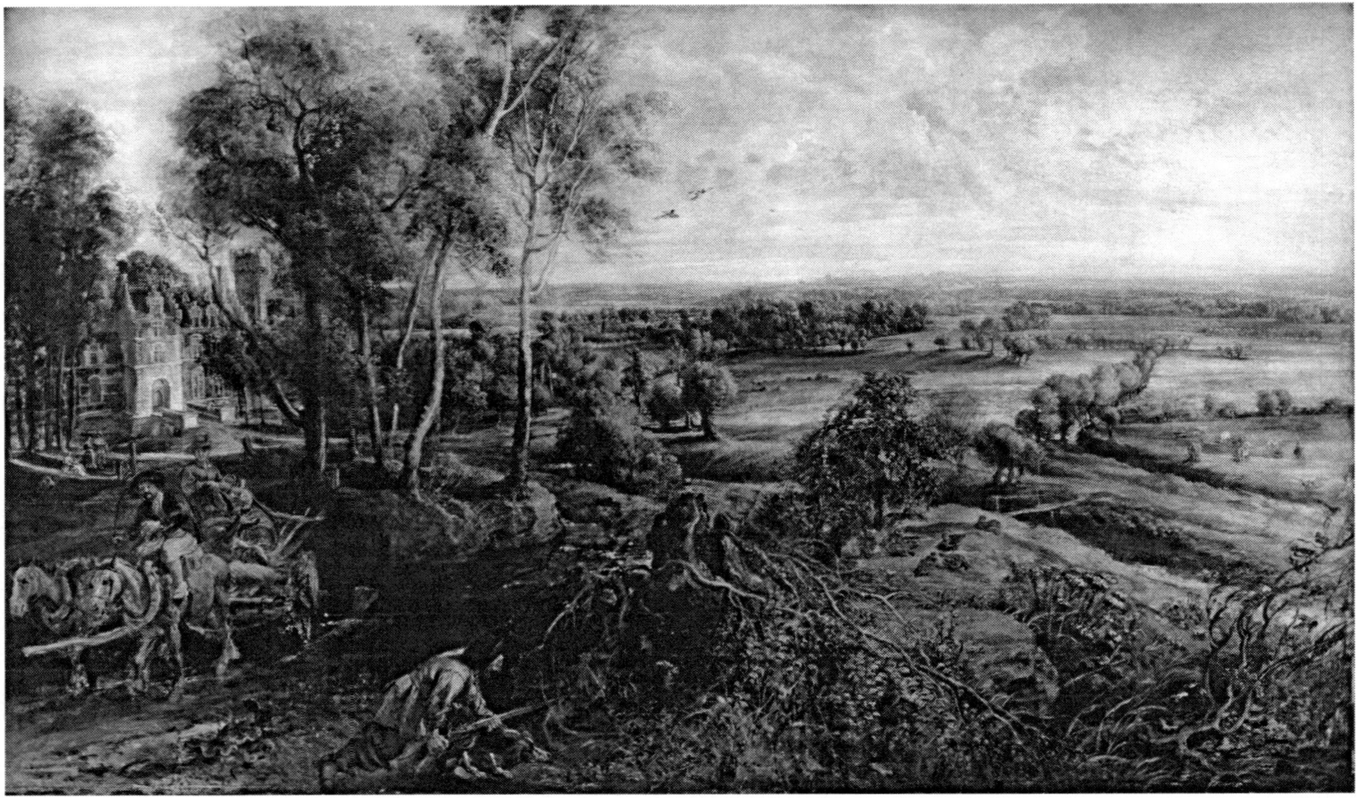

**Figure 10.1** Peter Paul Rubens, *An Autumn Landscape with a View of Het Steen in the Early Morning* (probably 1636). The National Gallery, London. Gift of Sir George Beaumont. Picture reference NG66.

> Looking out on a vast landscape, I see a hunter and his dog in the shadows near me, as a farm wagon passes by, then catch sight of a small footbridge crossing a stream, and beyond that a group of grazing cattle. I look to see what the hunter's quarry might be, and notice several birds in the field. Examining them more carefully I identify them as partridges. . . . I pick out a blackberry bush in the foreground. I watch the clouds drifting lazily across the sky, and several birds circling above. Finally I catch sight of a village on the horizon, the town of Malines.

These words understood literally might describe a person's experience as he looks out on an actual rural scene. The viewer of the painting uses them to report her imaginative experience, what she imagines seeing as she scans the canvas. It is *as though* she is surveying an actual landscape for several or many minutes, for as long as she continues to look at the painting.

What I have said about Rubens's painting applies equally to landscape photographs, such as figure 10.2. It will be convenient to focus mostly on photographs, since I will be comparing them with photographic films.

The viewer sees the photographic surface. She imagines seeing a mountain. And she imagines her actual visual experience to be an experience, not of a picture but of a mountain. Lingering before the photograph, she might describe her experience in a narrative worthy of reporting an extended visual examination of the mountain itself:

> Looking toward the forbidding hulk of Mt. Geryon, I notice that it is almost entirely without vegetation. My eye is drawn to the jagged ridge line. Then I focus on the vertical fissures, looking for a climbing route to the top. Finally, I notice the mountains far in the background.

All this so far may seem pretty innocuous. But worries lurk in the shadows.

Motion pictures of static scenes can in principle be visually indistinguishable from still pictures of the same scenes. If a film is made of Mt. Geryon using a fixed camera, without zooming or panning, the motion-picture image is likely to be motionless for as long as it lasts, and may be indistinguishable from the still photograph. The scene Rubens depicted is mostly static, but the cart is moving slowly, presumably, and so are the birds and the clouds in the sky. Suppose we crop out these moving objects. If oil paint could be induced to change in controlled ways making oil-on-canvas motion pictures possible, a motion picture of the static scene, in that medium, might be visually indistinguishable from the cropped painting. No technological breakthroughs would be needed to produce

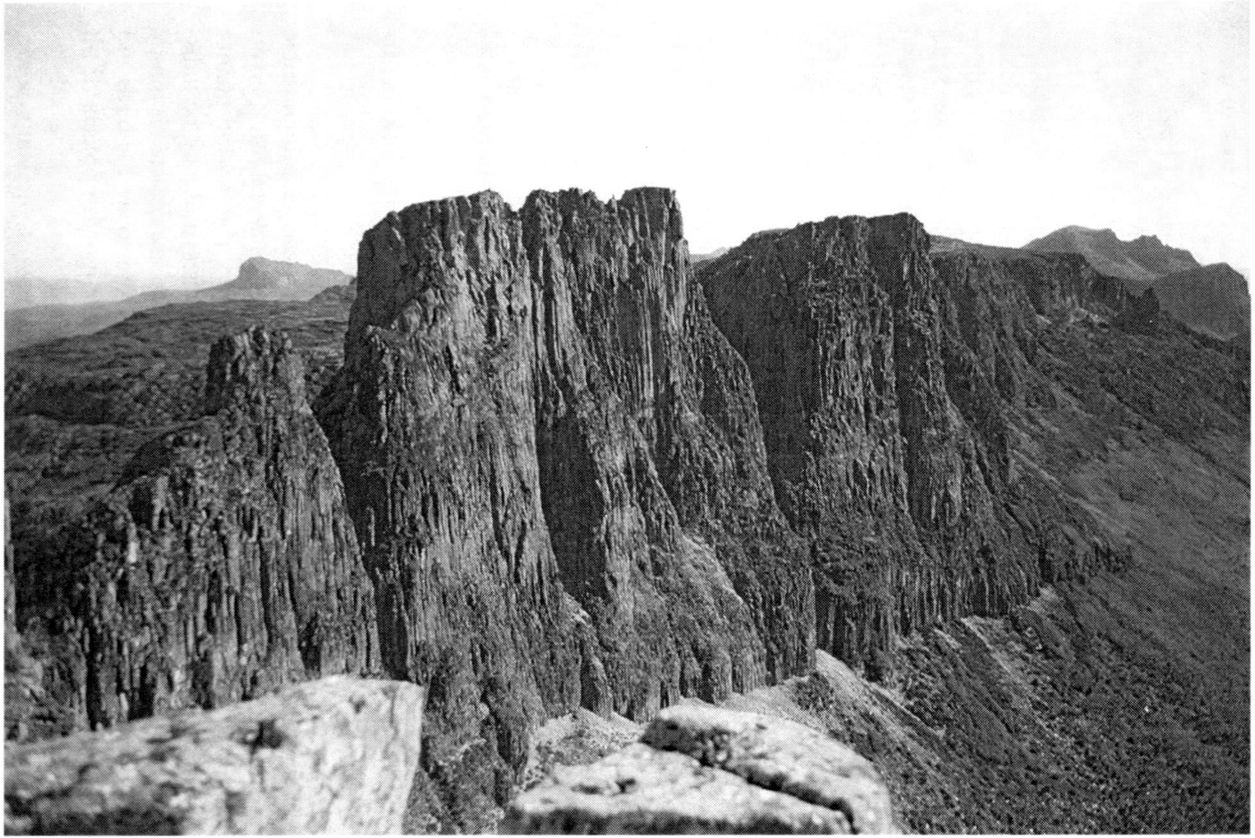

**Figure 10.2** Kendall L. Walton, *Mount Geryon*.

a photographic motion picture indistinguishable from a photographic reproduction of the painting.

Even if they can't tell them apart by looking, however, viewers are likely to experience a still and a motion picture of a static scene very differently – assuming that they realize that they are seeing a still picture in one case and a film, a motion picture, in the other. The two images do not appear *different*, but they appear *differently*. They afford different visual experiences without giving the impression of being different.[2] This difference is a symptom of fascinating and so far mostly unnoticed complexities in our experiences of still pictures generally. The above observations do not bring the difference out. What I just said about experiences of painted and photographic still pictures surely goes for motion pictures as well: Observing the filmed image of Mt. Geryon, one imagines seeing the mountain, and imagines one's actual perceiving of the image to be a perception of the mountain. One also imagines continuing to observe the mountain scene – for as long as the shot lasts.

What is it for a picture to be a still or a moving one? This question is trickier than it seems. Arthur Danto once wrote that "Moving pictures are just that: *pictures which move*."[3] He can't have meant this, however, for he offers (near) counterexamples of his own, including Andy Warhol's film, *Empire*, a single five-hour shot of the Empire State Building. Moving pictures do not necessarily move. And stills need not be still: Paintings fade over time, a picture drawn in sand erodes, an artist touches up his canvas or a restorer cleans it, pigeons deposit droppings on it. Also, both still and moving pictures can depict or represent either motion or stasis. The filmed mountain landscape depicts things as unmoving. Many still pictures depict motion; some do so with astonishing vivacity. Look at the examples shown in figures 10.3, 10.4, and 10.5. The difference between still and motion pictures consists neither in temporal properties of the images themselves nor in their representational content, but rather in the relation between the two, the relation between changes or lack of them in pictures, and changes or lack of them in picture worlds.[4]

What is it about images of the two kinds by virtue of which they depict motion or stasis? In the case of motion pictures, temporal properties of

2 See Robert Hopkins, "Aesthetics, Experience, and Discrimination," *Journal of Aesthetics and Art Criticism* 63: 2 (2005): 119–33.

3 Arthur C. Danto, "Moving Pictures," *Quarterly Review of Film Studies* 2 (1979): 15; italics in original.

4 There are likely to be differences in *depictive* content, as opposed to *representational* content, however. See below.

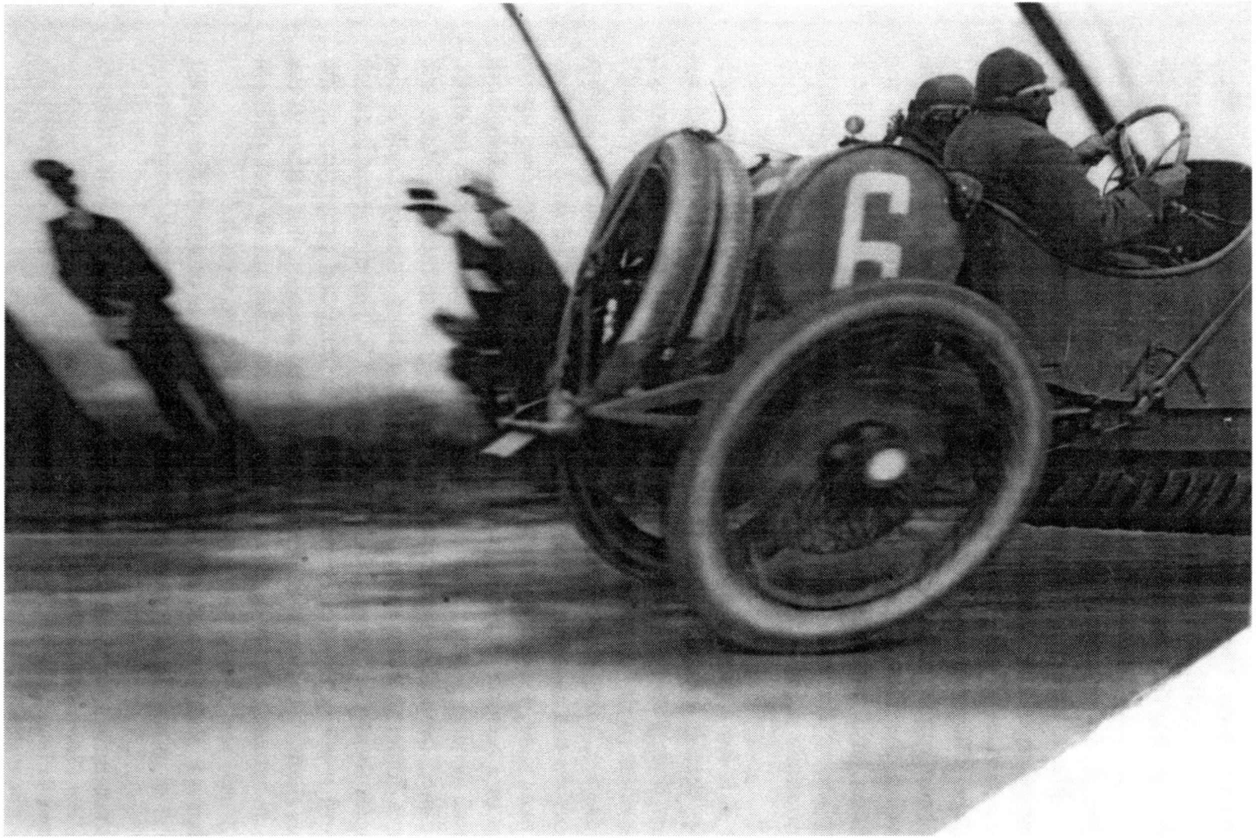


**Figure 10.3** Jacques Henri Lartigue, *Grand Prix of the Automobile Club of France*, 1913. The Metropolitan Museum of Art, Gilman Collection, Purchase, Ann Tenenbaum and Thomas H. Lee Gift. Accession Number 2005.100.125, Image Number DP 141227.

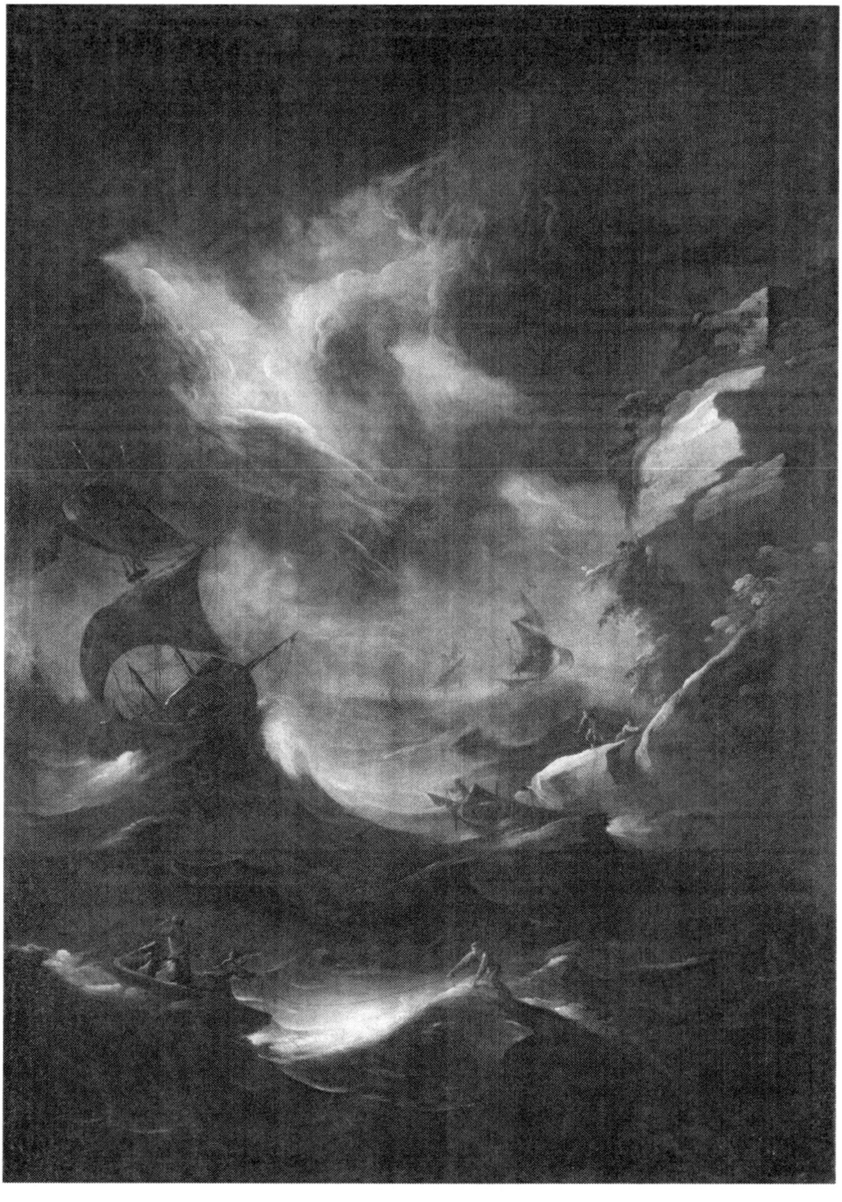

**Figure 10.4** Francesco Antoniani, *Marina in burrasca*, *c.* 1770, Banca Intesa, Inv A.B-00530A-A/BI.

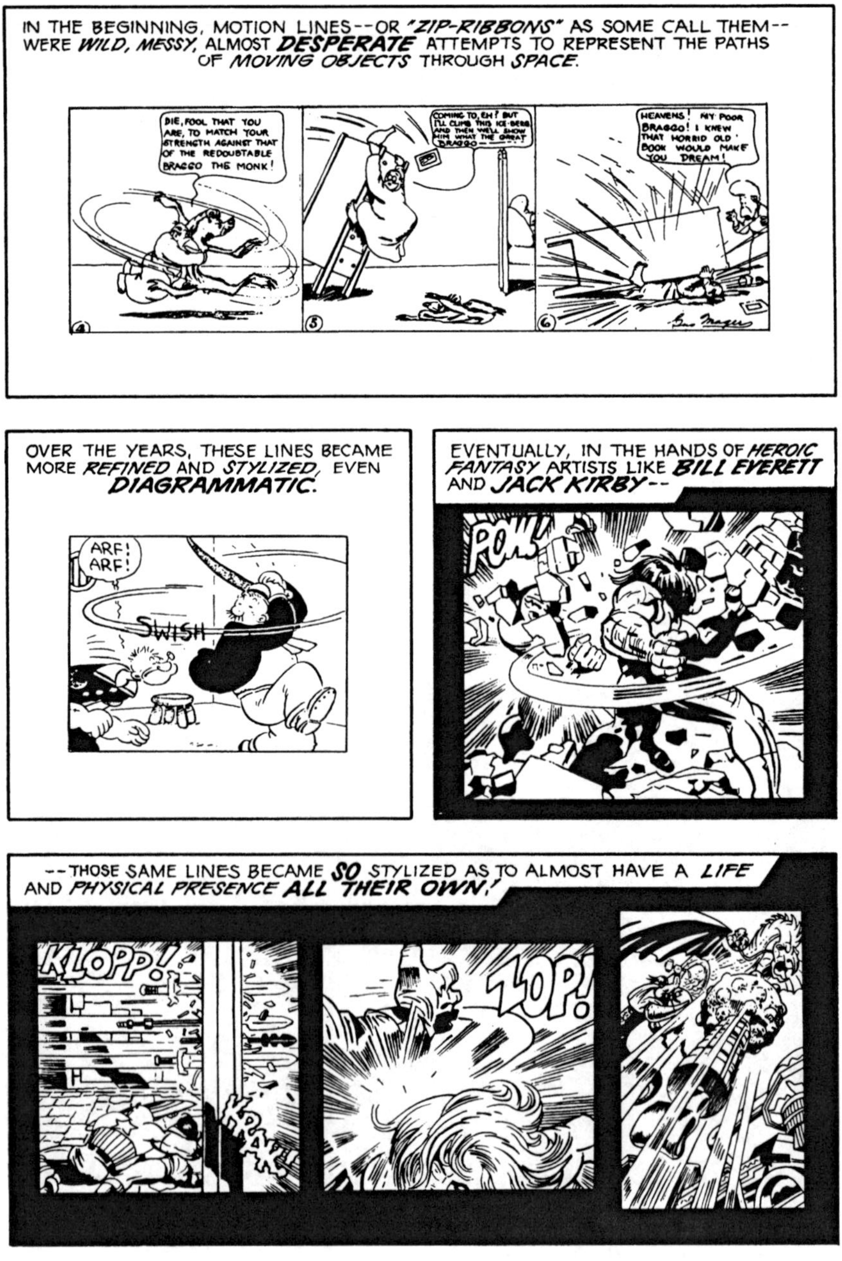


**Figure 10.5** Page 111 from *Understanding Comics* by Scott McCloud. © 1993, 1994 by Scott McCloud. Reprinted by permission of HarperCollins Publishers.

the images do the job.[5] Movement of the image of a horse, on a movie screen, depicts the horse as running. When the image stops, it depicts the horse as stopped. (I am supposing, again, that the motion picture is made with a fixed camera, without panning or zooming.[6])

Still pictures work differently; they depict motion or change without moving or changing themselves. And if a still picture – the configuration of marks on its surface – does change, the process of change does not have the representational significance it would have in a film. Fading paint or restoration work or pigeon droppings may alter a picture's representational content; what the picture depicts after the change may be different from what it depicted before. But a change in what something depicts is not necessarily a depiction of change. If an artistic prankster or exceptionally clever pigeons transform the surface of the Rubens so that it depicts airplanes in the sky instead of birds, it has not thereby depicted birds being transformed into airplanes, nor has it depicted birds being replaced by airplanes. We just have a picture which depicts, at one time, birds and, later, airplanes. The birds and the airplanes need not be understood to belong to the same fictional world. And at any or all particular moments in the changing image's history, it may depict things as unchanging. Whether a still picture depicts movement or stasis depends not on what happens to the image over time, but on features of the image that are present all at once. Blurry images in photographs often serve to depict motion. So do configurations of marks depicting objects in positions that we expect not to last – a dancer with his legs off the ground, a waterfall, a lightning bolt, a diver in mid-air. Cartoons use motion lines of various kinds. The multiple images in Duchamp's *Nude Descending a Staircase* – all present simultaneously – depict the woman's downward progression (see figure 10.6).

What is it about the still photograph of Mt. Geryon by virtue of which it depicts things as unchanging? Most obvious is the fact that the marks are such as to depict objects of kinds we would expect not to change – a massive, solid mountain, with no volcanic steam or dynamite sticks or strip-mining equipment in sight. Also, the images are not blurred, nor

5 As Gregory Currie, *Image and Mind: Film, Philosophy and Cognitive Science* (Cambridge: Cambridge University Press, 1995) and Gideon Yaffe, "Time in the Movies," in P. A. French and H. Wettstein, eds., *Midwest Studies in Philosophy: Meaning in the Arts*, 27 (Oxford: Blackwell, 2003), pp. 115–38 put it, films represent time by means of time, and more specifically, duration represents duration.

6 If the camera does move or pan or zoom, it is still true that temporal properties of the image are responsible for the depiction of temporal properties.

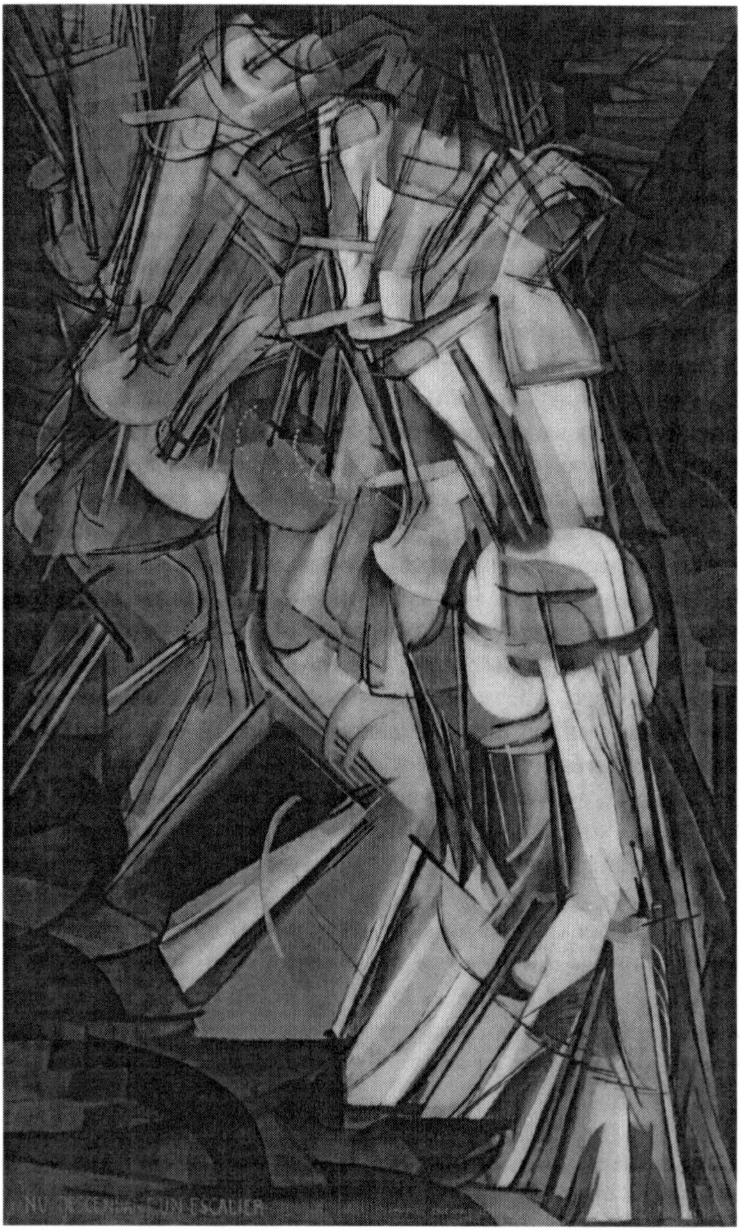

**Figure 10.6** Marcel Duchamp, *Nude Descending a Staircase*, 1912 (no. 2). Philadelphia Museum of Art: The Louise and Walter Arensberg Collection, 1950-134-59.

do they contain anything like motion lines. Again, all of these features (or absences thereof) are present in the image all at once.

Freeze frames in film – still pictures, in effect, inserted in the midst of moving ones – demonstrate dramatically the difference between still and moving pictures. For a moment, until she realizes that it is a freeze frame, the viewer may read the frozen image as depicting a frozen scene – an athlete or dancer stuck in mid-air, for instance. Once it is evident that the image is a still picture, once she understands it as such, all-at-once features of the unmoving image may induce her to see the athlete or dancer as in motion.

These examples suggest a general account of the difference between still and moving pictures, which I take to be correct: A picture is a *still* one if temporal properties of the image are representationally inert, if what happens or doesn't happen to the image over time has no bearing on its representational content. Motion pictures are pictures whose temporal properties do contribute to their representational content.

How might this difference between still and motion pictures explain the different experiences viewers enjoy of the indistinguishable images of Mt. Geryon?

Whether something counts as a still or motion picture will affect viewers' experiences if it affects what they take to be its representational content, of course. Freeze frames illustrate this. But the still and motion pictures of Mt. Geryon seem not to differ in representational content; both represent the mountain as unmoving, unchanging. Does the difference of medium, as I have characterized it – the difference in which features of the images are responsible for their content – account for the difference in viewers' experiences? Consideration of motion-depicting still pictures will help answer this question.

*Marina in burrasca* (figure 10.4) depicts only a momentary time slice of an ongoing event; that is what viewers of the painting imagine seeing. Yet one may look at the picture indefinitely, as long as one likes. If I gaze at it for five minutes, do I imagine spending five minutes observing an event that lasts but a moment? Do I imagine my five-minute visual experience of the picture to be a five-minute viewing of the momentary event? This would be rather strange (though not incoherent).

I have elsewhere proposed a more plausible way of understanding such experiences.[7] At each individual moment while I am observing the

[7] Walton "Experiencing Still Photographs: What Do You See and How Long Do You See It?" in *Marvelous Images* (New York: Oxford University Press), forthcoming.

picture, I see (in imagination) the momentary occurrence that the picture depicts, a short time slice of the ongoing event. And at each moment I imagine my momentary visual experience of the picture to be a glimpse of this momentary occurrence. I do not imagine anything of my five-minute visual experience of the picture as a whole; in particular, I do not imagine it to be a five-minute observation of the depicted event. I do not, in imagination, *watch* the instantaneous event for an extended period of time, for five minutes or for however long I observe the picture. I will sum this up by saying that, on this account, *Marina* is a *snapshot*.

At the climax of Michelangelo Antonioni's *Zabriskie Point* (1970), a huge explosion destroys the desert retreat of an evil real estate tycoon. The explosion is shown again and again in the film, so the viewers, repeatedly, imagine seeing it. But surely they do not imagine it is occurring repeatedly, or imagine seeing it repeatedly. They imagine, repeatedly, observing a single explosion at a single moment. The experience of looking at Antoniani's storm at sea is similar, except that the multiple successive imaginings are not discrete but continuous. Do they imagine seeing the same event again and again? No. They imagine, again and again, seeing it just once.

I should add that the moment in question – the duration of the depicted event, which the viewer imagines seeing – is not a mathematical instant, an extensionless point in time. That would make it hard to understand how viewers, in imagination, see things *move*. Some motion-depicting pictures depict longer moments than others do, although there is usually no fact of the matter about exactly how long the depicted moment is. Duchamp's *Nude Descending a Staircase* arguably depicts the entire action of descending several steps, perhaps lasting several seconds. Even so, the duration of what is depicted, what the viewer imagines seeing, is likely to be exceeded by the time she spends observing the painting. The former duration is limited, whereas there is no theoretical limit to how long one can look at the picture.

Although motion-depicting still pictures *depict* only momentary events, some of them *represent* events with much longer durations. A picture represents an event (in my sense) if it is fictional – true in the picture-world – that it occurs, i.e., if viewers are to imagine its occurring. They need not imagine *seeing* it occur. If they do imagine seeing it (and properly so), the picture not only represents but depicts the event (in my sense). It is fictional, in *Marina*, that a sailing ship is on the crest of a large wave. It is fictional also, by implication, that it will soon fall into a trough between waves, and perhaps that it will shortly break up and sink. Viewers imagine seeing it atop the wave, but not in the trough, although they probably see (in imagination) *that* it will soon fall into the trough, or infer that it will from what they see. The picture depicts the boat atop the wave, but merely represents it as falling into the trough.

It is tempting to construe all still pictures, including stasis-depicting ones such as *Mt. Geryon* and (the cropped) *Autumn Landscape*, as snapshots, and there are several good reasons for doing so. According to this hypothesis – the *snapshot* hypothesis – *Mt. Geryon* depicts but a moment in the life of the mountain; that is what the viewer imagines seeing, no matter how long she gazes at the picture. At each moment of her experience, she imagines her actual visual experience to be a sighting of the one momentary time slice of the mountain. She does not imagine anything of her extended visual experience as a whole, and she does not, in imagination, watch the mountain for an extended period of time. The picture may, nevertheless, *represent* the mountain as remaining (and remaining motionless, or nearly so) for an extended period of time – for the 5 or 50 minutes that a viewer might look at the picture, or more or less indefinitely. The viewer may imagine seeing, in her glimpse of it, that it will, or inferring that it will.[8]

(Some may prefer to say that it is fictional only that the mountain is *likely* to remain for 5 or 50 minutes or indefinitely, not that it definitely will or, for that matter, that it definitely won't. I prefer to say that, fictionally, the mountain definitely does remain static more or less indefinitely, and that features of the still image present at each moment, including the very first moment of the picture's existence, make this fictional. This accords with a common pattern in our understanding of many works of fiction: If it is fictional that $p$ is probable, it is frequently understood to be fictional that $p$, absent any indication to the contrary.[9])

[8] I am ignoring works from the Renaissance, for instance, that portray several temporally discrete events within a single frame. Masolino's fresco *Healing of Cripple and the Raising of Tabitha* (1424–5) depicts St Peter twice, once healing a cripple and again raising Tabitha from the dead. So it depicts (at least) two distinct moments. Alternatively, we could regard it as consisting of two different pictures, each depicting a single moment, although there is no saying exactly where on the fresco one picture ends and the other begins. These multiple images obviously function very differently from those in *Nude Descending*. The latter induce viewers to imagine seeing motion, whereas the former do not. To regard *Nude Descending* as a combination of several different motion-depicting pictures, each of which depicts one very short moment, would risk overlooking the importance of attending to them all at once, and recognizing their depiction of motion.

[9] Cf. Walton, *Mimesis as Make-Believe*, p. 164. That the mountain is unchanging for an extended period of time is an *implied* fictional truth (§4.2).

The snapshot hypothesis fits nicely with my proposal about how still pictures differ, in general, from motion pictures. When a viewer imagines his perception of a picture to be a perception of a depicted object or event, usually it is, more specifically, his perceiving of the picture's features by virtue of which that object or event is depicted, that he imagines to be his perceiving of the object or event. It is my perceiving of the particular marks on the surface of Rubens's canvas that depict a cart, those that prescribe imagining a cart, that I imagine to be my perceiving of a cart. All-at-once features of *Mt. Geryon*, features that are perceivable in a moment, are what make it fictional that the mountain is motionless, and it is the viewer's perceiving of these that she imagines to be her perception of the motionlessness of the mountain. All-at-once features (probably the same ones) are also what make it fictional that the mountain persists for an extended period of time, if anything does. But it hardly seems likely (I don't say impossible) that viewers should imagine their perceiving all-at-once properties, which they do in a moment, to be watching the mountain persist. Shall we say that at each moment of their experience, they imagine watching the mountain persist for 5 or 50 minutes or longer?

So maybe the viewer does not imagine watching the mountain persist for an extended period of time. She imagines catching only a momentary glimpse of it – and perhaps, in that glimpse, seeing that it will persist or is likely to, or inferring that it will from what she sees of it. If this is right, it accounts nicely for the impression that viewers experience the still and its motion-picture look-alike differently. The motion picture does depict an extended temporal segment of Mt. Geryon – five minutes or five hours of its life, if the shot lasts that long (more, or less, if it is in slow- or fast-motion). It is the persistence of the image on the screen that makes it fictional that the mountain persists for that duration. So naturally viewers imagine their perceiving the image's persisting to be a perceiving of the mountain's persisting; they imagine watching the mountain for 5 or 50 minutes of its history.

This conclusion – that all still pictures are snapshots – is much too quick. If it is right, extended narrative accounts of one's experience of still pictures, like those I mentioned earlier, are problematic, as they appear to describe temporally extended imaginative surveys of depicted scenes.[10] Such accounts certainly appear to be perfectly natural, and they seem to report experiences that are perfectly proper. Viewers of *Mt. Geryon* obviously *can*,

[10] Such narrative accounts could conceivably be construed in some less-straightforward way, on which they do not describe imaginative experiences of this kind.

if they choose, imagine catching much more than a glimpse of the mountain. As their eyes roam over the picture surface, they can imagine noticing first this and then that, looking for a likely climbing route, finding or not finding one, and so on. The photograph is visually indistinguishable from a stasis-depicting motion picture, and one can simply experience it as though that is what it is – as though it is a film shot that continues indefinitely, or as long as one cares to look at it. Even if the viewer is well aware that the image is a still picture, that its persistence is not what makes it fictional that the mountain persists, she might imagine her observation of the former to be an observation of the latter. I have no doubt that viewers of stasis-depicting stills do (sometimes?, often?, to a considerable extent?) engage in such imaginings. And the idea that it is somehow illegitimate to do so is not attractive.

But simply denying that stasis-depicting still pictures are snapshots, and insisting that viewers do (properly) imagine observing a stretch of the scene's history lasting perhaps as long as they look at the picture, would also leave us in an uncomfortable position. We already know that it would complicate the task of explaining the difference between experiences of still and motion-picture look-alikes. The discomfort doesn't end there.

*Mt. Geryon* arguably does not represent (let alone depict) the mountain as remaining *forever* the same. Signs of severe past erosion are evident. Presumably it is fictional that erosion continues, that it is probably occurring imperceptibly before our eyes, and that eventually the mountain will look very different from how it does now. Indeed, we might reasonably understand it to be fictional – part of the picture's representational content – that the appearance of the scene will be different shortly, when the sun sets or moves across the sky. If a viewer should observe the picture for hours or months or years, will she have to imagine suffering from an *illusion* that the mountain and its appearance are always the same?

It is hard to see how motion-depicting still pictures could fail to be snapshots. If *Marina* depicted a long-lasting scene, wouldn't it depict the sea and the ships as frozen in place, motionless during that time? Obviously it doesn't. It depicts the sea broiling wildly and the ships being tossed about; viewers imagine seeing things move. So shall we say that still pictures are snapshots when they depict motion or change, but not when they depict static scenes? That would be awkward, to say the least. The awkwardness is especially evident when both motion-depicting and stasis-depicting images are included within the same frame, as they are in figure 10.7.

Is this a snapshot of the smartly trotting horses, depicting but a moment of their existence, and yet a depiction of an extended period in the histories of the stone horses? Does the viewer (in imagination) catch

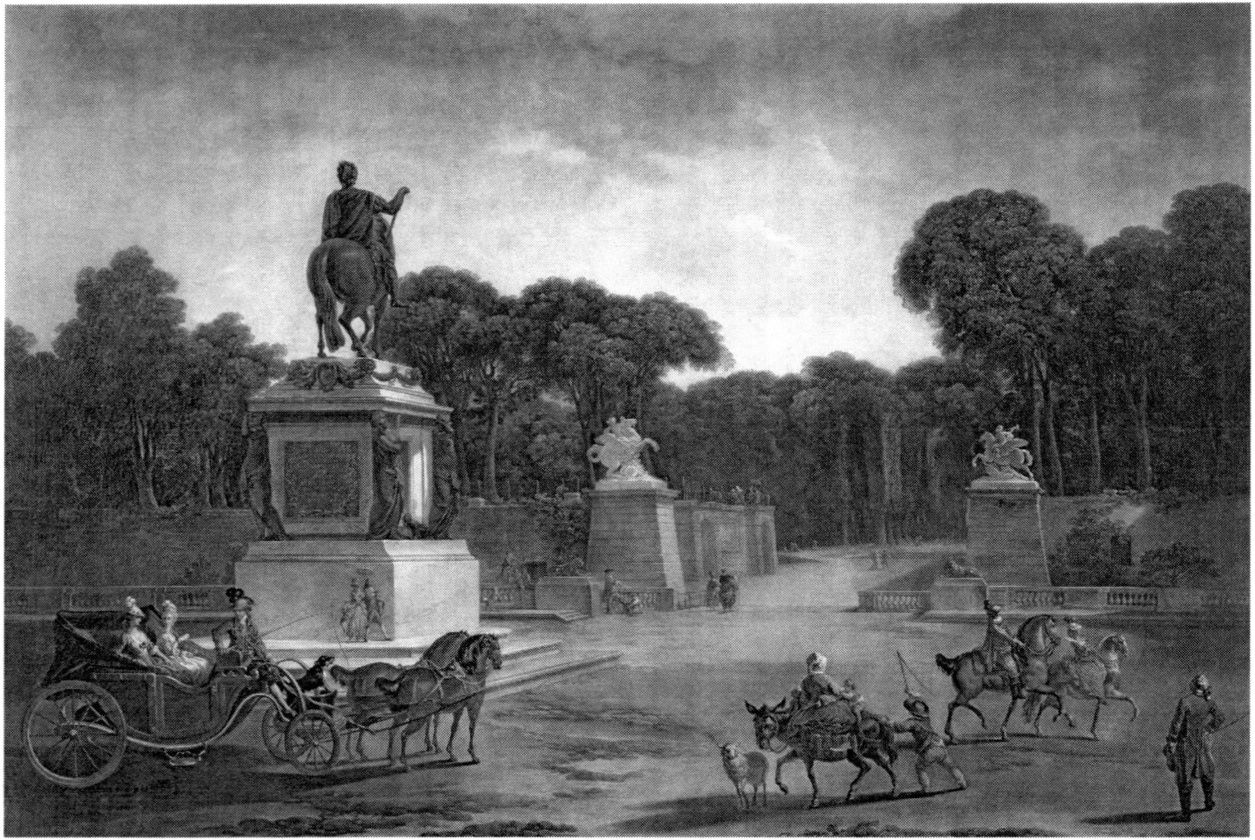

**Figure 10.7** Joseph de Saint-Quentin, J.-P. *Vue de la place Louis XV*. Reproduced in Jean de Cayeux, *Le Paysage en France de 1750 à 1815*. Editions Monelle Hayot, p. 97. ND1356.4.C381. Musée des Beaux Arts, Besancon.

but a glimpse of the moving horses, as they kick up a cloud of dust, but observe the equestrian statues continuously for as long as he cares to gaze at the picture? And what are we to say about the live horses temporarily at rest?

What shall we conclude? Given the conflicts built into the medium of still pictures, we should not expect any simple account of viewers' imaginative experiences to be adequate. Perhaps the most we can say, in general, is that people experience stasis-depicting stills in a complicated combination of ways, alternating imperceptibly between, or subtly intertwining, imagined glimpses and prolonged visual surveys of depicted scenes.

Viewers are not usually aware of these complexities or bothered by the conflicts. This is partly because, like so much of our mental lives, the imaginings our experiences of pictures involve, or some aspects of them, are implicit and not readily open to introspection – evident only when we pay unusual attention (if even then) or draw conclusions from what we say and do. Viewers rarely if ever even have the alternatives we have considered clearly in mind. Also, some of the questions I recently left hanging, questions highlighting the complexities or confronting the conflicts, are *silly* in the (slightly) technical sense I introduced in *Mimesis as Make-Believe*; they do not appropriately arise in the course of appreciation, appreciators are advised to avoid them. And they are likely not to have definite answers.[11]

What a picture depicts is (roughly) a matter of what viewers properly imagine seeing, when they experience it. If as I suspect there are no especially relevant propriety considerations affecting the kinds of experiences I have described, there will be complications and uncertainties about pictures' depictive contents corresponding to those characterizing viewers' imaginative experiences. We will have to be satisfied with the recognition that pictures like *Mt. Geryon* are ambiguous between depicting a momentary event and a longer period of the history of a scene, and with the realization that this is not a "clean" ambiguity – each of the readings interferes with the other.

Some may find these conclusions frustratingly messy and inconclusive. I think they reflect facts about pictures and our experiences of them which are messy and hard to pin down – facts which, partly for that very reason, may contribute to the immense fascination that many pictures have for us.[12]

11 Walton, *Mimesis as Make-Believe*, pp. 174–83.

12 This essay overlaps a longer one, "Experiencing Still Photographs: What Do You See and How Long Do You See It?"

# 11

# THE PROBLEM WITH MOVIE STARS

Noël Carroll

## Introduction

In *The World Viewed*, Stanley Cavell offers the brilliant critical observation that "In *Ride the High Country*, the pathos of the aging cowboys (Randolph Scott and Joel McCrea) depends upon their being enacted by aging men whom we can remember as young cowboys."[1] For Cavell, the earlier roles of stars can affect our reception of their subsequent characterizations. Humphrey Bogart's portrayals of protagonists with checkered histories, in movies like *Casablanca*, succeed so well, in part, because we recall, as Cavell puts it, his outlaw past[2] – that is, the series of films, such as *Angels with Dirty Faces*, where Bogart played heavies on the wrong side of right.

The phenomenon to which Cavell adverts is hard to gainsay. Once established, most movie stars, save perhaps chameleons like Daniel Day Lewis, come to us with an established persona, rooted in their previous films, and that persona can have expressive ramifications which we often use to fill in our sense of the character before us in the present instance. This is quite obvious with respect to parodies, such as *The Freshman* and *Analyze That* in which Marlon Brando's and Robert DeNiro's comic portrayals of gangsters play off their earlier dramatic portrayals of mafia chieftains. But serious films also exploit the penumbra of film history that follows the movie star on screen.

A very clear-cut example of this is Billy Wilder's *Sunset Boulevard*. Especially for its first audiences, the fading silent-movie queen Norma

1 Stanley Cavell, *The World Viewed: Reflections on the Ontology of Film* (New York: Viking Press, 1971), p. 75.

2 Ibid., p. 71.

Desmond had all the more resonance for being enacted by Gloria Swanson, whom many of the initial viewers of the film recognized as a genuine silent-movie star whose career was in eclipse. Likewise, when her butler Max asserts that he, along with D. W. Griffith and Cecil B. DeMille, were once the leading film directors in Hollywood, the line is particularly moving because it is spoken by Erich von Stroheim, who, as well as being a well-known actor, had indeed been a silent-film director of the highest stature. And for the viewer who might have forgotten these well-known facts of movie fandom, the creators of *Sunset Boulevard* include some footage of *Queen Kelly*, a film directed by Stroheim and starring Swanson.

Though *Sunset Boulevard* is quite overt in this matter, references to star personae, though in a subtler register, are quite pervasive. When a casting director ponders whether the audience will accept a certain actor in a certain role, she is thinking about whether, given the persona that the actor has forged thus far over his or her career, it enriches or, at least, meshes with a viable interpretation of the character at hand.[3]

Although I am reasonably sure that Basil Rathbone was pleasant enough with his friends and family, at a certain point in his career it would have been hard to imagine him portraying an affable, ordinary traffic policeman. Of course, he could have been cast as an extraordinary policeman whose self-confidence bordered on arrogance. But an ordinary, nice guy – never! And even if he could have, in some sense, pulled it off, the producers would have vetoed the suggestion. Glen Ford would be a better bet, they'd say.

Indeed, movies are often written with specific stars in mind. Sofia Coppola's *Lost in Translation* was said to have been conceived from the start with Bill Murray in the leading role. Here the author herself was using Murray's star persona to flesh out the character in the expectation that viewers would continue to do the same.

Movie stars have personae that accumulate associations as their careers progress, and it is part of the art of the producer, writers, the casting director, and so forth to match up current projects with suitable, ongoing, star personae. They do this because they know that viewers will use that information to round out their comprehension of and, in consequence, their affective response to the characters.

That we react to certain characters as we do is often abetted by employing actors whose careers are freighted with certain publicly available associations. We usually begin by presuming that a character played by

[3] This is true not only of stars, of course, but of stock players in minor roles, like Donald Meek (whose name says it all).

Gregory Peck is a decent guy because he appeared in so many films where he earnestly struggled to do the right thing. We presume that Clark Gable will stand up for his rights and for the rights of others because his screen persona is that of a stand-up kinda fellow. He is brash and aggressive, never passive. Confronted, he barks rather than whispers. He could never have been cast as Ashley in *Gone with the Wind*.

Responses of this sort are not flights of fan fantasy. They are premeditated effects; the film has been designed to elicit them through the way in which the relevant movie stars have been chosen for their roles.

Perhaps, all this sounds very obvious and unexceptionable. Reacting to movie stars in this way is a pattern of spectatorship that most of us pick up almost by osmosis, as we are inducted into the practice of movie-going. However, acknowledging the existence of this channel of communication between the screen and the auditorium can very quickly head us toward paradox.

Why?

Most popular, commercial movies – that is, the kind of movies in which movie stars star – are fictional. Furthermore, many of our responses to fictions, including fictional films, depend upon restricting our attention to the story world of the movie and to what it presupposes. It is fictional in the film that the hero is dangling over a precipice and it is presupposed in the fiction that, were he to fall, he would be crushed to death against the ground below. That is what we need to be thinking about at this moment in the movie, if we are to feel suspense.[4] We should keep our minds focused upon what is contained within the bounds of the fiction operator – that is, on what fills in the blank in the formula: "it is true in the fiction that ——." For, if we help ourselves to certain information that does not belong under the scope of the fiction operator, suspense will not obtain.

Which information? For example, film-viewing commonplaces such as that the hero always escapes from tight predicaments like the one just mentioned. If we dwelt upon our knowledge of that bit of motion-picture lore, we would not have call to fret about the plight of the hero. If we brought to mind what we know of how such popular movies are constructed, in other words, most of the curiosity required to sustain our interest in such films would evaporate.[5]

In order to be effectively drawn into the question of whether the boy will get the girl, we need to relegate to the back burner of our consciousness

4 For an account of suspense, see Noël Carroll, "Film, Genre, and Emotion," in Noël Carroll and Jinhee Choi, eds., *Philosophy of Film and Motion Pictures* (Oxford: Blackwell Publishing, 2006).

5 On the role of curiosity in sustaining audience interest in popular entertainments, see my "Narrative Closure," in *Philosophical Studies* (forthcoming).

our "real-world" knowledge that this is almost always how it goes when the top-billed star and starlet are thrown together. Yes, they bicker, but the veteran film viewer ***knows*** this is but a prelude to a kiss. And yet, we do not let that knowledge push its way to the forefront of our mind, since, were it to take over, it would be difficult to remain inquisitive about the outcome of this prospective courtship.

As we imaginatively entertain a fiction like this one, we need to bracket our quite-considerable command of the ways in which the plots in popular movie genres generally unfold. That is, in order for many movie plots to work their emotional magic upon us, we need to put our fund of movie lore on hold. We must discount our grasp of the principles that govern popular-movie plot construction when it comes to entertaining the probabilities of what is likely to transpire or not in the fictional world; since that involves knowledge that is outside the legitimate scope of the fiction operator.

But isn't it precisely that sort of movie lore that we are mobilizing when we use a star's persona to fill out the character he or she is playing? Thus, it appears that successful movie-going both requires access to extra-fictional or external movie lore, while also demanding that we bracket such lore from our imaginative engagement with films. A contradiction seems in the offing.[6] The purpose of this essay is to avert it.

## The Problem

Although the recommendation – that successful engagement with a fiction requires us to focus imaginatively upon what falls inside the fiction operator – is, broadly speaking, correct, it is very important not to misinterpret this maxim. For, in order to understand any fiction, we must generally access information that is unstated and/or not shown in the work. We need not only to attend to what is explicitly given in the fiction, but also to what is presupposed by it. That is, we will have to fill out the description or the picture of the fictional environment with which the creator presents us; and to do this, we must go beyond the explicit boundaries of the fiction operator, strictly construed, albeit in a principled way.

But how will we know how to fill in what is presupposed by the fiction in a principled way? To a great extent, we achieve this by using our beliefs

6 This problem is broached by Jonathan M. Weinberg and Aaron Meskin in their "Imagine That!" in Matthew Kieran, ed., *Contemporary Debates in Aesthetics and the Philosophy of Art* (Oxford: Blackwell Publishing, 2006), p. 230.

about the actual world to help us along. When in the course of a movie about World War II, a British soldier fights alongside an American soldier and against a German one, it does not have to be explained to the typical American viewer that the "Tommies" were our allies; that is knowledge from the "real world" that the intended viewer uses to fill in or make sense of the fiction. Likewise, when we are shown that the fiction is set in the Forbidden City in Beijing, the average, prepared audience member does not have to be told that the Emperor is Chinese, since that is a belief about the actual history of the world that the viewer almost naturally brings to bear on the fiction on the screen.

In short, imaginative narratives make reference to the world outside the fiction in multiple ways and, in order to follow such fictions, cinematic and otherwise, audiences must employ and, indeed, are expected to resort to, many of their standing beliefs, convictions, (and emotions) regarding the extra-fictional or "real world" in order to flesh out what is presupposed by the fiction. Moreover, this involves not only historical and geographical facts, but also biological and social ones – such as, *ceteris paribus*, persons drained of blood die, and mothers are likely to attempt to protect their offspring.

These suppositions, of course, can be overridden by the presiding rules of a genre or explicitly by the specific way in which the narrative at hand evolves. For example, persons drained of blood may return as the Undead in vampire films. Nevertheless, to a perhaps surprising extent, following a fiction involves using what we believe about the actual world and how it works in order to fill in and make sense of what is on screen. Thus, what might be called the *realistic heuristic* is often our default assumption when processing a cinematic fiction.[7]

Generally, we respond emotionally to the situations in cinematic fictions and anticipate their likely outcomes in accordance with the realistic heuristic.[8]

7 I think that this idea originally stems from David Lewis, "Truth in Fiction," in *Philosophical Papers: Volume I* (Oxford: Oxford University Press, 1983), pp. 261–81.

8 This requires some qualification. Though we may start by assuming the realistic heuristic, it may have to be waived or, at least, modified, under certain conditions. In some instances, the genre in question mandates that the realistic heuristic be retired with respect to certain situations. For example, in a science-fiction adventure, such as an episode of *StarTrek,* space ships may travel through black holes, though we know that, in reality, an attempt to do so would be short-lived. Call this a genre dispensation. Similarly, in other cases, in order to render a fiction coherent, we may have to repeal the realistic heuristic in favor of entertaining the divergent beliefs of the culture that originally produced the fiction. So, although we may not believe that ghosts are possible, we may suppose they are in order to feel our way into Hamlet's plight.

We are not meant to calibrate our reactions to what transpires in the fiction in the expectation that it will abide by the rules that govern the plot construction of popular fictions. If we know that the boy will get the girl, or vice-versa, or that good always wins out, where's the *frisson* in that? So, we go with the realistic heuristic and the kind of probabilities it makes available.

We do not key our emotional responses to the conventional plot trajectories and their subtending probabilities which we know rule Hollywood-type plot construction, since they have little to do with our beliefs about what is probable in the actual world as it thrives outside our cinéplexes. That is, we do not typically deploy the movie-going lore pertinent to the plot construction of popular entertainments, unless we are watching a film about Hollywood plot construction (for example, *Boy Meets Girl*).

Standardly, the beliefs about how the fictional world works, upon which our cognitive and emotional responses to the movie depend, rely upon the realistic heuristic and not on film lore about plot construction. Although film lore about plot construction reflects how movies go, it does not reflect what we know of the way of the actual "non-cinematic" world. For, what we believe is probable of a movie-*qua*-movie is radically different from what we believe to be probable *in* a movie conceived of as a creditable fictional world.

But do the prescriptions of the realistic heuristic also preclude our using what we know of the past careers of movie stars in order to augment our affective response to the character before us on screen? When we recall John Wayne with a twinge of wistful recognition as a truly beautiful young cowboy while watching the (intentionally exaggeratedly) dilapidated and besotted version of him in *True Grit*, are we in violation of the realistic heuristic?

At first blush, it may appear that we are. For, supposing that the realistic heuristic discounts the transmigration of souls as an explanation, how would we account for any relation of continuance between the Ringo Kid, for example, and Rooster Cogburn? Nor is reincarnation a presupposition of the western genre, as it is of the mummy genre. So, isn't our melancholy in this case as ill-advised here as would be our invocation of the inevitable happy ending with respect to any number of suspense sequences? In both cases, we are going outside the fiction and our realistic default assumptions about how the fictional world works and is intelligible. In both cases, we are using what we know about movies in order to engender our reaction to the movie before us.

## Film, Photography and Allusion[9]

And yet, once again, it pays to re-emphasize that we do allow that fictions can make reference to the world outside the fiction. A fiction can make reference to air travel and invite us – even bid us – to use what we know about air travel in order to fill out the story. *United 93* does not explain to us what those metal carts that the stewardesses push are; it presumes that we know what they are and that we use that information to explain to ourselves why they are available for smashing in the door of the cockpit.

But the creators of fictions may not only refer to the actual world with *literal* intent – with the intention that we apply literally what we believe of the real world to the circumstances of the fiction. The creators of a fiction may also refer to things outside the fiction with what might be called *figurational* intent – that is, with the intention that we apply figuratively what we associate to the stretch of reality referred to by fiction to elements within the fiction, or even to the totality of the ongoing fiction as a whole.

A fiction, including a pictorial one, for example, may refer to Christ in order to encourage audiences to apprehend a certain character within the fiction in terms of attributes that they associate with Jesus, as is the case of the character played by Ian Hunter in Frank Borzage's *Strange Cargo*. Here the allusion to Christ is a way of underscoring the redemptive aura of the character. The use of figuration in this way does not violate the realistic heuristic, since it does not involve claims about what is literally true in the fictional world nor how it operates.

As I understand *Strange Cargo*, it is only committed to the view that the character is Christ-like, not that he is necessarily Christ; just as the monster in *Bride of Frankenstein* is pictorially associated with the crucified Jesus when the villagers chain him to a pole. The monster is not literally identified with Jesus here, though the allusion serves to analogize his situation to that of Christ's as the victim of an unruly and unjustified mob.[10] And, as this case should make abundantly evident, one can allude for purposes of figurative comparison in a fiction to things outside the

[9] On allusion, see Stephanie Ross, "Art and Allusion," *Journal of Aesthetics and Art Criticism* XXXX (1981): 59–70; William Irwin, "What is An Allusion?" *Journal of Aesthetics and Art Criticism* LIX (2001): 287–97; and William Irwin, "The Aesthetics of Allusion," *Journal of Value Inquiry* 36 (2002): 521–32.

[10] This sort of visual allusion is well precedented in painting, as when David figures the assassinated Marat as a Savior by arranging his limbs after the manner of those typical of the expiring Christ.

fictional world with no impropriety – not logical, conceptual, ontological, or even aesthetic.

Moreover, a fiction may also allude to a fictional character. During the movie *In Her Shoes*, the character Rose twice runs the dogs she has been hired to exercise up the steps of the Philadelphia Art Museum. In doing this, the film alludes to the fictional character of Rocky Balboa from the movie *Rocky*. Via this allusion, we are encouraged to regard Rose's new life – previously she had been an uptight, corporate lawyer – as some sort of personal triumph for her, as a similar run up that staircase had been for Rocky.

In a written fiction, an author may allude to a movie character, saying, for example, that so-and-so's muscles rippled like Maciste's. There is no reason to think that comparable allusions cannot be achieved pictorially as well, as the case of the allusion to Rocky during *In Her Shoes* indicates. Indeed, in both written and pictorial fictions, one can even allude to movie stars; the character played by Raymond Massey in the movie version of *Arsenic and Old Lace*, for example, is explicitly compared to Boris Karloff.

But what has this to do with our problem with movie stars? Namely: that in the cases before us, the images of the pertinent movie stars, among other functions, allude to the actors in question. That is, it is my contention that when we encounter established movie stars on screen, it is sometimes the case that we may experience them – and may be encouraged to experience them – in a twofold manner. On the one hand, they portray the character in the fiction before us; on the other hand, in certain cases, their image may also serve as an *allusion* to the screen persona they have cultivated over the course of their career. This, moreover, probably has to do with the photographic basis of the traditional fictional film which itself can be twofold in a parallel manner.

The traditional, photographically based image of a person in a fiction film both represents a character (as Cesar Romero *nominally portrays* Cortez in *The Captains of Castile*), while it also refers to (*physically portrays*) its actual model (in this case, Cesar Romero).[11] The same shot of Cesar Romero can appear in the fictional motion picture *The Captains of Castile* where,

[11] On the distinction between physical portrayal and nominal portrayal, see Noël Carroll, "Concerning Uniqueness Claims for Photographic and Cinematographic Representation," in *Theorizing the Moving Image* (Cambridge: Cambridge University Press, 1996), pp. 45–8. See also, Monroe Beardsley, *Aesthetics* (New York: Harcourt, Brace and World, 1958), especially ch. VI, sec. 16. See also Göran Hermeren, *Representation and Meaning* (Lund, Sweden: Scandanavian University Books, 1969), especially ch. II.

first and foremost, it represents or nominally portrays Cortez; or it can appear in a documentary on the TV program *Biography* where it refers to Cesar Romero (playing Cortez). Every image, populated with particularized people, in a traditional, photographically constructed fiction-film has at least this potential for doubleness.[12] In this respect, such images have built into them the possibility of referring (by way of physical portrayal) to the actual models of the characters that they nominally portray within the fiction.

Furthermore, as we shall attempt to demonstrate in the next section, it is possible to mobilize physical portrayal and nominal portrayal in the self-same shot or sequence of shots in a given film. Consequently, due to the possibility of simultaneously enlisting physical and nominal portrayal at once, it is conceivable that when movie stars nominally portray one character on screen, they may also, by way of the photographic physical portrayal of themselves, be referring, or, more precisely, *alluding* to their screen persona in a way that beckons us to bring to bear associations we have regarding their earlier roles upon the character currently on screen before us.

Were we to recruit what we know about the construction of popular plots – for example, that the hero always escapes in thrillers – we would not be able emotively to process the majority of fictional movies in the way they are designed to be assimilated. This is because they are designed to be imaginatively engaged in accordance with the realistic heuristic and the aforesaid strategies of plot construction are usually so improbable that they are scarcely realistic. In most cases, the mandated emotive uptake of a fiction requires the realistic heuristic, or the realistic heuristic modified by the relevant genre presuppositions, or something quite like them. If we track the story in terms of the principles of popular plot construction, as a script doctor might, there would not be any affective friction in the fiction.

Although most of us know the likely plot trajectories that shape popular films from Hollywood through Hong Kong and on to Bollywood, we do not take those structures to be part and parcel of the ontological laws that govern the pertinent fictional worlds. The relevant laws for following what goes on in most movies approximate what we would surmise deploying the realistic heuristic. Were we to allow knowledge of

12 The qualification "at least," above, signals our acknowledgement that a cinematic image might also *depict* a class or collection of objects. On depiction, see my "Concerning Uniqueness Claims." In virtue of depiction, said images have the potential not only for doubleness, but for *tripleness*.

movie-going lore about plot development to figure in our calculations of whether the heroine can save the infant from the mounting, enveloping flames, we would be treating the pertinent, popular plot-construction strategies as though they were literally principles that govern the fictional world (as opposed to principles that govern the fabrication of the fictional world in our real-world movie studios). However, those plot stratagems are outside the fictional world of the motion picture; they are not literally part of the fictional environment.

Contrariwise, allusions are not presented as literally elements of the fictional environment, nor do they intersect literally with the causal laws that we presuppose to be operative in the fictional world. Allusions are figurative asides. They are not of a piece with the literal content of the fictional world, but are of the nature of meta-comments about the literal content of the fictional world. Their relation to the fictional world is tropological not ontological.

If we were to adopt plot-construction strategies – such as: the boy always wins the girl – for following the evolution of the fiction, we would be treating those strategies as functioning causal patterns operating within the ontology of the fictional world. However, they actually belong to our world where the producer, often for financial purposes, demands a happy ending from his writers and director. Thus we should not think of them as material to the sequence of events as they emerge within the fiction.

Furthermore, neither are these strategies of plot construction to be understood figuratively. They are not, for example, usually allusions intimated by the discourse that conveys the fiction; since, although a fiction might allude to the "happy ending" motif, as Bertolt Brecht does at the end of *The Threepenny Opera*, we typically have no reason to believe that most fictions that exploit such plot constructions are alluding to the popular narrative conventions that determine them. Thus, movie-going lore about the conventional trajectories of popular fictions is generally out of bounds when it comes to our imaginative engagement with movies.

Knowledge of these tendencies is precluded by the realistic heuristic from our cognitive processing of how the fictional world of the movie literally works (unless the fiction itself is about how popular-movie-makers construct popular-movie plots). Moreover, except where marked appropriately, movies that employ these conventional structures are not to be taken to be referring to them figuratively. So, we may not access these plot schemas on the grounds that the movie is alluding to them. On the other hand, it may be the case that we can entertain the movie lore we know about star personae, since the image of the stars on the screen may be functioning as a trope.

Allusions do not refer directly to states of affairs or causal chains within the fictional world. They are *figural*. So just as the metaphorical dissolves in Eisenstein's *Strike* do not propose that the spy has literally turned into a monkey in the fictional world, when a movie image (containing a character played by Joel McCrea) alludes to Joel McCrea and his star persona, the image does not imply that Joel McCrea or any of his previous characters are inhabitants of the fictional world of *Ride the High Country*.

The movie lore that we are not mandated to access concerns the artistic strategies for construing the laws of probability that govern the story world from inside the scope of the fiction operator. However, that principle is not violated when we explore the figurative allusions available in the cinematic array.

So far, then, we have found a reason why certain prohibitions concerning our access to movie-going lore may not bar our remembrance of the star's persona when configuring our emotional response to the character that he or she is portraying on screen. The reason is that the photographically based image of the star is alluding to the star's persona that has evolved over his or her past roles and, moreover, this kind of figuration is perfectly compatible with a literal approach to what is true in the fiction. The star persona is part of the connotative dimension of the movie, as literary scholars use that phrase, rather than being part of the denotative dimension. This is surely a conceivable solution to the problem of movie stars. But how plausible is it to suppose that sometimes movies are really alluding in this way to star personae?

## The Movie Star as Allusion

Whereas our knowledge of movie lore can be applied to the fictional world when it is alluded to figuratively, as may be the case with star personae, knowledge of movie lore about popular plot conventions should not be enlisted literally in our processing of the fictional world. Perhaps this distinction gives us a way to explain why filling out the characters by reference to star personae is acceptable, while filling out the laws that govern happenings in said fictional worlds with reference to our knowledge of popular plot conventions, like the happy-ending motif, are not appropriate. But why think that star personae are actually used in this way? Why think filmmakers are alluding to star personae? What is the evidence?

We began with Stanley Cavell's inspiring analysis of the casting of *Ride the High Country*. One might balk at it on the grounds that the film does not explicitly invite us to recall the earlier careers of Scott and McCrea.

Why suppose that it is a donnée of movie-going that viewers should use established star personae to illuminate the characters before them on screen? Perhaps Cavell was simply allowing his mind to wander.

But one reason in favor of supposing that there is this donnée in operation is that there are some movies that explicitly invite us to access star personae. An incontestable example is Don Siegal's *The Shootist*, which starred John Wayne. This film opens in a way that almost seems to be informed by Cavell's interpretation of *Ride the High Country.*

The film concerns the last days of a gunman or shootist, named John Bernard Books (a character loosely based on John Wesley Hardin). John Bernard Books is played by John Wayne. The film opens with a montage of what is putatively John Bernard Books's earlier days. The viewer, however, recognizes that this montage is composed of shots from some of John Wayne's 68 other westerns, including cuts from *The Big Trail* and *Rio Bravo.* In short, we are overtly invited, indeed, nudged to formulate, our emotive response to John Bernard Books by recalling central moments in the evolution of John Wayne's star persona – we are almost instructed outright to attribute to Books associations we have formed over the years and over many films toward John Wayne, the actor portraying Books. For, in *The Shootist*, the earlier moments in the development of Wayne's star persona are recalled before our very eyes.

Nor can there be any doubt that this was intended. According to William Self, one of the producers of the film, George C. Scott was, at one point, being contemplated for the role of John Bernard Books. However, that idea was dropped immediately when it was learnt that John Wayne wanted to play the part. For, in Self's own words, it was anticipated that Wayne would bring an *iconic* dimension to the portrayal – where, by "iconic," Self appears to have in mind something like what I mean when I speak of a movie star's allusion to his or her star persona.[13]

Moreover, the producers of *The Shootist* intended the opening montage to set the tone of the film; as asserted by the film's screenwriter, Miles Hood Swartout, the creators of the movie wanted viewers to fill in Books's backstory[14] by alluding to Wayne's long tenure as an actor in westerns, thereby suggesting not only something of Books's courageousness, but also something of his righteousness and adherence to a cowboy code of honor.

13 Information about *The Shootist* in this essay derives from the short, "The Shootist Legend Lives On" on the 2001 DVD of *The Shootist*, which is distributed by the Paramount Widescreen DVD Collection.

14 Ibid.

At the time of the release of the film, this opening montage was sometimes compared to François Truffaut's use in *Love on the Run* of footage of Jean-Pierre Léaud from earlier films in Truffaut's Antoine Doinel cycle – such as *Bed and Board* and *The Four Hundred Blows*. However, Siegal's use of the Wayne footage is very different from Truffaut's use of the Léaud footage. For, Truffaut's footage is essentially a matter of flashbacks to earlier events (culled from earlier films in the same cycle) in the life of Antoine Doinel who happens to be played throughout this series of films by Léaud. There is no allusion to Léaud's star persona. On the other hand, John Bernard Books's celluloid biography is assembled from strips of film representing utterly disjoint fictional worlds. What they have in common is that all these different fictional characters were played by John Wayne and that all these films contributed to his established star persona as a western icon. For this reason, they function not only as ostensible flashbacks to Books's past, but also as allusions to Wayne's star persona.

Moreover, Wayne's is not the only star persona dragooned by *The Shootist*. In the final gun battle, Books is ranged against, among others, characters played by Hugh O'Brien and Richard Boone, stars of the TV series *Wyatt Earp* and *Have Gun Will Travel*, respectively. Since these actors never lost a fight in the programs that made them stars, we can use their star personae to surmise that they are very formidable opponents.[15] So even if one were skeptical about whether or not star personae are functioning allusively in a film like *Ride the High Country*, the possibility of this sort of figurative reference is virtually indisputable in the case of *The Shootist*, both in terms of its salient – shall we say "impossible to miss" – expressive orchestration of what is on screen and also on the basis of the subsequent documentary testimony of the creators of the film.

Likewise, in Ida Lupino's *The Bigamist*, there is also an important allusion to a star persona. The bigamist in the film, who is played by Edmond O'Brien, remarks that the social worker, who is investigating him, looks just like Edmond Gwenn. Of course, the social worker *is* being portrayed by the actor Edmond Gwenn. The point of this allusion is to insinuate that the social worker is benevolent, since Gwenn, recently the lead in *Miracle on 34th Street* (in which he played Santa Claus), possessed a star persona that radiated avuncularity. That this association is not a wayward or idiosyncratic one on our part, moreover, is made abundantly clear in the film when, on a guided bus tour of Hollywood, the bigamist is shown

15 Maybe there is even another layer of allusion here. Since Boone and O'Brien were essentially TV cowboy stars and Wayne was a movie cowboy star, perhaps it is being insinuated that Wayne belongs to a better class of gunfighter.

what we are told by the tour guide is the home of Edmond Gwenn who, in turn, is explicitly cited for his role in *Miracle on 34th Street* (a film, by the way, that the bigamist announces he enjoyed completely). In short, there can be no doubt that Lupino intends to be alluding to Gwenn's star persona in this film, most probably in order to incite our associations with him as a generous and caring figure – someone who, in other words, can be trusted.

In *The Shootist* and *The Bigamist*, there can be little doubt that the allusion to the star personae of the actors playing the pertinent characters is apposite, since the allusions are so out in the open, in a manner of speaking. Cases like this show that allusion to star personae is both an existing and a viable expressive device. But it would also appear that allusions need not be always as explicitly pronounced as they are in these cases.

In *Indiana Jones and the Last Crusade*, we are introduced to Indiana Jones's father, a scholar like his son, but decidedly more professorial, older, stuffier, and far less adventurous. Nevertheless, we readily accept that he charms the beautiful Dr Elsa Schneider almost as effectively as does his son.

But why do we feel so persuaded by this possibility? Probably because Indiana Jones's father is played by Sean Connery, a star with a persona linked associatively – since his days as James Bond – with being an irresistible seducer. Moreover, there can be little doubt that the producers of *Indiana Jones and the Last Crusade* considered the casting of their film with respect to the iconic status of its players no less than did the producers of *The Shootist.* They intend us to use the allusion to Sean Connery's star persona in order to influence our conception of the character of Prof. Henry Jones Sr, just as the creators of *The Shootist* deployed John Wayne's star persona in order to build up John Bernard Books's character.

In part because there is what might be called the practice of allusive casting, viewers test what they know of the star personae of actors they recognize in order to see whether it sheds light associatively on the characters in question. This, of course, does not always succeed, since sometimes actors choose to perform against the grain of their star persona, as Gregory Peck did when he played Dr Mengele in *The Boys from Brazil.* But where there are salient parallels between the character and the star persona, we regard that as a signal of an intended reference and allow the star persona to enrich our sense of the character.[16]

For, in the context where the practice of allusive casting is well entrenched and widely acknowledged – and where so much money hangs

[16] Salient parallels here would seem to be a reasonable clue since we presume, quite rationally, that the filmmakers know whom they have cast.

on getting the casting just right – a reasonable default assumption is that the intersection of the character with the star persona of the actor is not accidental, but rather is intentional. That is, within the context of Hollywood-type casting, a coherent mesh between a character and a star persona supplies us with the grounds for presuming that we are in the presence of an allusion whose full significance it is up to us to explore as we might explore a metaphor.

Undoubtedly, some are likely to dismiss the sort of associations evoked in viewers by star personae as wildly subjective. Of course, many viewers may have very personal associations with their favorite stars. Who cares if Cate Blanchette reminds you of your cousin? Nevertheless, there is also generally an intersubjective core of converging response regarding a great many star personae. Consider this thought experiment. You can cast any star, living or dead, as Mother Theresa. Would you cast Bette Davis or Pamela Anderson in the role? Would Greer Garson be a better choice? Which one would you choose? Now ask the person sitting next to you who of the three actresses she would choose? Isn't she likely to agree with you? Try it.

As indicated earlier, I think that the practice of allusion to the star personae of featured movie actors took root so spontaneously in traditional, photographically based motion pictures because of the possibility of that kind of film to produce images that could be taken equally as two different species of representations – as physical portrayals of their models and as nominal portrayals of fictional characters. The images in movies whose provenance is photography are, thus, potentially double-barreled. In many cases, this possibility lies dormant. But where the narrative context of a fiction triggers recognition in the character of aspects of the star persona of the actor, we permit ourselves to exploit further the star persona to enlarge our conception of the character expressively.

Perhaps some evidence for this hypothesis is that we seem far less prone to rely upon star personae when it comes to live theater than when viewing films. Orson Welles's star persona weighs heavily on his Falstaff in *Chimes at Midnight*. To our minds, this Falstaff is like Orson Welles, or, at least, like his star persona, in a way that illuminates this version of the character of Falstaff for us. But it is hard to think of theater actors whose history of roles infects their current performances so insidiously. Maybe the reason for this contrast is that theatrical representation does not possess the kind of representational doubleness that we have attributed to photographically executed films.

Whereas the film image physically portrays the actor himself on film while nominally portraying the fictional character, there is only one level of representation on the theater stage. The theater actor only nominally portrays the fictional character. Save some Brechtian-prompted experiments, the actor in theater does not standardly represent himself. He or she *is* himself and not a physical portrayal thereof. Typically, allusion to one's star persona does not seem to occur in theater, because theatrical representation does not possess the kind of doubleness of representation that we claim occurs in photographically engineered motion pictures.

One objection to this attempt to solve the problem with movie stars in terms of allusion might be that, if we are to suppose that there is an allusion to John Wayne's screen persona in a film like *The Shootist*, then we must take that allusion to be continuous throughout the film. That is, whenever John Wayne is on the screen, we must assume that the film is alluding to his star persona. But this is suspect, because, it may be argued, allusions are local not global.[17]

When Lloyd Bensten told Dan Quayle that he was no Jack Kennedy, that allusion was a one-off remark. Yet if *The Shootist* is alluding to John Wayne's star persona, it would appear to do so whenever Wayne is on camera.

However, this objection rides on a faulty premise. There is no reason to deny that allusions are continuous in the relevant sense. James Joyce's *Ulysses* is said to allude to the Catholic Mass. Allusions to the Catholic Mass are distributed progressively throughout the text from one end to the other. The allusion is not local but global. And if you reject this example, remember that the whole of Joyce's *Ulysses* involves a continuous network of allusions to Homer's *Odyssey*.

Similarly, in the indeterminately large number of fictions that allude to Christ by way of Christ-like figures, the characters are often Christ-like through and through and not just here and there. And, in a less exalted vein, the episode of *South Park* that eviscerates the 2004 presidential election in the United States, the allusion to the Bush/Kerry debacle, reconfigured as a contest between a giant douche-bag and a turd-sandwich, is continuous throughout.

## Summary

Many movie stars have what we have called star personae, clusters of associations that they have accumulated over their careers in virtue of the roles (and the kind of roles) they have played. Viewers often use these

[17] Michael Leddy, "The Limits of Allusion," *British Journal of Aesthetics* 32 (1992): 111–14. This article is discussed critically by William Irwin in his "What Is An Allusion?"

star personae to fill out their understanding of and response to the characters the actors are playing in movies that represent utterly distinct fictional worlds – as the fictional world of *Rio Bravo* is distinct from that of *The Shootist*. Furthermore, it seems that viewers are intended to do this by the established practices of casting.

And yet this raises a problem. In a great many cases, it seems as though viewers should put their knowledge of movie lore on hold, if they wish to enjoy a film in the way it is designed to be enjoyed. Forget that you know that in a Hollywood film the hero never dies in a car crash in the middle of the film. Dwelling on that piece of movie wisdom will stifle suspense.

But why is it appropriate to put our knowledge of star personae to work when watching a movie, but not our knowledge of how popular plots go 99.9 percent of the time? Why is access to one kind of movie lore legitimate and access to the other kind not?

In this essay, I have tried to resolve this apparent problem with movie stars by arguing that the invocation of star personae is a matter of figuration. Films allude to star personae; the history of the star's previous roles and the characters he played are not presented as literally connected to the character. Moreover, the possibility of alluding to the star persona appears to grow out of the capacity of the photographically based motion picture to physically portray the movie star who is nominally portraying a character in the fiction.

# 12

# PICTURES OF KING ARTHUR: PHOTOGRAPHY AND THE POWER OF NARRATIVE

Gregory Currie

We are used to the observation that photography is not painting by other means, and that its adoption of painterly styles and genres rarely produces anything worthwhile. Are there limitations to what photography can represent, as well as to how it represents? What of those once-admired attempts to use photographs to represent something other than the object before the lens? Such efforts have been derided for their dressing-up-box dramatics, as with Julia Margaret Cameron's illustrations for Tennyson's Arthurian poems.[1] But put aside shortcomings in composition, technique, and taste. Is there something in photography's very nature that makes it an unsuitable medium for fictional illustration? Writing 60 years ago, Gernsheim, Cameron's biographer, gave a confidently modernist judgment:

1 In 1874 Julia Margaret Cameron undertook to produce a set of photographs for inclusion in a cabinet edition of Tennyson's *Idylls of the King*. From some 180 negatives, Cameron offered 13, but only 3 were used, and they not directly; woodcuts were taken instead. The publisher then agreed to put out a volume of photographs, along with extracts from Tennyson's poems. There are pictures called *The May Queen*, *Vivien and Merlin*, *The Parting of Sir Lancelot and Queen Guinevere*, *Sir Galahad and the Pale Nun*, and 9 others. One of the photographs, for the front piece, is a portrait of Tennyson. A second volume appeared soon after. In all, 26 illustrative plates appeared. (Julia Margaret Cameron, *Illustrations to Tennyson's Idylls of the King and Other Poems*. Messrs. King & Co, 1875.) Cameron had produced a few photographs for an edition of Tennyson's *Enoch Arden and Other Poems*, published in 1864.

> We realise now that photography is not the right medium for story-telling and that any attempts to illustrate the unreal by a medium whose sole contribution lies in its realism must inevitably be doomed to failure.[2]

Gernsheim does not ask how this statement coheres with the use of what is, after all, a photographically derived method in cinema, which he presumably does not mean to condemn as "not the right medium for story-telling;" there is a conflation here of story-telling and story-illustration which we need to sort out. Nor is it right to say that all there is to photography is its realism; photographs, I shall argue, are capable of representing unreal things. But I am with him in seeing a tension between the realism inherent in the photographic method and the illustrative purpose Cameron intended for her pictures, though it is no a priori matter how that tension is to be resolved. What exactly is this tension and how might it manifest itself in the response of the viewer? Answering these questions will require us to sort out exactly what sorts of representations photographs are, and how they stand to some other representational kinds.

It will turn out that our problem has connections to the now-familiar problem of *imaginative resistance*. Why is it that we are resistant to imagining certain things that fictions present, notably (but not exclusively) moral evaluations? Fictions where donkeys talk or arithmetic is proved consistent by finite means don't challenge us, but fictions where cruelty is virtuous do.[3] I will argue that our problem involves resistance to engaging in the imaginative project we take Cameron's photographs to suggest. And while our resistance here is not a straightforwardly ethical one, it does depend on a negative response to that project. At the end of this essay I'll ask what there is of interest here for those who don't share the response.

[2] Helmut Gernsheim, *Julia Margaret Cameron: Her Life and Photographic Work* (London: The Fountain Press, 1948), p. 61. On the role of photography in Victorian texts, including the Cameron–Tennyson collaboration, see Carol Armstrong, *Scenes in a Library: Reading the Photograph in the Book, 1843–1875* (Cambridge, MA and London: MIT Press, 1998). A more detailed biography is Victoria Olsen, *From Life: Julia Margaret Cameron and Victorian Photography* (London: Aurum Press, 2003).

[3] There is now a large literature on this problem; one might begin with Kendall L. Walton, "Morals in Fiction and Fictional Morality," *Aristotelian Society*, suppl. vol. 68 (1994): 27–50; Richard Moran, "The Expression of Feeling in Imagination," *Philosophical Review* 103 (1994): 75–106; Tamar Szabó Gendler, "The Puzzle of Imaginative Resistance," *Journal of Philosophy* 97 (2000): 55–81. For a recent take, see my "Framing Narratives," in D. Hutto, ed., *Narratives and Persons* (Cambridge: Cambridge University Press, 2007).

## Sitters and Sources

We need a reminder of some basic facts about photography and how it differs from painting.[4] They seem very similar when we invoke a description often applicable to both: a person stands before an artist, who has either a camera or some painting materials, and who proceeds to make a picture of that person. This way of putting it suggests that we have processes with the same inputs and outputs, differing only at the intermediate stage. But the description marks only the contingent intersection of two very different categories. A painter does not need a *sitter*: a person who both poses for and is the subject of the painting. For painters may take as their subjects long-dead or nonexistent people, or those merely unable to be present at the session. They might do this by using a *model*: a person who serves the painter as a guide to her act of painting of another subject – an historical or mythological one perhaps.[5] But a model is also dispensable; I can paint a picture with X as its subject in many ways: by having X in front of me (the sitter), by having in front of me someone who looks, in relevant respects, like X (a model), by having a photograph of X or a photograph of someone who looks like X, or from memory, or from imagination guided by a description. Any one of these things is merely an aid to the process. What is essential is something else: the right kind of intention, embodied in the right way. Paint distributed on a canvas in such a way as to resemble Durham Cathedral but caused by accidental spillage rather than by an intending agent is a fool's painting, and depicts nothing. And paint incompetently distributed by an intending agent where no one can reasonably be expected to recognize the cathedral is a painting, but not one that depicts that cathedral.

With photography, there need be no such intention. There can be an accidental photograph, as when the mechanism is unintentionally pressed, or connected to a trip wire with no notion of when and by what it will be triggered. In such a case we end up with an image – a representation – of something no one planned to represent. The mechanism itself is a product of design, so there is intention somewhere along the line.[6] But

4 For simplicity, I shall speak of painting throughout, though the real contrast is between photography and "hand-made" images of all kinds.

5 For convenience, I restrict the argument here to human subjects. But the same argument applies to objects of other kinds. A plastic sword can serve as the model for a painting of some real sword, or for a painting of a mythical one.

6 Though we can imagine natural cameras: a plant with a light-sensitive surface and petals that form a sort of shutter; see Robert Hopkins, *Picture, Image and Experience* (Cambridge: Cambridge University Press, 1998), p. 73.

the fact that the wind-blown paint was manufactured will not make the result a representation of Durham Cathedral. Nor is competent execution relevant to deciding what is represented in the photograph. The photograph may be unrecognizable, while the accidental paint-spill has all the clarity and detail we expect from a super-realist work. Still, the photograph is, and the painting is not, *of* the cathedral.[7] With the photograph, there is a direct, causal relationship between the cathedral and the image which results from the process, and that makes it a photograph of the cathedral, independently of what anyone intended or what anyone could recognize in it.[8]

We should not think of photography in terms of models and sitters. They are just two of the kinds of things which may play a role in guiding the actions of the painter. Other things might be as helpful: good brushes, a good night's sleep before the session. The person who stands in front of the camera, on the other hand, plays an essential role in the production of the photograph. That person is the *source* of the photograph: the thing that the mechanism registers when the photograph is taken, whether the photographer knows it or not, and without which there is no photograph. It is better to say: with painting we (sometimes) have models and sitters; with photographs we (always) have sources. Sources are not special kinds of sitters; these things occupy quite different causal roles.[9]

Photographs are devices for producing representations by registering the presence of something – the source – that stands before the lens. That

7 See Kendall L. Walton, "Transparent Pictures: On the Nature of Photographic Realism," *Critical Inquiry* 11 (1984): 246–77, and reprinted in this volume (chapter 1). While there are no accidental paintings, there can be accidents *in* painting; the painter paints one thing thinking it is another. There is a sense in which she painted something other than what she intended to paint. But there is another sense in which she painted exactly what she wanted to paint. She wanted to paint *that* cathedral – the one directly in front of her – and that is what she painted, even if she was mistaken about which cathedral it is.

8 Because photographic representation is unconstrained by what a viewer will see in it, photographic representation is not depictive representation. A photograph represents non-depictively, even though it may look just like a painting, which certainly is depictive. But some photographic representations are also depictive representations. Those are photographs for which it is true that (1) the maker intended something to be seen in the picture and (2) an appropriate audience can be expected to see that thing in the picture. (Hopkins takes photographic representation to be a species of depictive representation: *Picture, Image and Experience*, ch. 4.)

9 See Wollheim, "Seeing-as, Seeing-in and Pictorial Representation," in *Art and its Objects* (Cambridge: Cambridge University Press, 1980), pp. 207–8. Wollheim holds, I think, that for photography there is a model and a sitter, and they are always identical.

is the photographic means by which representation is achieved. A representation is photographic when it represents by photographic means, and such means confine us to the representation of the source. With painting, nothing to do with its mode of representation confines it to the painterly representation of things implicated in the process of making the picture. There is no source for a painting. The limit of photographic representation is what is in front of the camera; the limit of painterly representation is the limit of thought.[10]

## Different Ways to Represent

It's tempting to say

(1) While a painting can represent anything the artist intends to depict, given appropriately skillful execution, a photograph can only ever represent its source.

If (1) is true, we can say, with Gernsheim that "Mrs Cameron attempted the impossible."[11] She took a photograph of (as it happens) Emily Peacock got up in appropriate dress, and presented it to us as a photograph which represents the May Queen (see figure 12.1). But according to (1), the photograph could not represent this, because the May Queen was not the photograph's source.

[10] A very different approach is taken by Dominic Lopes – *Understanding Pictures* (Oxford: Oxford University Press, 1996) – for whom paintings and photographs are to be classed together as information-based representations for which the key notion is causal origin and not maker's intention. The representation of nonexistents in pictures is then explained, following Evans, in terms of make-believe. Lopes says that a theory of depiction which gives prominence to intention cannot explain why, in the case of a model-based picture such as Rembrandt's *Bathsheba*, we give primacy of representational role to Bathsheba rather than to Hendrickje Stoffels, who Rembrandt certainly wanted to be recognized as the model (p. 164). I believe the theory can explain this: what the public context of the work, including its title, suggests about the maker's intention is that he intended recognition of Hendrickje to be achieved by at most a limited and specially informed group of viewers. And Lopes himself has trouble accounting for relative judgments of representational salience: his account of *Bathsheba* appeals to the notion that Bathsheba is the origin of the testimony-transmitted information made use of by Rembrandt, while Hendrickje was an aid to the transmission of that information. That might equally be true in the case where Rembrandt calls the picture "Hendrickje as Bathsheba," for which the representational priority would, intuitively, be reversed. The difference would be in Rembrandt's intentions, not in the facts about the causal roles of information emanating from the two representees.

[11] Gernsheim, *Julia Margaret Cameron*, p. 61.

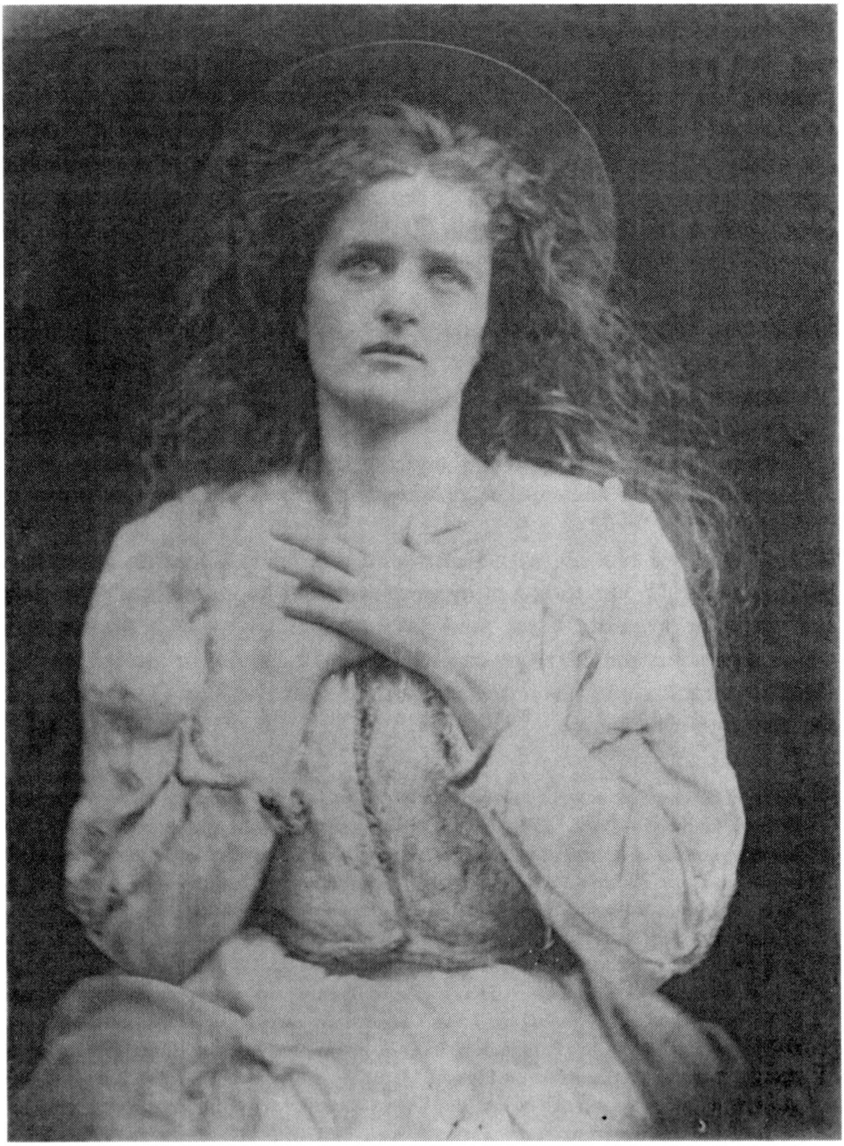

**Figure 12.1** Julia Margaret Cameron, *The May Queen*, 1874. Albumen print. George Eastman House, museum purchase, GEH NEG: 2893276:0024:0004.

But (1) is not true, and does not follow from what has been said about the two mediums. We should grant that photography, because it is a device for recording something, requires a source. But why assume that a photograph can represent only its source? Why should not a representation of one thing be also a representation of another? Later, we'll see that we do often treat source-based images as multi-representational. (1) is plausible only so long as we are held by two principles, one of which is wrong:

(2) A photograph can represent by photographic means only its source.
(3) A photograph can represent only that which it represents by photographic means.

(2) is true. "Photographic means" are just the ordinary operations of camera and film; these operations enable something, the source, to be represented only if it projects light into the camera and onto the film.[12] But (3) is not true, for there are many ways to get one thing to represent another; all we need do is *use* the one as a representation of the other. I said that the paint spillage that looks like a painting of Durham Cathedral does not depict that cathedral – it does not achieve the status of being a representation by painterly means. But it is well suited to being used as a representation of that building; if I know that it offers a fair likeness to the cathedral, I can suggest to someone that they examine it in order to get a good idea of what the cathedral itself looks like. Roughly speaking, anything can be used as a representation of anything, though not everything is a candidate for being a natural or convenient representation of everything else (a point I return to later).[13] A painting

12 The photographer can produce an image in other ways, by directly scoring the film surface for example. Certain works of Stan Brakhage are of this kind. But the argument here concerns the normal use of photography, the use we might describe as its proper function, or the function that photography performs and which accounts for the persistence of photography as a widespread representational practice.

13 See below, note 22. I agree with Dretske – *Explaining Behavior* (Cambridge, MA: MIT Press, 1988) – that whether something is a representation depends upon it functioning as an indicator. But I do not agree with him that indicator content must depend in a law-like way on the condition of that which it indicates. The accidental picture functions, or might function, well as an indicator of various things about the cathedral, but it does not depend in a law-like way (or in any other way) on the state of the cathedral, since it was produced by an accident in which the look of the cathedral played no part whatsoever. If the cathedral had looked different from the way it does look, the picture would not have looked any different. (Perhaps the accidental picture serves as an indicator only by taking its place within a system of use which involves being approved by some reliable person as a means of conveying information about the cathedral; in that case *being an indicator* is a property the picture comes to have at the same time, and in the same way, as it comes to have the property *being a representation*.)

of your house can be used as a representation of my house – or as a representation of your car or my bicycle or anything else, as long as we can find a way of using the picture to convey information about these things.[14] And a photograph which has as its source someone other than the May Queen can be used to represent the May Queen, simply by being used so to represent.[15]

When something is a representation by virtue of the process that went into its making, I shall call it a *representation-by-origin*. What we call "representational painting" is a form of representation-by-origin, because the process of making such artifacts involves (i) the intention that something be depicted, and (ii) being made in such a way that an appropriately chosen audience will be apt to see that thing in the picture. That thing is then what the picture depicts.[16] Photography is also a form of representation-by-origin because the process that goes into making a photograph involves the leaving of a visible trace on a surface by exposure of that surface to light emitted or reflected from the source; the source is then what the photograph represents. Something that is not a representation-by-origin may still *represent-by-use*, as a pepper pot may represent a regiment by being so used in the course of my explaining the battle to you.[17] And something which is a representation-by-origin of X, may also be a representation-by-use of Y. A small plastic figure representing Napoleon might be used to represent his army in my table-top explanation of the battle.

Note that what can be represented-by-origin in painting may not always be so represented in photography. A painting can represent-by-origin the May Queen, because all that is required is a suitably embodied intention

14 Thus in our earlier example, the Durham Cathedral-resembling picture won't be a painterly representation – a depiction – of Durham Cathedral, but it could easily come to be a non-depictive representation of it by being used, for example, to provide information about that cathedral.

15 Wollheim makes the point that a photographic representation may also represent in other ways ("Seeing-as, Seeing-in and Pictorial Representation," pp. 208–9).

16 Following Wollheim (ibid., pp. 205–6), it is standard to define depiction partly in terms of a condition of correctness, which for Wollheim amounts to saying that the picture depicts *a* (an *F*) only if an informed and competent viewer can see *a* (an *F*) in the picture. Other theories generally include a comparable clause: see e.g., Lopes, *Understanding Pictures*, p. 153.

17 Strictly speaking, the categories of representation-by-origin and representation-by-use are not disjoint; something which represents by convention might have a process of making which is, in effect, a process of establishing its use as a convention. Here I am concerned with the distinction between things which represent-by-origin and things which represent-*merely*-by-use – i.e., things which do not get their use as part of their process of making.

so to represent, and the embodiment of depictive intention is what the activity of painting strives to achieve. But a photograph cannot represent-by-origin the May Queen; it can do so only by use. Two pictures, one a painting and the other a photograph, may both represent the May Queen, and there need be no significant difference between the ways they look – they might be impossible to tell apart just by looking. Still, there would be a significant representational difference between them, since only one is a representation-by-origin of the May Queen.

## Representational Dissonance

We may now start to analyze the unease I expressed concerning Cameron's photographic project. On seeing, say, Cameron's photograph called *The May Queen*, I understand a certain effect to be intended: that I should attend with interest and attention to the picture as a representation (by use) of the May Queen. But I find this hard to do; I find my attention constantly dragged to its being a representation (by origin) of Emily Peacock. The source – Emily Peacock – has a high degree of attention-grabbing capacity, or what psychologists have called *pop-out*. But attending to the photograph as a representation of the May Queen is not merely hard; there is a sense of the ridiculous that goes with the attempt and its difficulties – like to trying to pretend that the actor on stage is Captain Hook while noticing that his beard is falling off. I have a sense of *representational dissonance*: a sense that the picture is intended to serve as a vivid and engaging representation of something – the May Queen – which it fails to be.

This proposal immediately confronts a problem. There are contexts in which photography seems perfectly well suited to create representations of fictional, mythical, and otherwise nonexistent things. With the moving images of film there seems to be nothing self-defeating or even problematic about the project of using photographic means to represent fictional characters. In these situations we do not, typically, experience representational dissonance; we do not experience pop-out on the part of the actors who are the sources of the film image. How can that be?

Before I answer, I need to say more about the relation between photography and film images, and about why we would expect both to be subject to pop-out of the source. I don't mean to equate a cinematic image with the series of photographs you might find on the film strip; we do not look at the film strip when we are watching a movie, we watch the screen. The cinematic image is something that exists only under conditions of projection and is – literally, in my view – a moving image; an image which reproduces the movement of its source.[18] So a cinematic image is not, as I use that term, a sequence of photographs. However, a cinematic image belongs to the same class of representations that photographs belong to – source-based representations. What is represented by cinematic means is not determined by the maker's intention, but by facts about what was in front of the camera at the time the image was produced. Representation by the cinematic method is representation of a source, and anything else that we think of as being represented in a cinematic image, such as a character of a fictional narrative, is there because it is the product of representation-by-use. And while this is true of cinematic images because they depend upon a photographic method – cinematic images being produced by taking large numbers of closely spaced photographs – this is simply one way in which a form of representation may be source-based. Video technology produces a source-based representation which is not dependent on a photographic method. But for the sake of simplicity, I'll consider just the case of film.

Why, precisely, would we expect photographs and cinematic images to be subject to pop-out of the source? I will give two reasons, both of which depend on their being source-based representations. One is this: with photographs and film images, the source is the thing which the object represents-by-origin, and there is a tendency for us to think of something as very saliently representing an object when it represents it by origin – perhaps even as representing it intrinsically, or essentially, much as we tend to think of a computer as essentially or intrinsically having the function of doing computations and only incidentally as something to block a hole in a wall. It is this tendency which helps a painting to be so naturally thought of as representing a mythical object like the May Queen even when we know that there was a living model for the painting; the painting represents-by-origin that which it is intended to represent, and the painting is intended to represent the May Queen; so that's what we most naturally see it as representing. The second reason is that source-based representations like photographs and film images are peculiar in their degree of intimacy with the things they represent-by-origin. A photograph

[18] On the reality of movement in cinematic images, see my *Image and Mind: Film, Philosophy, and Cognitive Science* (Cambridge: Cambridge University Press, 1995), pp. 19–47. For dissent, see Andrew Kania, "The Illusion of Realism in Film," *British Journal of Aesthetics* 42 (2002): 243–58. For an interesting extension of the claim that cinematic motion is real, see also Trevor Ponech, "External Realism about Cinematic Motion," *British Journal of Aesthetics* 46: 4 (2006): 349–68.

is connected more intimately, more powerfully, and more directly with its source than a painting is with its model. The source of a photograph leaves a direct trace upon the photograph itself, the photograph being in this respect like a footprint or shadow.[19] Thus photographs, even indifferently composed and executed ones, are generally thought to bring us closer to their subjects than paintings do, especially in cases where the subject has emotional significance for us. I grant that Emily Peacock has little emotional significance for me, compared with that of the people I know and am close to. Nonetheless, she is a human being, and there are powerful mechanisms wired into us for responding emotionally to conspecifics. So we can expect that photographs, on account of being traces, will tend to provoke a high degree of pop-out of their sources, where these are human, or otherwise emotionally engaging objects. [20] The same goes for film images. There is, in general, much less pop-out where the source lacks appreciable emotional grip on the viewer. This is born out, I think, by the case of other attempts to illustrate Tennyson's poetry; the collected poems of 1884 contains pictures of appropriate natural scenes with no human figures, and here there is little representational dissonance generated.[21]

Putting these two reasons together, we can say that, for source-based representations like photographs and film images, it is *doubly* difficult for us to allow much salience to what is represented merely by use. First of

19 See Walton, "Transparent Pictures," and especially his discussion of Bazin.

20 This line of thought can be given a stronger formulation by those who think that photographs are transparent: that photographs provide a way for us to see – literally see – the object which stood before the lens (ibid.). Someone who believed this would be able to argue for the natural dominance of the source in photography, since on their view seeing the photograph is a case of seeing the source itself. I happen not to agree with the proposition that photographs are transparent. But advocates of transparency can certainly agree with me that there is something in the nature of photography itself which makes it hard for us to see the May Queen as the *subject* of this picture, for we agree that photographs make their sources highly salient objects. If they can make an even stronger case for this than I can, then they may have some advantage in explaining representational dissonance. But it would be a distraction from the main issue to try to settle that here. For objections to the transparency thesis, see my *Image and Mind*, ch. 2. See also Walton, "On Pictures and Photographs: Objections Answered," in R. Allen and M. Smith, eds., *Film Theory and Philosophy* (New York: Oxford University Press, 1997); Gregory Currie and Ian Ravenscroft, *Recreative Imagination* (Oxford: Oxford University Press, 2002), pp. 30–1; Jonathon Cohen and Aaron Meskin, "On the Epistemic Value of Photographs," *The Journal of Aesthetics and Art Criticism* 62 (2004): 197–210.

21 *The Works of Alfred Lord Tennyson, Illustrated with Photographs* (London: Robert Riviere & Son, 1884).

all, the source is what the image is seen as intrinsically or essentially representing; secondly, the source (assuming it is the right kind of emotionally involving source) is what the image is vividly and immediately seen as representing.[22]

Given this, why do cinematic images *not* produce the same unsatisfactory effects as illustrative photographs in the Cameron style? The tendency of source-based representations to display pop-out of the source can be dampened by getting the viewer to do things which raise the salience of what is represented-by-use. These are precisely the things that the viewer of a movie is encouraged to do, but which the viewer of a Cameron-style photograph is not. In the case of the film, but not in the case of the illustrative photographs, the viewer is provided with a fluent and absorbing imaginative engagement with the image which serves to focus the mind on the represented character at the expense of the source. Let's unpack this idea.

In the case of film, and in the case of photography, the kind of use to which we are expected to put the image is an imaginative use. But beyond this generality, the two uses are very different. In the case of film, the imaginative use is an attractive and engrossing one; we are soon lost in the images, for they, along with the sound that accompanies them, are our means of access to the narrative itself. Engaging with the images, we are absorbed in a dynamic process of imagining; what we imagine about the world of the story and its characters now depends on what we imagined at previous stages in the movie in ways that correspond in part to

22 We need some distinctions within the category of representations-by-use. Our photograph is a representation-by-use of the May Queen, but its being so is significantly related to its being an representation-by-origin of Emily Peacock. It is well suited to serve as a representation-by-use of the May Queen *because* it is a certain kind of representation-by-origin of Emily Peacock: the way that the photograph visibly represents its source makes it a natural candidate for being a representation of the May Queen. If somehow we found a way to use the photograph as a representation (by use, of course) of Buckingham Palace that would not be because it is the sort of representation-by-origin of Emily Peacock that it is. If, for some reason, we want a photograph of someone that will serve as a representation of the palace, this photograph of Emily Peacock is no better suited to the task than many other photographs of many other things. Let's say that Cameron's photograph of Emily Peacock is a *highly natural* representation-by-use of the May Queen, and a *highly unnatural* representation-by-use of Buckingham Palace (supposing that it does get used to represent that building). I have suggested that things which represent-by-use tend to be seen as not essentially or intrinsically representing those things. But there is room for more and less in this tendency, and the tendency is likely to be more marked the more unnatural a case of representation-by-use we are dealing with.

the ways in which later events of the film depend, fictionally, on earlier events. Being drawn into this complex – and absorbing – imaginative project, the role of these images in representing fictional things becomes very salient to us, and naturally eclipses (in all but unusual circumstances, some of which I will mention in a moment) their role in photographically representing their sources. After all, the narrative concerns the characters and not the sources – as *Casablanca* concerns Rick and Ilse, not Bogart and Bergman, who play them.

There is a great contrast here with any imaginative project that we are likely to associate with Cameron's photograph *The May Queen*. The most we seem to be asked to do is to imagine that it is a picture of the May Queen, or perhaps to imagine that we are looking at the May Queen when we look at the photograph. There is a thin, static quality about this sort of involvement with the representing object; in particular, there is not a clear schedule of activities advancing over time, because the photograph plays no role (or at most a very minimal role) in our engagement with the narrative, which is given instead by Tennyson's poem, to which the photograph is merely an adjunct. There is little that is appealing or absorbing about this imagining and we are likely either to refuse it altogether or, if we engage in it, the imagining is so thin that it does little to raise the salience of the May Queen as represented object over that of the source, Emily Peacock.

We can say, generally, that when photographic images are associated with a narrative, there will be unity, or disunity, or some degree of unity or disunity between the photograph and the narrative. There is a high degree of unity when the photographs play a significant role in presenting that narrative to us, as they standardly do in film; a low degree when they play little or no such role. Imaginative projects with a high degree of unity tend to be appealing and, when we engage in them, absorbing. Those with a low degree of unity tend to be less appealing and more difficult to take on in an absorbing way. In the case of Cameron's photographs, the degree of unity is very low, and our level of active engagement with the photographs is correspondingly low; we barely participate in the use which makes them representations of characters from the story. So the tendency to attend most to what is represented-by-origin (the source) is likely to prevail. With filmic images, on the other hand, the degree of unity is very high, and our level of active engagement with them is correspondingly high; we participate very actively in the use which makes them representations of characters from the story. So that same tendency is likely not to prevail. And this means that the still photographs created for the purpose of illustrating a narrative create a sense of representational dissonance, while cinematic images created to present a narrative generally will not. We sense in the former but not in the latter case a failure on the maker's part to achieve the intended degree of salience for that which is represented by use alone.

## Varying the Conditions of the Project

I've been trying to explain a certain response to photographs. Such a project ought, surely, to lead to testable results. And my theory is testable; it makes predictions about how someone who reacts in this way *would* react if the conditions of the photographs in question were varied in certain ways. These predictions might be tested against actual cases, but that is not what I propose to do here. Instead, I offer scenarios of variation which the reader may imagine, and then see how, in imagination, he or she reacts.

Cameron might have done various things, even prior to the cinematic age, which would have increased the degree of unity between her photographs and Tennyson's narrative. My theory predicts that the dissonance effect would weaken as the photographs gain increments of unity with the narrative. How might that have been achieved? Cameron might have presented the photographs independently from Tennyson's text, as an interpretation of the poem, as a film generally is offered as an interpretation of its literary original, if it has one. One would then look to the photographs, in sequence, to convey a narrative to some extent their own. With so few photographs it is doubtful that a narrative of any richness or interest could be sustained, but Cameron might have added substantially to their number.[23] If we imagine a succession of photographic projects here, each successively a little more "narrative sustaining" than the last, I think we can see that, as we progress through these projects, the intuition that photography is the wrong medium for a project of this kind weakens. And long before we get to its natural limit – a Muybridge-style sequence of images somewhat like a film strip – the complaint that she should have used painting rather than photography ceases to have any appeal, whatever other objections there might be to the project.[24]

23 Disregarding here the many great difficulties that photographic production presented at this time. Cameron was notorious for her long sittings, required by the lighting and background she preferred, and potential candidates for her photographs often fled, knowing the long hours of servitude that awaited them.

24 In this context, one thinks of the photographic novel, popular in France.

So far I have focused on the difference in respect of the dissonance effect as between photographs and cinematic images. But there are differences in this same respect between individual works within a given medium. The dissonance effect is not always of the same strength for any two photographs which have the duality of representational role which makes dissonance a possibility: representation-by-origin and representation-by-use. And occasionally, cinematic images induce dissonance because of the pop-out of their sources. So while it is true that the dissonance induced by still images like those of Cameron is high and the dissonance of cinematic images is low, there is room for variation of dissonance in both media. With film, dissonance occasionally becomes noticeable because a particular actor has a high degree of pop-out; the actor may be playing wildly against type, be currently in the news, or be in some other way inappropriately cast – suppose Rick in *Casablanca* had been played by Sidney Greenstreet.[25]

Some of Cameron's photographs are more dissonance-inducing than others, because the degree of pop-out of the source is affected by factors that vary between them. Photographic style and technique play a role: when a photograph is poorly executed or composed, or unwise decisions are made about the sources, pop-out is sometimes increased – *Sir Galahad and the Pale Nun* is a notable example in the Cameron *oeuvre*. But other choices that were available to Cameron might have reduced the degree of pop-out that we find with her pictures. Instead of having photographs which provide lots of information about facial features and expression, build and pose, thus emphasizing the identity and characteristics of the source, Cameron might have produced instead pictures of very dimly

[25] As Robert Black pointed out to me, filmmakers sometimes intentionally induce something like a dissonance effect by giving – and making it clear that they intend to give – a high degree of pop-out to certain sources. In *Monty Python and the Holy Grail* (Gilliam, Jones 1975) John Cleese and Graham Chapman perform in ways which emphasize their unsuitability to the roles they are playing. I call this "something like a dissonance effect" because, as I have defined it, dissonance occurs only when there is a contrast between the actual salience of something represented, and its *intended* salience, and in the Monty Python case the salience of the actors is intended. In this film the contrast is between the actual (and intended) salience and the kind of salience which is standard for, say, an historical-fiction movie. We could have defined dissonance so as to cover this sort of case as well, but to keep the argument from becoming yet more complex I have chosen the simpler definition of dissonance in the text above. (It is possible to see ironic references to Cameron's project in the Monty Python version of the Arthurian story, and I like to imagine that the degree of pop-out given in the film to its actors was inspired by the similar (but this time unintended) effect of Cameron's photographs. Note also a slight resemblance between Eric Idle and the Galahad-source, whoever that is, in Cameron's *Sir Galahad and the Pale Nun*).

visible subjects where these sorts of features are not easily discriminable; compare Cameron's *The May Queen* with an imagined photograph by her of Emily Peacock in the distance in bad light.[26] Again, we can imagine a succession of projects here, right up to the point where one cannot with confidence distinguish the figures from the setting in which they stand. And once again, I think, the sense of discomfort with these photographs as illustrations decreases with the decreasing clarity and identifiability of the sources.

We can summarize all this as follows. Illustrative photographs in the manner of Cameron are subject to a certain effect, representational dissonance, which is produced by their sources having a high degree of pop-out. But the degree of pop-out of a photograph's source can be varied by a range of factors, some intrinsic to the image itself, and some which are better described as aspects of the image's context. One factor – a contextual one – is what I have called the unity of the image – its role in the presentation of a narrative. Cinematic images tend to have high degrees of unity, and this makes for a reduction in the pop-out of the source. And a still photograph may have a source with relatively low pop-out if, instead of merely illustrating a narrative, it plays a role in the presentation of that narrative – if, in other words, that photograph is provided with a raised level of unity. But the pop-out of the source of a still photograph can be varied in other ways as well: through stylistic choices and variations in the level of technical execution, and through variations in the kind and quantity of information it conveys about its source.

In that case, different aspects of an image can have countervailing effects on pop-out, and the degree of dissonance is in that case the product of a number of distinct factors standing in complex relations to one another. A comprehensive theory of all this would be hard to construct. But one thing strikes me. Of all the factors that might be in play, unity with narrative makes a disproportionately strong contribution to the degree of pop-out of the source, and hence to the degree of dissonance we experience. When pictures are highly unified, as they typically are in a film, other factors do little to create a dissonance effect.[27] We may know

26 It has been suggested that Cameron attempted some moderation of the pop-out effect by using soft focus; see Michael Bartram, *The Pre-Raphaelite Camera: Aspects of Victorian Photography* (Boston: Little, Brown, 1985), p. 132.

27 Little, that is, by contrast with the very high degree of pop-out we experience with Cameron's still photographs; there are interesting things to be said about the ways in which sources in cinematography affect our experience of the film; compare *Black Hawk Down*, with its ensemble of relatively unfamiliar actors and deliberate refusal of sharp individuation, with the star-strewn *The Thin Red Line*. For a discussion of the ways in which films sometimes exploit our knowledge of an actor's previous movie-history, see Noël Carroll's contribution to this volume (chapter 11).

the identity of the actor very well, and not be much affected as a result by dissonance. But when unity is very low or non-existent, as it is with Cameron's photographs, an uncomfortable degree of dissonance will tend to be felt, even where the picture is technically and stylistically excellent, and even where the source is photographed in a way which provides only minimal information about that source.

## The Power of Narrative

I have said that unity with a narrative makes a disproportionate contribution to degree of pop-out in a photograph's source. There is a more general point to be made here about the powers of narrative. It is widely recognized that narratives are able to exert a peculiar power over us. Ideas that are unengaging, tedious, and even ridiculous outside the context of a narrative can be utterly absorbing when framed within one. Human beings are great consumers of narratives of the supernatural, adopting a variety of attitudes towards such stories from sustained belief to frivolous imagining, with many attitudes at indeterminate stages between. But very few of us have any interest in theories of the supernatural, and would get little diversion or instruction from a treatise on ectoplasm and its relation to telekinesis. And theological speculation along systematic lines brings few converts compared with the power of religious stories.[28]

This is a point about *content*. When we say that narrative makes certain ideas more attractive than they would be when presented in some non-narrative context – within the context, say, of a theory – we are talking about the content of the narrative. But narrative has a similarly enhancing power with respect to the *vehicle* of representation. Where the photographs do not themselves constitute a narrative – where they are at best an adjunct to a narrative in some other medium – their use as representations of things which belong not to the photographic realm but to the independently expressed narrative seems at best anomalous and at worst absurd. But this impression can be very dramatically altered by having the photographs (or cinematic images) constitute the means of narration itself. When that happens, there need be no sense of the anomalous or the absurd; the narrative, conjoined very tightly to the photographs

[28] See G. Currie and J. Jureidini, "Narrative and Coherence," *Mind & Language* 19 (2004): 409–27.

themselves, justifies their use and makes the whole issue of their representing the non- or no-longer existent recede from our minds, pushed aside by the interest of the narrative itself.

## Turning the Argument on its Head

I have sought here to explain a certain response to Cameron's illustrative photographs, one which I experience myself. Others, I have learned, do not all experience it to a very notable degree, and some tell me that they do not experience it at all. The way I have put the argument suggests that I am building a case which privileges my response as the appropriate one. After all, I have said that, while the imaginative use to which we are invited to put the images of a fiction film are fluent and absorbing because of their dynamic relationship to the narrative, the imaginative use to which we are invited to put Cameron's photographs is "thin and static."

But there is another way to see the matter. Someone who has no problem with Cameron's illustrations, who feels no sense of representational dissonance on seeing them, can claim that my imaginative responses are simply too unsubtle to allow me to appreciate the imaginative invitation these photographs offer. "You," they will say, "are capable only of responding imaginatively to large-scale, vividly described projects. You probably admire crudely dramatic orchestral pieces like the 1812 Overture, and fail miserably to engage with minimal chamber pieces. You are unable, or unwilling, to imagine anything unless your imagining is supported at every step by loud instructions. You should not be claiming that there is an imaginative barrier here; you should be admitting that there is an imaginative hurdle, and that you are insufficiently competent to clear it." I have some conviction that this is a mistaken diagnosis, but I do not have any arguments to refute it.

Does this matter? No. My argument can easily be reframed as an attempt to explain, rather than to justify, the response I have: I find something problematic in Cameron's pictures; according to me the explanation is that I experience a sense of representational dissonance in their presence, and this in its turn is because I find the imaginative project which those pictures present for me a thin, static, and hence unrewarding one. If you don't find anything problematic in the pictures, my suggestion is that this is because you find the imaginative project to be, not thin and static, but challengingly minimalist. Or perhaps it seems relatively rich and effortless to you, because your imaginative powers are so much greater than mine. Or perhaps you agree with me that it is thin and static and you find something rewarding in thin-and-static imaginative enterprises. In all these ways, your response is accommodated within the explanatory framework I have offered, for on my account you are someone whose positive response to the imaginative invitation of the photographs reduces the pop-out of the source. We don't need to decide who, if any-one, is right.[29]

[29] Earlier versions of this essay were read at a conference on Cognitive Values in Art at the University of Nancy, and at the University of Nottingham in Autumn 2006. Thanks to Robert Black, Pierre Demeulenaere, Robert Kirk, Peter Lamarque, and Jerry Levinson for comments.

# 13
# THE NAKED TRUTH
## Arthur C. Danto

> "Is it true the natives think the camera steals their souls?"
> "Some of them. The sensible ones."
>
> Pat Barker, *The Ghost Road*[1]

Not so long ago I was discussing aesthetics with the junior faculty of a northern university, when one of them said, as a kind of joke, that whenever she saw a job opening in aesthetics posted, she could not suppress the thought that the department wanted someone who could do nails. She clearly came from a language community in which the term serves as the generic business name of enterprises ministering to the cosmetic requirements of patrons who would, if they lived in the United States, instead have had recourse to what, evidently without thinking it the least odd, we designate as "beauty shops." And her amusement derived from the appropriation, in one language, of a term that has come to mean, in another language, primarily a branch of philosophy, concerned, as the dictionary tells us, with "a theory of the beautiful and of the fine arts." It is more than slightly ludicrous to think of cosmetology as applied philosophy, and the permanent wave as an exercise in practical aesthetics, as if one might assure graduate students in aesthetics that they might always find employment in a tight market by trimming hair – or for that matter "doing nails" – just as students of logic are assured that careers in computer programming are fallback options in case academic positions are not to be had. The ludicrousness of applying a discipline almost defined

[1] Pat Barker, *The Ghost Road* (New York: Dutton, 1995), p. 86.

Reprinted with permission from Jerrold Levinson, ed., *Aesthetics and Ethics: Essays at the Intersection*, Cambridge Studies in Philosophy and the Arts (Cambridge: Cambridge University Press, 1998), pp. 257–82.

by the contrast between the aesthetic and the practical is given an edge of slight revulsion by the image of the philosopher with clippers and rouge pot.

The philosophical beautician – or practical aesthetician – would of necessity be engaged in the activity of flattering the appearances, which Plato had already decreed as repugnant in the *Gorgias*, where no deep differentiating line is allowed to be drawn between the art of the hairdresser and that of the Sophist. It is this perhaps that explains the mild shudder: what better characterization of the beauty shop could we find than Plato's way of putting the vaunted practice of the Sophist down as "making the worse as the better case?" The beautician does what she can to make silk purses out of the sows' ears who wish under false colors to win contests in the skirmishes of flirtation.

There is no dialogue titled *to' Aesthetikos – The Beautician* – but it would not be difficult to imagine a conversation – it might be a pendant to the *Ion* – in which Socrates, true to character, undertakes the dialectical brutalization of the somewhat effete hairdresser who takes on the defense of appearances. It would take very few ironic pages before Socrates would score the point that ringlets and pomades will not make anyone better but at most momentarily happy, and that we ought to turn from appearance to reality, from what we aspire to look like to what we should aspire to be, and instead of a life of ephemeral attractiveness we should seek one of abiding goodness and justice. After all; it was Socrates' mandate to establish that it was better to be than to appear just, even if, in the limiting case, the just man should appear maximally unjust and the unjust man appear the embodiment of justice, as in the case, Colin McGinn pointed out to me, of Dorian Gray. But Aesthetikos might profess puzzlement: he cannot see how our unhappiness with the appearances nature dealt us has anything much to do with goodness and with justice: there just is the human propensity to look askance at ugliness, even if beauty is only skin deep, and why should the just man badly endowed not enhance his hopes for happiness by rectifying his appearances in such a way as to deflect the propensity to suspect the ill-favored, gain the trust of others, and actually do the just things his appearances render difficult? Possibly we would be better off if we could be indifferent to our appearances, but, Aesthetikos continues, this is tantamount to saying that we would be better off if we were not human. To be human is to care about how we are seen, and that means that, as humans, we endeavor to see ourselves as others might see us, and seek, so far as possible, to assure that they will find us, if not attractive, at least not unattractive. Our preoccupations with aesthetics might be something of a distraction, but hardly equivalent to leading unjust lives! And Aesthetikos, who happens to be a student of

Gorgias himself, driven into cosmetic engineering because of the sparsity of paying jobs in Sophistry, presses his point. "Look at you, Socrates, with your belly hanging out and your dirty feet bare like that! If anyone *looks* indifferent to looks, it is you! Nobody would hire you if they wanted a lawyer! Nobody would hire you for anything, especially when you run about the marketplace saying to everyone in earshot that you don't know anything except how ignorant you are. You are an absolute master of appearances, and through the way you look get people to relate to you precisely as you wish. It would really be a fit punishment were the rulers to make you get a haircut, put on a pair of decent sandals, and lose a bit about the middle! You would probably prefer execution to changing your looks." The dialogue breaks off here, but it is very popular in the classroom, where there are predictably lively undergraduate discussions of the instructor's beard and blue jeans, or the ethnic jewelry and Andean pocketbook affected by the professor of multiculturalism, though shunned in the School of Accounting.

I shall memorialize Aesthetikos by designating as *aesthetikoi* those whose profession it is to enable individuals to achieve the looks that in their view represents them as they are, and letting the representationality of looks serve as a bridge between cosmetology and the mimetic arts in general. Needless to say, the look is capable of deceiving others, especially in causing them to believe its possessor younger and more attractive than reality underwrites, and it is the inducing of false beliefs that has doubtless made of *aesthetikoi* and their patrons targets of moralistic condemnation down the ages. It certainly establishes a philosophical fellowship between Ion and Aesthetikos, as it does between them and the legions of poets and imitators swept into the camp of enemies of the truth in the great dialogue that succeeds *to' Aesthetikos* in the order of Platonic composition: Book 10 of *The Republic*. It does not matter that aesthetic mimesis is of an ideal, usually, which the acquirer of the false look falls short of, sometimes far short of, on her own. Mere works of art, however we fault them on Platonic grounds, in general do less damage than looks achieved through the mediation *at aesthetikoi*, which trap the unwary, as we see, for sad example, in the cruel case of the second Mrs. Dombey's meretricious mother, Mrs. Skewton, whom Dickens refers to as "Cleopatra" when she is made up to face the world:

> Mrs. Skewton's maid appeared, according to custom, to prepare her gradually for night. At night, she should have been a skeleton, with dart and hourglass, rather than a woman, this attendant, for her touch was as the touch of Death. The painted object shrivelled underneath her hand; the

> form collapsed; the hair drooped off; the arched dark eyebrows changed to scanty tufts of grey; the pale lips shrunk; the skin became cadaverous and loose; an old, worn, yellow, nodding woman, with red eyes, alone remained in Cleopatra's place, huddled up, like a slovenly bundle, in a greasy flannel gown.[2]

But of course the deception can be vastly more serious than anything padding, coloration, and false curls can achieve. Plato tips his hand at the end of Book 10, when he has Er watch supposedly purged souls choose their next lives. He tells us of a man who chooses the life of a tyrant, obviously the life painted in glowing colors by the Sophists Socrates wrangled with throughout, those who, like Callicles and Thrasymachus, tell us that the best life is the one in which a person can do what he wants with impunity. The assumption is that each of us really wants power and sex, whatever the appearances – and what Socrates has wanted to argue is that this is itself the most dangerous appearance of all: it represents a morally ugly life as beautiful – and when the duped soul sees the reality he has chosen "he began to beat his breast and lament over his choice." The Sophists have, in their portrayals of life, as usual made the worst appear better, given the natural appetites of those they deceive. This, by the way, might give Plato an answer for Aesthetikos. He has given Socrates his unprepossessing look in order that the reality of the good, just life he exemplifies be the one his readers choose. The point is to *be* like Socrates, since no one would choose to *appear* like him. "And it shall be well with us both in this life," Socrates tells Glaucon, "and in the pilgrimage of a thousand years which we have been describing."

In one of her *Matisse Stories*, A. S. Byatt has her heroine, a middle-aged university lecturer, patronize a beauty shop because of a print of Matisse's *Pink Nude* she sees through the window. She would sincerely attribute her patronizing the establishment to the artistic taste of the patron when in fact it is the sexual voluptuousness of Matisse's nude that draws her in, but we learn this, as she does, only late in the story. The lecturer affects a certain plainness in her appearance, wearing her hair straight and somewhat severe. One day she comes in to have her hair done, for she is to be on TV, and in the midst of the washing she lapses into a memory of intense lovemaking with an Italian student, when she was young. On this occasion, the *aesthetikos* has turned her over to an assistant, who does not know her preferences, and when she emerges from her memory

2 Charles Dickens, *Dombey and Son* (London: Penguin English Library, 1979), p. 472.

she sees herself in the mirror wearing rather an elaborate coiffure, an architecture of curls and whorls, the kind, indeed, appropriate to a women of her age and her attainment. She throws a fierce tantrum, smashing the tinted mirrors with jars of gel. When she calms down it is clear to us, and it becomes clear to her, that her straight hair was a memorial to vanished youth and to that moment in her past when she and her flesh were as one, as in the Matisse. It is no longer appropriate, much, as Aristotle observes, as the young man's scarlet cloak is unbecoming when worn by an elderly man. The lecturer is not endeavoring to deceive nor disguise, but the look she has, with the collaboration of the *aesthetikos*, made her own has had a double meaning she only now is able to see through. It is meaning rather than mimesis that must be appealed to in seeing what appearances are in the moral lives of humans. When the curled replaces the straight in the lecturer's appearance, there is no question that she is being truer to what she is; it would be like putting aside scarlet cloaks and acting one's age. But that is because she now identifies with the meaning carried by the curled as against the more private meaning carried by the straight.

This might offer Socrates the basis of a reply to Aesthetikos. He can defend his looks by saying there is no stigma in carrying a potbelly when one has passed the age in which it is suitable to wrestle naked in the palaestra, where the belly would reduce effectiveness and would in any case be less – aesthetic. So his present lumpy middle is a way of signaling acceptance of middle age: diet and exercise would doubtless make him slim, but this would be a kind of scarlet cloak – part of the paraphernalia of youth. Socrates would be right, were he to have recourse to such an argument, but he would have lost the match, for he has conceded meaning to appearances of a kind his older way of contrasting appearance with reality was too coarse to capture. We live in a world of appearances, he would have to concede, but they define what we are at any given moment, and the *aesthetikoi*, like artists, are laborers in the field of symbolic reality. When Socrates first sets out to design his republic, the whole form of life to be lived by its inhabitants, while it ministers to basic needs, does so in a way to transmit to potential conquerors that this is not a polity worth the conquest. It has none of the gold and plate that countries go to war for. Nothing we do as human beings is innocent of meaning, and a Platonic Form of human reality that left meanings out of reckoning would be radically inadequate. The radical tack of turning one's back on appearances is a formula for ineffectiveness. The right tack would be to engage with the Sophists, but to make the better appear the better. And what else, after all, do the Socratic dialogues try to do? There is a truth in appearances that ensures as deep an affinity between Aesthetikos and Socrates as the falsity in appearances gives Aesthetikos his standing in applied Sophistry.

Byatt's dowdy lecturer turns out to be transformed by her coiffure into a grudging attractiveness, as an evidently unwonted kiss from her husband that evening demonstrates. Nor is attractiveness altogether alien to her personal agenda of looks. It is just that the attractiveness she wants is only symbolically facilitated by the style she affects: it is the attractiveness of a lank, humid female in the coils of young fleshly love. *She*, before her enlightenment in the beauty salon, would have justified her dowdiness by appeal to "what is fitting" for a person of her station, dedicated in almost Platonic fashion to higher scholarship. It is a kind of uniform of the professor who would suppose that she had left behind what she continues to live for in her heart of hearts, smouldering beneath the clinkers of middle age. Indeed, her husband tells her she looks twenty years younger, and the wry irony is that in seeking to retain her youth by means of straight hair, she made herself into something of a crone. The enlightenment is an accident, benign or cruel only the subsequent narrative of her life, beyond the narrative boundaries of the short story, could reveal. Byatt leaves her at a fork in her life path, where competing coiffures point, like signposts, in conflicting directions. And the enlightenment raises the difficult question of whether the truth inadvertently released to her consciousness by the well-meaning *aesthetikos* was a good thing. Conscious or unconscious, the projection of our image of ourselves through a system of symbolic appearances is something the ethical rights and wrongs of which are infrequently discussed, though everyone has intuitions in the matter, and the intuitions in a certain way are universal. In the domain of human rights, the moral inviolability of the body, appealed to in connection with torture and rape, and in connection as well with cruel and unusual punishment, is widely conceded. But what of the symbolic body, the body presented symbolically under a system of signals that convey the meaning a person intends to have acknowledged by others? The kind of meaning mediated by the mirror in the *aesthetikos*'s salon where patron and artisan collaborate on the production of an image?

In addressing this question, I want to make the mirror central: it is to one's mirror image that one assents or dissents, depending upon whether one believes that it expresses the truth of what one is. When Byatt's lecturer sees reflected back a woman in a stylish coiffure, she has no doubts of the optical truth of the mirror image, but only of its moral truth – its *truth to* what she believes herself to be. And in a way her rage is explained less by the fact that the image is *false to* the belief than that the belief itself is false. She is no longer a student, no longer a girl; she has, as the mirror shows, taken on attributes she has systematically denied through affected plainness. Mirrors, like cameras, always tell the truth, optically speaking, but they do not always tell the moral truth, as I am using that somewhat uncomfortable phrase. I have in mind the distinction, made much of by Virginia Woolf in the character of Jennie in *The Waves*, between composing one's face before the mirror, so that one sees, hopefully, what one intends to see, and catching a glimpse of oneself in a mirror – one's mouth sullen one's posture slack, one's belly out – and, using the mirror as a monitor, adjusting one's features, throwing one's shoulders back, sucking one's stomach in. One arranges oneself to conform with the mirror image that commands one's assent. Of course, the discrepancy may in the end conduce to the acknowledgment of the glimpsed image: one has taken on weight, and taken on years, and allowed the history of sorrows to show in one's features. And at that point one might have recourse to the *aesthetikos*, to diet and hair dye, a tuck here and a tuck there, a regimen of exercise, so that the distance between the glimpsed and the rehearsed mirror image closes. Or one just accepts the glimpsed image, in which case the distance may close again, this time in the opposite direction: one stops resisting gravity, age, and letting one's features tell the bitter story of one's suffering. When this happens one has stopped caring. One is beyond the hope and fear that open space for applied aesthetic mediation.

Such a state is by no means contemptible. It can even be a basis for admiration. We all know one or two persons whose indifference to appearance is the objective correlative of their dedication to higher matters: the distinguished thinker with unkempt hair and cigar ashes on his stained vest, the visionary who so internalizes the urgency of her mission that she throws on whatever garment is at hand and makes obeisance to cosmetic imperatives by running her fingers through her hair. And probably that was Socrates' situation as well, so bent as he was on the pursuit of self-knowledge that we can imagine him throwing a scarlet cloak over his shoulders, not because he was an older gentleman feigning youth but because the scarlet cloak happened to be at hand. The admirability of indifference, on the other hand, does not itself define a universal ideal, though certainly if it were universal, there would be one modality of vulnerability to which human beings would no longer be exposed, and one modality of suffering. They – we – would no longer be vulnerable to a certain form of ridicule, and no longer be subject to the pain of mockery. And with this I approach the ethics of aesthetic degradation, where persons are degraded through their looks. The unkempt visionary and the disheveled thinker are obvious targets of ridicule and objects of mockery. But their unconcern, the absence of care, immunizes them against the suffering ridicule and mockery are intended to inflict. Doubtless this can ground an imperative of aesthetic asceticism, a further way to indemnify ourselves against suffering, a corollary of the kind of Hellenistic philosophy that sought such indemnification in its various stratagems to stultify pain. But that is tantamount to enjoining sainthood as the solution to moral problems. And it is a variant on blaming the victim. It appears as if it is our own fault if we are open to suffering of this order when surely there is a moral misdemeanor in inflicting it. Surely it entails a violation of respect for the person, even if it is "one's own fault" that one is vulnerable to it. Theft remains a moral transgression, even if we would be immune to it were we to forgo worldly possessions. One cannot exonerate thievery by enjoining Hellenistic wisdom against the transgressed. Besides, there is something brave in keeping up appearances in difficult times. One of Sartre's characters insists on shaving in the prison camp, as a way of showing that his spirit is not in captivity. Winnie, in Beckett's *Happy Days*, applies lipstick amid the ruins. Colette's Julie de Carneihan knows that as long as she wears seductive lingerie, all is not lost.

I have read that when Elizabeth the Great grew old, she could no longer bear to look at her image in the mirror. So she left the daily task of applying makeup to her ladies-in-waiting, who, in the cruelty of their youth, placed a spot of red on the queen's nose, to make her look foolish. One can imagine their stifled giggles as the queen, believing herself cosmetically armored, set forth to the ceremonies and duties of her day, made up like a clown. I take it that the queen must have ordered all mirrors removed from the court, and that none would dare to tell her that she had been betrayed. Cruelty is cruelty, even if it was the queen's own fault that she left herself, through vanity, open to this practical joke. Had she known the truth, she would have felt at once degraded and betrayed, where the betrayal consisted in co-opting the vanity that would keep her from acquiring that knowledge. The queen was hurt even though she in fact felt no pain: she was hurt through the subversion of her appearances, where she was made on the scale of dignity, to look opposite to what she believed herself to look.

A case like the smutched queen helps us thus to see the moral inadequacy of Hellenistic theories, which tended to identify hurt with felt hurt and went on to argue that what you do not know – do not feel – does not hurt you. It is difficult to see how the queen's ignorance exonerates the ladies-in-waiting, whose action, because of its gratuitousness, has a quality of evil. It is a standard intuitive counterexample to Utilitarian moral theories that if they are right, it is morally acceptable to make a promise to someone one knows will die, all the while intending not to keep it, giving the promisee a pleasure she would not have had had the promise not been made, and none of the pain that knowledge that the promise was broken, was insincere, would cause, since death removes the possibility of that knowledge. Absence of knowledge cannot neutralize the moral quality of an action, though the knowledge would, in this case, constitute part of the action's wickedness, inasmuch as were the queen to discover what had been done, that would not merely add a truth to the body of truths in her possession: it would be a hurtful truth, and lodge, like an arrow, in the flesh of the queen's self-esteem. So in my view one has to build the pain into the indictment, even if the pain is never felt. And the controlling factor in the case would be the mirror image, even if mirrors had been systematically removed from the precincts of the court. The self-image with which the queen would have been presented, had she seen it, is hurtful to her even if she has not. It is hurtful because it makes her ridiculous, an object of derision and contempt, of mockery and hurtful, if suppressed, laughter. And all that for the mere entertainment of mischievous attendants!

I want to interject a word on the immateriality of death to the relevance of appearances as a source of moral concern. I am not thinking merely of the cosmetic interventions of the mortician, who seeks to leave an image of the departed in the minds of the mourners which is of a piece with the eulogy that paints the departed in becoming colors. For reasons far too deep for me to understand, it is a human reflex to want to establish an image of the departed, as if death is not final if the image itself lives on in the minds of those left behind. I am thinking, rather, of cases such as this: a wave of suicides among young women in a town in ancient Greece was ended abruptly when it was decreed that anyone who took her own life would be carried naked to the graveyard. Nakedness in young men was not merely accepted but flaunted, but a woman's nakedness was a source of intense humiliation. It would not be a factor in not wanting to be seen naked that one would not know one was because dead. It would be even more painful to contemplate because one would be helpless to cover oneself. A New York medical examiner under the Koch administration was discharged because he entertained his wife and a group of her friends by showing them the reputedly anomalous penis of a famous actor when the latter had been taken to the morgue. Athena robbed Achilles of a gloating pleasure by preserving the body of the dead Hector against decay. And in general how we are to be remembered after death is an incentive to behave a certain way while alive, even if we know that we will not know how others represent us. Part of what concerns us is that the representations should be true. And this brings us back to the idea of the controlling image. The exposed maidens want to be remembered as virtuous, and for them being seen naked is inconsistent with that. The displayed actor wants to be remembered for interpretations and perhaps his romantic looks, but having his penis smirked at by strangers is inconsistent with that. Hector would want to be remembered as a hero, not a mass of decaying flesh, and Athena performed the function of mortician, keeping his beauty intact until he could be buried. Burial is a way of letting decay take place out of sight, so that the image is uncontaminated by it.

My interest in the rights of individuals over the way they appear, and my appeal to the endorsed mirror image as that through which the subject identifies himself, as how he wishes to be seen and of course thought of, was aroused by a certain concern with photographic images. Two concerns, in fact. The first is that there is no immediate assurance that a photographic image coincides with a look, just because there are differences between the speed with which visual images register and the speed with which photographic images do, so that there may be no way in which we can see something the way the camera shows it. This establishes a difference between the glimpsed mirror image, when we take ourselves by surprise, and being taken by surprise by a photograph of ourselves looking different from the way we would have looked had we composed ourselves for the camera. The difference is that it is unclear that what the "candid camera" shot shows and what the inadvertently glimpsed mirror image shows are on the same level, both being visually true. They are not on the same level because we cannot see with the speed of the camera, and what the camera accordingly shows may not be the way we look, where "looks" are indexed to what is available to the unaided eye. The second concern is where the photographer asserts her authority to show the subject as she sees the subject, rather than the way the subject sees herself: where the photographer, as it were, asserts the rights of the artist over the rights of the subject. Both of these concerns may be violations of the right to control one's representations of oneself – the right, as it were, not to allow our appearances to be used without our consent – where consent consists, canonically, in endorsing an image as ours. This is not an absolute right, and it can be overridden. But I want to see how far the claim that it is a right can be taken. For if there is this right, then there are grounds for a certain moral criticism of images that violate the right.

Elizabeth's ladies-in-waiting transformed the queen into a sort of walking caricature of herself, but there is a clear difference between what they did and an act of iconoclasm, in which someone smears with red paint the nose of a statue of the queen or a painting. The desecration is intended to cause pain – it is a way of showing disrespect – but the evaluation of the action is qualified by considerations of political expression, which have to be balanced against the right of a subject to be portrayed a certain way. And iconoclasm has to be further distinguished from a caricature in which the queen is painted as having a red nose, where a further matter of artistic freedom complicates the issue. There are pictorial practices in which the relationship between an individual and her picture is considered to be one of identity, so that a desecration of an image is an attack on the individual whose image it is. Iconoclasm more or less presupposes this identity, but caricature does not: caricature makes a statement about its subject that may be injurious enough, since it asserts, by pictorial means, a proposition through exaggeration: the red nose can be taken as an assertion of alcoholism, or "bad blood," or mere disfiguring blotchiness: an assertion that the queen is a sot, a syphilitic, a hag. Being depicted in these ways is certainly painful enough when the assertions are true – but what if they are maliciously false?

In a show of student work from the school of the Art Institute of Chicago some years ago, someone exhibited a painting of Chicago's black mayor, Harold Washington, wearing nothing but frilly underwear. It was an exceedingly cruel painting, implying secret vices on the mayor's part or suggesting a metaphor for which there was no obvious interpretation that corresponded to any known fact of the mayor's character or behavior. It was *merely* cruel: the painter wanted to hurt the mayor through damaging innuendo, and to justify his so doing not with reference to any truth but with reference to artistic freedom. An artist could paint what he wanted – and he wanted to paint Mayor Washington in a brassiere and panties. Shortly after the opening, a group of black aldermen entered the gallery and simply removed the painting, causing as great an uproar in the press as the painting itself had caused. The argumentation was predictable. Everyone in the art community regretted that the painting had been done, but saw no alternative but to show it once it was done. The premise was that any obstacle to its display was censorship and a violation of the artist's freedom of expression, however painful the content of what was expressed. The artist's First Amendment rights were at stake. But what of the subject's right to control over his image? I believe Washington had died by then, but as I have argued, that does not affect the right.

My own sense is that the aldermen's solution was correct. The painting was, literally as well as metaphorically, false, and it violated Washington's right to correct representation. The painting in question was essentially pictorial libel, as much so as it would be libel if a newspaper columnist, merely arguing freedom of the press, were to print an article claiming that Harold Washington wore women's underwear. One reads these days that J. Edgar Hoover liked to flit about in black cocktail dresses and fishnet stockings – but there is evidently testimony to this effect by people who actually saw him so garbed. The artist did not claim knowledge, but merely the freedom to assert pictorially what he did assert. He did not, as it were, believe it true. He simply did it as an act of aggression. The discussion on freedom of expression has from its inception allowed exceptions, notoriously in the example of shouting "Fire" in a crowded theater. I take it that the example intends the case of so shouting when there is no fire: in the situation where there is fire, shouting might save lives. It would be valuable to have some further examples, this perhaps being one, given the realities of racial antagonism in Chicago at that point. The removal of the painting would not open room for anyone to take down any painting found distasteful. The aldermen did not find this painting merely distasteful. They took it down because it falsely represented the mayor and appeared to justify false beliefs about him, and so violated the mayor's right not be falsely represented. Freedom of artistic expression is as limited as shouting in theaters is. My view would be that rights have to be balanced out. Merely, for example, because someone finds the representation of nudity offensive does not override a gallery's right to exhibit an artist's nude paintings. Injured sensibilities do not constitute a right to remove the agency of injury. There is no slippery slope at the top of which is the action of the aldermen with, farther down, the cancellation of the exhibition of Robert Mapplethorpe's photographs. There is no abstract right to remove offensive images, any more than there is an abstract right to exhibit them. We have to proceed case by case.

For the most part, the sorts of cases I am interested in discussing *do* not arise with photographs, though the technology of computer simulation certainly would raise them: a simulated photograph of Mayor Washington in feminine underwear closes certain of the gaps between painting and photography. The kinds of cases I am thinking about do not raise the specter so much of libel – they do not connect with legal matters at all. But they do involve moral judgments and hence a form of criticism on moral grounds that leaves artistic freedom untouched. There is a question of artistic autonomy somewhat parallel to the legal questions of artistic freedom. And in the case of photography there is probably an evenly matched contest between the right of an artist over his images and the right of the subject over his appearances. I will bring this out by considering two ways in which this conflict might arise, only one of which raises interesting philosophical questions.

I want to contrast two photographs of the transvestite Candy Darling – aka James Slattery – a superstar, or at least a star, in various Andy Warhol films, who formed part of the flamboyant chorus of misfits that surrounded Warhol in the 1960s. Born in Massapequa on Long Island – the son of a policeman – Candy Darling achieved a triumph in Warhol's 1968 film *Flesh*, in which she and another transvestite, Jackie Curtis, read bits of gossip to one another from movie magazines as Joe D'Allessando, his back to the viewer, is apparently receiving oral sex. Of the transvestites in Warhol's stable, Candy Darling had perhaps the deepest vocation to be a female movie star: as a youth, he wanted to be Lana Turner, then, somewhat later, Kim Novak. He dyed his long hair blonde, had a willowy figure, and displayed, as if by upbringing, the most ladylike demeanor. Candy Darling – who had by then a devoted following – died of cancer in 1974, and I shall respect her memory by using the feminine pronoun. The photographs are respectively by Richard Avedon and by Peter Hujar. Avedon's picture, *Andy Warhol and Members of the Factory* – a rather large polyptych of 1968 – shows a number of figures, all of them male, naked. All but one of the women, several other men, and Warhol himself are fully clothed. Candy Darling is grouped with the naked males, and she stands, in makeup and garter belt, and with her long hair, looking like Venus in Botticelli's famous panel, but with a penis. It is an aggressive picture, like so many of Avedon's, and particularly so in the case of Candy Darling, whom it is clear the artist means to "uncover" or "expose": as if, had he left her clothed, the viewer would not know she was a man. Instead, she looks like something of a sexual freak. Candy Darling clearly had a fragile personality, and for someone who lived the fantasies of movie magazines and Hollywood allure, it would have been too much to ask her to resist the opportunity to be photographed by someone whose name signified fashion, beauty, and glamour. So for the sake of that opportunity, Candy Darling betrayed her true identity. When I speak of Avedon as aggressive, I mean that he did not simply disregard Candy Darling's values, he forced her to surrender them. I find it an exceedingly cruel image, but given that the subject was co-opted, there is no serious parallel between it and the painting of Harold Washington *en travestie*.

I contrast Avedon's image with a photograph by Peter Hujar, *Candy Darling on her Deathbed* (1974). It is an extremely moving picture of Candy Darling, in a black nightgown and mascara, dressed as it were for the occasion, with bouquets of flowers by her bedside and a single rose beside her on the sheet. She has arranged herself in the Hollywood pose required by a glamorous expiration and is clearly playing a role, that of *la dame aux camelias*, dying a beautiful death. Hujar has photographed

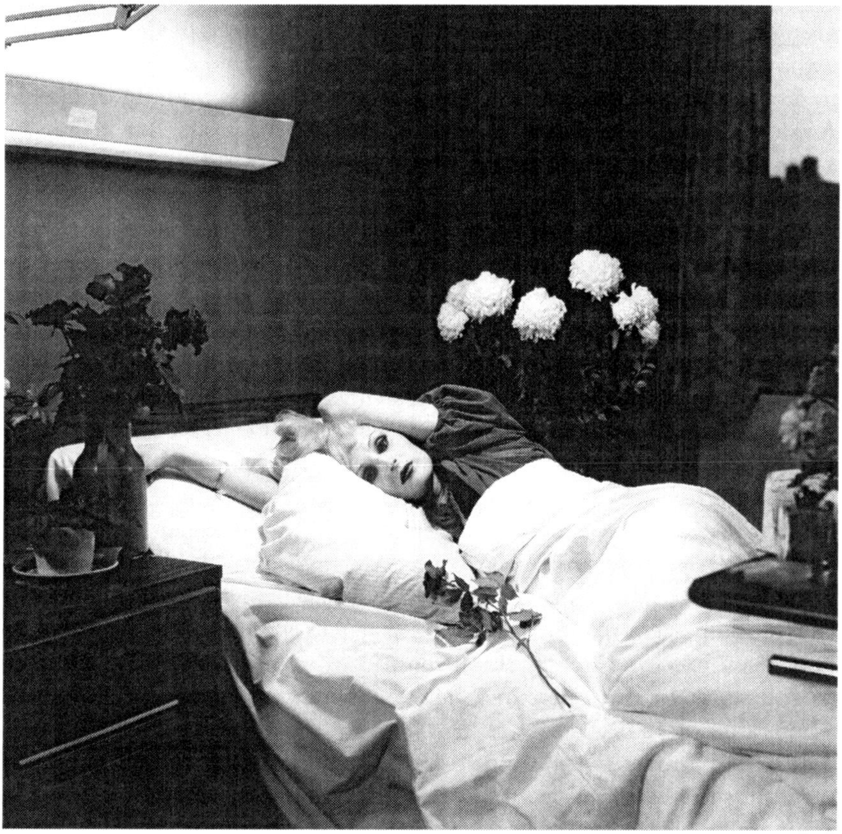

**Figure 13.1** Peter Hujar, *Candy Darling on her Deathbed*, 1974. Gelatin-silver print. © The Estate of Peter Hujar, courtesy Matthew Marks Gallery, New York.

her the way she would have wanted to be shown, and he has added something of his own: the black closes in on the beautiful lady as she leaves the world like a poem ending. Hujar lived in the closed world of transvestites, the world so marvelously recorded by Nan Goldin (who was also part of it), and accepted their values without question. I regard this as his masterpiece, and one of the truly great photographs of the century. What I admire is the profound respect he displayed for Candy Darling's project, and the way he presented this death portrait as an authentication and a gift. Hujar had deferred to the image Candy Darling would identify as her and submerged his artistic will to that of the subject. Avedon violates the subject's will to his own ends. He has whited out the background, which is a signature manner, displaying the truth of Candy Darling without qualification. Hujar has used the shadows to lend drama and pathos to fit the role and the fact of a dying beauty. There is nothing of libel in Avedon's image – he shows us what is after all, the truth. But it remains a morally bruising artistic action whose harshness is not mitigated by the so-called autonomy of the artist.

My second example also turns on the claims of artistic autonomy, and may again be illustrated by the work of Richard Avedon. But it turns on a certain feature to which the high-speed camera gives rise in the sense that it produces images that do not correspond to the way subjects look, mainly because looks are indexed to certain limits on the visual of which nobody was especially aware until the invention of high-speed photography, where the camera shows things we are unable to see. But it is what we *are* able to see under normal conditions that defines a look. This can be brought home by considering a whimsical charge by the Russian émigré painter, Alexander Melamid, that the cave paintings recently discovered in the Ardeche were fakes. They were, Melamid argued, because nobody knew how to paint animals in motion before photography, the influence of which on whoever did the painting makes it impossible for them to have been executed before the invention of photography. The allusion, of course, is to the celebrated images of moving horses by Eadweard Muybridge of 1877.

It is well known that the unaided eye cannot answer certain questions regarding the locomotion of animals – for example, whether a horse in flying gallop ever has all four legs off the ground at once. It was in order to settle this (and decide a bet) that Muybridge set up a bank of fourteen cameras whose shutters were triggered by a horse running in front of them, tripping attached threads. These photographs were published in 1878 under the title *The Horse in Motion*, and it is doubtless to these that Melamid refers. They and the subsequent images in *Animal Locomotion*, published in 1887, made Muybridge famous, and when he projected them by means of his zoopraxinoscope – a technical forerunner of the modern motion picture mechanism – the illusion of motion was quite thrilling. No one who has seen Muybridge's images, however, which are stills showing arrested motion, would have the slightest temptation to see any resemblance between them and the running beasts of the Ardeche caves.

The reason is easy to state. We really don't see animals move the way Muybridge shows them moving, or else there would have been no need for the photographs in the first place: it was because no one knew the disposition of horses' feet when they run that Muybridge hit upon his awkward but authoritative experiments. Muybridge's published images had an impact on artists like Eakins and the Futurists, and especially on Degas, who sometimes shows a horse moving stiff-legged across the turf, exactly the way it can be seen in Muybridge's photographs, but never in life. Far more visually satisfying are the schematisms artists evolved down the centuries for representing animals in motion the way we *feel* they move. And what is striking about the Ardeche animals is the presence of such schematisms twenty centuries ago. Muybridge was, of course, positivistically contemptuous of the use of schematisms. His photographs showed how differently the horse uses its legs in the amble, the canter, and the gallop: it was, he told audiences, "absurd" to depict a galloping horse with all four feet off the ground. But a famous painting, which he made merry with – Frith's *Derby Day* of 1858 – shows no fewer than ten horses in this visually convincing but locomotively false posture. The animals at Ardeche dash headlong through space, vastly more like Frith's – or Gericault's or Leonardo's – than the reality Muybridge's photography disclosed. And the philosophically interesting point is that we do not really know what a horse in flying gallop looks like, since it does not look like Muybridge's unquestionably true images and unaided perception cannot support any existing description. That is why schematisms are indispensable. The schematism in a certain sense corresponds to the canonical image of the subject – the image of who the subject thinks he is.

Muybridge reproduced his images sequentially, like panels in a comic strip, so that we get, with qualification, some sense of a total movement, whether of an animal or a human. The qualification is that the point of view on the moving subject is distributed across the several cameras, so that it is as if we get concatenated glimpses by distinct observers, which are never fused into a single coherent movement. This was regarded as a blemish on Muybridge's achievement by Thomas Eakins, who invented a form of the modern motion picture camera by attaching a rotating disk with two apertures to a camera, thus referring the successive images to a single point of view. When a device was contrived for projecting them at a certain speed, so that the individual images fused into a single motion, one could no longer answer questions about the relative position of the feet in flying gallop: that could be answered only by stopping the film and examining what we now refer to as a still. But the still does not correspond to anything the unaided eye is able to take in: we do not see, as it were, in time-stop fashion. The motion picture camera (including Muybridge's prototype) is accordingly an optical device for arresting motion if we arrest the motion of the film and study the frame. It shows us things that are not part of the normal visual world, like the microscope does. When the microscope was invented, there were those who seriously raised the question whether God meant for us to see things as it enabled us to see them. In 1877, that kind of question was no longer asked, though a somewhat similar one was, namely whether God intended us to see one another naked. Indeed, that got to be a very vexed question in Philadelphia, where Muybridge was invited by Eakins, at that time the director of the Pennsylvania Academy, to lecture. But this takes me ahead of my story. The point is that Muybridge had, as it were, invented the still without having quite invented moving pictures. Up to that point there was a relatively simple correspondence between ordinary perception and the photograph: the photograph shows the world as we perceive it visually. The still, by contrast, shows the world as we are not able to perceive it visually. It shows us the world from the perspective of stopped time – the *fermata*, to use the title of Nicholson Baker's novel about a man able to stop time and explore the nakedness of women without their knowledge. The still is a kind of invasion into a world in which our eyes have no natural entry point.

In consequence of this contribution of Muybridge's, photographs became divided into two main classes, stills – which imply a reference to motion – and what one might, having in mind Fox Talbot's phrase "Nature's pencil," call "natural drawings." Talbot, after all, invented photography because of his own limitations as a draftsman: the camera was to do by means of light what he did by means of pencil – only, of course, more accurately and better. I am not recommending that we change our vocabulary to fit a distinction language has chosen to disregard. I make the distinction to draw attention to photographs that take normal perception as canonical, and photographs that disregard normal perception in showing us things the eye cannot see. Since the same kinds of cameras are used in making both kinds of photographs, with mechanisms for altering exposure by means of lens openings and shutter speeds, it gets to be a matter of the attitude of the photographer. Avedon makes stills, Hujar makes "natural drawings." And this in effect is the result of how they treat their subjects. Hujar posed his subjects as if he were a painter. They were not supposed to move. They *held* the pose, in the interest of an image that was a matter of negotiation between artist and subject. The controlling factor was what the subject wanted to look like, which the artist helped realize. Candy Darling was typical of the society of misfits and sexual fantasists from which Hujar drew his subjects (and his friends). They dressed for their portraits. Men wore women's clothing, or they posed in such a way as to proclaim their sexuality. And Hujar was unwavering in taking them at their own assessment, which is what gives his photographs their power and their truth. For what it is worth, my sense is that gay photographers are naturally drawn to "natural drawings," largely because of the fact that they are so singularly sensitive, through their sexual orientation, to appearances: the gay photographer and the *aesthetikos* probably share a sexual preference. Avedon has no interest in the sitter's wishes. He is after something the sitter may be unable to identify with at all. *Tant pis.* The sitter is a means to the attainment of an image that Avedon will not hesitate to claim is the truth of the sitter, a revelation or discloser of who she is. But often, typically, the image is false.

Avedon's portraits are stills, then, even if not cut from a filmstrip. What makes them stills is that they are of moving objects. In a sense, the world, as Buddhists might say, is in unremitted motion: even a rock is different from instant to instant as sunlight and shadow induce their changes. Those are changes we do not see, any more than we see grass growing. They are too slow, the way a horse's movement is too fast for us to see the way its legs go. The changes I refer to in the case of portraits are the changes in the human face as it moves from expression to expression. One does not register these motions, which is why the artistic discipline of physiognomy never sought to deal with them: it dealt with fear, anger, joy, hope, and the like. Nadar collaborated with a physiognomist to capture the basic facial expressions, which Cindy Sherman astutely observed looked all alike – which means, probably, that there were schemata for these, as for horses in flying gallop, though the same expression would take on different readings in different contexts.[3] Edgar Wind, for example, demonstrates in *Hume and the Heroic Portrait* that the expression that means wild sexual abandon on the face of a maenad means intolerable grief on the face of a *Mater Dolorosa* at the base of the Cross.[4] The "smile" we are urged to show by the photographer is as close as most of us can come, if that far, in complying with a schema. Probably the photograph of a real smile is a natural drawing, since the smile assumed for purposes of being photographed is willed, where real smiles are not. The *still* of a smile is probably a record of a fleeting facial expression that merely looks like a smile.

Most of what the human face shows is not so much expressions as transitions between expressions, and with ASA 160 and shutter speeds of a sixtieth of a second we can capture stages in these changes that the eye

[3] See Michael Kimmelman, "Portraitist in the Halls of Her Artistic Ancestors," *New York Times*, May 19, 1995.

[4] Edgard Wind, "The Maenad Under the Cross: Comment on an Observation by Reynolds," in *Hume and the Heroic Portrait: Studies in Eighteenth Century Imagery* (Oxford: Clarendon Press, 1986), pp. 74–6.

never sees. Avedon gets his severe effects by overexposure – he sets his openings about two f-stops above what a light meter would recommend – and then underdevelops. (Mapplethorpe kept his camera at f16, whatever that means here). The result is that faces are defamiliarized, all the more so as the typical Avedon portrait strips away the sitter's entire context. They are not the faces we know, if we know the subject, and certainly not what the subject sees in the mirror. My feeling is that in making stills Avedon asserts his autonomy over the subject, all the more so when he displays the image as the subject – for example, *Isaiah Berlin, Philosopher* – when anyone who knows the subject knows that this cannot be he. It is, moreover, false to say that he sometimes looks like this. He never looks like that to the eye. He only does so to ASA 160, f22 at 30 – which, of course, does not see. Apologists often say, "In a hundred years, nobody will know what Berlin – or anybody Avedon photographed – looked like." But given the natural authority ascribed to the photograph, namely "Photographs never lie," this is how people a hundred years from now will believe someone looked. And that is to use artistic authority in the propagation of a falsehood.

A photograph for which we are unprepared will often show us things we would not know about ourselves, of course, and we have to admit its higher authority than our own self-deceived self-image. "I saw you in the paper," someone tells the narrator in a story by Michael Byers. " 'I've gained a little weight since you knew me,' I said. My picture had been on the inside front page. I was on the stage, receiving a plaque from the principal and superintendent. My suit jacket had been open and my stomach loomed out in its striped shirt, my tie barely reaching to the third button. I had been shocked by the picture, unpleasantly, but strangely fascinated, too, as if I were seeing myself for the first time in years."[5] But it will often lie as well. Candid shots, taken in a certain glaring artificial light, do not necessarily show people as they in fact are. Their expressions are unnatural, their gestures as wooden as Muybridge's horses' legs. They look like terrible people. I find this in Garry Winogrand's images, which in my view are often unmeritedly punitive. Catching people unawares does not automatically assure us that we have achieved the truth. Cameras do not lie, but photographers do, making "the better case look worse."[6]

[5] Michael Byers, "Settled on the Cranberry Coast," *Prize Stories, 1995*, ed. William Abraham (New York: Doubleday, 1995), p. 166.

[6] An instructive example is the recent work of photographer Philip-Lorca diCorcia. "DiCorcia, 43, hides several synchronized strobe lights on signs or buildings, places his camera on a tripod and steps aside. . . . This technique allows his subjects no warning that they're being photographed, which seems to rankle New Yorkers more than most. 'They think I'm violating their rights,' says diCorcia, a New Yorker himself. 'Maybe I am.' " *New York Times Sunday Magazine*, May 18, 1997, p. 69.

I cannot recall reading a discussion of nakedness in the canonical litsrature of philosophical ethics, a surprising omission in view of the fact that the first discovery made by Adam and Eve upon partaking of fruit from the Tree of Knowledge of Good and Evil was that they were naked and that nakedness was something of which to be ashamed. The phenomenology of perception at Genesis I is brilliant: when their "eyes were opened," the disobedient pair saw nothing they had not always seen, including one another's naked bodies. But for the first time they saw themselves *as* naked, and hence as in a condition that called for hiding. "Who taught you that?" God wants to know, for he realizes that this is not so much a new truth as a special perspective on old truths. They have, as the serpent promised, become "as gods, knowing good and evil." And it is surprising that philosophers have not paused long enough in their endless mooting of promise keeping and truth telling to ask wherein the wrongness of being naked lies. My own sense is that the contrast with their prior state would be the same, even had Eve and Adam, in finding that they were naked, suddenly felt proud of their bodies. So that instead of making aprons out of leaves and hiding from God, they might have twisted flowers in their pubes, like Connie Chatterly and her lover. Shame and pride alike contrast with the state of innocence from which they had fallen. God would have known that they had knowledge only the gods had a right to, either way. And in particular, insofar as it is wrong to be seen naked, it is wrong to be shown naked, however the person in question happens to feel about his body.

Obviously there is something wrong in showing a person in some state of which the person is ashamed. Patricia Morrisroe describes an episode in her biography of Robert Mapplethorpe in which, untypically, the artist took photographs of someone against the latter's will: a particularly fat man let himself in for some masochistic thrills at the hands of leather-clad sadists, who forced him to submit to having the seance documented. It is not clear that the man was ashamed of the episode – it was very likely the acting out of a fantasy – but he was clearly ashamed of having it shown, and Mapplethorpe was wrong to show him this way, even if one is tolerant about what consenting adults do to one another in the name of sex. On the other hand, there exists a horrifying photograph of three Jewish women, stripped bare by the Nazis, waiting, terror in their eyes, to be executed. One would tend to think the humiliation forced upon these pathetic women vastly worse than the witness borne by the act of photographing it, and thus that the photograph stands today not as a self-indictment but as an indictment of inflicted shame. An enlargement hangs in a museum in Israel, devoted to what the Jews were made to endure by the Nazis. However, there is an Orthodox objection to the image, not because the women are ashamed of their nakedness, but because they are naked – as though the whole point of showing it were morally unacceptable because nakedness is morally unacceptable. Showing nakedness is morally disallowed by the rabbinate, even if there are compelling moral reasons for showing it.

In 1877, a writer in Philadelphia argued that it might be granted that "practice in every department is necessary to the thorough artist" without this committing one to the proposition that "what must be painted in the life-school, may surely be shown to the public." No, the writer continues, "To paint well the human figure, models are necessary: but . . . we deny that to paint the human figure utterly naked *is* to paint it well. And to paint it in any condition of exposure that lowers our sense of the dignity of the human being should be forbidden by directors of the life-schools." And he concludes with the rhetorical "Has a Hanging Committee no right of refusal if the *technique* be correct?"[7] This was in an era when there were serious problems regarding nudity in the "life-school" itself, when male models were required to wear loincloths, and female models given the option of wearing masks. Eakins (who has left us some powerful drawings of masked female nudes) was forced to resign the directorship of the Pennsylvania Academy because he removed the loincloth in the presence of female students, and he created a scandal a decade later when he did the same thing at Drexel in a course he had been invited to give on anatomy. His defense was based on pedagogical necessity: to learn to paint the male figure "well," one has to be able to follow the musculature all the way through, which even the minimal garment renders impossible. But no such argument justifies exhibiting a painting of a human male without a garment: the painted nude must as a matter of course be anatomically correct, but it is not the purpose of the painting to teach anatomical correctness. And this was the Philadelphia editorialist's point. What artistic justification could there be for "lowering our sense of the dignity of the human being" that nudity evidently a priori does?

One might think that little could be less compatible with the dignity of the wearer than an apron of leaves of the sort to which Eve and Adam resorted to hide their nakedness. And one of the tasks of artists, compelled by convention to depict the male nude in the achievement of the kind of historical painting that secured preferment in the salons, was to find a way of concealing the penis without reducing the dignity of the figure represented by means of a ludicrous garment: the wide scabbard worn diagonally across the groin, a fortunate twig, an architectural fragment

7 In David Sellin, *The First Pose* (New York: Norton, 1976), p. 58.

would be typical academic stratagems. But the question of why nudity as nudity reduces human dignity remains to be answered. One is dealing, after all, with generic nudity, presumably, so that the kinds of considerations I have been pursuing in the body of this text would have no particular application: there is no one whose will is violated by her being shown nude. The painting of, say, Themistocles nude, where the artist employed a nude model, is not a painting of that model, not even if the artist copied that model's features exactly. And the same considerations apply to photographs of naked models, which were "legitimized" by photographing the figure next to a classical column, so that one could title it (say) "The Dream of Alcibiades." That way, men with certain tastes could glut their eyes on luscious youths, and draw as a kind of moral loincloth over their prurience the always acceptable excuse that they were admirers of the Classical. And of course this worked with female models as well: piety and family values disguised the real object of depicting, in *Roman Charity*, a young matron offering her breast to her imprisoned father, to keep him from starving. Eakins was revolted by these subterfuges in viewing the Salon of 1868:

> The pictures are of naked women, standing, sitting, lying down, flying, dancing, doing nothing, which they call Phrynes, Venuses, nymphs, hermaphrodites, houris, and Greek proper names. The French court has become very decent since Eugenie had figleafs put on all the figures in the Garden of the Tuileries. When a man paints a naked woman, he gives her less than poor nature did. I can conceive of few circumstances wherein I would have to paint a woman naked, but if I did, I would not mutilate her for double the money. She is the most beautiful thing there is – except a naked man. . . . I hate affectation.[8]

Eakins would have muttered something about nakedness being "natural," and hence a representation of someone naked would itself have to be natural. His marvelous painting of the nude model in *William Rush Carving His Allegorical Figure of the Schuylkill River* of 1877 solves the problem of showing nakedness without resorting to artifice. But not being artifactual is not equivalent to being natural in the intended sense: nakedness had not been natural in the whole long history from Paradise to Philadelphia, at least in the Judeo-Christian tradition. If anything is natural to human beings it is to wear clothes. And when Eakins depicts naked males in his painting *The Swimming Hole*, he is clothing his figures

[8] Ibid., p. 47.

in a form of nudist philosophy. When nakedness was natural to Adam and Eve, they did not think of nakedness as natural, since clothing had not been invented.

Eakins's powerful painting of William Rush and his model really solved the problem of how to show nakedness when artists no longer had the taste to set naked figures in classical landscapes: what they did was to paint models as models, rather than as Phrynes, Venuses, and nymphs. Artist-and-model, or model alone, became standard motifs in Modernist art, and the nude (typically female) figure became part of the vocabulary of studio interior, like the still life – or studio exterior, like the landscape – which turned out to be so attractive in the free markets of art from the late nineteenth century until very recently, when the life of the artist began to undergo powerful changes. Nude, still life, and landscape, for example, formed almost the entire range of Cubist and Fauvist canvases. In effect, by showing the nude as model, artists made an end run around the distinction that the Philadelphia critic took as canonical – between the studio and the gallery. The viewing public was given the privilege of the insider's view of naked flesh, not placed in edifying mythological and historical surroundings, but as so many planes and tones and shapes. The beginner in the life class was advised not to be shocked, but to look on the body as if it were a still life, an arrangement of forms. This of course did not prevent the artist from painting still lifes as if they were bodies – painting apples as surrogate breasts, as Meyer Schapiro insists Cézanne did.[9] Cubism and Fauvism were far over the horizon in 1877, but it is difficult to believe the Philadelphia writer would have understood their way of showing nudity as – showing nudity. He presupposed a naturalistic representational style. As in photography. In modernist representation, the nakedness of figures is, as it were, covered by the *style*.

In painting the model as model, artists painted women working, where nakedness was the condition of labor. That was not, of course, "natural," in the nudist sense of the term. But neither was it an assault on the woman's dignity, unless modeling itself was, given that she understood that in posing she very likely would be shown. And indeed, other than as models, there was no "natural" circumstance under which people would encounter nakedness in the regular course of life – except in the intimacy of the bedroom. The disjunction of artist's studio or bedroom then meant

9 Meyer Schapiro, "The Apples of Cézanne: An Essay on the Meaning of Still-Life," *Art News Annual* 34 (1968). Reprinted in *Modern Art: 19th and 20th Centuries* (New York: Braziller, 1978).

that unless shown as a model – which turned out to be in its own way an edifying context, as much so as the sylvan glade, the classical landscape, the picnic of the gods – the depiction of nudity was ipso facto associated with sex. And it is this, as much as anything, that must underlie contemporary feminist animadversions against the depiction of naked women as objects of "the male gaze." It must be a residue of received ideas from 1877 that in the 1990s females avert their eyes from naked men. In any case, in 1992, the directress of the National Museum of American Art – part of the Smithsonian complex – ordered the removal from an exhibition titled "After Muybridge" of an early work by the Minimalist master Sol Lewitt that showed the figure of a naked woman receding in space as one moved from porthole to porthole in a kind of stylized peepbox. It was claimed that the photograph, which was about as sexual as any of Muybridge's galloping horses or leaping men, was degrading to women.

The church fathers, Saint Augustine especially, saw the moral root of the discovery by Adam and Eve of nakedness as really the discovery of desire and of the clotting of reason by passion. Augustine's inference was that in Paradise there was no passion, that Adam planted the seed of his kind as coolly and as dispassionately as he would plant seeds in the ground, by sowing. For the first time Adam and Eve saw each other with desire, and they were ashamed of that feeling and, derivatively, of the state that occasioned it. The solution was to regain rationality by whatever improvised garment lay ready to hand, leaves as it happened. But it was too late. Sexualized beings could no longer look on one another save as potential objects of passionate desire. And that means we no longer see one another as rational beings seeing rational beings. Genesis was wise enough to recognize that this cut across the gender gap: both Adam and Eve undertook to screen their nudity from each other, at least until the privacy of whatever served them as bedroom: they had no business running about the garden in the "cool of the day" when their maker took a proprietary stroll. Nakedness belonged to the night – hence not under the full illumination allowed by the skylight in Philadelphia's Memorial Hall at the time of the centennial exhibition of 1876.

The knowledge of good and evil meant, in the language of the Bible, opening the eyes, and that meant seeing one another sexually. That is our condition, for better or worse, and the Bible simply takes it as something to be explained. Acknowledging it is not the same thing as returning to a state of innocence, but it is better, in my view, than seeing it as inimical to our dignity, for if the human being is a sexual being, the dignity of human beings must be consistent with that. No doubt we exploit one another through our sexuality, but the moral path to dignity is to recognize that sexuality itself is not exploitative but possibly fulfilling, at least along one of the dimensions of what it means to be human. But then neither is it exploitative to depict human beings as sexual, though by that I have in mind something rather stronger than merely showing human beings as naked. As far as showing a subject naked, the morality of that is altogether a matter of how the subject feels about himself as seen that way. Pauline Bonaparte was proud of her body when she posed for Bernini, but the *Man in Grey Polyester Suit* was sufficiently ashamed of his opulent sexuality that he made Mapplethorpe agree to crop his head when he photographed his immense penis hanging out of his fly. Pride and shame, those postlapsarian feelings, define the morality of the situation once the objections to generic nakedness have been removed – if they have been removed.

# EPILOGUE

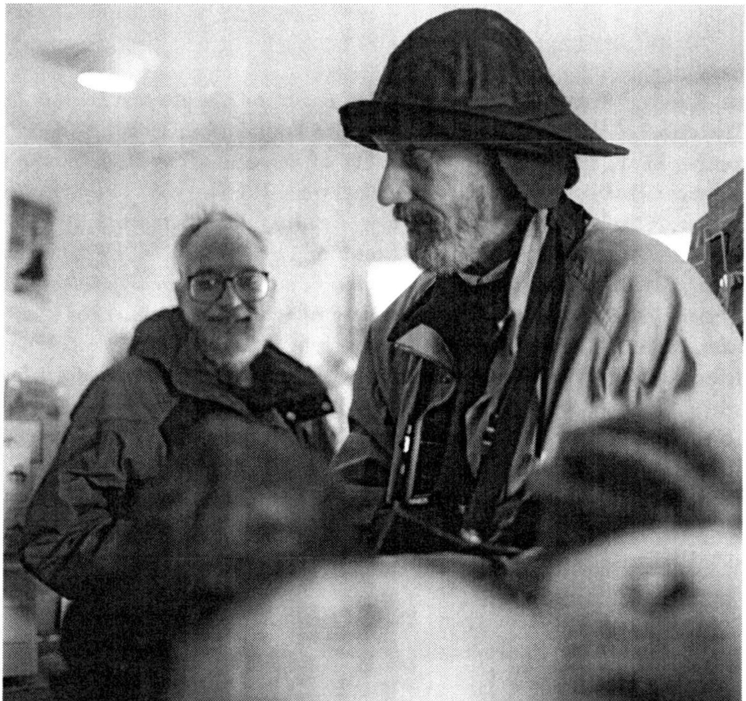

**Figure 14.1** *Make-Believe Mariner*, Kendall L. Walton and Patrick Maynard at Cape Spear, Newfoundland, September 2002. Photograph by Scott Walden.

# BIBLIOGRAPHY


Adams, Robert, "Beauty in Photography," in *Beauty in Photography: Essays in Defense of Traditional Values* (New York: Aperture Foundation, 1996).

Anscombe, G. E. M., "The Intentionality of Sensation," in R. J. Butler (ed.), *Analytical Philosophy* (Oxford: Basil Blackwell, 1965).

Armstrong, Carol, *Scenes in a Library: Reading the Photograph in the Book, 1843–1875* (Cambridge, MA, and London: The MIT Press, 1998).

Arnheim, Rudolf, "Melancholy Unshaped," in *Toward a Psychology of Art: Collected Essays* (Berkeley, CA: University of California Press, 1967).

Arnheim, Rudolf, "On the Nature of Photography," *Critical Inquiry* 1 (1974): 155.

Arnheim, Rudolf, "The Two Authenticities of the Photographic Media," *Journal of Aesthetics and Art Criticism* 51 (1993): 537–40.

Arnheim, Rudolf, *Art and Visual Perception* (Berkeley, CA: The University of California Press, 1954).

Arnheim, Rudolf, *Film as Art* (Berkeley, CA: The University of California Press, 1957).

Barber, Charles, "From Transformation to Desire: Art and Worship After Byzantine Iconoclasm," *Art Bulletin* 75 (1993): 7–16.

Barker, Pat, *The Ghost Road* (New York: Dutton, 1995).

Barthes, Roland, "The Photographic Message," in *Image/ Music/Text*, translated by Stephen Heath (New York: Farrar, Straus, and Giroux, 1977).

Barthes, Roland, *Camera Lucida: Reflections on Photography* (New York: Noonday Press, 1981).

Bartram, Michael, *The Pre-Raphaelite Camera: Aspects of Victorian Photography* (Boston, MA: Little and Brown, 1985).

Bazin, André, *What Is Cinema?*, translated by Hugh Gray (Berkeley, CA: The University of California Press, 1967).

Beardsley, Monroe, *Aesthetics* (New York: Harcourt, Brace and World, 1958).

Belting, Hans, *Likeness and Presence: A History of the Image Before the Era of Art*, translated by Edmund Jephcott (Chicago and London: University of Chicago Press, 1994).

Belting, Hans, *The End of the History of Art?*, translated by Christopher S. Wood (Chicago, IL: University of Chicago Press, 1987).

Blocker, Gene H., "Pictures and Photographs," *Journal of Aesthetics and Art Criticism* 36 (Winter 1977).

Bonnefoy, Yves, "Foreword," in *Henri Cartier-Bresson: Photographer* (Paris: Delpire, 1979).

Brentano, Franz Clemens, *Psychology from an Empirical Standpoint*, translated by Antos C. Rancurello, D. B. Terrell, and Linda L. McAlister; edited by Linda L. McAlister (London: Routledge & Kegan Paul; New York: Humanities Press, 1973).

Brubaker, Leslie, "Icons Before Iconoclasm?," in *Morfologie sociali e culturali in Europa fra Tarda Antichità e Alto Medioevo, Settimane di Studio del Centro Italiano di Studi sull Alto Medioevo* 45 (Spoleto, 1998): 1215–54.

Budd, Malcolm, *The Aesthetic Appreciation of Nature* (Oxford: Oxford University Press, 2002).

Byers, Michael, "Settled on the Cranberry Coast," in William Abraham (ed.), *Prize Stories 1995: The O. Henry Awards* (New York: Doubleday, 1995).

Cameron, Julia Margaret, *Illustrations to Tennyson "Idylls of the King" and Other Poems* (London: Henry S. King, 1875).

Carlson, Allen, "Nature, Aesthetic Judgement, and Objectivity," *Journal of Aesthetics and Art Criticism* 40 (1981): 15–27.

Carroll, Noël, "Concerning Uniqueness Claims for Photographic and Cinematographic Representation," in *Theorizing the Moving Image* (Cambridge: Cambridge University Press, 1996), 45–8.

Carroll, Noël, "Film, Genre, and Emotion," in *Philosophy of Film and Motion Pictures*, edited by Noël Carroll and Jinhee Choi (Oxford: Blackwell Publishing, 2006). Carroll, Noël, "Narrative Closure," in *Philosophical Studies* (forthcoming).

Carroll, Noël, "On Being Moved by Nature: Between Religion and Natural History," in Christopher Pinney and Nicholas Thomas (eds.), *Beyond Aesthetics* (Cambridge: Cambridge University Press, 2001).

Carroll, Noël, *Philosophical Problems of Classical Film Theory* (Princeton, NJ: Princeton University Press, 1988).

Cartier-Bresson, Henri, *The Mind's Eye* (New York: Aperture, 1999).

Cavell, Stanley, *The World Viewed: Reflections on the Ontology of Film* (New York: The Viking Press, 1971).

Chiarenza, Carl, *Passages and Transformations* (Rochester, NY: George Eastman House, 1995).

Chisholm, Roderick M., *Perceiving: A Philosophical Study* (London and Ithaca, NY: Cornell University Press, 1957).

Cohen, Jonathan and Meskin, Aaron, "On the Epistemic Value of Photographs," *Journal of Aesthetics and Art Criticism* 62:2 (2004): 197–210.

Cormack, Robin, *Painting the Soul: Icons, Death Masks and Shrouds* (London: Reaktion Books, 1997).

Croce, Benedetto, *Estetica* (Boston: Nonpareil Books, 1978).
Currie, Gregory and Jureidini, Jon, "Narrative and Coherence," *Mind and Language* 19 (2004): 409–27.
Currie, Gregory and Ravenscroft, Ian, *Recreative Imagination* (Oxford: Oxford University Press, 2002), 30–31.
Currie, Gregory, "Framing Narratives," in Daniel Hutto (ed.), *Narrative and Understanding Persons* (Cambridge: Cambridge University Press, 2007).
Currie, Gregory, "Visible Traces: Documentary and the Contents of Photographs," *Journal of Aesthetics and Art Criticism* 57:3 (Summer 1999): 285–97.
Currie, Gregory, *Image and Mind: Film, Philosophy and Cognitive Science* (Cambridge: Cambridge University Press, 1995).
Cutting, James, "Reconceiving Perceptual Space," in H. Hecht et al. (eds.), *Looking into Pictures: An Interdisciplinary Approach to Pictorial Space* (Cambridge, MA: MIT Press, 2003).
Danto, Arthur C., "Animals as Art Historians: Reflections on the Innocent Eye," in *Beyond the Brillo Box: The Visual Arts in Post-Historical Perspective* (Berkeley, CA: The University of California Press, 1992).
Danto, Arthur C., "Moving Pictures," *Quarterly Review of Film Studies* 2 (1979).
Danto, Arthur C., "Seeing and Showing," *Journal of Aesthetics and Art Criticism* 59:1 (Winter 2001).
Danto, Arthur C., "The Artworld," *Journal of Philosophy* 61(1964): 571–84.
Dickens, Charles, *Dombey and Son* (London: Penguin English Library, 1979).
Dretske, Fred I., *Explaining Behavior* (Cambridge, MA: The MIT Press, 1988).
Dretske, Fred. I., *Knowledge and the Flow of Information* (Cambridge, MA: The MIT Press, 1981).
Dretske, Fred. I., *Seeing and Knowing* (Chicago, IL: Routledge & Kegan Paul, 1969).
Dutton, Denis, *The Forger's Art: Forgery and the Philosophy of Art* (Berkeley, CA: University of California Press, 1983).
Eisenstein, Sergi, "Word and Image," in *The Film Sense*, translated and edited by Jay Leyda (New York: Harcourt Brace Jovanovich, c1975).
Feagin, Susan and Maynard, Patrick (eds.), *Aesthetics* (Oxford: Oxford University Press, 1997).
Fodor, Jerry A., "Observation Reconsidered," in *A Theory of Content and Other Essays* (Cambridge, MA: The MIT Press, 1990).
Fodor, Jerry A., *The Modularity of Mind: An Essay on Faculty Psychology* (Cambridge, MA: The MIT Press, 1983).
Friday, Jonathan, *Aesthetics and Photography* (London: Ashgate Publishing Company, 2002).
Gendler, Tamar Szabó, "The Puzzle of Imaginative Resistance," *Journal of Philosophy* 97 (2000): 55–81.
Gernsheim, Helmut, *Julia Margaret Cameron: Her Life and Photographic Work* (London: The Fountain Press, 1948).
Gibson, James J., *The Ecological Approach to Visual Perception* (Boston, MA: Houghton Mifflin, 1979).

Gladwell, Malcolm, "The Physical Genius," *The New Yorker* (June 2, 1999).
Goldberg, Vicki (ed.), *Photography in Print: Writings from 1816 to the Present* (New York: Simon and Schuster, 1981).
Goldman, Alvin I., "Discrimination and Perceptual Knowledge," *Journal of Philosophy* 73 (1976): 771–91.
Goldman, Alvin I., "Perceptual Objects," *Synthese* 35 (July 1977): 269.
Gombrich, Ernst H., *"Meditations on a Hobby Horse" and Other Essays On the Theory of Art* (London: Phaidon Press, 1963).
Goodman, Nelson, *Languages of Art: An Approach to a Theory of Symbols* (Indianapolis, IN: Hackett Publishing, 1976).
Goosens, William K., "Causal Chains and Counterfactuals," *Journal of Philosophy* 76 (September 1979): 489–95.
Grice, Paul, "Meaning," *Philosophical Review* 66 (July 1957): 377–88.
Hampshire, Stuart, "Logic and Appreciation," in William Elton (ed.), *Aesthetics and Language* (Oxford: Blackwell, 1959).
Heiferman, Marvin and Kismaric, Carole (eds.), *Talking Pictures: People Speak about the Photographs that Speak to Them* (San Francisco, CA: Chronicle Books, 1994).
Hermeren, Göran, *Representation and Meaning* (Lund: Scandanavian University Books, 1969).
Hopkins, Robert, "Aesthetics, Experience, and Discrimination," *Journal of Aesthetics and Art Criticism* 63:2 (2005): 119–33.
Hopkins, Robert, *Picture, Image and Experience* (Cambridge: Cambridge University Press, 1998).
Humphreys, G. W. and Riddoch, M. J., "From What to Where: Neuropsychological Evidence for Implicit Interactions Between Object- and Space-Based Attention," *Psychological Science* 14:5 (2003): 487–92.
Irwin, William, "The Aesthetics of Allusion," *Journal of Value Inquiry* 36 (2002): 521–32.
Irwin, William, "What is an Allusion?," *Journal of Aesthetics and Art Criticism* 59 (2001): 287–97.
Kania, Andrew, "The Illusion of Realism in Film," *British Journal of Aesthetics* 42 (2002): 243–58.
Keller, Ulrich F., "The Myth of Art Photography: A Sociological Analysis," *History of Photography* 8 (Oct.–Dec. 1984): 249–75.
Keller, Ulrich F., "The Myth of Art Photography: An Iconographic Analysis," *History of Photography* (Jan.–Mar., 1985): 1–38.
Kim, M.-S. and Robertson, L. C., "Implicit Representations of Space After Bilateral Parietal Lobe Damage," *Journal of Cognitive Neuroscience* 13:8 (2001): 1080–7.
Kimmelman, Michael, "Portratist in the Halls of Her Artistic Ancestors," *New York Times*, May 19, 1995.
Kitzinger, Ernst, "The Cult of Images in the Age Before Iconoclasm," *Dumbarton Oaks Papers* 8 (1954): 83–150; reprinted in W. Eugene Kleinbauer (ed.),

*The Art of Byzantium and the Medieval West: Selected Studies by Ernst Kitzinger* (Bloomington, IA, and London: Indiana University Press, 1976), 90–156.

Kitzinger, Ernst, *Byzantine Art in the Making: Main Lines of Stylistic Development in Mediterranean Art, Third to Seventh Century* (Cambridge: Harvard University Press, 1977).

Kracauer, Siegfried, "Photography," in Alan Trachtenberg, *Classic Essays in Photography*.

Kracauer, Siegfried, *Theory of Film: The Redemption of Physical Reality* (New York: Oxford University Press, 1965).

Leddy, Michael, "The Limits of Allusion," *British Journal of Aesthetics* 32 (1992): 111–14.

Lewis, David, "Truth in Fiction," in *Philosophical Papers: Volume I* (Oxford: Oxford University Press, 1983), 261–81.

Lewis, David, "Veridical Hallucination and Prosthetic Vision," *Australasian Journal of Philosophy* 58 (September 1980): 241.

Lewis, David, *Convention: A Philosophical Study* (Cambridge, MA: Harvard University Press, 1969).

Lifson, Ben, "Garry Winogrand's Art of the Actual," in Garry Winogrand, *The Man in the Crowd: The Uneasy Streets of Garry Winogrand* (San Francisco, CA: Fraenkel Gallery, 1999).

Lopes, Dominic, "The Aesthetics of Photographic Transparency," *Mind* 112 (2003): 433–48.

Lopes, Dominic, *Understanding Pictures* (Oxford: Oxford University Press, 1996).

Lossky, Vladimir, *The Mystical Theology of the Eastern Church* (London: James Clarke, 1957).

Macé, Gérard, "Preface: The Lightest Baggage," in Henri Cartier-Bresson, *The Mind's Eye* (New York: Aperture, 1999), pp. 8–11.

Malcolm, Janet, *Diana and Nikon: Essays on Photography* (New York: Aperture, 1997).

Martin, Edwin, "On Seeing Walton's Great-Grandfather," *Critical Inquiry* 12 (1986): 796–800.

Mast, Gerald and Cohen, Marshall 2nd (eds.), *Film Theory and Criticism: Introductory Readings* (New York: Oxford University Press, 1979).

Matturri, John, "Windows in the Garden: Italian-American Memorialization and the American Cemetery," in Richard E. Meyer (ed.), *Ethnicity and the American Cemetery* (Bowling Green, OH: Bowling Green State University Popular Press, 1993).

Maynard, Patrick, "Drawing and Shooting: Causality in Depiction," *Journal of Aesthetics and Art Criticism* 44:2 (Winter 1985): 115–29.

Maynard, Patrick, "Talbot's Technologies: Photographic Depiction, Detection, and Reproduction," *Journal of Aesthetics and Art Criticism* 47:3 (Summer 1989): 263–76.

Maynard, Patrick, "The Secular Icon: Photography and the Function of Images," *Journal of Aesthetics and Art Criticism* 42 (Winter 1983): 155–69.

Maynard, Patrick, "The Time It Takes," in Jan Baetens (ed.), *The Graphic Novel* (Leuven: Leuven University Press, 2001).

Maynard, Patrick, *Drawing Distinctions: The Varieties of Graphic Expression* (Ithaca, NY: Cornell University Press, 2005).

Maynard, Patrick, *The Engine of Visualization: Thinking Through Photography* (Ithaca, NY: Cornell University Press, 1997).

Metz, Christian, *Film Language: Towards a Semiotics of Cinema*, translated by Michael Taylor (New York: University Of Chicago Press, 1974).

Moran, Richard, "The Expression of Feeling in Imagination," *Philosophical Review* 103 (1994): 75–106.

Nelson, Robert S., "The Discourse of Icons, Then and Now," *Art History* 12 (1989): 144–57.

Nicoll, Allardyce, *Film and Theatre* (New York: Arno Press, 1972).

Olsen, Victoria, *From Life: Julia Margaret Cameron and Victorian Photography* (London: Aurum Press, 2003).

Ousterhout, Robert and Brubaker, Leslie (eds.), *The Sacred Image East and West* (Urbana, IL and Chicago, IL: University of Illinois Press, 1995).

Pinker, Steven, *How the Mind Works* (New York: W. W. Norton & Co., 1997).

Podro, Michael, *The Critical Historians of Art* (London: Yale University Press, 1982).

Ponech, Trevor, "External Realism About Cinematic Motion," *British Journal of Aesthetics* 46 (2006): 349–68.

Railton, Peter, "Subjective and Objective," *Ratio* 8 (1995): 259–76.

Ritchin, Fred, *In Our Own Image: The Coming Revolution in Photography* (New York: The Aperture Foundation, 1999).

Robertson, L. C., "Binding, Spatial Attention, and Perceptual Awareness," *Nature Reviews Neuroscience* 4 (2003): 93–102.

Robertson, L. C., *Space, Objects, Minds and Brains: Essays in Cognitive Psychology* (New York: Psychology Press, 2004).

Robertson, L. C., Treisman, A. M., Friedman-Hill, S. R., and Grabowecky, M., "The Interaction of Spatial and Object Pathways: Evidence from Balint's Syndrome," *Journal of Cognitive Neuroscience* 9 (1997): 691–700.

Robinson, Henry Peach, *The Elements of a Pictorial Photograph* (London, 1896).

Rogers, Sheena, "Truth and Meaning in Pictorial Space," in H. Hecht et al. (eds.), *Looking into Pictures: An Interdisciplinary Approach to Pictorial Space* (Cambridge, MA: MIT Press, 2003).

Ross, Stephanie, "Art and Allusion," *Journal of Aesthetics and Art Criticism* 40 (1981): 59–70.

Savedoff, Barbara, "Abstract Photography: Identifying the Subject," *Exposure* 37:2 (2004): 25–34.

Savedoff, Barbara, "Escaping Reality: Digital Imagery and the Resources of Photography," *Journal of Aesthetics and Art Criticism* 55:2 (Spring 1997): 201–14.

Savedoff, Barbara, "Frames," *Journal of Aesthetics and Art Criticism* 57:3 (Summer 1999): 345–56.

Savedoff, Barbara, "Transforming Images: Photographs of Representations," *Journal of Aesthetics and Art Criticism* 50:2 (Spring 1992): 93–106.

Savedoff, Barbara, *Transforming Images: How Photography Complicates the Picture* (Ithaca, NY: Cornell University Press, 2000).

Schapiro, Meyer, "On Perfection and Coherence in Art," in Feagin and Maynard, *Aesthetics* (Oxford: Oxford University Press, 1997).

Schapiro, Meyer, "The Apples of Cézanne: An Essay on the Meaning of Still-Life," *Art News Annual* 34 (1968). Reprinted in *Modern Art: Nineteenth and Twentieth Centuries* (New York: Braziller, 1978).

Scharf, Aaron, *Art and Photography* (London: Allen Lane, 1968).

Scruton, Roger, *Art and Imagination: A Study in the Philosophy of Mind* (London: Methuen, 1974).

Scruton, Roger, *The Aesthetic Understanding: Essays in the Philosophy of Art and Culture* (London: Methuen, 1983).

Sekula, Allan, *Photography Against the Grain: Essays and Photo Works 1973–1983* (Halifax, NS: The Press of the Nova Scotia College of Art and Design, 1984).

Sellin, David, *The First Prose* (New York: Norton, 1976).

Shannon, C., "A Mathematical Theory of Communication," *Bell System Technical Journal* 27 (1948): 379–423.

Snyder, Joel and Allen, Neil Walsh, "Photography, Vision, and Representation," *Critical Inquiry* 2 (1975).

Sontag, Susan, *On Photography* (New York: Farrar, Straus, and Giroux, 1977).

Szarkowski, John, *Looking at Photographs* (New York: MoMA, 1973).

Tagg, John, *The Burden of Representation: Essays on Photographies and Histories* (Amherst, MA: University of Massachusetts Press, 1988).

Talbot, William Henry Fox, *The Pencil of Nature* (London, 1844).

Tennyson, Alfred Lord, *The Works of Alfred Lord Tennyson, Illustrated with Photographs* (London: Robert Riviere and Son, 1884).

Tomasello, Michael, *The Cultural Origins of Human Cognition* (Cambridge, MA: Harvard University Press, 1999).

Trachtenberg, Alan (ed.), *Classic Essays in Photography* (New Haven, CT: Leete's Island Books, 1980).

Trachtenberg, Alan, "Likeness as Identity: Reflections on the Daguerrean Mystique," in Graham Clarke (ed.), *The Portrait in Photography* (London: Reaktion Books, and Seattle, WA: University of Washington Press, 1992).

Walden, Scott, "Objectivity in Photography," *British Journal of Aesthetics* 45:3 (July 2005): 258–72.

Walker, Ian, *City Gorged with Dreams: Surrealism and Documentary Photography in Interwar Paris* (Manchester: Manchester University Press, 2002).

Walton, Kendall L., "Categories of Art," *Philosophical Review* 79 (1970): 334–67.

Walton, Kendall L., "Experiencing Still Photographs: What Do You See and How Long Do You See It?," in *Marvelous Images* (New York: Oxford University Press), forthcoming.

Walton, Kendall L., "Fearing Fictions," *Journal of Philosophy* 75 (January 1978): 5–27.

Walton, Kendall L., "Looking Again Through Photographs: A Response to Edwin Martin," *Critical Inquiry* 12 (1986): 801–8.

Walton, Kendall L., "Morals in Fiction and Fictional Morality," *Proceedings of the Aristotelian Society*, Supplementary Volume 68 (1994): 27–50.

Walton, Kendall L., "On Pictures and Photographs: Objections Answered," in R. Allen and M. Smith (eds.), *Film Theory and Philosophy* (New York: Oxford University Press, 1997).

Walton, Kendall L., "Transparent Pictures: On the Nature of Photographic Realism," *Critical Inquiry* 11 (1984): 246–76.

Walton, Kendall L., *Mimesis as Make-Believe: On the Foundations of the Representational Arts* (Cambridge, MA: Harvard University Press, 1990).

Warburton, Nigel, "Authentic Photographs," *British Journal of Aesthetics* 37: 2 (April 1997): 129–37.

Warburton, Nigel, "Individual Style in Photographic Art," *British Journal of Aesthetics* 36:4 (October 1996): 389–397.

Warburton, Nigel, "Photographic Communication," *British Journal of Aesthetics* 28:2 (Spring 1988): 173–81.

Weinberg, Jonathan M. and Meskin, Aaron, "Imagine That!," in *Contemporary Debates in Aesthetics and the Philosophy of Art*, edited by Matthew Kieran (Oxford: Blackwell Publishing, 2006), p. 230.

West, Shearer, *Portraiture* (Oxford: Clarendon Press, 2004).

Westerbeck, Colin and Meyerowitz, Joel, *Bystander: A History of Street Photography* (Boston, MA: Little Brown, 1994).

Willats, John, *Making Sense of Children's Drawings* (Mahwah, NJ: Lawrence Erlbaum Associates, 2005).

Wind, Edgar, "The Maenad Under the Cross: Comment on an Observation by Reynolds," in *Hume and the Heroic Portrait: Studies in Eighteenth-Century Imagery* (Oxford: Clarendon Press, 1986).

Wollheim, Richard, "Seeing-as, Seeing-in and Pictorial Representation," in *Art and its Objects* (Cambridge: Cambridge University Press, 1980).

Wollheim, Richard, "Style Now," in Bernard William Smith (ed.), *Concerning Contemporary Art* (Oxford: Oxford University Press, 1975).

Yaffe, Gideon, "Time in the Movies," in P. A. French and H. Wettstein, *Midwest Studies in Philosophy 27: Meaning in the Arts* (Oxford: Blackwell Publishing, 2003).

Zemach, E. M., "Seeing, 'Seeing', and Feeling," *Review of Metaphysics* 23 (September 1969).

Ziff, Paul, "Reasons in Art Criticism," in *Philosophic Turnings: Essays in Conceptual Appreciation* (Ithaca, NY: Cornell University Press, 1966).

# INDEX

Lightning Source UK Ltd.
Milton Keynes UK
UKOW03f1215040714

234575UK00005B/57/P

9 781444 335088